GERMANY
AND THE
UNITED STATES OF AMERICA
DURING THE
ERA OF BISMARCK

GERMANY
AND THE
UNITED STATES OF AMERICA
DURING THE
ERA OF BISMARCK

By

COUNT OTTO ZU STOLBERG-WERNIGERODE

Translated from the German

Published by
THE HENRY JANSSEN FOUNDATION
READING, PA.

Under the Auspices of
THE CARL SCHURZ MEMORIAL FOUNDATION, INC.
225 SOUTH FIFTEENTH STREET
PHILADELPHIA, PA.

The original translation from the German was made
by Otto E. Lessing, Ph.D. Special thanks is due
Mrs. Natalie Summers, Herbert E. Angel and Ernst
Correll, Ph.D., of Washington, D. C., for final correc-
tions and for the Index.

Printed in the United States of America

TO THE MEMORY

OF

MY MOTHER

INTRODUCTION TO AMERICAN TRANSLATION

I

W HEN Count zu Stolberg-Wernigerode told me some years ago of the work he was doing in preparation for a volume on the United States and Germany in the time of Bismarck, I was convinced that he would make a very valuable contribution to a subject on which surprisingly little of a comprehensive nature had been written. When his book appeared in German in 1933 it more than lived up to my expectations. He was not content to rest on a thorough examination of printed materials—newspapers, monographs, memoirs and letters of German immigrants—but carefully examined the archives in Washington and Germany for more authoritative official information. Some of this interesting and wholly new archival material he has printed in the appendix, showing how monarchical Europe looked for guidance to the American democratic experiment in federal government, how the crisis of the Franco-Prussian War was viewed by American representatives abroad, and how George Bancroft stood in pleasant friendly relations with the Iron Chancellor. All this material Count zu Stolberg-Wernigerode has woven together into a clear, thoughtful and scholarly book which cannot fail to be of great interest to students of American as well as German history.

Today, when the World War and its aftermath have unfortunately left so much bitterness in so many minds, it is pleasant to learn from this impartial and very readable volume that the first century of German-American relations—from the formation of our Constitution to the fall of Bismarck—was on the whole a hundred years of serenity and cordiality. This was naturally so. During the first fifty years there was no serious rivalry or friction; our trade

vii

was slight; we were busy building up our own country at home; and our contacts with the thirty-odd German states were relatively few. There developed therefore a cordial but not intimate friendliness between the two peoples. It was fostered by the memory of Frederick the Great's cordiality to us during the American Revolution and by the services of Steuben and other German officers. It was fostered also by a certain affinity between Americans and Germans, based on many similarities of culture and institutions: Protestantism, federalism, liberalism, emancipation from English influence, and the pervasive common factor of German immigration into the United States. Furthermore, as the author so well suggests in the two parts into which his main study is divided, during the second fifty years two great questions were developing parallel to one another in the two countries—the struggle for national unity, which was settled here by the Civil War and in Germany by the three wars of '64, '66, and '70; and the spread of the industrial revolution which gradually led both countries to branch out as world powers, Bismarck reluctantly taking African colonies in the '80's, and the United States following suit a little later with the acquisition of the Philippines in 1898.

This volume is also to be welcomed as an admirable introduction to further studies in German-American relations which have appeared subsequently, such as Edith Lenel's biography of her grandfather (*Friedrich Kapp, 1824-1884*, Leipzig, 1935), and Alfred Vagts' monumental work (*Deutschland und die Vereinigten Staaten in der Weltpolitik*, New York, 1935) on the years after Bismarck's fall when serious friction arose between the two countries which had so long been on cordial terms.

SIDNEY B. FAY,
Harvard University.

II

With a view to enlighten his own people in regard to the diplomatic background that preceded the World War, Count Stolberg has presented in this work a body of historical materials as valuable and fascinating for American as for German readers. Years of painstaking investigation in state archives abroad and in this country, careful examination of manuscript collections and private correspondence prepared the author for his important task. As an historian he was not satisfied with a mere compilation of documents; he has studied them critically and given his interpretation, with remarkable fairness and sympathy. Diplomatic relations (*Beziehungen*) do not, however, exhaust the field of his inquiries, though his materials are drawn mainly from that source; he wishes to sketch a complete picture of an epoch that sowed the

seed for the future, the age of Bismarck. Belonging to the historical school of
the Bismarck biographer Professor Erich Marcks, Count Stolberg sees in
Prince Bismarck the great architect of the German Empire who built not alone
for his own generation but for that coming after, giving to the reign of
William II an inheritance of prestige and power, yet also of responsibility.

In Part I the author reaches back to the eighteenth century, when the imper-
ishable names of Frederick II and General Steuben stand out for friendship
and service to the American colonists in their struggle for freedom. Our
attention is called to the fact that as nations both the United States and
Germany had their beginnings about the same time, German national feeling
arising strongly with Frederick the Great contemporaneously with the union
of the thirteen American colonies. Sympathy and good feeling prevailed
between the two young nations also throughout the nineteenth century. Not
alone political, but educational and social influences were at a high tide in
the days when Young America sought an alma mater at German universities.
The life-long friendship between Motley and Bismarck founded while fellow-
students at Göttingen, bore fruit in vital diplomatic decisions of later years.
Contemporaries and successors of John L. Motley, as George Bancroft, Bayard
Taylor, Andrew D. White, inspired with German ideals of scholarship and
admiring the constructive statesmanship of the Iron Chancellor, came to the
helm of diplomatic affairs and established that prolonged era of friendly
understanding, peace and good will between Germany and the United States
which created a noble precedent that cannot be effaced whatever errors in the
future may cloud its memory. Germany's confidence in the Union cause was
undoubtedly strengthened by the brilliant representatives of America that
Bismarck had learned to appreciate and admire. Her purchase of the bonds
of the United States Government in that despairing period 1863-64 was
followed subsequently by America's recognition of the justice of Bismarck's
attitude in the Franco-Prussian War and American satisfaction with the founding of the German Empire in 1871. Impressive was the settlement of difficult
problems (as that of the conflicting naturalization laws) between Bismarck
and Bancroft (1867-73), as compared with the mess made of all things by
A. A. Sargent (1882-84), a machine politician.

Credit must be given Count Stolberg for unfamiliar and new material
introduced in Part II, "A World Power in the Making." The United States
and Germany awoke late to the absurdity of isolation, to the importance of
international trade, colonies, sea power. Germany arrived twenty years too
late to get her share of unclaimed land for her surplus population when she
started to search for it. The newcomer was then looked upon as a landgrabber,
perhaps nowhere more than in the United States, who had entered into the

game herself as a rival. The great German immigrations to America in the nineteenth century were a gain to the United States, a bloodletting for Germany, an economic, financial and social loss. Differences necessarily arose between the nations, one interested in the exportation of her raw products, the other desiring reciprocity for her manufactured goods. Bismarck always succeeded in steering his ship of state clear of difficulties, making it a definite policy to preserve the time-honored friendly relations with the American people. Though he is said to have considered the Monroe Doctrine an international impertinence (*Unverschämtheit*), he was always very careful not to irritate American sensitiveness on this policy. In the later years of Bismarck's chancellorship there were many troublesome questions at issue between the two countries: the high tariff, most-favored-nation privileges, export of German sugar, embargo on American hogs, unpleasant contacts in the West Indies, Hawaii, the Carolines, Samoa; but Bismarck frequently preferred to yield to an obstinate antagonist rather than sacrifice friendly relations with the United States; this was not only a tradition but a purpose with him.

Count Stolberg closes with Bismarck's retirement (1890). After we have studied the accurate historical picture so clearly outlined in this scholarly work, the question arises within us: Was diplomacy in less skillful hands after the great Atlas had laid down his heavy load, after carrying on his strong shoulders the world's affairs for a generation? Was the next quarter century unfortunate in possessing diplomats less wise and less inclined to preserve the century-old friendship between the United States and Germany? Certainly the age of Bismarck contended with difficulties equally great, for fate decrees that between powerful, ambitious nations rival interests frequently clash. It is the office and privilege of diplomats to bring about understanding not conflict, and fortunate it is for both parties when diplomats are friends. We get the impression that while Count Stolberg never departs from the correct methods of the judicial historian, he is patriotically German in the best sense and at the same time has deep sympathy and understanding for America. His is the type of Motley and Bancroft, ambassadors of good will. The present work is a contribution to better understanding of the interrelations between the German and American peoples. The Henry Janssen Foundation and the Carl Schurz Memorial Foundation, Inc., are to be congratulated upon making it accessible in an English translation to American readers and students.

ALBERT BERNHARDT FAUST,
Cornell University.

PREFACE

THIS translation was made possible through the generosity of the Henry Janssen Fund, administered by the Carl Schurz Memorial Foundation in Philadelphia, whose Director, Dr. Wilbur K. Thomas, took special interest in this work. I should like to express my deep gratitude to Mr. Henry Janssen, of Reading, Pa., and to all the officers of the Henry Janssen Fund and the Carl Schurz Memorial Foundation.

Besides the German State Archives in Berlin, Potsdam, and Frankfort on the Main the following sources were used: The archives of the Department of State in Washington, D. C., the collection of manuscripts in the Library of Congress, the Bancroft Collection of the New York Public Library, the private papers of Andrew Dickson White in the library of Cornell University, and finally, because of the peculiar nature of my problem, consular reports.

I regret being unable to express my appreciation individually to all those who so kindly assisted me in my work during my sojourn in the United States in 1927 and 1928. I am under special obligation to Mr. Herbert Putnam, Librarian of Congress, as well as to Mr. Tyler Dennett, then Chief of the Division of Publications in the Department of State. Both gentlemen facilitated my work in every way possible. To Mrs. Maddin Summers, Chief of the Archives Section in the Department of State in Washington, I owe a debt of gratitude of a particularly pleasant kind. In the first few months of 1928, when I took up my work in the Department of State, Mrs. Summers generously placed at my disposal her great professional experience. After my return to Germany she continued to furnish much valuable information to me. In addition I owe to Mrs. Summers a considerable part of such material as I had not sufficient time to collect personally while in the United States. I am

xi

therefore glad to state that I could not have completed my book in its present form without her intelligent coöperation.

A few words of explanation may not be out of place as to the first chapter, which gives an account of the relations between Germany and the United States from their beginnings until the War of Secession and which does not belong to the subject proper. It seemed necessary for a general understanding of later developments to discuss early relations in detail and to bring together, from a uniform point of view, information scattered through various books and articles. My narration of the War of Secession and its causes will hardly contain anything new for American readers, but it did not seem feasible to omit that chapter lest the general continuity of the whole book be broken.

Except for minor essays such as Snyder's recent study, *Die persönlichen und politischen Beziehungen Bismarcks zu Amerikanern,* the relations between Germany and the United States in the era concerning us have been extensively discussed only in Jeanette Keim's *Forty Years of German-American Political Relations.* I am glad to have this opportunity of calling attention to this competent study, which served me well in many ways. As her book appeared during the World War, the writer could not use the sources in the German and American archives, but had to limit herself to available published literature.

The extensive bibliography at the end of this book will, I hope, encourage German and American scholars to take an interest in this or a kindred subject. The translation in principle makes use of the original text for literal quotations; in the case of extracts from sources the sense of the originals is accurately rendered.

This American version of my book is issued with the sincere desire that it may promote mutual understanding and friendly relations between the two countries.

THE AUTHOR.

Munich, August 1937.

CONTENTS

xiii

INTRODUCTION

THE present book owes its origin to the World War. The entrance of
the United States into the war was an experience, especially for the
younger German generation of the period, both revolutionary and unexpected.
American participation in the war would not fit in with the ideas our
generation had been taught in school. We had received but vague impressions
of American history and the foundation of the American commonwealth. The
fact that the United States had become so decisive a factor in the outcome of
the war and so disastrous a one for Germany forced us to study the early
relations between the two countries. Superficial explanations such as were
offered from various directions did not afford us much satisfaction. For an
understanding of the present we evidently had to explore the past. It
seemed the more necessary, however, to be on our guard against the tempta-
tion of judging the past by recent events, and vice versa. For this reason I
was glad that the nature of my subject compelled me to begin my story far
back in the past. In limiting myself to a definite period I enjoyed the advantage of grouping the material, otherwise obscure and hard to grasp, around
the personality of Bismarck. It was a matter of relative completeness. I do
not, however, claim that all the problems touched upon were solved. The
interest in the subject has recently been growing to so gratifying a degree
that no doubt valuable additions and searching analyses in detail may be
expected.

In choosing a title for this book, the word "relations" was purposely
avoided. For not merely relations in the narrower sense are to be accounted
for, but similar phenomena in both countries are to be reported and examined
as to their internal connections. It seemed advisable, then, particularly in the

initial chapters, to give more space to other European countries than the subject in itself demanded. It was a characteristic feature of American-German
relations that, politically speaking, they were indirect for a long time, being
largely determined by the politics of other powers, primarily Great Britain.

The simultaneousness of significant events of American and German history, however, is too evident to be overlooked. The later German Reich
developed from the success of Frederick the Great of Prussia in the Seven
Years' War. The simultaneous war against France by Great Britain, in alliance
with her colonies, decided the future of North America. When France lost
Canada the predominance of Protestantism in North America was assured. A
hundred years later, in 1864, German and American soldiers again were fighting in wars on either continent. The causes that led up to the American Civil
War and the Danish War were indeed quite different. But the final issues
were the same on both sides of the Atlantic: restoration of national unity.
The battles for the Düppel entrenchments and for Richmond laid the corner-
stones for unified national states. When their struggle for unification had
ceased, both Germany and the United States were confronted with the problem of concentrating their powers on internal affairs. Germany turned to
problems of world politics earlier than the United States. At first the beginnings of Germany's colonial policy did not find a corresponding parallel in
the American Union. On the contrary, in the seventies and eighties of the
nineteenth century American policy appears to be self-sufficient, limited to
internal affairs, and without foreign aspirations. America still needed its full
energy for the great westward advance in its own continent.

But, after all, that period was a time of preparation. Even then American
claims of the future were announced and, incidentally, against Germany.
Scarcely had the North German Federation been founded in 1867 when
Charles Sumner, chairman of the Committee on Foreign Relations, asked to
be notified in case the North German Federation should intend to acquire a
naval station in the West Indies. Scarcely had the echo of the last shot in
France died away in 1871 when the United States Government suspiciously
made inquiries at its Berlin Legation as to Germany's intentions in Venezuela.
In vain did Carl Schurz, during the great Senate debate in 1871 regarding
the island of Santo Domingo in the West Indies, which President Grant
wanted to annex, seek to convince his fellow-citizens that Germany did not
think of acquiring Santo Domingo. Even at that time the opinion was current
that the newly united Reich was compelled to divert its surplus population to
foreign territories. There was some apprehension also that American interests
might thus be affected. After Germany had seriously started to take part in
the general competition for colonies, the United States was ever ready to raise

objections and protests concerning potential claims of its own. While the great majority of Americans maintained an attitude of indifference or even aversion toward matters of foreign policy, a few politicians, like Secretary of State James G. Blaine and the diplomatist John A. Kasson, preserved the tradition of imperialism that had existed so strongly before the Civil War.

Bismarck therefore had to take American interests into consideration on various occasions: during the West African Conference of 1884, in the Caroline Islands dispute of 1885, and in the Samoa problem from 1875 to 1889. In the era of Bismarck the United States was not as yet a world power. However, bordering both on the Atlantic and the Pacific, its commerce turned to the same sea routes and groups of islands used and claimed by the other great powers. Considering German affairs with those facts in mind, we may say that it would have been an extraordinary advantage for Germany had its unification taken place twenty years earlier. In that case the Germans would have had an undisturbed period of transition for adjusting themselves to industrial conditions as revolutionized by technical science. In its quest for colonial territories for its surplus population, Germany also would probably not have encountered so much resistance as was later the case. Great Britain's freedom of action at that particular time was very much limited because of the internal reorganization of its empire and because of political differences with France and the United States. Moreover, Germany joined the ranks of the great national states at a period when world business had already undergone a transformation. Germany was compelled, as it were, to make its purchases in the midst of the season instead of at clearance sales, and to pay with unpleasant friction, and later on even with compensations, for every little advantage in the matter of colonies.

As early as the eighties it was impossible to avoid minor conflicts with the United States. How deliberate and cautious were Bismarck's beginnings in colonial policy—groping along, under the necessity of helping German industry and the German merchant! However moderate his policy was, it could not prevent temporary disturbances of relations when an untenable triple administration—Britain, Germany, and the United States—in Samoa brought about disputes and when consular representatives, far removed from their home countries, carried on a policy of their own liking. The United States thought it had achieved a victory over Bismarck when he finally retreated in the Samoa question in 1889. In reality he never for a moment had thought of a war against the Union. It remained one of his leading ideas to cultivate a traditional friendship and to give the greatest possible consideration to American sensibilities.

A different factor, however, was destined in the course of time to give

American-German relations a changed aspect. Beginning in the eighties, industrial rivalry between the two countries became more and more noticeable. Before the foundation of the Reich the trade of the United States with the individual German states was not nearly so important for America as was its trade with other European countries. Later Germany rapidly rose to a high place. The development of their industries had different consequences for the two countries. Germany became a country importing foodstuffs and raw materials while the United States continued to possess its own supplies. It was the great storehouse for Europe and yet at the same time was in a position to underbid competition with cheap industrial products. This enabled the United States arbitrarily to dictate laws of commerce. It refused reciprocity when Germany had granted it. Its radical protective tariff in the nineties was hard for the German partner to bear. The events of 1884 must be regarded as a foreboding of the industrial struggles which intermittently continued until the World War. The fact that German restrictions of imports caused a great deal of irritation in the United States and led to diplomatic negotiations clearly shows how important a market Germany had become for the United States. As economic questions were closely connected with the interests of immigrants, they no doubt helped create an unfriendly sentiment, at least in certain groups of the population. The atmosphere of mutual irritation which surprised Andrew Dickson White so much when in 1897 he again came to Berlin as an ambassador, is to some extent attributable to that situation.

It was, however, Great Britain that always held the key position in the relations between Germany and the United States. I hope that I have succeeded in bringing out that fact in my book. The opinion entertained of each other by the Germans and Americans as it continually developed was influenced by British opinion even after the American communications system had largely made itself independent. As early as the Bismarck era we may observe indications of an Anglo-Saxon community of interests on the American continent and still more so in the Pacific, a community of interests certain to become of political importance and of influence on American-German relations at the moment when the world powers began to shift the center of their political objectives from the Atlantic to the Pacific Ocean.

PART I

TOWARD NATIONAL UNITY

CHAPTER I

RELATIONS BETWEEN GERMANY AND THE UNITED STATES PRIOR TO THE AMERICAN CIVIL WAR

THE modern era was shaped by two events—the discovery of America and the Reformation.[1] The religious struggles that shook the sixteenth and seventeenth centuries were supplemented by the fight for the possession of America. The great powers strove for expansion. National territories had to be enlarged after two religious camps had been established. It was for this reason that America affected the fate of Europe so deeply. The demands of commercial policy and the quest for new trade routes to the Orient brought about the discovery of the new continent, but not until the seventeenth and eighteenth centuries were the actual problems of colonization taken up. Successively and side by side, Portugal, Spain, the Netherlands, Great Britain, and France fought for domination of the New World. Great Britain finally triumphed, not because she was stronger, but because she was less closely tied to Europe.

The Germans had no share in those decisions of world politics. While Germany had fostered the Reformation, she had not as yet become a nation. Religious schism only hastened political disintegration. The rise of the western powers, beginning centuries earlier, continued at an accelerated pace after the Reformation. The Reformation shifted the united front from the west to the east. The greatness and power of the medieval Reich were founded on the idea of the unity of the Christian west. That unity, though it later proved to be a myth, had allowed the Germans to fulfill their mission for the civilization of Europe, despite frontiers geographically disadvantageous and ethnographically obscure. But, as that unity was gradually superseded by the rise of nationalist tendencies, it became more and more evident that

[1] Cf. Rein, *Der Kampf Westeuropas um Nordamerika im 15. und 16. Jahrhundert.*

Germany was not a clearly defined territory. The west and the east settled their differences on German soil. Like America, Germany for centuries became a battlefield both in a real and symbolic sense. Lack of room for expansion came to be a decisive factor in German history. Germans who wished for travel and adventure went abroad to serve foreign masters, and in America they found a refuge from oppression and a new home when their native land would no longer support them. It was directly traceable to the effects of the Thirty Years' War and to the French invasions under Louis XIV that so many inhabitants of the Palatinate responded to William Penn's call to Pennsylvania. In the course of the nineteenth century the number of German immigrants had increased to millions. They did not come as soldiers under a flag of their own, but together with the Anglo-Saxons they spread civilization throughout North America. They undeniably performed valuable services as pioneers. They were particularly well qualified to hold their ground under most trying conditions, and on exposed frontiers they were unsurpassed, being frequently more inclined than the restless, adventurous Anglo-Saxons to develop and defend the territory once it had been conquered. The area chiefly peopled by German immigrants, between the Piedmont Plateau and the Great Valley, is a monument to German enterprise and industry.[2]

Consequently it is incorrect to say that the Germans had no share in the formation of the United States. Many German colonists fought in the ranks of the American militia in the war with France for Canada, the first step toward the Declaration of Independence. This was, of course, the case to an even greater degree in the War for Independence, when a German state, Prussia, directly influenced the fate of America. The peace of Aix-la-Chapelle was merely a breathing spell in the centuries of warfare between Great Britain and France. The two powers had been practically in a state of war since 1755. Their colonial systems, developed side by side on American territory, were so different that controversies were continuous. The British colonies felt their safety menaced by the Indians allied with the French. The question as to whether North America was to be predominantly Protestant or Catholic demanded an answer also, for Protestant New France had succumbed to the Spaniards in a stream of blood shortly before St. Bartholomew's night.[3]

The Westminster Convention of January 16, 1756, between Great Britain and Prussia, had its origin in the desire of the British King to protect Hanover from European entanglements. A pledge by both Russia and Prussia

[2] Cf. Faust, *German Element in the United States,* which has an extensive bibliography.

[3] Cf. Rein, *Der Kampf Westeuropas um Nordamerika im 15. und 16. Jahrhundert,* 232.

4

seemed to guarantee that end. Frederick, being of the opinion that a combination of Russia, Austria, and Saxony would depend financially on Great Britain, hoped that the convention would in time drive a wedge into the impending coalition. Both parties were disappointed. Russia, considering the convention an affront, canceled her obligations in connection with Hanover. Frederick likewise gained nothing, the hostile coalition being welded together all the more closely.

Hence Britain regarded the Prussian alliance as a very undesirable handicap at the outbreak of the European war in 1756. As a matter of fact, the King of Prussia, hard pressed as he was, needed far more help than he was able to give. From the British point of view it was only logical for George II, through the Convention of Kloster Zeven, to attempt to rid himself of the burden of Hanover. With Frederick's victory at Rossbach, however, the situation changed completely. The dark years of 1756 and 1757 had brought many setbacks to Britain; in the second year of the Seven Years' War, particularly, one disastrous report after another arrived in London. On August 16, after Kolin, Hastenbeck, and Calcutta, came the news of the evacuation of Ostend and Nieuport, and the loss of Louisburg was reported on the thirtieth. From India came the only favorable report. On September 23 word arrived that Colonel Clive, who had been sent from Madras to Bengal, had conquered Chandarnagar, the French station on the Hooghly. The climax of disasters was reached when the naval action against the French coast failed. What the glad tidings of Rossbach meant to the depressed spirit of the British may therefore be easily imagined. At once Frederick became a welcome ally. Pitt realized from that moment that Prussia's victory or defeat was certain to have a decisive influence on the world war which Great Britain was waging.[4] In a certain sense, the fall of Quebec in 1759 brought the war in America to an end, but in the last analysis the victories against the French armies on the Rhine and Frederick's unexpectedly tenacious resistance made French interference in the European war the great mistake that cost France her colonial empire in America.[5]

It is interesting to observe how profoundly America realized the important effect of the Prussian victories on the American war. After Rossbach the connection of the struggles had indeed been strongly emphasized by the British. Pitt had sounded the call for a holy war, and Parliament had responded.[6]

[4] *Cambridge History of the British Empire,* I, 460ff.; Lodge, *Great Britain and Prussia in the Eighteenth Century,* 74ff. For the impression of the battle of Rossbach on the British, see Ruville, *William Pitt,* II, 183.

[5] The opinion that it was a mistake for France to take part in the European war is shared, for example, by Bradley, *The Fight with France for North America,* 140.

[6] Cobbett, *Parliamentary History of England,* XV, 785ff.

Feeling ran so high that prayers for the success of Frederick's armies were offered in the churches of New England. "For," said a preacher in Boston, "his victories are ours." [7] James Sterling, a clergyman in Kent County, Rhode Island, eulogized Frederick in a poem as a "royal comet" and a new Arminius.[8] The German colonists were of course most strongly impressed of all. Twenty years later, Steuben, on his journey through Pennsylvania to Washington's headquarters, found indications of admiration and affection everywhere. German taverns in and near Philadelphia were called "The King of Prussia," and Steuben found the picture of his monarch in not a few residences.[9] Contemporary American literature praised Frederick as an arbiter, as the wisest man of Europe, and as a prince whose mental superiority logically caused him to ally himself with the Americans. Washington, in a letter to Lafayette, called it the highest honor imaginable to be received honorably by so great a statesman and general as Frederick.[10] The story that Frederick sent Washington a ceremonial sword is suggestive of America's esteem for Frederick as was the ephemeral plan for making his brother, Prince Henry, king of the liberated colonies.[11]

Frederick's fame and authority were indeed the real reason that, during the War for Independence, the American commissioners so persistently sought his sympathy, nay, his recognition of the insurgent colonies.[12] The political importance of the German Reich and its individual states should not be overestimated, however. France, being Great Britain's strongest opponent, indisputably was most important to the colonies; then came Russia, Spain, Portugal, and the Netherlands. Prussia and Austria were really last in order.[13] The shortsighted policies of the petty states were not conducive to increasing the prestige of the Reich. Their traffic in mercenaries with Britain, morally so objectionable, was a political mistake as well. Even considering the ideas

[7] *Boston Evening Post,* June 27, 1793.

[8] Wilkins, "Early Influence of German Literature in America," in *Americana Germanica,* III, 156.

[9] Kapp, *Frederick William von Steuben,* 100.

[10] Kapp, *Friedrich der Grosse,* 12. Cf. Benjamin Franklin's opinion of Frederick: "Three Monarchys the most powerful in Europe besides the Swedes, on his Back at once; no Magnamity (sic) but his own could think of bearing it; no Courage but his that would not sink under it, no any less Bravery, Skill and Activity than his that would equal to it." (To David Hall, London, Apr. 8, 1759) in Victory, *Benjamin Franklin and Germany,* 13, *Americana Germanica,* no. 21.

[11] Cf. Krauel, "Prince Henry of Prussia," in *American Historical Review,* XVII, 44.

[12] Cf. Kapp, *Friedrich der Grosse;* Haworth, "Frederick the Great," in *American Historical Review,* IX, 460ff.

[13] John Adams, in a letter to the President of the Continental Congress Aug. 4, 1779, describes the situation in that sense. John Adams, *Works,* VII, 99ff.

characteristic of the times, that traffic was indefensible. It demonstrated the pitiful weakness of the Reich so clearly, and disapproval both inside and outside the borders of Germany was so vehement that all attempts at justification failed miserably.[14] Those German mercenaries, however, possessed a sense of soldierly honor strong enough to gain recognition from their enemies for their bravery.[15] Still another concern of the American commissioners was to keep Germany from meddling in French politics. The alliance with France was of paramount importance.

The political attitude of Frederick, therefore, was of considerable consequence. It was a fortunate coincidence for the rebellious colonies that the Prussian King, embittered against Great Britain after the Seven Years' War, welcomed British troubles in America. He realized at once the seriousness of the revolution for Great Britain, but nevertheless did not wish to commit himself in any way. The fact that he once prohibited British auxiliaries from passing through his territory was primarily a gesture against the unfriendly British policy in Danzig. We cannot ascribe undue emphasis to that prohibition in itself.[16] By that time the American commissioners were no longer greatly disturbed about consignments of German troops, for a storm of protest against the sale of German soldiers had arisen inside and outside the Reich, and the petty German princes could hardly risk having too many troops withdrawn from their territories.[17] Nevertheless, Frederick's vigorous statements about the traffic in soldiers were more than merely a tactical device. The leader of the strongest German state, disgusted with the petty and egotistic methods of the German courts, became the spokesman for general criticism. Thus, the Prussian King, interested first of all in the Prussian State, fought also for political morality and national honor. Praise for Frederick from those who in their hearts protested against that disgraceful traffic was quite justified.

[14] Cf. Benjamin Franklin to John Winthrop, Paris, May 1, 1777, in Wharton, *Revolutionary Diplomatic Correspondence*, II, 311.

[15] Cf. Lowell, *Hessians and Other German Auxiliaries of Great Britain in the Revolutionary War.*

[16] Cf. Reimann, *Neuere Geschichte des preussischen Staates*, II, 651.

[17] Kapp overestimates the importance of the prohibition in *Friedrich der Grosse*, 70f.; Kapp, *Soldatenhandel deutscher Fürsten nach Amerika*, 157ff. Haworth, in his article cited, emphasizes the provisional nature of the prohibition. Cf. also Arthur Lee to the Committee of Foreign Affairs, Berlin, June 11, 1777: "The consequence of the Prince of Hesse's conduct is beginning to be a lesson to the other German princes, so that it is not probable they will draw any more supplies from them. The country of Hesse is depopulating so fast, from the apprehension of being forced into this service, that the women are obliged to cultivate the lands." Wharton, *Revolutionary Diplomatic Correspondence*, II, 335.

On other matters Frederick managed to resist the blandishments of the American envoys.

There were noncommittal conversations about a potential mutual trade, which, however, did not proceed very far. The King, in a Cabinet order, wrote to Schulenburg on March 12, 1777, that trade could not be protected without a navy.[18] The Americans obtained only the promise of Minister von Schulenburg, on January 16, 1778, that Prussia would recognize the independence of the colonies as soon as France had set the good example.[19] But Frederick was unable to keep even that promise, for his attention was demanded by the outbreak, in 1778, of the Bavarian War of Succession. Now he did not dare risk open opposition to Great Britain, for he had to prevent the Hanoverian army of 30,000 men from joining his enemies.

For this same reason, too, Austria had to exercise extreme political caution. The American commissioner judged conditions correctly when, in September 1778, he declared it unlikely that either Berlin or Vienna would take sides openly.[20] From the American point of view there was the more serious possibility that France would be forced by treaty to participate in the war and would thereupon withdraw from the American war. The Americans were greatly relieved when France disavowed her continental obligation, and when armed conflict was avoided despite Frederick's advance into Bohemia. "We apprehend that America has at present nothing to fear from Germany," said John Adams.[21] It will not suffice to describe Frederick's attitude toward the rebellious British colonies as one of friendship. Prussia's benevolent neutrality toward France was the sole consideration—unless Prussia's influence in the Netherlands because of the Governor's Prussian wife be mentioned—and that was a fortunate coincidence attributable to the general grouping of the powers.

Prussia's sole, but great gift—Germany's contribution to the struggling colonies—was a former Prussian officer, Friedrich Wilhelm von Steuben, who in 1777 offered his services to the Americans.[22] He had fought in the Seven Years' War and was wounded at Rossbach. After the war he had been rewarded by the King. Just why Steuben left the Prussian service we cannot

[18] Kapp, *Friedrich der Grosse,* 22.

[19] *Ibid.,* 52.

[20] William Lee to Committee of Foreign Affairs, Paris, Sept. 12, 1778, Wharton, *Revolutionary Diplomatic Correspondence,* II, 714ff.

[21] John Adams, *Works,* VII, 19. Hanfstaengl, *Amerika und Europa von Marlborough bis Mirabeau,* 68, attaches too great an importance to the report. It is contradicted by the calm statements of the American commissioners in 1778.

[22] Cf. Kapp, *Frederick William von Steuben.* We are very much in need of a new Steuben biography which should, above all, give a detailed account of his life in Germany.

tell. It may have been because of personal disagreements, but more likely he wearied of the monotonous garrison life. He became lord chamberlain of the Prince of Hohenzollern-Hechingen, and then he joined the court of Karl Friedrich of Baden. Through the French Minister of War, Count St.-Germain, the plan was evolved for sending Steuben to America.

The American militia was in need of a trained, experienced officer; St.-Germain, having watched Steuben since the Seven Years' War, considered him the proper man. In America Steuben would require a rank higher than he possessed, but negotiations to that end did not result in a definite contract, and the French let him depart with their good wishes, but with no promises.

Consequently it was first the envoy of France, and second the officer of the Great King, who was honorably received and feted in America. Nevertheless, the fame of Frederick had preceded him. Americans of German extraction welcomed him most cordially. Washington came from his headquarters to meet him. Steuben's name became the byword of the day.

The military situation of the rebels was not absolutely desperate when Steuben arrived at headquarters in Valley Forge. Boston had even been evacuated by the enemy after the British surrender at Saratoga. But the American militia was dwindling. The troops lacked the most essential necessities and, above all, the proper spirit. Whole groups of recruits were deserting and going home. With the enemy before him, Washington had to gather a new army. Steuben did not understand a word of English and had no time to adjust himself to conditions quite foreign to him. He began by training small units of men. He himself set the example, and example meant everything. What he had to give to the Americans was a knowledge of discipline and the Prussian sense of duty, but he avoided Prussian methods because they did not fit into that environment. Thus he succeeded in making astonishingly great progress in a short time. He transformed a gang of men into soldiers of an army. Steuben encountered many difficulties. Not until March 5, 1778, was he appointed inspector general. A foreigner, his position was coveted. Washington, however, realized Steuben's value. His rules of drill were universally adopted. At the front, too, he withstood the most difficult conditions. He was given command of the Virginia militia with whom he had to hold his ground against trained British regulars. Steuben was in command of the trenches on the day when the surrender of Yorktown decided the war in favor of the colonies. In the army report he was given special mention. The grandson of General Greene rated Steuben's military achievements in the War for Independence highest after those of his own grandfather and Washington.[23] It was no doubt because of Steuben's personal influence that the

[23] Greene, *German Element in the War of American Independence*, 85.

Americans developed the military self-confidence which they needed to succeed.

After the war that had ended so favorably for the colonies, many people in Europe dreamed of new commercial possibilities. Joseph II, in particular, let his imagination rove in that direction, having entered into conversations with John Adams even during the war. Trieste, Fiume, and the Austrian Netherlands were mentioned as bases for enlarged commerce. John Adams, while staying at The Hague, was in favor of a treaty, although the House of Hapsburg, as he said, was an enemy of the Bourbons. As Emperor of the German Reich, Joseph II was a factor not to be overlooked.[24] But such nebulous plans vanished. Negotiations with Prussia progressed far more successfully. Frederick shared the general optimism regarding trade, and though he had held aloof during the war, he now insisted energetically on the conclusion of a treaty once political obstacles had been removed. Since he had but recently acquired possession of East Frisia, he was interested in making Emden an important trade center.[25] During the war an exchange of Silesian linen for Virginia tobacco had been considered. Congress, greatly favoring commercial treaties for political reasons, commissioned its three European representatives, Franklin, Jefferson, and Adams, to negotiate treaties of friendship and commerce with the German Reich, Prussia, Denmark, Portugal, Spain, the Holy See, and Tuscany. A series of treaties, it was thought, would undermine the solid structure of the British mercantile system and afford protection from British arbitrariness on the seas in case of war.

In November 1783, Frederick had instructed his minister in Paris to approach the American envoys.[26] When the Paris negotiations reached an *impasse,* he asked Thulemeyer to consult with Adams at The Hague. The Americans were chiefly interested in having private property protected in naval wars, while Frederick, in return for anticipated commercial advantages, was ready to meet the American demands inasmuch as Prussia could hardly be involved in a great naval war. Thus the Prussian-American treaty was concluded on September 24, 1785, enunciating for the first time the principle of "free ships—free goods." In principle, permanent confiscation of private property was to be made impossible. Some humanitarian statements on the treatment of prisoners of war came from the pen of Franklin. Washington declared the treaty with Prussia to be the most liberal treaty ever concluded

---

[24] Hanfstaengl, *Amerika und Europa von Marlborough bis Mirabeau,* 115ff.; John Adams, *Works,* VIII, 95ff.

[25] John Adams, *Works,* VII, 107f.; Victory, *Benjamin Franklin and Germany,* 14.

[26] Cf. Kapp, *Friedrich der Grosse,* 86ff.

between sovereign powers:[27] "It is perfectly original in many of its articles; and, should its principles be considered hereafter as the basis of connexions between nations, it will operate more fully to produce a general pacification than any measure hitherto attempted amongst mankind." It is indeed its spirit which makes that treaty such a remarkable document. It was a unique event in the development of the law of maritime war, for Prussia and the United States in their first treaty had thus declared the inviolability of private property on the high seas. Many other opportunities were to come for joint action in that respect, but Prussia did not always make full use of them.[28]

At first, however, the treaty existed for the most part on paper. In the prolonged war between France and Great Britain the rights of neutrals were abused more arbitrarily than ever. None suffered more painfully than the young American Republic. Placed as it was between the two powers, there was considerable danger that it might be involved in war with either Great Britain or France. In the Jay Treaty of 1794 with Britain, the Americans surrendered the principle of "free ships—free goods." That act was resented in Paris, the Directory declaring that it would no longer adhere to former agreements. In 1797 diplomatic relations were severed. One group of Americans, consisting of Alexander Hamilton, Gouverneur Morris, and John Quincy Adams, whose father was President at the time, demanded war with France, while another strong party, led by Jefferson, was decidedly opposed to it. During that tense period the Americans carefully watched Prussia. Morris in particular, who, as a special American envoy, had witnessed the French Revolution from its very beginnings and had been profoundly disgusted with the reign of terror in Paris, sought to evolve a plan for a general coalition against France. He considered Prussia the most important continental power for the realization of such a combination. When he arrived in Berlin in 1796, he told Haugwitz, the Prussian Minister of State, that he considered Prussia the master of the destiny of Europe. Using Hanover as bait, he tried to bring Prussia into an alliance with Great Britain. He persistently clung to that idea, not being discouraged even by the skeptical British envoy, Lord Elgin, who clearly saw that Prussia was politically dependent on France. Again and again Morris sent word to the British Minister, Lord Grenville, that Hanover should be joined to Prussia. The Reich, he said, was practically nonexistent. Events along the Rhine and in Italy had wrought confusion in Vienna. France could profit by that situation. The fate of Europe was in the hands of the Prussian Government. If Great Britain wanted Prussia's support

[27] Washington, *Writings,* IX, 182.
[28] See *post,* p. 49, footnote 9.

11

she had only to surrender Hanover. In view of the circumstances, the latter plan could not possibly succeed. Haugwitz did not commit himself, having bound Prussia too closely in a system of neutrality.[29]

While Morris's mission cannot be identified with official American policy, it undoubtedly influenced John Quincy Adams when he arrived in Berlin in 1797. Had it not been for Morris's high opinion of Prussia's importance, the President would hardly have thought of sending his son to Berlin. But the policy upon which Adams and his son proceeded was different. They wished to revive the principle of armed neutrality, the doctrine of Catherine of Russia, which, during the Seven Years' War, had also proved so eminently useful to America. The United States held high hopes for its commerce if armed neutrality was guaranteed by a coalition of the northern powers. John Adams, in a letter of June 2, 1797, did not restrict his son to Berlin,[30] but John Quincy Adams, coming from The Hague, soon learned that his mission in northern Europe could be easily accomplished from Berlin, where he could also negotiate treaties with Russia and Sweden. The President was not especially interested in renewing the commercial treaty with Prussia unless articles 12 and 13 could be revised. As he informed Secretary of State Pickering on September 30, 1798, he thought it too dangerous to allow France and her colonies to procure all of their supplies—even American products—from Prussian, Swedish, or Danish ships at a time when America might be forced into a war.[31] For this reason his son, on July 11, 1798, proposed to the Prussian State Ministry that article 12 be changed so that neutral property on enemy ships would not be free. The Prussian Government, however, rejected that proposal, asserting that Prussia could not forego her trade with the present belligerent powers, especially with regard to East Indian and West Indian goods. Berlin likewise feared that the northern powers, and especially Sweden, would not consent to such a change.[32] Adams, not greatly disturbed, was willing to compromise. A definite settlement was deferred for the time

[29] Morris, *Diary and Letters,* II, 174ff.

[30] "The part which the King of Prussia means to take, either during the war, or at and after the peace, and what his relations are to be in future towards France and England, will be important for us to know. The Emperor of all the Russias, too, and the Emperor of Germany, are important luminaries for the political telescope to observe. In short, what is to be the future system of Europe, and how we best can preserve friendship with them all, and be most useful to them all, are speculations and inquiries worthy of your head and heart. You have wisely taken all Europe for your theatre, and I hope will continue to do as you have done. Send us all the information you can collect. I wish you to continue your practice of writing freely to me, and cautiously to the office of State." John Adams, *Works,* VIII, 545.

[31] *Ibid.,* VIII, 598f.

[32] Haugwitz to Adams, Aug. 1, 1798.

being. As for the existing war, it was agreed that warships and privateers of belligerent powers should treat neutral merchantmen as generously as the conduct of war permitted and that they should follow the universally recognized principles and rules of international law. A few other provisions were modified somewhat, but in general the treaty of 1799 closely resembled the treaty of 1785.[33]

To his chief assignment, the observation of conditions in northern Europe, Adams gave his keenest attention.[34] Like Morris, he was greatly irritated by the arrogant policies of the French Directory. He could not understand the vacillating policy of his own country. He did not, however, wish Great Britain to be strengthened by a general coalition; armed neutrality best seemed to meet the existing situation. Adams hoped it would be easy to secure Prussian adherence to that policy. He viewed the situation thus: Prussian policy since the Peace of Basle had been based on the principle of neutrality and to this Prussia owed her present strong position. When Adams arrived in Berlin, France had just issued her decree against neutral shipping. The time seemed propitious for suggesting a coalition of the northern powers to protect their endangered commercial interests. A letter of March 20, 1798, to William Vans Murray clearly sets forth his views of the general situation. He considered cooperation of the northern powers, including Prussia, quite possible, as there were tempting opportunities for them in the West Indies. Not since the discovery of America, he said, had there been such a chance for rearranging the trade relations of Europe.[35] As a matter of fact, Haugwitz was not altogether unwilling. He promised to report as soon as the replies from the courts had come in. Adams admitted that, if France insisted on her decree, were only three possibilities: to accept the loss of trade quietly, to throw themselves into the arms of Great Britain, or to evolve an arrangement that would be for their common interests. Adams gained the impression that Haugwitz favored the last alternative,[36] but he soon discovered that the Prussian Government could not be relied upon to follow any strong course of action. Nevertheless, he remained in Berlin until 1801 to keep his Government informed regarding northern European politics. With the turn of the century, when the United States succeeded in coming to a provisional agreement with the First Consul, John Quincy Adams shifted his antagonism to

[33] Kapp, *Friedrich der Grosse,* 144f.
[34] Cf. J. Q. Adams, *Writings;* and *Memoirs,* I, 193ff.; and Dept. State, *Letters of J. Q. Adams, Minister of U. S. to Berlin, 1799-1801.*
[35] J. Q. Adams, *Writings,* II, 270.
[36] *Ibid.,* II, 257ff.

Great Britain, painfully rueing the lack of an understanding among the northern powers, in view of British supremacy on the high seas.

Adams meanwhile visited Silesia, the province which he considered the most interesting part of Prussia and the only one worth while for commercial relations.[37] In 1801, his father failed to be reelected and, since it no longer seemed necessary to have an observer in northern Europe, his Prussian mission came to an end. Congress had heretofore been interested but slightly in the commercial treaties with Prussia.[38]

With Adams's departure from Berlin, direct political relations between the two countries ceased for a time and Austria, under Metternich, assumed control of affairs. From the American point of view Prussia, throughout the South American wars for independence, was regarded as Austria's vassal.[39] Metternich, considering himself the protector of Europe, attacked most vehemently the Monroe Doctrine of 1823: "If this flood of evil doctrines and pernicious examples should extend over the whole of America, what would become of our religious and political institutions, of the moral force of our governments, and of that conservative system which has saved Europe from complete dissolution?" [40] Thus American democracy found the Metternich system arraigned against it. American ideology particularly hated those elements which were embodied in the combination of Metternich and Austria: political reactionism, Catholicism, and suppression of nationalities. A sort of secret war was waged between Austria and the United States until the revolutionary years of 1848 and 1849. The Americans went so far as to intervene directly in the Hungarian war for independence of 1848, sending a special delegation to meet the rebels. This had serious diplomatic consequences.[41]

The fact that Austria was considered a source of political evil enhanced Prussia in American opinion. The part that Prussia had played at this period of American history automatically heightened the esteem in which Prussia was held. Above all, Prussia was long considered the chief protagonist of Protestantism on the Continent. Like the reception of the Huguenots by the Great Elector after the repeal of the Edict of Nantes, Frederick's struggle

---

[37] Adams to Pickering, Leipzig, Oct. 4, 1800, Dept. State, *Letters of J. Q. Adams,* I. Cf. for that journey J. Q. Adams, *Letters on Silesia.*

[38] Pickering to Adams, Philadelphia, Jan. 7, 1800: "That it [the treaty] has not been sooner decided upon, seems to be owing to the little interest which any treaty with Prussia could excite; she not being a maritime power, nor as yet connected with us by commerce." Dept. State, *Instructions, Prussia,* 5: 277.

[39] Perkins, *Monroe Doctrine, 1823-1826,* 167.

[40] *Ibid.*

[41] Curti, *Austria and the United States 1848-1852,* 150ff.

for the cause of Protestantism in the Seven Years' War was still remembered. George Bancroft, the greatest American historian of the first half of the nineteenth century, in his *History of the United States,* assigned a place of honor to Prussia. With partiality, but grandly, he interpreted democracy as a sort of institution by divine grace, declaring the rise of the American people to be a triumph of Protestantism. The Brandenburg-Prussian State to him connoted a country that had achieved a victory for Protestantism in Europe similar to that in North America. After the Thirty Years' War, so he reasoned, only America and Brandenburg were places of refuge for the German Protestants. Washington, Pitt, and Frederick alike had fought for the liberty of the world.[42]

Similarly, John Motley's *History of the Netherlands* became a graphic account of a Protestant-Germanic war of liberty against the Roman-Catholic tyranny of Spain. Prussia, in American eyes, continued to be identified with the idea of intellectual liberty. Despite her "political reactionism," so distasteful to American opinion, she enjoyed, at least in New England, a certain degree of esteem because of her system of general education, freedom of thought, and high state of the sciences. It is hardly a discovery to note a distant relationship between the puritanic and the Prussian principles of living, a similar ethical conception of work, which facilitated an understanding, especially with northern Germany. Many an American who toured Germany in the first few decades of the nineteenth century was astonished to see how simple, "how republican," were the habits of daily life, how much leeway absolute monarchy granted to the personal liberty of the individual.[43] Even general conscription was sometimes enviously lauded as an excellent method of education for truly democratic citizenship.[44]

While American opinion of Prussia, within those limits, took a rather definite form, American ideas of Germany in general were more than vague. This was but natural, for the lack of a representative German type and of

[42] Bancroft, *History of the United States,* X, 83ff.

[43] "The badges of monarchy being thus remote, and the nobility who reside in the province having generally their houses in the country, the manners of the people in the towns have more of a republican than of a monarchical cast; and the general equality among the people gives them a social turn, which I have seldom seen in other parts of Germany." J. Q. Adams, *Letters on Silesia,* 177. Buchanan, too, after a Rhine journey in Aug. 1833, said: "There is great freedom of speech allowed throughout the Prussian dominions, and in those east of the Rhine the king is popular notwithstanding the violation of his promise to give them a constitution." Cf. G. T. Curtis, *James Buchanan,* I, 219; cf. Greeley, *Glances at Europe,* 266.

[44] See John Bigelow, *Retrospections,* IV, 429ff.

cultural centers, such as were possessed in particular by Great Britain and France, made it very difficult to form an opinion. Moreover, aside from inadequate means of communication, it was chiefly British sources upon which Americans had to rely for information about the various phases of life in Germany. In the first few decades of the nineteenth century Americans had no distinct idea of Germany's intellectual development. English translations of a number of German books had appeared in America before 1826, for instance, Goethe's *Hermann und Dorothea* and *Werther,* the latter even reach ing several editions. But the number of Americans who had as much as a reading knowledge of German was small indeed. As was the case throughout Europe, French culture dominated the upper classes of society. Ignorance of the German language was so widespread that George Ticknor could not find a German instructor when he sought to study the language after reading Madame de Staël's book on Germany, an English translation of which had appeared in New York in 1814.[45]

A second factor which influenced American opinion was the German immigrant. Appraisal of German colonists was unconsciously transferred to all Germans in general. While their efficiency and sense of order were admired, such qualities as the Americans disliked most were indiscriminately characterized as "Dutch," a designation with a touch of disdain, for the Hollanders as a rule were considered phlegmatic, hard drinkers, and rude in their treatment of women.[46] On the other hand, the Americans were influenced by the ideas brought from the home country by the German colonists, whose attitude toward Germany frequently was full of resentment since they had been forced to emigrate because of economic, religious, or political conditions. American opinion all too often reflected an image distorted or dependent on temporary political situations. It was difficult for Americans, enjoying as they did the opportunities of vast undeveloped areas, to appreciate conditions peculiar to Europe, and to Germany in particular, resulting from lack of room for expansion.

While American opinion of things German was consequently vague, intellectuals frequently felt the spell of Germany. Reports of travelers indicate as much; the novelist Henry James, for instance, writing from Homburg on July 28, 1873, describes an evening in the Kurgarten that gave him a feeling of inspiration such as he had never experienced in Italy. William James, in a letter to Oliver Wendell Holmes from Berlin, September 17, 1867, speaks of his sympathy for the Germans, with whom association was so pleasant because

[45] Wilkens, in *Americana Germanica,* III, 156ff.
[46] Not always, but frequently, the word "Dutch" had a derogatory meaning. Cf. Wendte, *America and Germany,* 14.

of their qualities of righteousness and lack of prudery and avarice, which impressed him favorably.[47]

The intellectual classes of New England society, especially, realized their direct or indirect indebtedness to German culture. The most prominent representatives of New England literature—Emerson, Longfellow, and Thoreau—had either visited Germany themselves or were strongly influenced by German thought. Transcendentalism as founded by Emerson could not be imagined without Kant and Hegel. At the same time, the opinion of the few Americans who in the first part of the nineteenth century studied German literature was invariably affected by a prejudice they were unable to overcome. This was the moral viewpoint peculiar to a mode of thinking tinged with puritanism, the thesis that all mental culture was devised exclusively to serve the improvement and education of mankind. Even Emerson, more liberal-minded than the others and an admirer of German science, did not pass this barrier.[48] In a well-known essay he criticizes Goethe for not having fathomed the depths of genius. Goethe did not, he says, venerate the Supreme Unity; he was incapable of entirely surrendering himself to moral sentiments.[49] George Bancroft, who did much to promote in America an appreciation of German cultural achievements, criticized Goethe because he had "more frequently sketched the sorrows which spring from the imagination, and the vices of refinement" than "sentiments of tenderness and true humanity . . . He never was carried away by a holy enthusiasm for truth or freedom." [50] Only Bayard Taylor, who was partly of German extraction and who had married a German, was absolutely free from that bias. In an essay "Weimar in June" he defended Goethe's attitude toward women. No poet, he says, was ever so much misunderstood in that respect as was Goethe.[51] Taylor's translation of *Faust* is the admirable work of a man capable of thoroughly identifying himself with the spirit of a foreign country.

[47] Henry James, *Transatlantic Sketches*, 362; William James, *Letters*, I, 98ff.

[48] Cf. Emerson on German science, in his *Journals*, IX, 30f.: "I think the Germans have an integrity of mind which sets their science above all other. They have not this science in scraps, this science on stilts. They have posed certain philosophical facts on which all is built, the doctrine of *immanence*, as it is called, by which everything is the cause of itself, or stands there for its own, and repeats in its own all other; 'the ground of everything is immanent in that thing.' Everything is organic, freedom also, not to add, but to grow and unfold."

[49] Emerson, *Works*, IV, 270.

[50] ". . . Instead of describing sentiments of tenderness and true humanity, he has more frequently sketched the sorrows which spring from the imagination, and the vices of refinement. . . . He never was carried away by a holy enthusiasm for truth or freedom." Bancroft, *Literary and Historical Miscellanies*, 193, 201.

[51] *Atlantic Monthly*, XXXIX, 61ff. (Jan. 1877).

German opinion of Americans was likewise strangely vacillating and unsettled during that period.[52] That opinion, too, was strongly influenced by the impressions of German emigrants. Enthusiastic approval or severe criticism was often determined by the fulfilled hopes or bitter disappointments of people who had migrated from Germany. From the narrow limits of his native country the German would longingly look forward to the land of vast territories, only to be repelled by a cold and indifferent atmosphere when once in America. Those at home revolting against existing conditions looked to America for support and comfort. The American War for Independence was consequently received with great approval in Germany, the advocates of *Sturm und Drang* vying with the classicists in exuberant eulogies.

For the age of rationalism the establishment of the American state was of significance because there "man, by free agreement, created a State wherein he was free to determine his own destiny." [53] The feeling was current that a new stage in the development of mankind had been reached. The opinion of romanticism, however, was quite to the contrary. According to its conception of an organic state, America could not be considered a state. As for young Germany, opinions were divided. Some of its members, like Börne, professed their sympathy, while others, like Heine or Gutzkow, disliked America. Lenau's attitude was quite contradictory. His romantic soul praised America's still primitive nature, but, confronted with its concrete reality, his enthusiasm vanished. After his sojourn in the United States, he asserted that the Americans, exclusive devotees of materialism, had no souls. Nor did nature in America, he thought, have feeling or imagination.[54] Kürnberger, in his political novel *Der Amerikamüde,* struggled against excessive enthusiasm for America. He, too, denied that the Americans valued spiritual things but admitted the importance of the materialistic principle which, in his opinion, dominated America.

Interest in mutual trade relations was at first less keen in America than it was in Germany. Between 1810 and 1820 the percentage of American exports to Germany dropped considerably. Britain as well as France meant far more

[52] Hildegard Meyer, *Nord-Amerika im Urteil des Deutschen Schrifttums bis zur Mitte des 19. Jahrhunderts,* 8, and Weber, *America in Imaginative German Literature;* Hatfield and Hochbaum, "Influence of the American Revolution upon German Literature," in *Americana Germanica,* III, 338ff. (1899); Bancroft, *History of the United States,* X, 89ff.

[53] Hildegard Meyer, *Nord-Amerika im Urteil des Deutschen Schrifttums bis zur Mitte des 19. Jahrhunderts,* 12ff.

[54] Baker, *Lenau and Young Germany in America.*

to American export trade.[55] It was not even considered worth while to maintain a diplomatic representative in Berlin. Consular offices, too, were not established to any great extent until the twenties. The Prussian point of view, however, was different; Prussia soon found it necessary to have a permanent observer in America. That circumstance resulted from the American tariff policy, which dated back to 1816. Through the efforts of Prussia's representative in Washington, Friedrich Greuhm, the act of Congress of March 3, 1819, permitted Prussian ships to enter North American harbors on perfect equality with American ships. But that reciprocity was limited as to duration.[56] Then came an interval without a treaty when a diplomatic mission seemed advisable, the Prussian Ministry of Commerce being especially interested (July 28, 1822). Dr. Niederstetter became the Prussian chargé d'affaires at Washington. At first he tried to continue the work of Greuhm. But a bill for equal treatment of Prussian and American ships failed to pass Congress. Under the circumstances the Prussian Government desired to conclude a treaty. Noncommittal discussions had been held before. It was a fortunate coincidence that John Quincy Adams occupied the White House at that time, he being unique in that he was to some extent informed about the possibilities of commerce with Germany. The Prussian Government desired a treaty of reciprocity which was to stipulate the principle that the flag protects the cargo in case of naval war. It wished to avoid, however, a reformulation of the principle of "free ships— free goods" but expressed the hope that the matter should be interpreted liberally in case of war. Niederstetter was authorized to state that his Government in principle held to the former regulations. Thus the draft submitted by Secretary of State Henry Clay contained but one article on the immunity of private property while all other maritime articles of the two former treaties were dropped. The President found that objectionable. He recommended a supplementary article which was to sum up all those regulations that might prove useful in future. Niederstetter proposed to insert article 18 of the commercial treaty of 1783 between the United States and Sweden which provided that a ship was to be returned to the original owner if it had been seized by privateers of the other country and had not been in enemy hands for more than 24 hours.[57] The President approved, but the Secretary of State wanted a somewhat more exact definition of blockade. However, Niederstetter had no instructions on this point. Before ratification he proposed to

[55] Fisk, *Die handelspolitischen und sonstigen völkerrechtlichen Beziehungen,* 54, calculates the drop of American exports to Germany between 1810 and 1820 at 3.21 percent.

[56] Greuhm's *Memorandum,* Berlin, May 22, 1822.

[57] Malloy, *Treaties,* II, 1731.

supplement the treaty by three more articles: elimination of privateering, definition of blockade, and a list of articles of contraband. The American Government, however, evaded the issue.

Thus the treaty of May 1, 1828, was concluded,[58] with a few amendments being added in 1829. Article 5 of the treaty was based on the most-favored-nation principle. No higher duties, accordingly, "shall be imposed on the importation into the Kingdom of Prussia of any article, the produce or manufacture of the United States, than are or shall be payable on the like article being the produce or manufacture of any other foreign country." The same regulation was made regarding exports. According to article 9 the treaty became a treaty of reciprocity. It contained the reciprocity clause the United States had used in many treaties before: "If either party shall hereafter grant to any other nation any particular favor in navigation or commerce, it shall immediately become common to the other party, freely, where it is freely granted to such other nation, or on yielding the same compensation, when the grant is conditional." [59]

At the same time the United States was negotiating with the Hanse towns. Navigation companies in Hamburg and Bremen had had much intercourse with America as early as 1800.[60] Young Americans came to study "commerce" in Hamburg and to get additional training in the local Academy of Commerce. Many Hanseatic merchants went to America at that time. The years between 1795 and 1799 had brought prosperity to Hamburg and Bremen as they profited from their neutrality in the war between Britain and France. They became the most important marts for tropical articles. But that prosperity did not last. The European war, and particularly the continental blockade, seriously interfered with navigation. The last American sailing ships appeared on the Elbe at the close of 1808. Not until after 1813 could ocean traffic be gradually resumed. Transatlantic trade did not reach its former proportions for some time. Nevertheless, Hamburg established a consulate general at Philadelphia in 1817. New York received its first consul from Bremen in 1815. The great revival of commerce with America came as a result of the struggle of the South American colonies for independence. "Hamburg has acquired colonies," they said at the time. Hanseatic enterprise vigorously took advantage of the tempting business opportunities. Even though South American interests prevailed, trade with North America was on the increase.

---

[58] Prussian Ministry of the Interior to the Prussian Ministry of Foreign Affairs Aug. 22, 1827; instructions to Niederstetter, Oct. 16, 1827. Cf. J. Q. Adams, *Memoirs*, VII, 515ff., and Malloy, *Treaties*, II, 1496.

[59] Kapp, *Friedrich der Grosse*, 123ff.; Malloy, *Treaties*, II, 1497, 1498.

[60] Wätjen, *Aus der Frühzeit des Nordatlantikverkehrs*, 3ff.

Between 1820 and 1827 the total value of goods carried to North America from German ports amounted to $14,250,000, while sundries and staple commodities having a total value of $18,000,000 were shipped from thence to German ports. On the conclusion of a treaty with Brazil in 1828, an economic agreement with the United States was reached after prolonged difficulties quite similar to those in the Prussian negotiations. The commercial treaty, as prepared by the Hanseatic Minister in Paris, Vincent Rumpff, was concluded on December 20, 1827, with an additional article of June 4, 1828. The text of the treaty was very similar to the Prussian treaty, article 2 containing the most-favored-nation clause regarding customs and article 9 the reciprocity clause.[61]

After that the Hanse towns decidedly took the lead in trade relations with the United States. A radical change took place especially with regard to the proportion of commerce carried under the two flags. More and more the German flag superseded the American flag. Of the number of ships that sailed from American seaports to the Elbe, Weser, and Trave in 1829-30, 14,728 were American and 10,262 were Hanseatic and other ships. In 1840-41 the ratio was 14,123 American to 46,147 Hanseatic and other ships.[62] Besides economic depressions in America and the preeminence of the internal trade for American business, causes for that development, as a modern historian of economics points out, were to be found in the rising importance of emigration traffic.[63] Bremen was more important than Hamburg because it depended on the tobacco trade, and it came to be the greatest trade center for tobacco imports from North America. The export of tobacco attained such importance that the United States wished to conclude new agreements with the Zollverein and other German states as well. For the first time the United States sent to Berlin its representative, commissioned to enter into closer relations with the Zollverein. The American market had become very important to Germany, German exports between 1834 and September 30, 1836, amounting to $14,840,192.[64]

The Americans wished to pay for German goods with increased tobacco exports. On March 25, 1844, an agreement with the Zollverein was reached, the United States agreeing not to charge a rate of duty higher than 20 percent on agricultural and industrial products of the Zollverein states. The Zollverein, in its turn, granted a reduction of duty on lard and tobacco.[65] The

---

[61] Cf. text in *Hamburger Handelsarchiv*, 1864, 26ff.; Miller, *Treaties*, III, 387.
[62] Wätjen, *Aus der Frühzeit des Nordatlantikverkehrs*, 13.
[63] *Ibid.*, 14f.
[64] Fisk, *Die handelspolitischen und sonstigen völkerrechtlichen Beziehungen*, 83.
[65] *Ibid.*, 89ff. Cf. also Daniel Webster, *Writings and Speeches*, XII, 85ff.

United States, however, was not satisfied with that; agreements with other German states, not members of the Zollverein, were sought. Negotiations were carried on by A. Dudley Mann, who was to play so prominent a part on the Confederate side in the Civil War. A treaty with Saxony was concluded on May 14, 1845, one with Hanover came in the following year, and successively followed treaties with Oldenburg on March 10, 1847, with Mecklenburg-Schwerin on December 9, 1847, and with Mecklenburg-Strelitz on December 2, 1853. The treaty with Hanover was of particular importance in that it contained a provision permitting the ships of the contracting parties to carry products for other countries besides their own. American efforts to induce the Zollverein to adhere to that treaty failed.[66] The favorable development of commercial relations between the United States and individual German states during that period is no doubt due in part to Friedrich List, the father of the Zollverein. List had come to America in 1825; in 1832 he became American consul in Leipzig and subsequently served in other German cities.

It may be imagined what great hopes for increased commerce were raised by the expected unification of the whole of Germany in 1848. In that year negotiations were indeed carried on at Frankfort looking toward a universal German customs union. The several states had sent delegates to Frankfort. The Reich Ministry of Commerce had planned a Reich Customs Act and a Reich Customs Law.[67] Negotiations with the United States for a commercial treaty were looked upon with favor, America being greatly interested because of her tobacco trade. The provisional government sent Friedrich Ludwig von Rönne, formerly Prussian Minister Resident in Washington,[68] to America; but as he had to wait until the beginning of 1849 for his credentials, much valuable time was lost. In fact, negotiations never began. The political situation had changed so much to the detriment of the provisional government that the Department of State hesitated to give offense to Berlin and Vienna. To be sure, commerce was not the sole reason for the intense interest Americans took in the German Revolution. A German national state of liberal tendencies, they thought, would closely approach American ideals. The Ameri-

[66] Buchanan's instructions to Mann Mar. 27 and Aug. 12, 1846, and Jan. 9, 1847, Dept. State, *Special Missions*, 1, 239, 245, 248; also June 26, 1847, and May 29, 1848, Dept. State, *Instructions to Diplomatic Agents, Germany*, 1ff., 14ff.; Buchanan to C. T. Gevekoht, Nov. 11, 1847, Dept. State, *Notes to German Legation*, 6, 172ff. Cf. Bemis, *American Secretaries of State*, V, 224f.

[67] Delbrück, *Lebenserinnerungen*, I, 221. Cf. Hawgood, *Political and Economic Relations between the United States of America and the German Provisional Central Government*, 38ff.

[68] In 1834 Rönne was Prussian Minister Resident in Washington.

can Government had accredited its Minister to Berlin, Andrew J. Donelson, to Frankfort at the same time, expressly stating that this measure was by no means directed against Prussia. Donelson, in an introductory speech, was more than optimistic in speaking of the insolubility of the Union—15 years before the Civil War. But he was justly proud of the fact that the American Constitution served as a model for the discussions of a federal German constitution. The German public at that time was indeed greatly interested in the Constitution of the United States.[69] Political pamphlets circulated during 1848 and 1849 frequently suggested that the public law of the United States be transferred to the German law then in the making, either entirely or in part. Such wishes were by no means restricted to publicists more or less given to sentimental argumentation and admiration of the Union as a prototype of democratic government. Serious politicians, too, recommended such a transfer as advantageous. Count Robert von der Goltz, for example, later German Ambassador in Paris, in a memorandum of April 18, 1848, pointed out that the political organization of the North American Union and its members contained numerous elements quite congenial to German conditions. They would need only to be adjusted to monarchical principles to furnish most excellent material for the foundations of a permanent German constitution. The influence of the American Constitution is quite evident from the discussions in the National Assembly. The constitutional committee extended the so-called *"Siebzehner-Entwurf"* on the American model and improved and supplemented it in some cases. A. Dudley Mann was enthusiastic in his reports on the influence of American ideas. But it speaks well for his clear vision that his original enthusiasm very soon subsided as he recognized the menace of radical tendencies on the triumph of the national movement. His reports, therefore, became less and less optimistic. After his recall, there was only a secretary of legation left in Frankfort.[70]

American politicians, too, because of their own problem of Federal rights and States' rights, very attentively watched the struggle of the Germans for national unity. On April 18, the Prussian Minister, Baron von Gerolt, reported that the American statesmen had recognized the fundamental difference

[69] Cf. Scholl, *Einfluss der nordamerikanischen Unionsverfassung auf die Verfassung des Deutschen Reiches vom 28. März 1849.*

[70] The following reports from Donelson are noteworthy: To Buchanan, Frankfort, July 26 (enclosure, note to Schmerling July 24) and Sept. 14, 1848; Berlin, Oct. 26 and Dec. 14, 1848, and Feb. 3, 1849; Frankfort, July 1 and 8, 1849; Dept. State, *Despatches, Germany*, 1, nos. 1 and 4, *Prussia*, 5, nos. 97, 108, and 118, and *Germany*, 1, nos. 16 and 18, respectively. Reports of A. Dudley Mann from Munich Mar. 13, 1848, no. 13, and from Frankfort Apr. 25, 1848 (private), Dept. State, *Special Agents*, 14. Cf. Bemis, *Secretaries of State*, V, 325f.

in the development of Germany and France. John C. Calhoun repeatedly stated that, as to the European continent, he expected establishment of constitutional government by Germany and not by France. In a letter of May 28, 1848, to the Prussian Minister von Gerolt, he wrote in detail on the forthcoming national German constitution. He cautioned him against conferring too much power on the central government. Germany's foreign policy, defense against attacks from without, preservation of peace, and internal relations among the several states, he said, should be intrusted to the central government; but it should not be given more authority than necessary for any of the purposes mentioned.[71]

Thus, there was once more between the two countries a live, direct connection aside from merely economic considerations. Mutual interest was increased by the many political refugees who criticized European affairs from their new American viewpoint. But in the last analysis this constituted but a brief interlude. The breakdown of the national movement in Germany brought a severe reaction, and the cultivation of commercial relations between the United States and the individual German states again took the lead.

Nevertheless, the year 1848 marked a new chapter in the relations between the two countries. The problem of national unity was coming to a head. In America, the differences between the North and the South threatened to break up the Union. In Germany, the year 1848 demonstrated the fact that a unified national state would be possible only if either of the two great powers, Prussia or Austria, assumed control. Such similarity of political developments was increased by the large number of Germans who looked for a new home in America during those decades. Since a majority of those immigrants settled in the North, they continually strengthened the anti-slavery movement. Social motives and more especially religious motives had influenced emigration in the seventeenth and eighteenth centuries; to these political considerations were now added. Emigration for political reasons should not be overestimated as to numbers; naturally it was always exceeded by emigration brought about by social causes. But it gave the immigrants in America new ideals. The political refugee, driven from his native country by political evils, retained a far more intense interest in events in his fatherland than did the ordinary emigrant. Frequently he was not as eager to renounce his allegiance to Germany as earlier emigrants had been.

The German element had been able to retain its national characteristics only in regions, like Pennsylvania, where it established centralized settlements.

[71] Appendix to Gerolt's report to the Prussian Ministry May 29, 1848, cf. appendix, *post,* p. 277; Calhoun, *Correspondence,* in American Historical Association, *Annual Report,* 1899, II, 748ff.

Only in Pennsylvania did it seem for a time as though the German colonists might be able to impress not only their social but also their political characteristics upon the country. Benjamin Franklin's worried letter to his British friend Peter Collinson, May 9, 1753,[72] complaining of the preponderance of the German element in Pennsylvania, will forever be a remarkable testimony to the strength of German colonization in a section of the United States. In general, however, the German settlers were unable to form separate cultural units. The reasons are readily understood. The majority of German immigrants did not come from the middle classes, as did the Anglo-Saxons, but from the lower strata of society. They scarcely possessed a common language. Innumerable dialects differentiated them from one another. They did not come as colonists into a culturally inferior country, but as refugees or victims of want. In many cases they had no greater desire than to be severed from their native country forever. The overwhelming expanse of natural riches of the new country contributed—as was the case with all other nationalities—to a rapid absorption of national individuality. The German element therefore could not, in the long run, triumph in an unequal fight with an Anglo-Saxon element which was racially united and numerically far superior. It is utterly incorrect to suppose that there was ever a possibility of gaining supremacy for the German language anywhere in the United States, even in States most extensively settled by Germans.[73]

Not always did the loss of the German language cause complete alienation from the fatherland, even after two or three generations, not to mention the fact that mastery of their native tongue gave the German immigrants a different position in the country of their choice.

It is hard to estimate the contribution of the German element to the development of the American nation. German blood became an ingredient of the national life, the intangible and indefinable characteristics being justly important. For an answer to the question as to what extent German immigrants affected the political development of the country, we must depend on an

[72] Benjamin Franklin, *Works,* VII, 66. The letter, written out of Anglo-Saxon resentment, should not be taken quite literally. Nevertheless, it shows that the German element had established itself there.

[73] There is a legend, sometimes taken seriously even today, to the effect that, except for one single vote, the German language might have been at one time declared the official language of the State of Pennsylvania, and that Friedrich August Muhlenberg's vote decided against it. This absurd story was refuted by Faust in his article "Vergangenheit und Zukunft der deutschen Sprache in Amerika," in *Monatshefte für deutsche Sprache und Pädagogik,* XVII, pt. 7, 235ff. (Sept. 1916). It is correct only in that both English and German were used in the middle of the eighteenth century for certain resolutions of the Pennsylvania Assembly.

abundance of individual observations, but a final opinion cannot be written as yet. Undeniably Germans influenced local administration and reforms of certain phases of public life, such as civil service and forestry, but their influence on governmental affairs is less evident. Not until the end of the nineteenth century was there a President of German descent. In contrast to the Irish, we do not find many Americans of German descent among the highest officials. The prominent position occupied by Carl Schurz remained an isolated case despite a considerable number of members of Congress and other officials of German extraction. In neither of the two great parties did the Germans exercise an influence corresponding to their numerical strength. Americans of German descent did not possess the Anglo-Saxon instinct which derives political power from loyalty to a party. Relatively independent, the German voter was considered unreliable. American politicians used to complain that the German element failed in political matters. Henry Clay at one time said on that point half jestingly: "The Germans are very honest people, fine farmers, and very industrious. I consider them a blessing to the country in which they settle. The only thing I do not like," he added quite in good humor, "is their politics." [74]

On the whole, German immigration was regarded favorably. People realized the value of those diligent and reliable laborers and artisans. The capital which the German immigrants produced in the form of labor was a substantial asset to American business. But the strong Anglo-Saxon race would not tolerate alien forms of civilization; it found undesirable the preservation of habits other than British. This point of view was strongly manifested as early as June 4, 1819, in a letter from John Quincy Adams to Maurice de Fürstenwaerther, answering a question of April 22 concerning the opportunities offered immigrants.[75] Similarly, too great a concentration of foreigners in one place was not favored. In 1729 the Governor of Pennsylvania promulgated a law against an excessive influx of immigrants which, under the circumstances, could only have been directed against the Germans.

Actually, unfriendly acts against the Germans did not occur until the thirties and forties. The "Know Nothing" Party originally had sound principles. After Jackson's Presidency the American party system was so corrupt and degenerate that something had to be done to stop the shameless practice of misusing the votes of ignorant immigrants. But this nativist movement turned its spite against the Germans, who made up by far the largest number of immigrants. Serious riots occurred. During a celebration in New York in honor of a German woman singer a torchlight parade was broken

[74] Koerner, *Memoirs*, I, 350.
[75] J. Q. Adams to Maurice de Fürstenwaerther, Philadelphia, June 4, 1819.

up. The office of a German newspaper in St. Louis was threatened when its editor criticized the nativist movement. Emerson's magazine *The Dial* took occasion to satirize the anti-German sentiment.[76] Thus, the immigrants of that period had to contend with more difficulties than ever before. Their troubles were greatly increased by the different ideology of the intellectuals among the new immigrants. For the first time—this cannot be emphasized too strongly—large numbers of people came to America who were opposed to the prevailing orthodox views.[77]

The Germans of 1848 were children of rationalism, radicals in politics as well as in religion. Those immigrants, most of them, hoped to return soon to their native country. They judged American things by European standards. Disappointment was inevitable. But the more harshly they criticized, the more isolated they became. Their constant nagging and their bickerings with the Germans who had immigrated in the thirties did not increase their popularity.[78] They invited ridicule, a few of them demanding that America should annex Europe, although this demand contained an instinctive insight into the connections between events on both sides of the Atlantic. The situation of those Germans was an extremely critical one. They faced a life full of either sterile disappointment or complete absorption in the masses of those who already had renounced their heritage. At this point they suddenly discovered a new ideal: it was the great historical truth that on foreign soil they had nearly the same mission to perform as the one for the sake of which they had left Germany. For it was at the beginning of the fifties that the question "Union or Secession" entered its decisive phase of development, while the problem of slavery had aroused the sense of justice of innumerable people. Taking part in that struggle with the same ardor that had made them fight for the unity and civil liberty of Germany, the Germans became the personal representatives of the close connection between their fatherland and the country of their choice. Carl Schurz, the most prominent man of that group, although always independent of the masses, could never have been called a citizen of two worlds had he not experienced in his own soul the destiny of two countries.[79]

Thus we reach the starting point for a detailed discussion of our subject. At the outset, we shall have to form an idea of the American crisis and its effects on European conditions.

[76] Koerner, *Das deutsche Element in den Vereinigten Staaten,* 319; Bacourt, *Souvenirs d'un diplomate,* 120f.

[77] Goebel, *Der Kampf um die deutsche Kultur in Amerika,* 86.

[78] For those controversies see *Der Deutsche Pionier,* VII, 112ff.

[79] Schurz, *Der Deutsche und der Amerikaner,* 97ff.

CHAPTER II

THE EUROPEAN POWERS AND THE
AMERICAN CIVIL WAR

E VER since the birth of the Union there had been latent possibilities of secession. The struggle over the Constitution, the vehement clashes between the advocates of a strong centralized government and the champions of state sovereignty barely concealed dissensions caused by territorial conditions. The Constitution, in the end, proved to be a compromise, a *modus vivendi;* it gave the central Government just enough power to keep the Union together but not enough for a solution of the increasingly urgent national problems. Such a situation at the outset of American history was probably fortunate. Domestic colonization called for unrestrained utilization of all available forces. Somewhat paradoxically expressed, the Union at that period did not disintegrate because the idea of unity was not as yet sufficiently developed to afford opposition to any counterpressure of particularist tendencies. The delimitation of powers was not a live issue until the Northern States agitated for a strong Federal Government as the only means of keeping the Southern States in check. When the break came the adherents of the Union idea endeavored to prove that secession was a violation of the Constitution. The champions of the theory of nullification, with as much sagacity or sophistry, were able to defend their thesis that the creators of the Constitution had admitted secession to be a fundamental right of the States, or that they had at least left the question open.[1] Such matters, however, can be decided only by force, not by legal arguments. A victory for the Southern secessionists would have obliterated the political future of the Union. Hence a peaceful separation was possible only at a period when the instinct for power was not

[1] C. F. Adams, *Trans-Atlantic Historical Solidarity,* 27ff.; Jefferson Davis, *Rise and Fall of the Confederate Government,* I, 121ff.; Beard, *Rise of American Civilization,* II, 47ff.

markedly developed. Possibly, but not very probably, psychological conditions for a peaceful separation existed throughout the forties. After that period the desire for unity had become so general and so strong that secession was out of the question. Furthermore, as the utilization of steam power revolutionized industry, the tendency toward centralization increased. Europe had the same experience. Technology destroyed old political connections. Removal of existing customs barriers was sought instead of the erection of new ones. The changed conditions called for a firmly consolidated national state.

As long as two factions were fighting each other, foreign politics also suffered greatly. For a certain period we may still consider that division of duties was geographically determined—while the North protected the Canadian border, the South guarded the territory along the Gulf of Mexico. Somewhat similarly, a sort of balance between Prussia and Austria had been established. But in that respect, too, things changed. Immediately after the Mexican War of 1848 opinions differed as to the division of the spoils. The South wished to have the number of slave-holding States increased, while the North, of course, resisted vigorously. It was evident that to keep the ship from being wrecked national politics could be managed only from a political center. Such was the situation in America; the same relations obtained between Prussia and Austria after the war of 1864 for Schleswig-Holstein. Power alone was able to effect a decision. Bismarck, at that time formulating the expression "blood and iron" for the only possible solution of the great problems of the period, in the last analysis meant the same thing as did William H. Seward, subsequently Secretary of State, in his speech on the "irrepressible conflict between opposing and enduring forces."

Unfortunately for the United States, the differences between the North and the South were regional as well as economic and social. Therein lay the real significance of the slavery question. Originally, slavery had not in principle separated the North from the South. There had been opponents of slavery as early as colonial times. Virginia was first in passing resolutions against the slave trade. As late as the second decade of the nineteenth century, the American South considered slavery a necessary evil the elimination of which was open for discussion. The invention of the cotton gin and other machines changed the situation. Strong doubts have been raised as to whether the development of cotton production was really, economically speaking, fortunate for the South. But developments were inevitable. The whole region adjusted itself to the raising of cotton. This again made slave labor immensely more valuable, since the negroes were eminently fitted for just that kind of work under difficult climatic conditions. At the beginning of this new development there was some opposition which the small planters and the poor whites directed against the rising aristocracy of the big planters. But the new economic order proved to be stronger.

Slavery now became the very foundation of Southern civilization, which assigned a definite place to everybody, giving even inferior white people a feeling of self-reliance and personal liberty necessarily lacking in countries of free labor. "Wherever there are large numbers of slaves," Burke wrote, "those who are free are by far the most proud and jealous of their freedom." [2] In contrast to European traditions, however, society was not grouped in separate castes. The old South was more correctly called a democratic oligarchy. Political and social power was controlled by a comparatively small group of planters, but side by side with them there existed the community of free white people who considered themselves a privileged class superior to the negroes. The South clung to democratic ideals. Jefferson and Jackson came from the South; nowhere else could more fanatic adherents of the Constitution and the republican form of government be found than there.

Developments in the North were radically different. Technology had changed the country on a grand scale. The interests of the farmers demanded free land and the interests of capital an increase in markets. Free labor meant prosperity for both groups. For this reason the remnants of slavery in the North could be removed relatively soon and without friction. Everything was in a state of change in the North; all forces were moving in free competition. But the wave broke on the dam of the South which would not participate in unrestricted industrialization. Thus the social and economic contrast constantly widened. The dynamic pressure of the economically progressive North resulted in ever-increasing resistance from the agrarian South. Feeling menaced, it isolated itself entirely from the North. Its leaders consistently endeavored to fortify its political power. This in turn raised a feeling of growing danger in the North. But a comparison of the opposing forces leaves no doubt that the South had better reasons for fearing the superiority of the North than vice versa. For the offensive against slavery meant nothing else for the South than an attack against a national property of approximately four billion dollars. If political and social supremacy were transferred to the North, the whole structure of the old South would inevitably be shaken to its very foundations.

The South was indeed able to set up a number of arguments for its cause. It could not be denied that the condition of the slaves was constantly improving. The high prices paid for them necessitated good treatment. In general, especially in the central States, patriarchical relations between master

2 Wilson, *Division and Reunion,* 105.

and servant prevailed, an unwritten treaty of loyalty which proved its value even through hard times. First of all, the South raised the question of what should be done after a sudden emancipation of the slaves. Three million colored people lived in the South next to six million whites. White supremacy, once slavery was abolished, so it was argued, could be maintained only by use of the most brutal means. The South had given the country its ablest leaders. Nine out of thirteen Presidents had come from the South by the time the Civil War broke out. Nearly all the prominent Senators were southerners. New England, to be sure, also possessed great writers and artists. But the atmosphere of the South was more refined and cordial than the atmosphere of the North. The paternalistic system prevented the worst abuses of capitalism. Personal responsibility for the welfare of the economically weak had a strongly educational influence which, for one thing, made possible the development of a high type of womanhood. Even people of a spiritual bent of mind felt justified in defending slavery or at least in acknowledging it as an inevitable fact. Under pressure from without there developed a regular philosophical school which taught slavery to be a providential and natural institution. Thus we find only relatively insignificant counter-currents, with everybody submitting to the overwhelming force of existing conditions. Even an organization as strong as the Methodist Church was disrupted by the regional differences. The Democratic Party likewise came near dissolution shortly before the war broke out.

The problem of slavery in itself was perhaps least suited for a decision by force of arms. But the struggle over slavery had torn open such a chasm and had created such an atmosphere of misunderstanding that the few level-headed people who tried to prevent the clash on its eve did not succeed. Otherwise it would be inexplicable that the election of Lincoln as President should have caused the break. Realizing how difficult of solution the problem of slavery was, he did not intend to interfere arbitrarily with the sovereign rights of the several States. But his election was merely the final signal. Both groups felt so seriously menaced that the unbearable tension forced the issue. The North had the spirit of the times in its favor, while the South was by no means a decaying shell, but a very live organism. It was ready to risk everything for its rights. On the eve of the war, in a crowded church in Richmond, later the capital of the Confederacy, one of the best-known clergymen preached that the slaves had been intrusted to the white people by the Lord, with the same earnestness and power of conviction as Sunday after Sunday all New England churches prayed for the abolition of slavery.[3] The tension was so great that the collision was certain to be terrible. It was to be the

[3] Dodd, *Cotton Kingdom,* 109, footnote.

greatest world catastrophe between the Napoleonic wars and the Great War.[4]

It will suffice to sketch briefly the military and political development of the War of Secession. The South had relied on two factors: the shortage of cotton ("King Cotton") was expected to have a decisive influence on world markets, and Great Britain and France would inevitably be drawn into the fight against the Union, or, at least, in their own interest, be forced to recognize the independence of the seceding States. The South was completely in error. The shortage of cotton indeed caused serious crises in certain European countries; but the South underestimated the power of adjustment and reorganization of world business just as did Germany with regard to world tonnage in the Great War. Nor could the South attain recognition by the European powers as an independent federation of states. Only a decisive triumph could have given the South such recognition; but the South won only partial victories. Thus we may say that the seceding States had, after a short time, lost the war politically and economically. However, as the blockade cut off the rebel States from the outside world, there developed the belief, peculiar to garrisons of besieged fortresses, that successful sallies would convince the enemy of the uselessness of his efforts.

From the very beginning forces were distributed quite unequally. Nine million people, three million of whom, being slaves, could be used only for economic warfare, fought against twenty-two million in the North. Nearly the entire steel and textile industries as well as most arsenals were in the North, which also possessed more than two thirds of all the capital in the banks of the Nation. Neither the North nor the South had ready a trained army. They had to form them and produce the corresponding war materials from the ground up. The superiority of the Union on the seas proved to be a fatal factor to the South, as the blockade deprived it of essential supplies. It became evident how much the South depended on the North, whereas it had previously entertained the opinion that it controlled the North economically. As early as 1862 prices for such essentials as butter, tea, coffee, and oats rose to excessive heights.

At first both parties rivaled each other in their devotion to their respective causes. At the beginning of the war it was considered a duty of honor for the young men of well-to-do families to volunteer for service in the army. As to military leadership, however, the South was far superior. The organization

---

[4] For the causes of the conflict, see Wilson, *Division and Reunion;* Rhodes, *History of the United States,* I, 357ff.; C. F. Adams, *Trans-Atlantic Historical Solidarity,* 27ff.; Beard, *Rise of American Civilization,* II, 3ff. Among the special literature the works of Dodd, *Cotton Kingdom, Jefferson Davis,* and *Lincoln or Lee,* deserve foremost mention.

of its society was such as to encourage natural selection of leaders. Personal connections often existed between the men in command and the men they commanded. In Robert E. Lee, particularly, the Confederate army possessed a man whose respected strategic talent and great personality gave its leadership a stability lacking in the North, where the commander-in-chief constantly changed, especially at the beginning of the war.

For years the military situation was uncertain. The Confederates had the initial advantage of the great victory of Bull Run. On the other hand, the naval superiority of the North was demonstrated by the conquest of New Orleans, which cost the South the control of the lower Mississippi. The situation in general was rather obscure for the reason that the war had to be fought on two entirely different fronts. Whereas, generally speaking, the Confederate cause was steadily declining, some great successes appeared on the surface. The defeat of the Union armies at Fredericksburg in December 1862 and at Chancellorsville in May 1863 revived failing hopes in the South again and again while increasing the internal crisis in the Union. After Chancellorsville, Lee was able to advance through Maryland. Washington, Philadelphia, and Pittsburgh seemed seriously endangered for a moment. Opposition to the Lincoln administration had grown very strong since the autumn of 1862. The elections in the fall of that year nearly everywhere resulted in successes for the Democrats, who were opposed to a continuation of the war. The Union, too, after the stream of volunteers had dwindled, was compelled to resort to general conscription, the enforcement of which was as difficult as in the South, if not more so, owing to the mixture of races in the large cities. As early as September 22, 1862, conciliation was made impossible by the declaration of emancipation. It was no doubt an emergency measure, born of the moment, for the defense of national unity and for the purpose of influencing the critical attitude of foreign countries.

Such was the state of the contest at the beginning of July 1863 when the belligerents faced one another at Gettysburg. A decisive victory for the South might possibly have resulted in a tolerable compromise. The route to Washington would have been open, the reelection of Lincoln very uncertain, and financial failure of the Union practically inevitable. Lee had concentrated the best army of the whole war at Gettysburg, almost exclusively veterans accustomed to fight and to conquer. For the first time he was his enemy's equal numerically. On the first day of battle he neglected to occupy the commanding heights of Cemetery Hill, so that on the morning of the second day Union troops were able to take a strong position there. Despite the warnings of his staff, Lee, trusting the offensive power of his troops, risked a frontal attack. By evening he had won some partial successes. On the third day, however,

33

after a terrible cannonade, the general attack against Cemetery Hill started, and Longstreet's division was crushed by the defensive fire of the Unionists, the 11th Army Corps with its many Germans distinguishing itself. Nor was Hood's attack against the left wing of the battle line more successful. While the outcome of the three-day battle did not mean a complete defeat for Lee, the moral effect on his troops was all the greater. They had sacrificed in vain nearly one half of their effectives, dead, wounded, or captured. The political consequences of the battle were equally fatal. The latent crisis within the Union was ended. In November 1864, Lincoln was reelected by an over-whelming majority.

In spite of Gettysburg, the South continued the fight for another eighteen months. Its population proved its high qualities more clearly than ever. Before the war broke out the South had boasted of its superiority. The Confederates were right to a certain extent in feeling strong and safe. Compared to the difficulties encountered, the achievements of the army and people were very great. Lee's troops were admirable fighters. But the South was not united within itself. Certain Governors practiced sabotage openly on the pretense that general conscription was incompatible with the sovereignty of states. Toward the end of the war the number of deserters steadily increased. As in the case of Germany in the World War, the blockade deprived the South of its most essential imports. The comparatively small number of inhabitants made it necessary for nearly all able-bodied men to serve in the army so that the supervision of the slaves put an almost superhuman burden of responsibility on the shoulders of the women. Nevertheless, the self-sacrificing devotion of all classes of society was so great as to carry on the fight to the bitter end. For, after Gettysburg, it is safe to say the struggle was doomed to failure. While the South spent its strength more and more, the North, with its inex-haustible resources, was able to recover again and again despite many a subsequent setback. In retrospect, such a struggle may look like a suicidal gesture; but it was after all a pathetic expression of the inward power of a proud people unwilling to surrender until the very last. The greatness of exertion was equalled by the suddenness of the collapse which, dramatically and yet unexpectedly, came with the capitulation of Lee in April 1865. The best elements of the people in the South bore their misfortune not without proud self-control. When Lee with a small group of companions, a few days after his capitulation, rode across a bridge near Richmond through crowds of people lining the road, they uttered a sympathetic murmur, but not a word of condemnation.[5]

The complete defeat of the South prepared the ground where the extreme

[5] C. F. Adams, *Trans-Atlantic Historical Solidarity,* 168.

capitalism of modern America was to develop. While the ethical ideal of abolition was realized, simultaneously the last obstacle in the way of an unrestrained spirit of enterprise was removed. The North, too, had over exerted itself during the long war. But its industry and agriculture had been strengthened. The work of settling the West did not pause for a moment, although only a limited number of new settlers came into the country. The war sealed an alliance between the capitalists of the North and the farmers of the West. The opposition against free land ceased definitely.[6] The South, on the other hand, reckoned only losses. It had spent all of its resources for the conduct of war. If for no other cause, its prosperity was ruined by the devaluation of its currency. The disastrous end of the war made its misfortune complete. Securities became worthless; the emancipation of the slaves cost the South a national fortune of four billion dollars without any compensation. That may be considered the greatest confiscation of property between the French and Bolshevist Revolutions.

The degree of impoverishment is illustrated by a page in the *North Carolina Advertiser* of December 16, 1865. There no fewer than twenty-six great manorial estates of from one thousand to fifteen thousand acres were offered for sale, nearly all of them with an additional notation that parcels of any size of that land could be had.[7] Numerous plantations were deserted because of the heavy war casualties and the emigration of many who, embittered by the unhappy outcome of the war, no longer wished to stay. This situation provided great business opportunities for those speculators of the North who during the war had devoted their attentions to the stock exchanges rather than to the battlefields of Fredericksburg, Vicksburg, and Gettysburg.

It is a moot question whether or not the South might have been saved from such depths of disaster had not Lincoln been assassinated on April 14, 1865. Lincoln's considerate policy of moderation encountered strong opposition, and as a result of the overwhelming victory the radical elements threatened to gain the upper hand. But Lincoln enjoyed the loyal support of his grateful people. At any rate, he was the only man capable of mastering an extraordinarily difficult situation. His assassination consequently was a misfortune for the South. His death enabled irresponsible demagogues to stir up mob instincts. The South showed passive resistance to the liberation of the slaves. Nevertheless, the so-called reconstruction laws of 1867 were outrageous. It was due to them that the South, under force of arms, was delivered up to the arbitrariness of its former slaves and of unscrupulous beneficiaries of

[6] Beard, *Rise of American Civilization*, II, 114f.

[7] Schmoller, "Nationalökonomische und sozialpolitische Rückblicke auf Nordamerika," in *Preussische Jahrbücher*, XVII, 587 (1866).

the catastrophe. Not until then came an atmosphere of hatred and suspicion from which the colored people suffered most. The South resorted to self-help at the moment of greatest danger when the graft of negro governments cried to heaven and when the safety of white women was menaced by former slaves. The Ku Klux Klan was found to be the means of repelling the onslaught against white civilization. That secret society terrorized the country for years. It could not be suppressed until, owing to its excesses, it lost the sympathy of the population which had openly supported it for some time. Reaction set in; special laws of individual States disfranchised the colored people politically and separated them socially from the whites.

The North had assumed somewhat naïvely that the sympathies of all good people in Europe naturally supported it in its struggle for "justice and liberty." Slavery by that time had certainly become obsolete in Europe. Its abolition was completed by the Russian emancipation of peasants in 1861. *Uncle Tom's Cabin* [8] had made a profound impression on Europe, but, apart from the question of slavery, Europe had many complaints to make against the Union. Even liberal groups were vexed more and more by the fact that the "Yankees" constantly arraigned European institutions before American tribunals or went so far as to interfere directly with European developments. One thing, in particular, was felt to be an inconsistency which grew more evident as time went on: the Americans, so proud of their own perfection and so confident of their future, were menaced by a collapse of their political system that belied their arrogance. Thus, Europeans were more and more inclined to think that the North American Republic would not keep together forever, wondering why the United States so strongly championed the liberal movement in European politics whereas they could not settle their own problems. When the war finally broke out, it seemed rather strange from the European point of view that abolition of slavery was not declared to be the objective of war from the outset. Europe did not sufficiently understand the difficulties of political institutions that did not allow the Federal Government, without violating the Constitution, to interfere with the self-determination of the several States; nor did Europe understand the uncertain attitude of the border States, which undoubtedly would have joined the South had abolition been proclaimed at once.

More important still, the interests of some European powers were not linked with a victory of the North. For Europe, America was not only the country that absorbed its surplus population, but it was still the goal of political and economic expansion. Should Europe remain idle while a hitherto loosely connected and politically weak federation developed to form a unit

[8] C. F. Adams, *Trans-Atlantic Historical Solidarity*, 79.

under a strong central government and threatened to become an extremely dangerous competitor in the economic struggle, who, in view of existing conditions, would inevitably take control of the American continent? The objection may be raised that later developments could not be foreseen at that time. But such was not the case. The consequences for Europe of the outcome of the American war were clearly realized. French pamphlets, in particular, published during the Civil War, repeatedly warned of judging the conflict exclusively from the angle of the slavery problem. European interests, they said, required a permanent separation of the contesting parties. That would preserve for European powers possibilities of influence in America which would be lost forever once the Union were restored.[9]

However, conditions for concerted action were unfavorable. The European countries had no leader. Because of their profound internal differences they neither desired nor were they able to proceed together. None of the powers concerned would have dared even indirectly to intervene for slavery. Their attitude was not merely determined by the military situation, which, as stated before, was not very clear. Until the very last period of the war, distant observers might have concluded that the Union would not attain its objective. It was comparatively late when the representatives of the Union in Europe were able to report a pronounced change of public opinion in consequence of the changed military situation. Not until February 18, 1864, could Norman Judd, American Minister in Berlin, write home that the Europeans expected an ultimate suppression of the rebellion.[10] The American Minister at London, Charles Francis Adams, did not see a decided change until February 1865. A glance at the newspapers reveals the same situation. The possibility of a restoration of the Union was doubted for a long time.[11] The anti-slavery sentiment was one of the factors influencing policy.

Great Britain and France were foremost among European countries in their relations with the United States.[12] British-American relations had been anomalous since the War for Independence. Racial kinship, the common language,

[9] For examples, see Remont, *L'Union Américaine et l'Europe*, and Delorme, *Les États-Unis et l'Europe*. Bernhardi, in a note of Apr. 16, 1865, writes: "European interests made a disruption of the republic desirable as that country, as now constituted, might in time exercize a tyranny on the seas which would be very oppressive and which is already in its beginnings. For this reason the outcome of the war does not seem favorable to me." Cf. Bernhardi, *Aus dem Leben Theodor von Bernhardis*, VI, 194. C. F. Adams, in *Trans-Atlantic Historical Solidarity*, 112, states that European interests really called for interference.

[10] *Foreign Relations*, 1864, pt. IV, 203.

[11] C. F. Adams, *Trans-Atlantic Historical Solidarity*, 63.

[12] Cf. Dunning, *British Empire and the United States*, and Mowat, *Diplomatic Relations of Great Britain and the United States*.

and the struggle for Protestantism in the Seven Years' War established a feel-ing of solidarity.[13] The two powers had had no armed conflicts with one another since the War of 1812. But their relations continued to be strained because of vague stipulations of treaties (problems of boundaries and fishing rights) and because of American hopes for having Canada ultimately join the United States. Thus, mutual suspicion was certain to continue. Besides, there was very serious rivalry in Central America, somewhat checked by the Clayton-Bulwer Treaty of April 19, 1850, but never removed. American policy, on the other hand, without the advantage of experience, in many respects remained dependent upon Great Britain. It was no match for the superior British tradition. The United States, therefore, without realizing it, frequently was taken into tow by Great Britain's foreign policy. Occasionally an Anglo-Saxon community of interests was mentioned.[14] Psychological inhi-bitions against friendly relations gradually relaxed.

English literature was widely known throughout America, especially in the Southern States. There was hardly a library without its set of Shakespeare's works. Carlyle was nearly as well known in America as at home. Byron, Scott, Adam Smith, Ruskin, Dickens, and Shelley were popular. The British, in their turn, began to take an interest in American writers. Irving, Cooper, Poe, Prescott, Emerson, and Motley had their readers. Books discussing America seriously and interpreting it affirmatively began to appear in the British market in the thirties. The social boycott of Americans ceased, and individual Americans were admitted to exclusive British clubs.[15] By the time immediately preceding the Civil War, interrelations had decidedly improved. The visit of the Prince of Wales in the fall of 1860 was interpreted in the sense of a "good will mission." The *Times* on that occasion declared that new relations ought to be established between the two greatest empires in the world. The Prince, it said, had come "to bridge the bloody chasm which for near a century has gaped between them." He brought Great Britain's friendship for America, the "great cognate nation." [16]

The War of Secession, then, interrupted a trend toward improved relations.

[13] See Nicholas Murray Butler's enlightening remarks in his foreword to Dunning, *British Empire and the United States,* viii.

[14] Jefferson, for example, wrote to Monroe on Oct. 24, 1823: "Great Britain is the nation which can do us the most harm of any one . . . and, with her on our side, we need not fear the whole world." Belmont, *Survival of the Democratic Principle,* 147.

[15] Dodd, *Cotton Kingdom,* 62f.; Dunning, *British Empire and the United States,* 83ff.

[16] Mowat, *Diplomatic Relations of Great Britain and the United States,* 166f.

It emphasized once more the differences.[17] Any war limiting Great Britain's freedom of action on the high seas would naturally make her an interested party. The blockade of the seceding States by the Union navy meant a painful loss to British trade. The North erred in resenting the fact that Great Britain and France recognized the Southern States as a belligerent power. For, according to international maritime law, a blockade was permissible only in the case of a war as defined by international law.[18]

Official Britain, to be sure, sympathized with the South. Lord Russell was not the only one to think that the South was fighting for the British idea of state sovereignty and that the conflict should be regarded as a continuation of the movement, as started in 1776, for separation from the Empire. The aristocracy of Southern planters indeed boasted of their British descent with particular pride. The Virginia gentleman was more closely related to traditional British society than the Yankee business man which the North was developing at the time. Tory groups hoped for a collapse of American democracy, Lord Shrewsbury prophesying that the struggle would not end without the establishment of an hereditary aristocracy and a monarchy.[19]

Economic interests in particular made Britain depend on the South. About seventy percent of her total imports from the United States consisted of raw cotton. Great Britain had three times as many spinning mills in operation as the rest of Europe combined. The South, like Britain, was opposed to protective tariffs. At the beginning of the war, Great Britain still had a surplus of cotton. The 1860 crop had been the largest, amounting to four million bales, three and a half million of which reached Europe before the war broke out. At first the warehouses in Liverpool were stocked so abundantly that they sold cotton to districts in need of it. The British Government found no cause for interference as British merchants made enormous profits from raising prices. But the situation soon changed. During the first few months of 1862 only 11,500 bales were imported from America. An attempt at importing more cotton from India proved unsatisfactory because of its inferior quality. In the industrial districts concerned poverty increased, beginning in March 1862 and reaching its climax in December of the same year. According to estimates, approximately 500,000 people then depended on public charity, a number extremely high for those times. No government could have faced that danger inactively. It was but natural that there should be strong agitation to end the

---

[17] E. D. Adams, *Great Britain and the American Civil War.*
[18] Mowat, *Diplomatic Relations of Great Britain and the United States,* 169.
[19] Report of American consulate, Bremen, Nov. 9, 1860. Cf. C. F. Adams, *Trans-Atlantic Historical Solidarity,* 21, and E. D. Adams, *Great Britain and the American Civil War,* II, 276ff.

war by intervention. The fact that there was no intervention undoubtedly was influenced by the question of slavery coupled with the distrust of France and the troubled situation in Europe. The Union very cleverly appealed to the sentiments of the masses. A few prominent Americans, among them Harriet Beecher Stowe, the author of *Uncle Tom's Cabin,* began an endeavor in 1862 to win British public opinion for the North.[20] They succeeded in having the suffering population of Lancashire pass resolutions against slavery instead of demanding British intervention in behalf of the South. Among the clergy, too, the anti-slavery sentiment was widespread. "Bondage and the lash can claim no sympathy from us. God bless and strengthen the North; give victory to their arms," thus preached Spurgeon, the well-known clergyman, after the Emancipation Proclamation.[21]

However, it was the marked improvement of the situation in the industrial districts that proved the decisive factor. Imports from India made up for the cotton shortage to some extent. And from the latter part of 1863, the Danish crisis forced British policy to proceed with the utmost caution.[22]

Nevertheless, Anglo-American relations were at times seriously strained. Besides supplying contraband of war, a source of conflict in every war, Britain violated international law by permitting the building of an auxiliary cruiser for the Southern States. This cruiser, the *Alabama,* "escaped" from England just before the adverse decision of the British crown jurists was announced. Since that privateer most seriously interfered with Union commerce, endless controversies over the *"Alabama* Claims" plagued British politics for a decade.[23] Imminent danger of war, however, probably did not exist then. The nearest approach to war came with the *Trent* affair when the captain of the American warship *San Jacinto* seized the Southern commissioners, Mason and Slidell, on their way to England and France on board the British ship *Trent* (November 8, 1861). A storm of protest arose in Britain at that time because of the violation of the British flag. If the American Government had not yielded to the British demand for surrender of the two agents, war probably would have been unavoidable. But Secretary of State William H. Seward, who at the beginning of the war had not conducted the delicate relations with Europe with too much tact or skill, had in the meantime developed to be a statesman of respectable stature. Guided by Lincoln, he had learned to play the instrument of practical politics. In the *Trent* affair he was particularly disinclined toward a break, as all

---

[20] E. D. Adams, *Great Britain and the American Civil War,* II, 33ff.
[21] Rhodes, *History of the United States,* IV, 351.
[22] E. D. Adams, *Great Britain and the American Civil War,* II, 203ff.
[23] See *post,* p. 67ff.

competent foreign representatives warned that war with any European power was utterly out of the question.[24] There was also some apprehension in the North that Southern reverses might result in European intervention since Britain had hoped that the Southern States would resist successfully even without outside help.[25]

War sentiment was possibly still less pronounced in Great Britain. As is generally known the Prince Consort softened the originally aggressive tone of the Russell note in the *Trent* affair. Great Britain, more than busy with her extended empire, was interested in avoiding a military conflict which under any circumstances would have presented grave difficulties. The Queen's profound love of peace, strengthened by her sorrow at the death of her husband, reflected the general sentiment of the country. We may even say that the situation was reversed in the second part of the war. Britain increasingly feared an American attack against Canada, which fear greatly increased after the Union victory.[26]

As for Franco-American relations, intangible factors played an essential part from the very beginning.[27] Although American gratitude for French aid in the War for Independence had greatly cooled during the period of the Directory—a military conflict seemed almost unavoidable at that time—there were enough ties left to connect the two countries. The dominant intellectual influence which French rationalism exercised throughout the world did not fail, of course, to affect American society.[28] French culture and customs prevailed among the well-to-do classes as long as the seacoast States, naturally closely connected with Europe both economically and culturally, were in the vanguard. Yet, from the start there were opposing tendencies, offsetting a complete victory for the ideas of French rationalism. The bourgeois character of the American did not care for radical ideas. It was instinctively averse to the spirit of Jacobinism, to what was called French immorality and irreverence. The frontier—the peculiar American phenomenon of the time— the army of colonists moving westward, were but slightly touched by the frivolous spirit of the eighteenth century. Anti-religious tendencies were not tolerated on the frontier. It may be observed, furthermore, that American

[24] For example, see Dayton to Seward, Paris, Dec. 6, 1861: "We cannot afford, in any event and under any circumstances, to go to war with Great Britain, with the moral sentiment of the Great Maritime Powers of the world against us." Dept. State, *Despatches, France*, 51, no. 91.

[25] Goltz to Bismarck, Aug. 30, 1863. Lord Lyons, British Minister in Washington, also worked for peace. Cf. Newton, *Lord Lyons*, I, 29ff.

[26] See *post*, p. 69.

[27] Cf. Jones, *American and French Culture*.

[28] Cf. Thwing, *History of Education in the United States since the Civil War*, 132ff.

enthusiasm for the Declaration of the Rights of Man was constantly associated with an apprehension of the extreme tendencies characteristic of nearly all French revolutions.[29]

The French and the inhabitants of the Southern States felt a certain affinity for one another. The Latin and Catholic elements in the South and the temperament of its people motivated that feeling somewhat. But France's pronounced prosecessionist policy must be laid chiefly to Napoleon III. Napoleon, who had spent a part of his exile in Central America, had then become interested in a plan for a canal which was to separate Latin America from Anglo-Saxon America.[30] Bourbon and Napoleonic plans were resurrected in his mind. Dynastic and commercial interests were to be combined in a Latin American empire under the protectorate of France. Thus originated the disastrous Mexican plan. Napoleon, to be sure, disliked the Northern States for personal reasons. Ever since his election as Emperor he had been fanatically opposed by the North and treated with so many personal insults that he had become strongly resentful. The Prussian chargé d'affaires in Paris, Henry VII, Prince Reuss, on November 29, 1861, reported from Compiègne that the Emperor of the French did not express particular sympathy for the Union cause and for the Washington Government and that he favored separation of the Southern States from the Union for which reason he hoped to see the failure of the recently begun campaign against the South. The Emperor said that traditional French policy had naturally always favored the development of a non-European power counterbalancing the maritime and commercial influence of Great Britain. So long as the United States had simply fulfilled that mission, being of great service to France and the European continent, it was possible to let them do as they pleased. But of late they had been displaying a tendency to interfere in European affairs, and such arrogance would have to be resisted and stopped. He could therefore only hope that the North would not triumph over the South in the conflict. Secession of the South would curb the North without impairing the interests of Europe. Great Britain, however, would have to exercise the same consideration, and the Southern States of America, once united and consolidated, would always be powerful enough to balance Great Britain's supremacy on the seas. The Emperor made similar statements in 1862: He would not object to a division of the United States because it had recently begun to meddle in European affairs in so curt a manner that the European powers

---

[29] Curtis, "American Opinion of French Nineteenth Century Revolutions," in *American Historical Review*, XXIX, no. 2 (Jan. 1924), and E. B. White, *American Opinion of France;* Beard, *Rise of American Civilization*, I, 364ff.

[30] Vagts, *Mexiko, Europa, und Amerika*, 88.

would be pleased to have an ever-growing transatlantic power divided and consequently weakened.[31]

Napoleon's Mexican policy could succeed only if the Union remained disrupted. The South was not in favor of Napoleon's Mexican plans inasmuch as that very country had been occupying a considerable place in the imperialistic dreams of Southern politicians; but in case of victory over the North, the Southern States would have been too dependent on the favor of European powers, especially France, to thwart Napoleon's plans. No doubt France was even more interested than Great Britain in an independent Southern Confederacy. Had it been possible France certainly would have undertaken a military intervention. But Napoleon could not risk that much. Instead, he wished England to take the lead in recognizing the Southern States so as to keep his own position in Europe safe. Isolated action seemed dangerous to him from the very beginning. In October 1862, he assured John Slidell, the Southern commissioner, of his sympathy for the South, at the time excusing his inactivity on the ground that the European situation, particularly in Italy and Greece, was unsatisfactory.[32]

After the autumn of 1863 developments in Germany largely diverted Napoleon from America. From that time on an aggressive policy was still less feasible. Thus the nature of the Emperor's American policy is rather obscure. It may well have been Napoleon's conviction that his policy served the interests of his country best. France suffered economically nearly as much as Great Britain; during the period between 1861 and 1863 alone, French commerce fell off more than seventy-seven million dollars. The French silk industry suffered most. Numerous petitions from all over the country strengthened Napoleon's opinion that his policy was correct. On the other hand, there was particularly strong opposition in France to intervention on behalf of the South. Even people who openly sympathized with the South took exception to slavery, expressing their desire that measures for its gradual abolition would be undertaken soon. The semiofficial *Revue Contemporaine* even admitted that slavery contributed very materially to a prolongation of the war.[33]

Ever since the South American wars for independence, the relations between Spain and the United States had been troubled and, after the middle of the century, very much strained on account of Cuba, the coveted jewel of

[31] Reuss to Bismarck, Nov. 13, 1862, telegram.
[32] John Bigelow, *France and the Confederate Navy,* 126ff. Cf. Sears, *John Slidell,* 186ff.
[33] West, *Contemporary French Opinion on the American Civil War,* 135.

American imperialism.[34] Spain, however, could not openly oppose the Union because of her foreign difficulties and internal troubles. With Great Britain and France, Spain had intervened in Mexico but, like Britain, had cleverly withdrawn when serious conflicts with the Union seemed near. Among the colonial powers of Europe there was left only Russia whose benevolent neutrality could be depended upon, the latent British-American differences being the principal causes of the friendship. Russia's attitude toward the North is the best proof of the fact that it was not the problem of slavery as such but political considerations that determined the policies of the European countries in the War of Secession. The peasant emancipation of 1861 and Russia's fight against the Polish insurrection were favorite objects of comparison in America. But such comparison was in reality far-fetched. Judging by Russian statements the Union could safely depend on Russia's opposition to a conference for mediation.[35] Russia went still further: a Russian fleet appeared near the American coast in the spring of 1863. This measure was interpreted as a demonstration against European intentions of intervention. For a long time rumors were current to the effect that the commander of the fleet had sealed orders to join the Union navy in case of military action by Great Britain.[36]

[34] The so-called Ostend Manifesto of 1854 demanded the purchase of Cuba, and possibly its annexation, if the national peace and the existence of the Union so required. Cf. Sears, *History of American Foreign Relations,* 267f.

[35] Cameron to Seward, St. Petersburg, Aug. 19, 1862, Dept. State, *Despatches, Russia,* 19, no. 8.

[36] The reasons for Russia's naval demonstration have never been fully explained. According to an American theory, Russia wanted some of her warships out of the way when war with France seemed imminent. At any rate, it was not of practical importance in the American crisis. See W. F. Johnson, *American Foreign Relations,* II, 46ff.; Golder, "The Russian Fleet and the Civil War" in *American Historical Review,* XX, 801-812.

CHAPTER III

PRUSSIA, GERMANY, AND THE
WAR OF SECESSION

WHEN the War of Secession began, Germany carried no weight in world politics. The German Federation was in a state of disintegration. The conflict between Prussia and Austria was paralyzing both powers. Prussia was still torn by internal dissension. Germany had neither colonies nor a navy to protect her trade. And above all, she lacked a national leader. To appreciate the change of situation brought about by the advent of a great man, we should compare the year 1867 to the year 1861. It takes little imagination to see how differently the belligerents would have considered Germany's attitude in 1867. The Franco-German tension would have reacted on Franco-American relations; the Hanse towns would have enjoyed the support of the North German Federation which their commercial interests lacked before 1866.

In 1861 the belligerents had no reason to be particularly concerned about the political sympathies of the German states. The Washington Government exchanged polite notes with Berlin with reference to an undisturbed continuation of commercial relations. But ministers changed in Berlin with the beginning of Lincoln's Presidential term. Norman Judd, the new minister, was not one of those men whom governments entrust with important missions in times of great danger. The Confederates likewise showed only a relatively slight interest in Germany. They did not send a special commissioner but depended for their political information on A. Dudley Mann in Brussels. As he had negotiated commercial treaties with some of the German states and had served as American consul in Bremen (1842), he knew German conditions fairly well. But he reported on developments in Germany only rarely. After the experiences of 1848, he no longer believed that the German people were capable of uniting into a nation. The Congress of Princes at

Frankfort in 1863 gave him an opportunity to comment rather contemptuously on "schemes of dreamy professors."[1]

At that time Germany was represented by only two diplomats in Washington, the Prussian Minister, Freiherr von Gerolt, and the Minister Resident of Bremen, Rudolf Schleiden. Gerolt, having occupied his post since the beginning of the forties, had had sufficient time to become thoroughly familiar with things American. While not a man of superior gifts, he represented his country efficiently during the war. His personal conviction that the Union would have to be restored coincided with the trend of Prussian policy, greatly helping to strengthen the impression in Washington that Prussia was friendly.

Rudolf Schleiden was no doubt the abler man.[2] The son of a prominent family of Schleswig-Holstein, he had spent his youth in Bremen and his student years in Berlin and Göttingen. Not unlike Bismarck in that respect, he, though fond of things traditional, participated in contemporary movements with a vigorous mind. Being a "corps student," he remained outside the world of the "Burschenschaften," but in the controversy about the Göttingen professors he was an ardent partisan of the cause of free thought. During the years of revolution, Schleiden became plenipotentiary of the provisional government of Schleswig-Holstein in Frankfort and, as a good German patriot, he fought side by side with the historian Droysen for the future of his native country. Exiled by the Danish Government because of his activity, he was happy to accept an offer from his friend Johann Smidt, Mayor of Bremen, to go to Washington, in 1853, as representative of

---

[1] "It is hardly necessary to speculate upon the preponderance that would be secured to Germany by a closer union of the various Sovereignties she comprises, and upon the change that would be wrought in European affairs by the establishment of a compact nationality, numbering nearly 70,000,000 of inhabitants. Those who are most familiar with the German character and with the history of the times are the least inclined to believe in the realization of so ambitious a dream. Having been employed on a diplomatic mission to the various German Governments in 1848, I was an attentive observer of the efforts made at Frankfort, by the German people, in that year of Revolution, to secure liberal institutions and establish political unity. The obstacles which defeated the hopes of the patriots in 1849 have lost none of their power in 1863; the same rivalry between Austria and Prussia, the same wild schemes of dreamy Professors, the same sectional jealousy and class interests are observable now as then. Neither the habitual good fortune of the Habsburg's, nor the apparent unanimity of the people is equal to the task of welding into one efficient political federation the separate institutions and conflicting nationalities of which distracted Germany is composed." A. Dudley Mann to the Department of State in Richmond, Brussels, Aug. 28, 1863, *Pickett Papers,* Library of Congress.

[2] Cf. Schleiden, *Erinnerungen eines Schleswig-Holsteiners,* I, and Lutz, *Beziehungen zwischen Deutschland und den Vereinigten Staaten während des Sezessionskrieges.*

Bremen. His patron in 1861 expressed to Schleiden his appreciation of the latter's excellent and untiring work. Because of the dangers to commerce Schleiden watched the approaching catastrophe of war with growing apprehension. He could not ally himself with the North unconditionally. He saw too clearly that unleashed mob passions on both sides had increased the tension to an intolerable degree. A born aristocrat, he asked himself the Machiavellian question whether it was more cruel to make slaves of free men or to set slaves free.[3]

As is always the case on the eve of a great crisis, most diversified attempts were made in Washington to close the breach at the last moment. Gerolt, too, with more zeal than ability, took that precarious course. A customs union, in his opinion, was the best solution, he wrote his king April 8, 1861. Upon the urgent advice of a friend he tried to interest Schleiden and the British Minister, Lord Lyons, in an attempt at mediation. But like the French Minister, Mercier, the British Minister refused to participate in any joint action. Schleiden thereupon was unofficially offered to the Washington Government as a mediator. Having personal confidence in Schleiden, the President and Secretary of State Seward did not reject that offer. They asked Schleiden to speak unofficially to the Vice President of the Confederacy, Alexander Hamilton Stephens, for Lincoln was not ready to give definite promises. The meeting took place in Richmond on April 25. Schleiden realized from the very beginning that the general sentiment for war was rendering mediation very difficult. Stephens, however, during a three-hour conversation, appeared to be honestly anxious to have peace preserved, although intimating that he personally was not very hopeful and complaining of the Union Government for its lack of good will. The most important points were put down in writing. Stephens, lacking proper authorization, asked for time for reflection, and Schleiden, upon his return, reported the results of the conversation to the Secretary of State. While the latter was courteous, if reserved, the President did not reply to Schleiden's letter of April 27, placing Schleiden in a rather embarrassing position. He had to justify his independent action to his own Government while being aware that he should have given Stephens a prompt and definite answer so as to convince him of the sincerity of his attempt at mediation. But developments had meanwhile gone too far to make success possible for his efforts.[4]

[3] Lutz, *Beziehungen zwischen Deutschland und den Vereinigten Staaten während des Sezessionskrieges,* 38.

[4] Schleiden's official reports were not accessible to me, being used elsewhere. Prof. Wätjen of Münster, however, let me have some extracts dealing with Schleiden's mediation. Cf. Lutz, "Rudolf Schleiden and the Visit to Richmond, April 25, 1861," in

It was the chief task of the German representatives in Washington to secure protection for the commerce of their states during the war.

At first the American Government seemed willing to make a grand gesture. As long as there was some doubt about the attitude of the great powers, chiefly Great Britain and France, toward the blockade declared against the South, it was thought to be expedient to show the utmost consideration for the commercial relations with the neutral countries. Gerolt, for example, had a very encouraging conference with Seward at the beginning of the war. The Secretary of State assured him that the Government would respect neutral property, making that promise even in the event that blockade rules were violated.[5] Schleiden had been commissioned to have the Union honor the so-called Marcy amendment of 1856. Privateering had been abolished by the Declaration of Paris. A note by Marcy, the American Secretary of State in office at that time, had insisted that private property of subjects or citizens of a belligerent power should be protected from seizure on the part of the opposing power. Marcy had found the Declaration of Paris unacceptable. Countries not possessing large navies, he said, could not surrender their right of privateering so long as confiscation of private property in one form or another existed.[6] A meeting on December 2, 1859, of leading Bremen merchants demanded inviolability of person and property on the seas, including the nationals of belligerent countries, except for restrictions necessary for the conduct of war.[7] Bremen, consequently, approved the Marcy amendment and Schleiden was commissioned to negotiate on that basis. By the time the War of Secession broke out the matter had not required a practical decision. Afterwards, Schleiden, with increased vigor, attempted to hold the American Government to the Marcy amendment, which seemed the best means of protecting the commerce of the Hanse towns.

He seconded the suggestion of the British Minister that the Union should counteract the declaration of privateering by the Southern States by recognizing the Marcy amendment so as to obtain the sympathies of all Europe. That attempt having failed, Schleiden worked for a convention of one kind or another which should contain the positive elements of the Marcy amend-

---

American Historical Association, *Annual Report*, 1915, 207ff. Except for the treatise by Lutz, my account is based on Schleiden's letters to Lincoln on Apr. 27 and to Seward on Apr. 30, 1861, Dept. State, *Notes from Hanseatic Legation*, 1.

[5] Gerolt to King Wilhelm, June 10, 1861.

[6] For the Declaration of Paris and the Marcy amendment see Hatschek and Strupp, *Wörterbuch des Völkerrechts und der Diplomatie*, II, 511ff.; Moore, *Digest*, VII, 558ff.; and Bemis, *Secretaries of State*, VI, 145-294, 420-431.

[7] *Staatsarchiv*, X, no. 6.

ment. But no sooner had the great powers of Europe recognized the Confederacy as a belligerent power than the Department of State had its European representatives announce the adherence of the Union to the Declaration of Paris. Britain, France, and Prussia agreed.[8] Thus Prussia,* so to speak,[9] stabbed the Hanse towns in the back. Henceforth, further negotiations on the part of Schleiden were doomed to be futile.[10] Consequently, nothing remained but to protect commercial interests as cases arose. This was not an easy matter for the representative of the Hanse towns—in 1862 Schleiden took charge of affairs for both Hamburg and Lübeck—since he was unable to support his demands with the pressure of political power. In April 1862, Schleiden left for an extended leave in Europe whence he did not return until December 17. He left Washington definitely on April 6, 1864. His successor was Dr. Rösing, who later became consul general in New York.

Germany's economic interests and the hundreds of thousands of emigrants who settled almost exclusively in the Northern States, determined the general trend which German policy was obliged to follow during the North American conflict. The German states had no interest in seeking a division of the Union; on the contrary, Great Britain's interest in that rift called for caution.[11]

Cotton imports to Germany were not nearly so large as in the cases of Great Britain and France. Bismarck, to be sure, on January 14, 1863, stated in the Prussian Legislature that economic conditions would be perfectly satisfactory if it were not for the fact that individual branches of industry were suffering from the effects of the war in the United States.[12] Likewise, Chlodwig Hohenlohe, in a letter of April 15, 1865, to the King of Bavaria, wrote that the American war was seriously affecting the material interests of southern Germany in particular.[13] The existence of cotton spinning mills was endangered. For political reasons, the democratic population sympathized with the Northern States.

The longer the war lasted the more seriously were its effects reflected in Germany. People hoped for its speedy conclusion because the United States

---

[8] Schleinitz's orders to the Prussian Minister in Washington, *Staatsarchiv*, X, no. 43.

[9] Prussia had agreed to the Declaration of Paris as early as 1856. For criticism of its conduct, see Lammers, "Reform des Seekriegsrechtes," *Preussische Jahrbücher*, XXVI, 669ff.

[10] For Bremen's negotiations, see "Frei Schiff unter Feindesflagge," in *Staatsarchiv*, X, appendix.

[11] Cf. *Grenzboten*, 1861, II semester, I, 464f.

[12] Cf. Bismarck, *Gesammelte Werke*, X, 149.

[13] *Denkwürdigkeiten*, I, 147.

was of importance to the trade of the entire world.[14] All in all, however, Germany's national trade was not decisively influenced by the American war.

Public opinion, especially in northern Germany, inclined toward the Union. Carl Schurz and Count Galen, Prussian envoy to Spain, observed that a large number of Prussian nobles as well as the officers of the army sympathized with the Southern Confederacy, "hating democracy and wishing that the Republic of the United States, as the greatest and most attractive example of democracy, should fail. . . . But all the rest of the Prussian people, that is, an overwhelming majority of them, comprising the most intelligent, active, and progressive elements, were decidedly and vigorously in sympathy with the North and the Union. Moreover, the traditional policy of Prussia was to cultivate the most friendly relations with the United States. The government and the people at large were thus united in this sentiment. The attitude of the Prussian Government was therefore not only one of neutrality, but one of distinctly amicable, well-wishing neutrality." [15] Such formulations are always exaggerated. It is probably more correct to say that many people had neither sympathy nor interest for any party. As in England, the landowners considered the large planters in the South as members of an equal caste. Only in the Southern States, they thought, could a social organization exist similar to that of Europe. On the other hand, the sympathies of the young labor unions naturally inclined toward that party which was fighting for the cause of "free labor." Liberal bourgeoisie hated slavery. Aversion to forced labor probably was more deeply rooted and more general in Germany than in any other country. The same sense of justice which induced hundreds of thousands of Germans living in America to take part in the fight against slavery and to join the Union armies also inspired countless people in Germany to become partisans of the Union. The American Legation in Berlin, at the beginning of the war, was literally flooded with offers of volunteers for the Union army. A special bulletin had to be posted pointing out that the Legation was not a recruiting office.[16] From all parts of Germany the American consuls reported unmistakable evidence of good will. They were overwhelmed with felicitations on Lincoln's reelection as

[14] Annual report of the American consulate general in Frankfort Sept. 30, 1864, Dept. State, *Despatches, Frankfort on the Main,* 14, no. 388.

[15] Schurz, *Reminiscences,* II, 265f. Cf. Jordan and Pratt, *Europe and the American Civil War,* 195ff. Austrian sympathies were also largely on the side of the Union; cf. Motley to Seward, Vienna, June 22 and Oct. 1862, Dept. State, *Despatches, Austria,* 5, nos. 5 and 8, respectively.

[16] *Foreign Relations,* 1862, pt. 2, 546f.

President.[17] The South numbered its friends chiefly among the army officers. The King at one time was obliged to express his disapproval of a dinner given in honor of Confederate officers in Berlin.[18] A considerable number of Prussian officers would have liked to fight for the South.

Considering the press as an indicator of sentiment, which it was to a lesser degree than at present, we may say that the *Norddeutsche Allgemeine Zeitung* and *National Zeitung,* among the most important Berlin papers, were critical, while the *Kreuzzeitung* inclined toward the South. As for papers outside of Berlin, the *Frankfurter, Kölnische, Weser,* and *Augsburg Allgemeine Zeitung* were pro-Union, while some of the Catholic journals in southern Germany displayed more interest for the South.[19] The press of that period gave comparatively little space to American affairs. In partial explanation we may cite Germany's internal political situation and the struggle over the constitution in Prussia. But as we know today, those factors were not the decisive ones. The principal cause was deficient information. There were no cable connections between America and Europe. The quickest news service took at least twelve days.

Pamphlets and periodicals give us more reliable information about the sentiment among the intellectual classes, though relatively few brochures were published. Friedrich Kapp's treatise on slavery was widely read. The leading periodicals took pains to interpret the meaning of the American crisis to their readers. The *Preussische Jahrbücher* was particularly severe in its condemnation of the slave States. "The masses, and to some extent their egotistic leaders as well, degenerate to the point of brutality; the slave-holding populations insist on privileges that disgrace humanity, more because of a natural cruelty than for social or economic reasons which in our country, too, are used for disguising moral turpitude."[20] Germany's sympathies cannot go astray, asserted an article entitled "The Negro Question and Recent Events in America." "It is the free land of the Northern States of the Union where innumerable fellow countrymen of ours made their home." The author deals very harshly with Southern aristocracy. "It was," he says, "consistently planning to convert the whole Union into slave territory. . . . Now that the

[17] Consulate general in Frankfort to Department of State Nov. 21, 1864, Dept. State, *Despatches, Frankfort on the Main,* 14, no. 401.

[18] Bancroft to Seward, Berlin, Feb. 26, 1869 (detailed report on Prussia's attitude toward the War of Secession), Dept. State, *Despatches, Prussia,* 15, unnumbered.

[19] Letters from the American consulates: From Bremen Dec. 4, 1861, Dept. State, *Despatches, Bremen,* 11, no. 18, and from Hamburg Jan. 18, 1862, Dept. State, *Despatches, Hamburg,* 14, no. 18. Cf. Lutz, *Beziehungen zwischen Deutschland und den Vereinigten Staaten während des Sezessionskrieges,* 49ff.

[20] *Preussische Jahrbücher,* VIII, 2ff.

North at last is resisting that plan, fighting for the cause of free labor, now that a great nation is shaking off the yoke of an aristocratic power, it cannot fairly be doubted which side the sympathies of civilized Europe should favor." [21]

The *Grenzboten,* although more critical, as a matter of course rejected slavery as rigorously as did the *Preussische Wochenblatt.* Nor did the conservative organs support slavery so far as we can judge. Slavery found its advocates only in a few publications of a small but extremely conservative group within the church, who advanced arguments quite similar to those of the Southern theorists. This was by no means an accidental coincidence, for Thomas R. Dew, who had been a student at German universities, presumably had received many suggestions there for his doctrine of the inequality of men as a basis of social organization.[22] They mentioned St. Paul's direct recognition of slavery. "Ham was destined to be a slave," wrote Count Reichenbach in a pamphlet *The Crisis in the United States.* "That is taught by the Holy Scriptures as well as by profane history, by nature as well as by Revelation."[23] Were it not for the slavery problem public opinion might have been quite different. A few years later the historian Ranke told the American Minister in Berlin, George Bancroft, that save for the question of slavery there were many things to be said in favor of the South.[24]

At any rate, public opinion did favor the North as decidedly as could be desired. Germany was an arsenal for the North. The extent that immigrants, war materials, and money could be obtained from Germany was of considerable importance to the Northern cause. While the Union Government in principle refused to invite German subjects to enlist in the Union army, it promoted emigration in every way.[25] Indeed it was the main business of the American consulates to spread propaganda for German emigration at the German seaports. The consulate in Hamburg called attention to the importance of that city, ascribing the fact that the Union had very little influence there, to the American mistake of condemning all European ideas as such. Moreover, British papers were exerting a strong influence, while the American press was practically unknown. Everything should be done, the consulate urged, to regain the monopoly on immigration. The consulate consequently

[21] *Ibid.,* VIII, 629.

[22] Dodd, *Cotton Kingdom,* 49.

[23] Lutz, *Beziehungen zwischen Deutschland und den Vereinigten Staaten während des Sezessionskrieges,* 63.

[24] Bancroft's record of a conversation with Ranke Nov. 9, 1867, Bancroft Collection, New York Public Library.

[25] Kreisman to Seward, Berlin, Aug. 9, 1862, *Foreign Relations,* 1862, pt. 2, 546.

suggested that the public should be favorably influenced toward emigration by letters from German-Americans to their friends in the old country; they should write about the better living conditions in America.[26] Compared to pre-war figures, emigration of course decreased considerably during the war. Nevertheless, every year there crossed the ocean a few thousand people who performed valuable services for the Union as colonists and as soldiers.[27] Some irregularities occurred, however. For instance, Prussian subjects were induced to emigrate and, upon their arrival, were pressed into military service in order to fill the quota of Massachusetts. The Prussian chargé d'affaires, von Grabow, complained to the Secretary of State, emphasizing that the immigrants would be glad to report as volunteers but that "they refused to be sold as substitutes for American citizens of Massachusetts who did not themselves have courage enough to fight battles for their country and who, besides, cheated their substitutes out of their money."[28] Conditions were improved by a law of July 4, 1864, which provided that any contracts of immigrants with agents of foreign countries should be considered legal only if the immigrants voluntarily renounced the oath of allegiance to their native state, expressing their desire to become citizens of the United States. The Germans of Boston, in a special proclamation of August 26, 1864, warned people desiring to emigrate of the dangers in store for them.

It was not, of course, the recent immigrants who were of particular importance to the Union army but the enormous number of Germans who had come before the beginning of the war.[29] Their number was estimated variously, depending upon how large the circle of Americans of German descent was assumed to be. This much is certain, that the number of Union soldiers of German extraction exceeded by far their quota as compared to the

[26] From American consulate in Hamburg to Department of State Jan. 18 and Aug. 5, 1862, Feb. 12 and Dec. 1, 1863, Dept. State, *Despatches, Hamburg,* 14, no. 67, 15, no. 125, and 16, nos. 174 and 232, respectively; and from Bremen Apr. 16, 1861, Dept. State, *Despatches, Bremen,* 11, no. 13.

[27] German emigration:

1861	31,661	persons
1862	27,529	"
1863	33,162	"
1864	57,276	"
1865	83,424	"

Statistics in *Senate Documents,* 61st Congress, 3d session, no. 756, 27ff. Cf. the figures in Wätjen, *Aus der Frühzeit des Nordatlantikverkehrs,* 193.

[28] To Bismarck, Washington, Sept. 17, 1864.

[29] Cf. Kaufmann, *Die Deutschen im amerikanischen Bürgerkriege,* and Faust, *Das Deutschtum in den Vereinigten Staaten,* I, 432ff.

total population.[30] This necessarily had its greatest effect at the beginning of the war when a fighting force could be recruited quickly only from the ranks of volunteers. We need not assume that those many thousands of Germans enlisted only for reasons of idealism. There are always a considerable number of unencumbered young men among immigrants to whom war service seems more alluring than to old settlers with families and real property. Nevertheless, it remains a noteworthy fact that the German quota was exceedingly large. It is a strange coincidence that in 1864 German soldiers offered their lives for the organization of national states on two continents. There was, so to speak, a front line, extending from the Düppel fortifications to the Mississippi River.

Certain nationalists sought to belittle as much as possible the actual achievements of the Germans in the war. They invariably blamed the foreign soldiers, particularly the Germans, for all sorts of errors, irregularities, and desertions. The serious defeat of the Union army at Chancellorsville served as a basis for unjust accusations against the Germans. The 11th Corps, containing many Germans and commanded by Carl Schurz, had indeed retreated, but only because of the mistakes of the commander-in-chief. The other corps did no better. Nevertheless, misleading reports led a mob in Washington to knock down wounded soldiers of the 11th Corps as if they had fled out of cowardice. It was impossible for Schurz to have his report of vindication accepted, so the Germans were compelled to hold meetings of protest against those unfounded charges.[31] Nevertheless it was a great advantage for the Union army that there were so many trained soldiers among the Germans.[32]

The number of Germans living in Southern States during that period is estimated at only seventy-two thousand.[33] It has been stated that those Germans sided with the North almost without exception, but that is an exaggeration. A large number of them, no doubt, loyally offered their services to the Confederacy. A considerable number of volunteers, too, went South, as evidenced by German reports of the campaigns of the Southern armies. The purchase of arms from Germany was not difficult. Supplies were ample and

---

[30] Kaufmann, *Die Deutschen im amerikanischen Bürgerkriege,* 120, calculates the total number of Germans in the Union Army at 176,817 against a quota of only 118,402. The Irish, on the other hand, despite their large contingent of immigrants, supplied only 144,221 soldiers against a quota of 139,052. Cf. also Faust, *Das Deutschtum in den Vereinigten Staaten,* I, 433.

[31] Cf. Kaufmann, *Die Deutschen im amerikanischen Bürgerkriege,* 367ff.; Schurz, *Speeches, Correspondence, and Political Papers,* I, 223f. Cf. also Heusinger, *Amerikanische Kriegsbilder,* 64f., 119.

[32] Kaufmann, *Die Deutschen im amerikanischen Bürgerkriege,* 131.

[33] *Ibid.,* 139ff.

even certain central German governments were glad to obtain some business.[34] The Confederates had their agents in Germany but could not accomplish much so far as can be learned because of the strict control by the Union representatives. On the part of the Southern States attempts were not lacking to incline the Germans toward the South so as to stop the emigration and supply of arms to the North. The fact that the secessionists were worried about them is brought out by a letter of Henry Hotze, commercial agent of the Confederate States at London, December 17, 1864.[35] Its writer mentions his intention of going to Germany in a day or two. German sympathies were inconsequential to him, but it was Germany where the enemy would have to recruit a new army in the coming spring, and moreover, the North was speculating on the possible use of German gold to continue the war. For these reasons the writer wished to discredit Union securities and to divert the masses from emigrating to America. Similarly, E. M. Hudson, a former secretary at the American Legation in Berlin, who secretly worked in the Legation for some time even after the secession of the Southern States, published, in a German translation, political epistles by James Williams under the title *A Vindication of the Southern States of America.* Their propagandist purpose was expressly stated in the introduction. The letters were a clever collection of all possible arguments that could be advanced for the South. In particular, they painted in the darkest colors the conditions that would result from a sudden emancipation of the negroes. The *London Index,* the Confederate propaganda paper in London, jubilantly remarked that sentiment in Prussia was noticeably changing in favor of the South. Likewise, an anonymous person living in Berlin in 1863 asserted that the Governments and armies of both Austria and Prussia were very favorably inclined toward the Southern cause. He suggested that a special commissioner be accredited to the Governments of Austria and Prussia.[36]

But the readiness with which the Union bonds were received in Germany disproved his assertion. For Germany's financial support was particularly valuable to the Union. Its financial condition at times was very critical since lack of experience and the weakness of government authority resulted in fatal mistakes. The enormous demand for money necessitated loans in addition to increases in taxes and customs tariffs. Loans at first were not highly successful as they did not offer much inducement for speculation. We may

[34] American consular reports from Hamburg June 7 and Nov. 2, Dept. State, *Despatches, Hamburg,* 13; from Bremen Oct. 9, 1861, Dept. State, *Despatches, Bremen,* 11, no. 8.

[35] *Official Records of the Union and Confederate Navies,* series 2, III, 1209.

[36] Richardson, *Messages and Papers of the Confederacy,* II, 455.

imagine the troubles of the Treasury, for the indebtedness of the country rose to more than four billions of dollars during the war. The gold agio became a cause for alarm. The shortage of money was greatly intensified by a decrease of exports and would have been even worse had it not been for gold from California.[37] To obtain gold or its equivalent from abroad it became necessary for the Union to enter foreign money markets. For this purpose Robert J. Walker, at a critical hour, was sent to Europe on a special mission. He was a man of great ambition, of an untiring capacity for work, but of dubious character.[38] Walker at first was confronted with extraordinary difficulties. The secessionist cotton loans had been a decided success in London and Paris. Baron Raphael Erlanger, a relative of Slidell, the Confederate representative, furthered Southern interests throughout Europe with great energy and skill. Walker, on the other hand, was not even successful in having the *Times* open its columns to his propaganda. He influenced the international business world with a multitude of pamphlets in English, French, and German. By undermining Confederate credit he finally managed to frustrate a second Confederate loan of over $75,000. In Holland, whither Walker went in keeping with an old tradition, he did not fare much better. Apart from the unfavorable attitude of some of the principal countries of Europe, confidence in American financial policy was not overwhelmingly great.[39] He found his ground far better prepared when he arrived in Frankfort. The Union Government had early recognized the importance of Frankfort-on-the-Main as an international center of commerce. Lincoln very cleverly influenced public opinion there by having his consul general present numerous American publications to the Senate and make the most flattering inquiries about the secondary schools of Frankfort, which were to serve as models for the American school system.[40] A few Northerners were actually sent to Frankfort to advance the cause of the Union, under the direction of the very clever consul general William Walton Murphy. The anti-Bonaparte

[37] Average gold prices: Jan. 1862, 102.5; July 1864, 258.1, greenback rate. Cf. Graham, "International Trade under Depreciated Paper," in *Quarterly Journal of Economics,* XXXVI, 220-273, and Schmoller, in *Preussische Jahrbücher,* XVII, 188f.

[38] For Walker, see W. E. Dodd's article in *Americana,* XXVIII, 229.

[39] "I am sorry to say that our finances, which with our friends are always a subject of deep solicitude, are not regarded here with the same hopefulness that seems to prevail at home. It is believed we want less legal tender and more taxation. Confidence is wanting that we can maintain our financial system for any length of time if the existing disproportion between income and expenditure is suffered to go on." Pike to Seward, The Hague, Jan. 27, 1864, in *Foreign Relations,* 1864, pt. III, 308. Cf. D. R. Dewey, *Financial History,* 355.

[40] *Hundert Jahre Amerikanisches Generalkonsulat in Frankfurt,* 49.

French-language paper *L'Europe* was put at their disposal. It had among its staff of contributors men like Rev. Dr. John McClintock, former president of Dickinson College, Dr. E. H. Chapin, a New York clergyman, and Andrew Dickson White, later envoy and ambassador in Berlin.[41] The paper was intended primarily to give information to sympathizers in France and Belgium and at the same time to increase confidence in American bonds among German men of finance. This was the more necessary, for the lack of Northern military successes made people reluctant to buy American bonds. "A few more defeats," complained Murphy on September 15, 1862, "and we shall have lost our credit in Europe for years."

The work of the Union representatives was not always easy. As there were no telegraphic connections, the arrival of ships determined whether news could be published in time to influence the stock exchange favorably. The *Neue Frankfurter Zeitung* advertised American bonds very actively. On July 21, 1863, it especially emphasized the advantages of investing, since a bond with a par value of 100 cost the citizens of Frankfort only 70, while it yielded 8 percent interest. "The [American] people, with their energy and inexhaustible wealth, will themselves find means of fulfilling all national liabilities." Even after the price dropped to 45, it warned its readers, on July 10, 1864, against panic sales.[42] While painting the financial affairs of the Southern States in very dark colors, it expressed strong confidence in the future of the Union. An article of January 9, 1864, on the financial condition of the Confederate States serves as an example of the attitude of the *Neue Frankfurter Zeitung*. It spoke of the desperate situation of the Confederates: "All strength has been exhausted; it is only by extreme means such as have always been inspired by despair in its final stage, that Minister Memminger hopes to prolong the wretched life of the rebellion until the end of June." The author refers to the war as the most reckless rebellion known to history and forecasts that it will result in the ruin of its instigators. If that end has not been attained as yet, it is attributable to the military inexperience of the Northern States rather than to that heroism of the South so excessively praised by the British press.

Unquestionably, high finance was largely pro-Union. The Paris and Frankfort branches of the House of Rothschild made no secret of their sympathies. The Paris Rothschild expressly offered his services to the Union, while the Frankfort Rothschild complained bitterly to a lady regarding Baron

[41] A. D. White, *Autobiography*, I, 97.
[42] Frankfurter Zeitung, *Geschichte*, 108ff.

Erlanger's activity on behalf of the Confederates.[43] A few of the Frankfort banks had branches in New York through which they had already participated in placing the first few war loans.[44] Walker consequently found the doors open when he came to Frankfort in 1863. He was chiefly concerned with placing as large a portion as possible of the so-called "five-twenty" bonds of 1862. It was a particularly favorable coincidence that the German money market showed considerable receptiveness in the years 1863-64. The confidence of South German investors in the Austrian railway stocks had been shaken after the Austrian Government had granted subsidies to a number of private banks in order to encourage private capital to build railways in Austria.[45] An auditing of the construction accounts had also brought to light serious irregularities. Once confidence was lost, South German savings sought new outlets for investment.[46] For this reason they welcomed the American offer. But it also required pronounced sympathies for the Union to place about $250,000,000 worth of "five-twenty" bonds within a comparatively short time. Robert J. Walker, in an open letter to the American people on November 30, 1867, called attention to the importance to the economic warfare of the Union of the cordial reception in Germany of the American bonds. He even advocated that a new loan be placed in Germany instead of Paris or London. In the same letter he spoke of being supported by Count Bismarck, who was in his opinion as great a friend of America as he was of German unification.[47]

[43] Dayton to Seward, Paris, Dec. 5, 1861, confidential, Dept. State, *Despatches, France,* 51, no. 90; cf. A. D. White, *Autobiography,* I, 97f.

[44] *Hundert Jahre Amerikanisches Generalkonsulat in Frankfurt,* 49; *Geschichte der Handelskammer zu Frankfurt,* 1140f.

[45] Frankfurter Zeitung, *Geschichte,* 113.

[46] According to the report of the Aktionär, no. 4, July 1865, the largest part of the savings capital diverted from the Austrian railway stocks was invested in American war loans. Cf. *Geschichte der Handelskammer zu Frankfurt,* 1142.

[47] Walker, *Our National Finances.* As this document is but little known, its most interesting part is quoted as follows: "It was then, at the period of our deepest gloom and danger, that a still small voice was heard in our favor from Holland, where Franklin had negotiated our first loan. It was then that the still louder notes of hope and sympathy fell like music upon my ears from the great German Fatherland. I visited both countries, unheralded and unknown, in 1863. Satisfied that any public call for a loan would be defeated by the machinations of France and England, I never announced my official capacity, nor asked for any American loan. I published my financial essays over my own name, merely as an American citizen, exhibiting the vast resources, the wonderful progress of our country, and the certainty of our success in crushing the rebellion. These essays were sent by thousands to all the principal bankers of Europe. In a few months I visited again nearly every city of Holland and Germany, giving me an opportunity to discuss the question personally with these bankers, and

Richard Bartholdt, at one time a member of Congress, stated in his memoirs that the heads of the big German banks inquired of Bismarck whether loans to the Union were compatible with the interests of Germany. Bismarck answered that as much as possible should be given. There is no record of that statement to be found in German archives. But Bartholdt refers to a personal conversation with Bismarck. There is no good reason for us to question the veracity of Bartholdt's report of a conversation with Bismarck that actually took place in Friedrichsruh on September 26, 1895. With regard to the American war loan and Bismarck's opinion of the Civil War, Bartholdt reports as follows: "His reference to the many 'good services' on the part of Germany the advantages of which we had enjoyed, encouraged me to ask him about the Union bonds which the German financiers were said to have bought during the Civil War. 'Yes,' he replied, 'that is true. It was reported to me that Lincoln would be unable to prosecute the war unless Germany helped him. Your commissioners themselves related how they had been turned down in London as well as Paris. Now, we wanted to see the Union preserved. The North, it seemed to me, was right morally, but, aside from that, we were heartily in favor of a strong, prosperous, and united country on the other side of the Atlantic.'

" 'So the monarchical feeling was no hindrance to giving succor to a republic?'

"The Prince shook his head, smiling. 'Not in the least,' he said. 'To diplomacy the internal affairs of the other countries are a sealed book. The main object of statesmanship is, or ought to be, to make people happy and prosperous, to give them peace and plenty. Let the different forms of govern-

---

enforce the written arguments already made. The result was that in a brief period the *people of Germany,* emphatically the *great masses of the people,* took several hundred millions of our loan at the same rates as our own citizens. Let it be remembered that this was a period of great apprehension as to the result of our contest, and that the credit of our greenbacks rested mainly on these bonds, in which they could be funded, and that the demand for them in Germany, as well as here, to organize the national banks, prevented our currency from disappearing in the gathering mists of depreciation. Our greatest peril was financial, and although the glorious deeds of our army and navy, and their gallant leaders, saved us on the ocean and the land, yet the Secretary of the Treasury was the real generalissimo of the contest. These German and other loans, based upon these United States five-twenties, constituted, to a vast extent, the *price we agreed to pay* to enable us to maintain the Government and preserve the Union." Oberholtzer, *Jay Cooke,* I, 513ff. estimates the American debt to Germany at 200 million dollars, to Great Britain at 100 million dollars, as of Mar. 1865. Schmoller, in *Preussische Jahrbücher,* XVII, 176, thinks that the American Government's indebtedness to Europe was not so large in proportion to the total debt.

ment vie with one another to accomplish that great purpose. We are not afraid of comparisons.' "[48]

In 1863-64 the purchase of Union bonds could hardly be called safe business, the fluctuations on the stock exchange being considerable.[49] Regarding the effect on the balance of trade, the *Neue Frankfurter Zeitung* of February 5, 1864, remarked: "At the end of the last calendar year, consequently, foreign countries were our debtors for so large an amount that even the recently developed disproportion between imports and exports can have reduced our assets but little."

Later, indeed, investment in American securities proved to be very good business, with the prices rising to 90 percent in 1867 and to as much as 96⅛ percent in 1870. The capital invested had increased from 39 percent to 140 percent. That profit aided Germany in her war with France, since a considerable part of the money for war loans was procured by the sale of American bonds.[50]

It is hard to judge to what extent the Erlanger group succeeded in Germany with their loans. The American consul general in Frankfort, on September 14, 1863, reported in that respect that he was skeptical whether a single capitalist had been won for the cotton loan. In Paris Erlanger accomplished his greatest transaction for the account of the South. James Murray Mason, the Southern commissioner in London, occasionally worried the American consul general in Frankfort by appearing in that city to promote the cotton loan. Erlanger probably met with some success as he had very favorable terms to offer. However, the financial success of the North was infinitely greater, a fact the more disturbing to the South as high hopes had been placed on the collapse of Union finances. A circular letter of the Confederate government of October 10, 1864, expressed disappointment at the strong participation of the German money market. Their European representatives were instructed to publish the financial situation of the North in order to meet the dangers menacing an early restoration of peace.[51]

[48] Cf. Bartholdt, *Steerage to Congress,* 75f. and 142f., which reference Mr. Lawrence Becker suggested to me.

[49] In a Senate debate Feb. 4, 1871, several speakers mentioned the risks for German investors. Cf. *Congressional Globe,* 41st Congress, 3d session, XLIII, pt. 2, 954ff.; and Gazley, *American Opinion of German Unification,* 331ff.

[50] Delbrück, *Lebenserinnerungen,* II, 188f.

[51] "For some months past the United States have been able to uphold their sinking finances by the sale of large amounts of public stocks in the German markets. These sales are reported to have reached a total varying from thirty to one hundred million of pounds sterling. There is no method within reach for approximating the true sum, altho' it is doubtless very large. We deem it advisable to present an analysis of the

Schleinitz, the Prussian Minister for Foreign Affairs, rejecting any rebellion in principle, had issued a declaration against the Confederacy. The American Minister was able to report the most positive assurance of Schleinitz that his Government would not recognize any "de-facto Government of the dis-affected States of the American Union."[52] The King, too, officially maintained that policy. He refused all petitions of officers who wished to enter the Southern army and, as mentioned before, he objected to a dinner in honor of Confederate officers visiting Berlin.[53]

When Bismarck, on September 24, 1862, provisionally took charge of the Prussian State Ministry, he found no reason to deviate from that policy. The offer of mediation made by Napoleon III, October 30, was the first diplomatic question to bring him into contact with American affairs. On a temporary visit to Paris, September 2, 1862, he telegraphed home that France would invite Great Britain and Russia to ask the United States to conclude a six-month armistice with the Confederacy. This information, not entirely accurate, was based on a statement by Prince Metternich.[54] Bismarck, when Prime Minister, treated the French plan with much reserve, merely wishing to ascertain "the impression made upon the United States itself by France's initiative and by the more or less outspoken rejection of it on the part of Great Britain." He also desired details as to the reaction of the South. On the 20th and 24th of February 1863, Gerolt informed him that the French proposal for mediation had aroused great indignation in Washington and in the Northern States, besides causing apprehension that recognition of the Southern States and French violation of the blockade were impending. Some years later, on March 13, 1884, in a speech before the Reichstag, Bismarck suggested that the policy of Prussia had been instrumental in wrecking a plan for intervention by certain powers.[55] Prince Metternich's impression, to be sure, was different. He wired from Paris November 13, 1862: *"La Prussie disposée à s'unir à la France dans la démarche projetée pour mettre fin à la guerre américaine après avoir sondé Washington et Londres."*

---

financial condition of the United States drawn from their official reports for the information of European capitalists, with some remarks on the probable influence of continued investments by them, not only in retarding the restoration of peace on this continent, but in destroying the resources on which alone they can rely for the security of investments already made." *Pickett Papers,* Library of Congress.

[52] Wright to Seward, Berlin, May 8, 1861, Dept. State, *Despatches, Prussia,* 11, no. 173.

[53] Bancroft to Seward, Berlin, Feb. 26, 1869, Dept. State, *Despatches, Prussia,* 15, no. 104.

[54] Bismarck to Bernstorff Nov. 8, 1862, confidential.

[55] Bismarck, *Gesammelte Werke,* XII, 407.

Bismarck certainly took great pains to maintain the best of relations with the Union. When the sinking of the ship *Essex* brought about some consternation in the Prussian business world, he personally asked the American Minister to settle the incident satisfactorily as soon as possible.[56] Occasionally he was made the authority for unfriendly newspaper articles,[57] and once he vigorously refuted such a charge with regard to the *Kreuzzeitung*. The Prussian Minister in Washington was commissioned to state to the American Government that: "the Royal Government felt, as always acknowledged to me by the local representatives of the United States, that throughout the war we never interfered with their interests but that we actually had our policy determined by consideration for the long years of friendly relations to the United States of America founded on principles of international law." [58] On February 20, 1865, Gerolt could assure Bismarck that the American Government was convinced of the friendly sentiment of the Prussian Government more than in the case of any other nation, in evidence of which most flattering indications on the part of the President and members of the Cabinet and Congress were constantly being received. John Lothrop Motley, Bismarck's friend of their Göttingen student days and once more associated with him after the early fifties, no doubt presented to him an ardently interested account of the American crisis as early 1855.[59] From the beginning of the war in his capacity as American Minister in Vienna, he strengthened Bismarck's confidence in the Union by his unshaken hope for victory. Werther, Prussian Minister in Vienna, reported on March 29, 1863, that Minister Motley of late had frequently informed him of the status of the American contest and that he improved the opportunity by having the complicated conditions there explained to him. During his Vienna sojourn in August Bismarck attentively listened to Motley's account of the American crisis, telling him that he would present it as his own opinion in due time.[60]

However, not even Motley succeeded in persuading Bismarck that right was exclusively on the side of the North. The latter compared the struggles in the Prussian Chamber with the American crisis, averring that the issues were not clear to either party. "Do you all know exactly why you are waging such furious war with each other? All certainly do not know, but they kill each

[56] Judd to Seward, Berlin, Nov. 25, 1862, Dept. State, *Despatches, Prussia,* 12, no. 35.

[57] Kreismann to Seward, July 30, 1864, Dept. State, *Despatches, Prussia,* 13, no. 23.

[58] Bismarck to Gerolt, Jan. 31; Gerolt to Bismarck, Feb. 20, 1865.

[59] *Bismarck-Jahrbuch,* III, 97ff.

[60] Motley, *Motley and His Family,* 213. Bismarck told ex-President Grant later that Motley had prophesied the Union would be restored without one village or hamlet missing, Young, *General Grant,* I, 416.

other *con amore*, that's the way the business comes to them."[61] Personally, Bismarck had many good things to say for the Southerners. In later years he used to speak of his personal sympathies for the highly cultured men from the South, probably thinking of his Göttingen student friends.[62] For example, Mitchell King, Bismarck's fraternity brother, was a Southerner. Bismarck was not a blind believer in the emancipation of slaves, considering inequality of individuals and races a fact. Divine Providence, he said, had allotted to the negroes a destiny different from that of the whites. But he condemned ill treatment of the weak with remarkable severity. He used horses and dogs as comparable cases where the system of training by means of whipping likewise was obsolete. It ill became the whites to use their superiority to contravene humanitarian ideas as well as to endanger practical profit. But the question as to what was to be done, after emancipation, with the negroes accustomed to slavery seemed indeed important to him. In an article inspired by Bismarck in the *Hamburger Nachrichten* of September 30, 1890 (evening issue), slavery among the Mohammedans and in America was judged differently. In America slaves were worse off than beasts of burden, all too often being treated with barbarous cruelty. With the Mohammedan peoples, slaves were more like domestics, well treated and quite content with their fate.[63]

Bismarck, however, expressly stated that he pursued a policy of benevolent neutrality toward the North. Although not at that time an official paper, the *Norddeutsche Allgemeine Zeitung* best expresses his attitude. In connection with the news of Lee's surrender, the paper, under date of April 28, 1865, wrote that in the American question it had always represented a point of view differing from the conservative as well as from the liberal party. It had not forgotten that President Lincoln and his Cabinet stood for legal authority. On the other hand, the admirable bravery with which the Southern States had resisted the enormous superiority of their opponents, could not possibly inspire excessive friendship for those people who thought they could avoid by means of force of arms and civil strife the necessary settlement of a social question. Clearly referring to the Prussian conflict, the paper called attention to the fact that it took the North four years of military efforts to build up an army and to lead its banners to victory. The author doubted whether the Union would succeed in retaining the conquered Southern States. That is, he said, the real test of the power of the republican constitution. He prophesied that it would not pass that test, that the republican government would not live to

[61] Motley, *Correspondence*, II, 126.
[62] Hofmann, *Fürst Bismarck*, I, 352.
[63] *Ibid.*, I, 293; Penzler, *Fürst Bismarck*, I, 261; *Bismarck-Jahrbuch*, III, 498ff.

celebrate its centennial, and that the year 1888 would see a different political organization of the Union than the one then existing. "We have often repeated that the breach between the North and South of the United States will never be welded together by blood." The *Kreuzzeitung* of April 26, 1865, feared that America would soon be a dangerous menace to the European countries.

CHAPTER IV

EFFECT OF THE WAR OF SECESSION
ON EUROPEAN POLITICS

THE overwhelming victory of the Union was certain to have its effect on Europe. For some time the Old World had skeptically watched the development of the United States, adjusting itself to the idea that the Union would inevitably disintegrate. After the war it was reluctantly forced to admit that the Union had demonstrated surprisingly great internal strength. Instead of being shaken, the Union had emerged from its severe crisis considerably stronger. For the first time in the modern history of the West there was now a great, successful republic, a fact which decidedly encouraged all European proponents of a republican form of government.[1] Furthermore, on the American continent monarchism was to receive a heavy blow a few years later. The collapse of the Mexican Empire, with the execution of a member of a sovereign European dynasty, was all the more injurious to the authority of European monarchs, since they were utterly unable to do anything but raise protests. A painful incident illustrates the situation. George Bancroft, in his memorial address to both houses of Congress and the diplomatic corps, on the anniversary of Lincoln's assassination, repeatedly called Emperor Maximilian of Mexico an adventurer. The Austrian Minister, Baron von Wydenbruck, greatly shocked, unofficially complained to the Secretary of State, who, however, caustically remarked that the Minister had no right to complain, Vienna having declared itself to be disinterested in Mexican affairs (Wydenbruck's report, February 13, 1866).

The young labor organizations in Germany hailed the victory of the Union. From the very beginning they had looked upon the war as a fight for free

[1] According to Lord Granville, the Revolution suggested to Europe the possibilities of democratic government—the American Civil War revealed to her for the first time the fact of democratic imperialism. Cf. Fitzmaurice, *Granville.*

labor. The address of condolence of the Berlin Working Men's Club upon the occasion of Lincoln's assassination, May 4, 1865, was not without veiled threats: "With liveliest interest we have watched the giant struggle for the rights of free labor which the United States of America has entered upon and has so nobly maintained during four years. With great joy we beheld the star-spangled banner issuing triumphantly from this battle for freedom and civilization, for we fully understood the vast import and bearing of the results thereby achieved. . . . But in giving expression of our deep sympathy in the death of Abraham Lincoln, we feel compelled at the same time to give utterance of our hopes and wishes to the effect that the freedom which has thus been sealed with the blood of one of the noblest men will only the more fully prevail, and that the star-spangled banner may wave in triumph wherever it is unfurled, in battling for the cause of freedom and civilization." The Berlin Artisans' and Mechanics' Union expressed itself still more plainly on May 21, when it wished that it might be possible "to achieve the fullest recognition of the principles of human rights, so that your enemies, who are ours likewise, will hereafter be deprived of all their noxious influence and power."[2]

For the moment, however, the impression on bourgeois democracy was more significant. Thiers became its leader in the French Chamber. Although frankly criticizing the crude manners of the Americans he said that America was a free country because the will of the nation was supreme and because the people showed so much greatness and devotion or made such sacrifices only for their own sakes, never for a ruler.[3] The American example even affected the princes of southern Germany. The Grand Duke of Hesse, for example, lauded the military system of the United States to Bancroft: "Your Nation is like a prudent man who uses an umbrella only when it rains and puts it aside the moment the rain is over. But we in Europe with our armies are like a man who holds up an umbrella in good weather as well as in bad, alike in sunshine and in storm." [4]

This explains why American representatives in Europe announced the victory of European democracy as imminent. Sanford, in a private letter to the Secretary of State, wrote from Spa, Belgium, August 31, 1866: "You see how the democratic wave increases in volume and strength here in Europe. The influence of our victories upon her destinies cannot be measured. Prussia, with its ultra divine right King going for universal suffrage and sweeping

[2] *Foreign Relations,* 1865, appendix, 498f.

[3] John Bigelow, *Retrospections,* III, 364.

[4] Bancroft to Seward, Berlin, Aug. 14, 1868, Dept. State, *Despatches, Prussia,* 15, no. 69.

away little 'by the grace of God' dynasties by the half dozen, to get ahead and lead this irresistible current, shows how potent it is. England must follow, and whether peacefully or through force depends on her aristocracy." [4a] Bancroft expressed himself similarly in his letters. The influence of the United States, he said, was great and constantly growing. Where twenty years before people did not believe that the American Republic could be preserved, there was now general confidence in the ability of the American Nation to cope with any difficulty whatever.[5] The Americans, however, greatly overestimated their direct influence. It was apparent in Great Britain, where the Government until the very last phase of the war had all too stubbornly doubted the possibility of restoring the Union. Turbulent meetings in Hyde Park indicated the disappointment of the British taxpayer with the shortsighted policy of his Government, pressing the reform of the national constitution farther and more completely than otherwise might have been the case.[6] The general tendency of the times was no doubt more influential than the American example. That trend called for the organization of national states and for consolidation of business. This necessitated concessions to the currents of liberalism.

Nevertheless, the influence of the American war and its consequences on contemporary European politics was considerable. Britain's freedom of action in Europe was hampered by her dispute with the Union over the *Alabama* claims. The controversy started as early as 1863. In a discussion of the European situation with Bismarck on April 24, 1863, the British Ambassador pointed out that Great Britain, "if a Franco-Prussian war should break out in the near future, even with the best of intentions could hardly help Germany because her relations with America were becoming so dangerously complicated as to menace the peace between the two countries."[7] No doubt the dispute with America had some bearing on Great Britain's conduct during the Danish crisis. Her apprehensions, toward the end of the War of Secession, increased to outright fear of an American attack. At the end of January 1865, when Gladstone advocated a limitation of naval reserves, a large majority of the

---

[4a] Dept. State, *Despatches, Belgium,* 9, private.

[5] Howe, *Bancroft,* II, 202, 206, 221f.

[6] "Every step in Great Britain toward breaking down the ancient system of privilege and restriction was an approach, however unintended, toward the democratic ideal. Every step in the United States toward national consolidation involved such development and fostering of special interests, however reluctantly, as to limit perceptibly the *laissez-faire* individualism of the democratic fact." Cf. Dunning, *British Empire and the United States,* 44; E. D. Adams, *Great Britain and the American Civil War,* II, 300ff.

[7] Bismarck to Werther, Apr. 24, 1863, *Gesammelte Werke,* IV, 111.

Cabinet opposed such a measure because of the sentiment in the Northern States.[8] As late as May 1, 1869, Lord Clarendon complained that the freedom of action of British politics was paralyzed by the American dispute.[9] As a matter of fact, British apprehensions were not at all unfounded. American public opinion was more antagonistic to Britain than to France, many people openly demanding humiliation of the former.[10] The situation in Canada was particularly precarious. Invasions by Irish Fenians were a constant menace. The British called Fenianism the ulcer of Ireland.[11] Throughout 1866 sentiment in Canada at least was such as to prefer independence to a war with the United States.[12] The Americans, for their part, fully realized how embarrassing the *Alabama* claims controversy was for Great Britain, and made the most of it.[13]

First of all the British Government had assumed that recognition of the Confederacy as a belligerent power had been permissible under international law. For this reason Lord Russell rejected in 1865 a general court of arbitration for the American claims. He merely wished to have submitted to a neutral court of arbitration the question as to whether the British Government had acted deliberately, that is, in good faith. A mixed commission was to discuss all problems between Great Britain and America accruing from the Civil War. The Department of State, however, rejected this British counter-proposal. But as British navigation interests clamored for an understanding because of the menace to trade relations, an agreement on principles was concluded in 1868. On January 14, 1869, the Johnson-Clarendon Convention was signed. According to the convention, a mixed commission of four members, two of whom were to represent each government, was to examine the justification for all claims advanced by the Union since 1863. This convention failed of ratification because in the meantime there had been a change of Presidents and the new administration was interested in thwarting the diplomatic successes of its predecessor.

---

[8] Victoria, *Letters,* second series, I, 249. For British nervousness, cf. Bemis, *Secretaries of State,* VII, 156.

[9] Victoria, *Letters,* second series, I, 594.

[10] Gerolt to Bismarck, Oct. 29, 1866.

[11] Bernstorff to King Wilhelm, Mar. 28, 1866.

[12] Gerolt to Bismarck, Mar. 9, 1866. For the Canadian independence movement, see Dunning, *British Empire and the United States,* 178ff.

[13] For example, Henry Adams wrote to Charles Francis Adams, London, Oct. 20, 1865: "We hold at this moment the whole foreign policy of England in our hands. She can't express even an opinion. If she tells Count Bismarck that he'd better mind his eye, the Count winks at us, and puts on his heaviest cowhides, and administers to her a licking that excoriates her figure." Henry Adams, *Letters,* 122.

Moreover, new Fenian riots had again shaken confidence. Although the American Government at the last moment had prevented an invasion by Fenians, London knew very well that the Irish filibusters had received secret aid from official and unofficial sources. However, it cannot be denied that the British themselves were to blame to some extent for the cession of Canada being so openly discussed in the United States. Many Englishmen at that time freely declared that the British colonies in general and the North American ones in particular were troublesome luxuries which should be disposed of as soon as possible. Ever since the American War for Independence, many had lost faith in the perpetuation of the colonial empire. It was a great mistake for the British even to discuss the possibility of Canadian independence.[14] The British Minister in Washington, Sir Edward Thornton, for one, had expressed himself to the effect that Great Britain would not keep Canada if she did not wish to stay.[15] Motley received a similar impression from conversations with the British Prime Minister in London.[16] A speech by Charles Sumner, chairman of the Committee on Foreign Relations, April 13, 1869, set forth certain conclusions from that situation. He thought the moment auspicious for action. Severely attacking Great Britain for her conduct during the Civil War, he said that money alone could not repair the wrong Britain had inflicted on the American Nation. Besides claiming $110,000,000 outright, Sumner injected into the debate the suggestion of indirect compensation by means of the cession of Canada. On the same day, Motley, a friend of Sumner's, went to London as American Minister. British public opinion was greatly agitated because of Sumner's tone as well as because of the large sum of money he had claimed. Likewise, the Americans keenly remembered the wrong Great Britain was thought to have committed. There were not a few people who wanted to call Britain to account; they placed high hopes on the American Navy, thinking that the new ironclads were superior to the British fleet.[17] The British Government was therefore considerably handicapped by strained

[14] Cf. Dunning, *British Empire and the United States*, 183ff. Lord Lyons, in 1870, was very pessimistic about the future of British North America; cf. Newton, *Lord Lyons*, I, 292. Seeley, the British historian, was foremost in combatting that tendency; cf. his *Expansion of England*.

[15] Pierce, *Charles Sumner*, IV, 409. Cf. Moore, *Digest*, I, 581.

[16] Motley to Fish, London, July 16, 1870, confidential: "He [Lord Granville] admitted that the matter of Canadian independence was a fair subject for discussion, especially as members of the Government had openly pronounced opinions thereon in Parliament . . . I expressed in conclusion the conviction that the independence of British North America would remove the main obstacle to permanently peaceful and friendly relations between the United States and the British Empire." Dept. State, *Despatches, Great Britain*, 104, no. 390.

[17] Gerolt to Bismarck, Oct. 29, 1866.

relations with America just before and during the Franco-Prussian crisis, when it should have been concentrating its whole attention on European developments. As a result, the war between Germany and France strengthened the desire for a speedy understanding.[18] The Treaty of Washington was concluded in May 1871, but new difficulties continued to interfere until the Geneva decision was handed down. Thus, Great Britain was troubled with the *Alabama* dispute for nearly a decade.

Not until 1869 did the *Alabama* claims case become of much importance to Bismarck's policy. Its significance may have increased after his friend Motley's arrival in London; once he inquired why the *Kreuzzeitung* was attacking Motley.[19] While Bismarck immediately understood the objective of Sumner's speech, he did not for a moment think of utilizing his knowledge to the detriment of Britain. On the contrary, on June 24 he instructed Bernstorff to discuss the German attitude with the British statesmen when the opportunity presented itself.[20] Even before, in instructions to Reuss, May 7, he had made his calculations as to how the British-American tension might possibly affect the general political situation in Europe. After mentioning Britain's Irish troubles, he dealt with the danger of a conflict with the United States. Britain, he thought, would not necessarily be prevented from actively interfering with continental politics, even though she had to take America into consideration. "The British know that they are in a position to eliminate the ultimate objective of the American conflict and to reduce to a minimum all other points of difference by deciding to cut loose the British colonies in northern America from the union with their mother country, placing them on their own responsibility. The British statesmen of all parties probably have been entertaining such ideas for a long time, and for most of them it is merely a question of finding the proper moment and the proper method. Friendly relations with America will easily develop, allowing Great Britain a perfectly free hand for her European interests. It is my observation that, regardless of the momentary excitement because of the *Alabama* affair, sentiment in America itself and among the masses is more unfavorable toward France than toward Britain because of the Emperor's Mexican policy and his intended official recognition of the Southern States."[21] Reuss discussed these instruc-

[18] "The relations of England with Germany too are any thing but satisfactory, and the impatience of Mr. Bull to get on better terms with the United States, which he has lately exhibited, has left the impression that there is a coalition forming between England, France & Austria on the one hand and Russia & Germany on the other, which is to result in a fight." John Bigelow, *Retrospections,* IV, 473f.

[19] The *Kreuzzeitung,* Oct. 13, had called Motley an "ornamental person."

[20] Bucher to the Foreign Office, Varzin, Oct. 16, 1869, telegram.

[21] Bismarck, *Gesammelte Werke,* II, 73.

tions with Gortshakoff, the Russian Chancellor, who shared Bismarck's opinion: the American threat should not be taken seriously, their bark being worse than their bite.[22] Bernstorff and Clarendon agreed with Bismarck's opinion that the Americans intended to acquire British America. Bernstorff, however, thought there was no danger of that since public opinion in Canada was opposed to annexation by the United States.[23]

For a short time, during the Franco-Prussian War, British-American dissension directly affected European politics. The Black Sea question, raised by Russia, in November 1870, made the unsettled *Alabama* dispute particularly embarrassing for Britain. Russia, at Bismarck's suggestion, thought the moment had arrived when the Black Sea Treaty of March 23, 1856, could be canceled.[24] Bismarck, who had been constantly afraid of intervention by the Czar, had intimated to St. Petersburg, through Grand Duchess Helen, that his Government would not be disinclined to support Russia's claims in the Black Sea. But it took some time to dissuade Russia from intervening in the Franco-Prussian War. After Great Britain, on October 21, 1870, had proposed that the powers call a peace conference, Russia, on October 31, presented a circular note to the signatories of the Treaty of Paris declaring that the Czar no longer considered the Black Sea clauses binding. As article 1 of the separate agreement of April 15, 1856, expressly declared any violation a *casus belli,* the circular note was a very serious matter. While certain members of the British Government realized to some extent that Russia could not forever submit to article 1, they thought that unilateral abrogation should not be tolerated. London was exceedingly irritated; for a time an open conflict seemed unavoidable.

It was indeed not impossible for the United States to take advantage of a British-Russian war to settle the *Alabama* conflict; this seemed the more likely after Motley's recall from London, in November, when it was assumed, though erroneously, that the American Government was about to pursue a more vigorous policy.[25] The British felt some uncertainty in that connection; Rothschild asked John Jay, American Minister in Vienna, whether the United States would declare war against Great Britain in case she participated in a war against Russia. Jay replied in the negative. The United States, as usual, would maintain strict neutrality, but owing to the sentiment still prevailing because of Britain's attitude in the Civil War, it would be difficult for the Government, even with the greatest precaution, to prevent ships from sailing

[22] Reuss to Bismarck, June 6, 1869, copy.
[23] Bismarck to Bernstorff, July 24; Bernstorff to Bismarck, July 31, 1869.
[24] Cf. Rheindorf, *Die Schwarze-Meer-(Pontus-) Frage,* 79ff.
[25] Bismarck to Bernstorff, Versailles, Oct. 16, 1870.

illegally.[26] The Russian Minister in Washington, Catacazy, was far more confident. The United States Government, he thought, did not feel disinclined to use the possibility of a Russo-British war to secure definite settlement of the *Alabama* problem and to give vent to long-restrained resentment against England. Mr. Fish even mentioned a defensive and offensive alliance between Russia and America and promised to send an American fleet to the Black Sea. However, those private statements of Mr. Fish should not be taken quite literally; the question as to the attitude of the Government was soon to be discussed in a Cabinet meeting. The Imperial Chancellor, while highly gratified by these first reports from America, would not entertain overly sanguine hopes in that respect. The American Minister energetically denied the rumor in St. Petersburg that the American Government had offered its entire fleet in the case of war, while the Russian Government, on the other hand, admonished its Minister in Washington not to hasten things too much but to give the Americans time to make their decisions. For the present the Americans should renew their former protests in Constantinople against neutralization of the Black Sea, thereby supporting the Russian *démarche.*[27]

Bismarck, whom Reuss had informed of the matter, had Bancroft asked confidentially from time to time whether he had formed a personal opinion with regard to America's potential attitude toward a Russo-British conflict.[28] Simultaneously he telegraphed to London that Great Britain would have cause for action only in the case of Russian aggression. A French newspaper seized the opportunity to spread the rumor that Bismarck had urged America to press its *Alabama* claims seriously. The Chancellor at once denied the rumor; no despatches of that kind had been written, nor was anything of the sort intended.[29] The hubbub over potential intervention by the United States seems to have had its source chiefly in the self-importance of the Russian Minister in Washington.[30] The Secretary of State, at any rate, very definitely declared

---

[26] Jay to Fish, Vienna, Nov. 21, 1870, Dept. State, *Despatches, Austria,* 11, no. 179. Cf. Morley, *Gladstone,* II, 400. The American press welcomed Russia's measure; cf. Rheindorf, *Die Schwarze-Meer-(Pontus-) Frage,* 100.

[27] Reuss to Bismarck, Nov. 19, 1870; telegram and report of the same date, secret, Nov. 20, 1870. Bismarck to Bernstorff, Versailles, Nov. 24, 1870, telegram. Bernstorff to Bismarck, Jan. 5, 1871. Telegram from Bismarck, same date. Curtin to Fish, St. Petersburg, Nov. 20, 1870, Dept. State, *Despatches, Russia,* 22, no. 86.

[28] Bismarck to Thile, Versailles, Nov. 20, 1870, telegram.

[29] Bernstorff to Bismarck, London, Jan. 5, 1871, telegram; reply on the same day.

[30] By that time Catacazy was already *persona non grata* in Washington, having seriously displeased the Government with his indiscretions. For this reason his reports to St. Petersburg do not deserve much confidence. A press notice, evidently originating near him, even asserted that the President had talked of an understanding with England for common action against Russia (Washington correspondence of the

that the Government of the United States would adhere to its principle "not to participate in the political disputes and conflicts among the European powers and that it would not use a war in which Great Britain might be engaged, for the purpose of enforcing the *Alabama* claims through an alliance with Russia against Great Britain, since the British Government was expected to settle the matter peaceably and satisfactorily."[31] Besides, Secretary of State Hamilton Fish thought the fisheries disputes with Great Britain far more important. That country was not inclined in the least to be drawn into a war because of the Black Sea question. In a three-hour conversation with Odo Russell, November 21, Bismarck expounded his plan for a conference, which both Russia and Great Britain accepted after conciliatory notes had kept the door open for an understanding.

Between the Washington agreement and the Geneva arbitration the German Government had one more occasion for considering the *Alabama* problem. Bancroft had thought at one time of suggesting Germany to his Government as an arbitrator in the *Alabama* dispute; but he abandoned that idea as he did not wish to jeopardize American-German relations by so delicate a matter. Thus he obtained the German Emperor as an arbitrator only in the dispute with Great Britain about San Juan. Originally, the American Government had been ready to compromise, but Bancroft strongly advised against it. The United States should insist unreservedly on its claim and the German Emperor was to decide the case definitely. As a matter of fact the German decision favored America, but Great Britain was not greatly vexed.[32]

Negotiations between the United States and Great Britain before the Geneva Court of Arbitration in 1872 attracted the attention of the German Government, particularly in that the Washington agreement had established a number of regulations for naval warfare but had left undecided the critical question—American indirect claims for compensation. The tension, therefore, was considerable and the negotiations did not proceed smoothly. On May 11, 1872, the German Empress wrote from Windsor Castle that a military conflict

---

Cincinnati *Enquirer*, no date). The American Government took issue with Catacazy's intrigues very decidedly. "He [Catacazy] has made himself busy, in season and out of season, in efforts to obstruct, embarrass, and defeat the recent negotiations between the United States and Great Britain for the adjustment of their mutual differences." Fish to Curtin, Nov. 16, 1871, Dept. State, *Instructions, Russia*, 15: 283. For the American dispute with Catacazy, cf. Moore, *Digest*, IV, 503 and 667f.

[31] Gerolt to Bismarck, Nov. 21, 1870.

[32] Foreign Office memorandum, Mar. 25, 1871; Bernstorff to Kaiser Wilhelm, June 4, 1872. Cf. Bancroft, *Denkschrift über den Kanal von Haro*, and message of President Grant, Dec. 5, 1871.

was not expected, for the American Navy could not offer prolonged resistance to the British Navy and would soon show its relative weakness in case of such a conflict. Public opinion in America, moreover, was decidedly averse to war. "Nevertheless, continued diplomatic controversies would result in a condition unfavorable for both world powers, in an insecurity of relations which would inflict serious losses on both nations and especially hurt American finances because they depend on the London money market." [33]

According to article VI, rules, of the Washington treaty of arbitration of May 8, 1871, the neutral government undertook "not to permit or suffer either belligerent to make use of its ports or waters as the base of naval operations against the other, or for the purpose of the renewal or augmentation of military supplies or arms, or the recruitment of men." [34] The new regulations chiefly benefited Great Britain, which would suffer little from such restrictions in case of war, having coaling stations of her own all over the world. Germany was more interested in those negotiations, as she had experienced the deficiencies of international law in consequence of the many breaches of neutrality on the part of Great Britain and the United States during the past war. [35] A unilateral development of the law of maritime warfare was not in the interest of Germany. Bismarck, therefore, on March 8, 1872, instructed Bernstorff, who shared his opinion, "to take the *Alabama* affair not merely from the British point of view as to which of the two contending parties is right in the present phase of the dispute, but to consider it in the light of our own interest as regards both parties in a decision of the international law controversy concerning neutral duties." The Ambassador was, therefore, to remark coolly to Lord Granville or other British statesmen "that the policy of both Britain and America during the last war lent a special interest to the negotiations now pending between the two countries and that we, for this reason, were observing the progress of the American claims with the desire of seeing general recognition of a stricter conception of neutral duties on land and on the high seas." When Bernstorff acted accordingly, Granville asked him whether neutral duties were to be made so difficult that it would be easier to conduct a war than to comply with them. Bernstorff denied that such was the intention, adding that the neutrality of the two countries now was a perfectly one-sided affair "being strictly observed only with regard to naval warfare, and we therefore necessarily wished to have the same strictness applied to war on land." Granville, not inclined to resume the controversy

---

[33] Kaiserin Augusta to Kaiser Wilhelm, Windsor Castle, May 11, 1872 (extract).

[34] Malloy, *Treaties,* I, 703.

[35] The Berlin Chamber of Commerce, in Sept. 1870, passed a resolution for the reform of the law of war.

thus alluded to, said it did not seem very reasonable for other countries to shut down completely certain branches of their industries while two powers were at war with each other; moreover, it was much easier to control and prevent a ship from leaving a port than to prevent the transportation of every case of arms or munitions of war, because that would require far more extensive and more difficult inspection.[36] Bismarck was satisfied that the purpose of his instructions had been achieved with that conversation, that is, by inducing the British, or at least Lord Granville, to think about their own policy. "That was shown by the vivacity with which he replied to you, and I hope that England will take occasion to reflect to the Cabinet in Washington, in the form of British arguments on the *Alabama* claim, America's attitude toward us during the war." On April 16, the Chancellor again formulated his opinion clearly, without expecting direct results. The Ambassador in conversation was casually to mention the German point of view: "that we would not join in stricter regulations for neutral duties in naval war alone." By tacit agreement during the long *Alabama* dispute, a distinction had been made between naval war and war on land, between Southern privateers equipped in British seaports and rifles supplied by British blockade runners to Southern land forces. The Chancellor was afraid that sanction of that arbitrary distinction would indefinitely obstruct development of international law in war along channels that seemed desirable to Germany.[37]

European or German policies were certain to be affected more directly by the French enterprise in Mexico. In retrospect, Napoleon's venture resembles a carnival joke, for to us today it appears utterly impossible that his Mexican plans ever could have succeeded. Only the mind of an ambitious adventurer seemed to have been able to conceive the hazardous plan of a French protectorate many thousands of miles distant from its base, with a form of government foreign to the American continent, save for Brazil. Difficulties were increased by the open antagonism of the United States and by the instability of Mexico's mixed population. Such considerations, nevertheless, do not do justice to the Mexican policy of Napoleon III. France was by no means the only country troubled by the everlasting revolutions in Mexico. Much international capital had been invested there, and influential financial groups demanded intervention.[38] In July 1860, the British Government proposed to the United States the presentation of a joint note to the government of Juárez and Miramón concerning the settlement of debts. The American Government refused. Thereupon, toward the end of 1861, British, Spanish, and French

[36] Bernstorff to Bismarck, Mar. 27, 1872.
[37] Bismarck to Bernstorff, Apr. 16, 1872.
[38] Cf. Moore, *Digest*, VI, 477ff.

ships were sent to Veracruz to occupy the customhouses. After obtaining separate debt agreements, Spain and Great Britain withdrew from the expedition in April 1862. Not until then did the French policy begin to take an independent course. The three powers at first had jointly guaranteed to the Mexican Government the privilege of electing a free government; but once the British and Spaniards had departed, the French troops proceeded from Veracruz by forced marches, occupying Mexico City in June 1863. A provisional government and the notables assembled under French protection declared an hereditary monarchy the future form of government of Mexico.[38a] At the beginning Napoleon rightly felt that he could not risk the Mexican adventure without British assistance. However, importunities of Mexican *émigrés,* augmented by those of the Empress, whose influence had already become very strong, made him determine to approve the election of Archduke Maximilian as Emperor of Mexico and to pledge French protection to Maximilian. It was believed that North America was too desirous of keeping on good terms with France to risk direct opposition.[39]

A more unfortunate choice than Archduke Maximilian could not have been made.[40] Thirty-two years old, blessed with the best of intentions, he could, as was to be shown, courageously resist dangers and die a hero. But he lacked a sense of reality and knowledge of human nature. As he blindly trusted Napoleon, he soon came under the varying influences of Mexican political parties. His policy was inconsistent and vacillating; ultimately it could scarcely have succeeded, even with the support of France. Affairs looked rather promising while the French troops under Marshal Bazaine stayed in Mexico, but when it appeared probable, then certain, that the French undertaking in Mexico was about to be abandoned, the situation became increasingly critical for Maximilian. From the outset the American Government had indicated rather clearly that it considered any intervention in Mexico undesirable.[41] This point of view was maintained throughout the Civil War, but Seward was very cautious in his intercourse with the French Government. His supercourteous notes, addressed to Napoleon, seemed even to level-headed John Bigelow to be too weak; whereupon Seward, in his sober way, replied that the moment was not auspicious for addressing hollow threats to the Emperor while Union forces on land and sea were retreating from the rebels instead of marching to Mexico.[42] The language of the American Government assumed a stronger

[38a] Perkins, *Monroe Doctrine, 1826-1867,* 400.
[39] Metternich reported in that sense from Paris, June 10, 1862.
[40] Cf. Corti, *Maximilian und Charlotte,* I.
[41] Cf. Moore, *Digest,* VI, 490.
[42] Rippy, *United States and Mexico,* 262f.

tone when the military situation had taken its decisive turn in favor of the Union. From the spring of 1865, Paris was given to understand that the United States expected an early departure of the French troops from Mexico. For a time, military intervention in Mexico was contemplated. General Sheridan "was sent with an army of about fifty thousand men to the line of the Rio Grande," [42a] but it soon appeared that an entirely new army would have to be organized for a military expedition. General John M. Schofield received the commission to do so; but the difficulties encountered led Seward in the summer of 1865 to seek a compromise. General Schofield was sent to Paris on a secret mission, while at home it was considered sufficient to support Juárez with volunteers and secret deliveries of arms. The general took pains to acquaint men in authority in Paris with the American point of view. In November 1865, the French Government offered a compromise: in return for the recognition of Maximilian in Mexico, the French troops were to be withdrawn. The Department of State's brusque rejection of that proposal left no further doubt in the minds of the French Government that nothing better could be done than to liquidate as quickly as possible the ill-starred Mexican enterprise. Thus General Webb, in November 1865, thought he had succeeded without much difficulty in reaching a secret agreement with Napoleon by which all French troops were to evacuate Mexico by March 1867.[42b]

In the meantime the German situation had become so difficult that no other choice was left to the Emperor. He could hardly have ventured to start a war with the United States at a moment when events of the greatest significance were foreshadowed in Central Europe. After the battle of Sadowa, at any rate, the Mexican burden could no longer be carried. When Empress Charlotte, troubled by evil forebodings, arrived in Paris in August 1866, she met a man not only ill but incapable of action because of the rapid succession of events. In vain she appealed to every person imaginable. The ministers remained indifferent. The Emperor shrugged his shoulders. The battle of Sadowa had decided the fate of Mexico.[43]

And what was the other side of the story? To what extent was Bismarck's policy influenced by the Franco-American tension because of Mexico? Did the Mexican enterprise lessen the preparedness of the French Army in Europe?

As a matter of fact, Franco-American relations became really critical only in the winter of 1865-66. For a liquidation of the Mexican enterprise as such the Emperor could count on the approval of the whole nation, including the

[42a] Schofield, "Withdrawal of the French from Mexico," in *Century Magazine*, vol. 54, no. 1 (May 1897), 128ff.

[42b] Perkins, *Monroe Doctrine, 1826-1867*, 502 footnote.

[43] Corti, *Maximilian und Charlotte*, II, 253ff.

army. Indeed, it seems that military circles had almost more sympathy for President Juárez than for Emperor Maximilian. The army instinctively realized that there were no laurels to be gained in Mexico. Nevertheless, Napoleon's prestige would undoubtedly be seriously undermined if he terminated the Mexican enterprise too suddenly. For this reason the Emperor tried to gain time. He pretended not to be worrying about America. But in December 1865, Empress Eugénie opened her heart to Goltz: a war between France and the United States would be for them and all of Europe a dreadful calamity which should be carefully avoided. But if such avoidance could be achieved only by national suicide of one of the parties, it would be preferable for them to kill off each other. France need not fear European democracy. Domestic issues would be immediately eliminated in case of war. Great Britain could not maintain her neutrality permanently in such a war since British commerce and navigation would be destroyed. The Empress also thought of a rehabilitation of the Southern States, for the Union had no Marshal Bazaine. The Emperor, too, seemed outwardly worried but little. The Americans will quiet down again, he said to Goltz, who noticed no preoccupation in the Emperor. The Foreign Minister, likewise, expressed himself very haughtily, but Count Robert von der Goltz, like the British Ambassador in Paris, Lord Cowley, was of the opinion that the French wished to avoid war at all hazards. News from London was less optimistic; Lord Clarendon considered war probable.[44]

Prussia certainly did nothing to stimulate war sentiment. On the contrary, Gerolt and Goltz offered their services for mediation, believing such a war detrimental to Prussian interests. Gerolt, whom the French Minister in Washington, in the course of a conversation, had informed of the impending danger of war, and who had noticed that Juárez was secretly receiving aid, asserted to Seward that such a war would be a misfortune for all parties concerned. Seward seemed embarrassed but did not interpret the situation as being so dangerous.[45]

As early as 1863 Goltz expressed forebodings that an unsuccessful expedition to Mexico might cause the Emperor to turn his attention to a larger field of activity (to King Wilhelm June 13). In January 1865, he requested Bigelow not to bring too much pressure to bear on France in the matter of evacuation. That would, he feared, drive the Emperor all the more readily into a European war.[46] After Gerolt's pessimistic reports of November 5 and 20 had been communicated to Goltz, he asked Bismarck's permission to talk

[44] Goltz to Bismarck, Dec. 29, 1865, and Jan. 12 and Feb. 1, 1866; Bernstorff to Bismarck, Jan. 3 and 31, 1866.

[45] Gerolt to Bismarck, Nov. 6, 1865.

[46] John Bigelow, Retrospections, II, 265.

to the Emperor and the French Foreign Minister in a conciliatory sense. He said he assumed that Great Britain would probably participate actively in such a war as an ally of France. "Accordingly, Germany's overseas trade would be completely destroyed, lacking a flag which might protect it, particularly so since the United States, which did not join in the Declaration of Paris, would issue letters of marque. Moreover, European democracy would be inclined to sympathize with America and thus might cause a revolutionary movement in Europe. To prevent the latter, Emperor Napoleon could hardly avoid reviving the Polish question. He would be the more inclined to do so with the consent of Great Britain who was anxiously watching Russia's progress in Asia, as the latter power was suspected of having added fuel to the fire in Washington. Very likely Russia would observe a benevolent neutrality at least toward America." [47] Bismarck's opinion differed from those of his two ministers. On December 6 he reprimanded Gerolt: His Majesty had the conservation of peace there as everywhere most sincerely at heart and His Majesty wished to have a war between France and the United States prevented. The minister, however, was not authorized to speak to the American Government in the way he had. He was not in a position to judge the effects of such a war on Germany's general policy. Even if the consequences were favorable in this case, they might be detrimental to the policy of His Majesty in other cases. Gerolt, on December 25, defended his action, saying that he had thought it proper to work for the preservation of peace between France and America, "the more so as, in my opinion, other European powers, including Prussia, would necessarily be drawn into such a war." On the 18th of the same month, Bismarck wrote to Goltz very fully: It would be desirable if he were to use the communications of the Minister in Washington in such a way as to show the French Government that the general instructions of the Prussian representatives and the chief objective of Prussian policy toward which Herr von Gerolt was moving, envisioned friendly relations with France. "If accompanied by expressions of our interest in the preservation of peace between these two great countries, such discussions, if reported to the American Government, will not give offense. Let me, however, expressly request that Your Excellency keep in mind and try to prevent the possibility of misunderstandings on the American side." Bismarck did not anticipate a break, but, should it occur, it would be doubtful whether Great Britain would make France's war her own, unless likewise offended by the United States. "From the England of the past I should have expected a resolute and far-sighted policy which would have preferred to expose British commerce to American privateers now in order to prevent future danger from that source; present-day

[47] Goltz to Bismarck, Dec. 11, 1865, confidential.

79

Britain, I rather expect, would not renounce material comfort without material necessity, nor would she courageously face the unpopularity which an alliance with France would presumably cause among all those who would suffer from a war with America." Great Britain might otherwise have taken part in the War of Secession. But even if he were mistaken in that respect, Bismarck was convinced that the war would not be accompanied by a democratic movement of any consequence in Europe. "The sympathies of democracy on our continent would rather turn to America than to the two belligerent European powers, especially Napoleonic France; both powers would therefore be interested in forestalling expressions of that sympathy and in suppressing the party which might entertain it."

Bismarck disagreed with Goltz's opinion that France was inclined to add a Russo-Prussian conflict to her American one. Furthermore, diplomatic measures need not be taken at this time in view of a possible Franco-American war. Emperor Napoleon could somehow prevent an unfortunate war which would be so unprofitable for France. "If the means chosen should be of such a nature as to impair French pride, I should indeed share the apprehension of Your Excellency that the Emperor might think he would have to make amends in Europe. In my opinion we can as yet judge so little how and in what direction his policy will move that the theories I might now express would certainly be very audacious." In subsequent instructions of January 5, 1866, Bismarck approved Goltz's relations with the French Emperor and M. Drouyn de Lhuys in a situation rendered difficult by the American problem, but recommended reserve in conversations with Bigelow. "We must by no means give Bigelow occasion to report home any Prussian partiality against America and in favor of France, for we must lay the greatest stress on excellent relations with Washington. But this desire for friendly relations with the United States as well as with France does not exclude the possibility that, if both powers should engage in a conflict with each other, we might exploit for the ends of Prussian policy our greater freedom from French control or the greater need on the part of France for an understanding with us. In this sense it is my request that Your Excellency on the one hand continue to utilize as carefully as ever all matters in connection with that question for strengthening our good relations with France and the confidence of Emperor Napoleon, and, on the other hand, to limit your influence on Mr. Bigelow—though not so noticeably as to infringe in any way upon Baron Gerolt's cultivation of our relations with America." [48]

Thus Bismarck, in his Mexican policy, likewise proceeded neither without

[48] Bismarck, *Gesammelte Werke,* V, 340ff., 351.

careful thought nor with excessive hopes. There are no indications which would show that he sought to increase the Franco-American tension. In any event he wanted to stay on good terms with the United States. While he allowed Gerolt to join the Austrian Minister in an attempt to save Maximilian's life, at the same time he instructed the Prussian Minister in Mexico to continue official relations for the present with the newly developing government in that capital, if he thought it compatible with the dignity of the Royal Legation. Prussia was indeed the first power to recognize the republican government in Mexico by resuming diplomatic relations. This step was taken in answer to the urgent requests of the German merchants who had in their hands a large part of Mexico's foreign trade. It was not by accident that Bismarck chose the United States Government as intermediary for that purpose. Bancroft, in his despatches to Washington, called attention to that evidence of good will.[49]

We need not exaggerate the actual danger of war between France and the United States. The French, in view of the European situation, were compelled to avoid such a conflict by all means. Only a pronounced desire for war on the part of the Americans would have brought it about. Possibly certain groups of American military men were not entirely averse to such a conflict; the Civil War had raised to prominence a considerable number of military leaders who were ambitious to add to their laurels. Similarly it might be imagined that Secretary of State Seward, firmly believing in the theory that domestic crises are best solved by foreign wars, personally would not have been disinclined toward another war.[50] At the same time he knew better than anyone else that he could never obtain the consent of Congress. In case of war all States of the Union would have had to be united immediately, and the former slave States could no longer have been refused admission to and representation in Congress; hence the radicals did not wish to have the Government thrust into a foreign war.[51] The American Ministers in London and Paris likewise worked for peace. As early as February 1865, Bigelow reassured Fould, the French Minister of Finance, regarding Mexico. It would be a mistake, Bigelow told him, to think that America did not know what disposition to make of her large army after demobilization. Every single man could make more money in civil life. Democracies were egotistic; they did not consider war a suitable cure for wounds inflicted on a people's soul. Bigelow, however, contributed a personal idea in his report: the Union would

[49] Bismarck to Magnus, Sept. 4 and 11, 1866; to Gerolt, May 2 and 29, 1867.

[50] Seward, before the Civil War, had suggested that the domestic crisis be settled by a foreign war.

[51] Gerolt to Bismarck, Feb. 12, 1866.

conquer Mexico some day, but not with the sword.[52] He made a similar remark to Goltz. Continuing his efforts toward mediation, he dined with Goltz on January 4, 1866, and was quite optimistic about peace. The French Government, he said, had delayed matters too long. America insisted on the evacuation of the army of occupation in Mexico, for those troops would never have reached that country had it not been for the war in North America. The Emperor would have to announce his decision voluntarily, without being requested to do so by a foreign power and without assuming an international obligation at its behest. Moreover, relations with Britain were menaced more seriously than were those with France. Goltz recounted this conversation to the Emperor, who was much interested. The American Minister in London, Charles Francis Adams, also thought that his Government would surely support Emperor Napoleon's wishes in that connection.[53]

It is safe to say that Napoleon's European policy was restrained by the general uncertainty as to what America would do in the case of a European war. For example, Bancroft as late as 1867 learned from a reliable source, among other things, that it was anxiety regarding the position the United States would take in the case of war which impelled Napoleon to keep the peace. Bancroft thereupon asked his Government not to relieve French foreign policy of that worry, a request with which the Secretary of State readily complied.[54]

The military aftereffects of the Mexican enterprise were a different matter. The Prussian military attaché in Paris, Freiherr von Loë, had a very pessimistic opinion of France's preparedness for war. His reports may be summed up in one sentence: the French Army is not prepared. He mentioned several causes such as the abuses in the high command and the defective recruiting system. But again and again he called attention to the unfortunate situation in Mexico, though not because of the number of troops involved, for there were only about thirty thousand French soldiers in Mexico. The insurrection that started in Algiers in 1864 was far more important in that respect. The military had hoped to be able to limit the number of effectives in Algiers to twenty-five thousand men, but at the beginning of the revolt it seemed doubtful whether seventy-five thousand men would suffice. "Algiers may call for 120,000 men from one day to another," Loë wrote to his King on May 25, 1864. In the

---

[52] Bigelow to Seward, Paris, Feb. 14, 1865, Dept. State, *Despatches, France,* 56, no. 30.

[53] Goltz to Bismarck, Jan. 5 and 12, 1866, confidential; Bernstorff to Bismarck, Jan. 12, 1866.

[54] Bancroft to Seward, Munich, Sept. 19, 1868, private, Dept. State, *Despatches, Prussia,* 15, no. 75. Foreign Office memorandum, May 2, 1867.

French Army the attitude toward Algiers differed from that regarding Mexico. While Napoleon III considered Algiers an Orleanist creation, complaining that he lacked eighty thousand men for his European policy, MacMahon was quite pleased with that situation, for he thought the continuous meddling with European affairs was dangerous and he wished to block that policy by keeping the army engaged in Algiers (Loë's report of January 1, 1865).

As mentioned before, the Mexican venture did not interfere greatly with the preparedness of the French Army as regards effective strength. The Government had sent no new troops there after 1865. But the unpopularity of the Mexican enterprise had a disastrous effect. Not daring to risk the flotation of loans for that purpose, the French Government was forced to retrench to the detriment of the development of the army organization. The effective strength of the Mexican formations had been doubled, but that could only be done by drawing on the regiments of the line. An especially evil feature was the heavy requirements of war materials and horses in Mexico. This no doubt caused a serious weakening of France's European army and its effects could be observed during the Luxemburg crisis. "So much, at any rate, is certain," Loë wrote on January 1, 1865, "that at the moment there are 110,000 French troops outside of Europe, which number does not include the corresponding depots in France, and that such a shortage would affect the situation considerably in the case of a European war. The authorities are fully aware of the fact that for years France has not been so greatly handicapped in her military influence in Europe than is the case at present, and the realization of that fact probably is a factor of no little importance in the general political attitude of the Government." Major von Burg reported from Paris on May 16, 1867, that the French military situation was probably never so bad as in March 1867. "Since no loans were to be issued for the expenditures for a six-year campaign in Mexico, all resources of the army and navy were made available to pay the expenses of that adventurous expedition which ended with the great political rebuff, submission to a simple menacing note of the United States. One thousand million francs, according to trustworthy information, are said to have been drained from the army and navy." The extraordinary efforts which France made during the Luxemburg crisis toward replenishing her supply of horses illustrated the situation.[55]

The Mexican problem no doubt influenced the decision of July 1866. In the Cabinet meeting of July 4, Drouyn de Lhuys had insisted upon presenting to Prussia demands for compensation. The Chambers should be called, a loan

[55] Of Loë's reports the following may be mentioned: May 25 and July 25, 1864, Jan. 1 and Nov. 21, 1865, Feb. 17 and Aug. 18, 1866. Cf. Loë, *Erinnerungen aus meinem Berufsleben*, 62ff.

of one billion francs issued, an army of 100,000 men sent to the eastern border, and the King of Prussia should be told that France would have to occupy the left bank of the Rhine if Prussia did not show moderation. The Empress approved these plans, while Rouher remained silent. Marquis de la Valette, Minister of the Interior, suddenly entered at that moment and submitted to the Emperor the question of whether he had the means of fighting a war with Prussia and Austria. He denied that the French Army was ready; it was short of essentials. Napoleon was forced to recognize the correctness of that objection, and Drouyn de Lhuys's plan was postponed. The right moment for a successful move was lost.

The Prussian military authorities no doubt considered Mexico in their calculations in the summer of 1866. Loë had reported that an army corps of thirty thousand men would remain abroad throughout that year.[56] On August 12, 1866, Loë wrote to his King that "despite that state of excitement the leading men in the army do not consider the moment auspicious for a war against Prussia. The equipment of the infantry which, I have reason to believe, is still in the experimental stage, and the situation in Mexico, again recently aggravated, no doubt are factors in causing that opinion to prevail. I know for certain that Marshal MacMahon expressed himself in that sense, but the Minister of War is also said to have spoken to the Emperor in a similar way."[57] The military attaché told General Froissard point-blank in August that France was not in a position to start a war. *"Il manque absolument d'artillerie, de trains, d'équipage, surtout de chevaux d'artillerie. C'est la conséquence du Mexique."*[58] Bismarck believed that Napoleon wished to make up for his failures in Mexico and Italy by acquiring Luxemburg.[59] "The Mexican troops have all returned. I repeat once more that the army is in no way prepared," Loë wrote on April 5, 1867.[60] Bismarck was not indifferent to the return of the French troops from Mexico. It was not, he thought, without significance and importance in governing relations with France. "I wish His Majesty's special attention called to that," Countess Bismarck, at his dictation, wrote to Keudell on October 21, 1866.[61] At any rate, it was generally thought in France that the Mexican enterprise had done a great deal of harm. Matías Romero, the Mexican Minister, reported from Paris on May 4, 1867: "Everybody now realizes that the insane expedition to Mexico led to

---

[56] Loë, *Erinnerungen aus meinem Berufsleben,* 83.

[57] Oncken, *Die Rheinpolitik Kaiser Napoleons III.,* II, 54.

[58] Loë, *Erinnerungen aus meinem Berufsleben,* 123.

[59] Vagts, *Mexiko, Europa, und Amerika,* 104.

[60] Oncken, *Die Rheinpolitik Kaiser Napoleons III.,* II, 289f.

[61] Keudell, *Fürst und Fürstin Bismarck,* 322.

an enlargement of Prussia, whose Prime Minister Bismarck took advantage of the time when the feet of France were chained to make Prussia one of the foremost military powers of Europe."[62]

[62] The relationship of the French policy in Mexico and Europe has not been treated in detail as yet. Oncken, in his essay *Amerika und die grossen Mächte,* 465, strongly emphasizes this relationship. For a good summary see Duniway, "Reasons for the Withdrawal of the French from Mexico," in American Historical Association, *Annual Report,* 1902, I, 315ff. The opinions of the French statesmen of the period are of little value as they were determined by considerations of national policy. Cf. Ollivier, *L'empire libéral,* VII, 486; Randon, *Mémoires,* II, 219ff. See a noteworthy essay by Romero, "The Fall of the Second Empire as related to French Intervention in Mexico," in the *Century Magazine,* vol. 54, no. 1 (May 1897), 138f., for the opinion that Napoleon's fall was hastened because of the prestige lost in Mexico.

CHAPTER V

THE UNITED STATES AND THE
UNIFICATION OF GERMANY

UNDER the circumstances Bismarck could not ignore the possibilities for the advancement of his policies as a result of the strained relations between Great Britain and France and the United States. While not expecting too much, he included them within the scope of his calculations. At no time was he so concerned about good relations with the United States as he was between 1866 and 1870.

A united front of the European powers would have been the greatest menace to his policy. He had to prevent that by all means in case the conflict with France became unavoidable, as he thought it would. Benevolent neutrality on the part of any nation would be an asset under such conditions. He did not expect material support from the United States; however, its friendship could be only advantageous. Bismarck cultivated that friendship consistently, which was not so difficult for him to do. As early as his Göttingen student days he had celebrated the Fourth of July with a group of Americans.[1] It was in Göttingen also that Bismarck made friends with John Lothrop Motley, later American diplomatist and historian, a friendship which was cemented for life in Berlin. If heartfelt affection is the decisive element in friendship, Bismarck's and Motley's friendship was ideal.[1a] Even Alexander

[1] With Coffin, his American student friend, Bismarck made the famous wager that Germany would be united within 20 years. When the time came for the bet to be paid, Coffin had died; Prenzler, *Jugendgeschichte des Fürsten Bismarck,* 64.

[1a] "Although Motley at that time had not yet mastered the German language, he was a fascinating *causeur* because of the wit, humor, and originality of his conversation. An enthusiastic admirer of Shakespeare, Byron, and Goethe, he would generously intersperse his conversation with quotations from his favorite authors. He loved to argue, often waiting for me to awake in order to continue a conversation on some subject of science, poetry, or practical life which we had interrupted late the night before, but in such discussions he never lost his sweet, lovable disposition." (Bismarck's analysis in later years.)

86

Keyserling did not receive such affectionate letters from Bismarck as did Motley in the sixties.[1b] We can easily understand why Bismarck was so closely attached to Motley: they met in the same turbulent period of their lives; they were temperamentally related; Motley's somewhat delicate nature was more than balanced by his vivid, ever-receptive mind and his vitality. Even at times when Bismarck's urge for physical activity was strongest, he occasionally liked to engage in sharp intellectual sword play. In that case he went to see the gifted American with whom he would carry on discussions for hours. Motley was the son of a prominent Boston merchant.[2] Born in 1814, he entered Roundhill School at the age of ten, where his teacher, George Bancroft, later American Minister in Berlin, introduced him to the German language and literature. As a schoolboy Motley translated poems by Goethe well enough to receive Frau von Goethe's recognition.[3] Motley, while attending various colleges, was less occupied with scholarly pursuits than with writing poetry. He arrived at Göttingen very immature, but thirsting for experience. The two friends came from different worlds, but they had basic feelings in common; not by mere chance did both admire Lord Byron as a hero. As a historian, Motley was always more interested in individual men than in people in general; his *History of the Netherlands* is really the story of William of Orange. Motley never felt quite at home in his own country, for the state of intellectual culture and the customs of society were not to his liking. It is characteristic of him that he preferred the company of British aristocracy. In *Morton's Hope,* one of his early novels, which he later disavowed, however, the hero, Otto von Rabenmark, unmistakably bears features of the Bismarck as Motley knew him in Göttingen, though unfortunately in a distorted form.[4]

[1b] For a considerable number of letters, cf. Motley, *Correspondence,* and *Motley and His Family.* A few letters are in *Bismarck-Jahrbuch,* III, 97ff., and IV, 209ff. A letter by Motley to Bismarck, Feb. 16, 1859, appears in Bismarck, *Anhang zu Gedanken und Erinnerungen,* II, 281ff. Letters from Motley to Bismarck prevail by far. According to Grund, "Bismarck and Motley—With Correspondence Till Now Unpublished," in *North American Review,* CLXVII, 369ff. (Sept. 1898), some of Motley's letters were destroyed by Bismarck. For information on their friendship, cf. Marcks, *Bismarck,* I, 87ff. and Whiteman, *Teutonic Studies,* 211ff.; Snyder, *Die persönlichen und politischen Beziehungen Bismarcks zu Amerikanern,* 1ff. and 18, footnote.

[2] For biographical data on Motley, cf. Holmes, *Writings,* XI, 329ff.

[3] *Ibid.,* XI, 340.

[4] The novel, *Morton's Hope, or the Memoirs of a Provincial,* seems to be accessible in only one copy in the British Museum; Motley destroyed all other copies. For this reason Snyder's extracts as quoted in *Die persönlichen und politischen Beziehungen Bismarcks zu Amerikanern,* 85ff., are the more valuable. In May 1858 the friends met again just when the Bismarcks were moving. When Motley wished to leave, Frau von Bismarck insisted that he stay, saying that his room was ready for him in their

But Motley, better than any other man, saw very clearly the genius in his friend, as his letters prove.

For decades, circumstances separated Bismarck from his American friend. Not until 1855 did Motley visit Bismarck in Frankfort, where he had come to study European archives for his *History of the Netherlands.* In the humorous vein characteristic of him he described that visit: Bismarck's pleasure in seeing him, his cozy, somewhat Bohemian-like family in Frankfort. They continued to exchange letters after that. On June 18, 1858, Motley sent Bismarck the first volume of his *History of the Netherlands,* and Bismarck, in reading it, recalled Motley's "melancholy eyes" and the "vivid glow of the narrator." [5] After years of scholarly study in Europe, Motley, in 1861, became American Minister in Vienna. As mentioned before, he was not without influence on Bismarck's opinion during the Civil War. On the other hand, Motley endeavored to utilize his friendship in a political way for his own country. In a letter of August 29, 1862, for example, he asked Bismarck to let him know whatever he could learn about the plans and intrigues of the French Emperor. He assured him of his strictest discretion if such were demanded. [6] The Vienna mission did not test Motley's ability very severely. Except for the Mexican affair, the mutual relations were undisturbed, and social functions, so important in Vienna, were quite in his line. Diplomacy, however, was not Motley's forte, as he often acted on impulse rather than on reason. He was unable to fill his subsequent position in London to the satisfaction of his Government. [7] At any rate, the friendship between Bismarck and Motley was chiefly based on common reminiscences of their student days. It made Bismarck feel years younger to see his companion of student pranks. [8] During a three-day sojourn in Vienna, in August 1864, he fairly revelled in reminiscences. But in that way, too, Bismarck received direct impressions of conditions in America. As Motley stayed in Vienna until 1867 and in London from 1869 to 1870, we may presume that finer threads were spun between them than is disclosed by official records.

Bismarck occasionally admitted his inclination toward Anglo-Saxon ways,

---

new home, and that he must come there. Bismarck and Motley met for the last time on the occasion of the former's silver wedding anniversary in 1872. Motley died two years later. Cf. Motley, *Correspondence,* II, 345ff.

[5] Bismarck to Motley, Frankfort, June 20, 1858; cf. Motley, *Motley and His Family,* 63ff.

[6] *Ibid.,* 133ff.

[7] Motley, in the Alabama negotiations in London, followed the instructions of Charles Sumner, his sponsor, rather than those of the Government. He consequently incurred the displeasure of the President.

[8] Motley, *Correspondence,* I, 221.

but it was only Americans, and not Englishmen, that he really called his friends.[9] While he was frequently irritated by British policy and politicians, he felt no such restraint in his intercourse with Americans. He was more at ease in their company. In the course of the war of 1870-71, he repeatedly mentioned the republican ideals of his early years to American generals, but we need not take such utterances more seriously than similar statements made to other foreigners.[10] No doubt he was attracted by the vitality and pioneer spirit of the Americans. He certainly succeeded in remaining on good terms with most of the American diplomats. Social relations with them often came to be more friendly than diplomatic custom called for.[11] Americans who were fortunate enough to know him intimately were not only filled with admiration for his statesmanlike ability but delighted to find him so unaffected, so natural, without any sham. But American opinion of Bismarck never became so clearly crystallized as in the case of Frederick the Great, who was directly connected with their history and whose image was so vividly presented to the English reader by Carlyle. American opinion of Bismarck vacillated. It varied with the political situation of the day. Moreover, it was strongly influenced by British opinion. In the necrologies of 1898, Bismarck was compared with Gladstone: on the one hand, Gladstone, the democrat, the man of the people and of peace; on the other hand, Bismarck, the man of power, the man of blood and iron. Such concoctions were prepared in the kitchens of British liberalism.[12] There is, however, one difference. No American government ever entertained such great distrust against the Chancellor as that through which

[9] Bismarck on one occasion said to White that he would have liked to be an English squire. Cf. A. D. White, *Autobiography*, I, 579.

[10] For such statements cf. Franz, *Bismarcks Nationalgefühl*, 103, footnote 52.

[11] For opinions of American Ministers regarding Bismarck cf. the following: Howe, *Bancroft*, II, 179ff. In the Bancroft Collection, New York (pt. "Minister to Germany"), I found a fragment evidently planned as part of a longer sketch, from which the following passage is worth quoting: "On the other hand, Bismarck's swiftness, instinctive correctness of judgment, like a flash, but with vehemence and moderation, which is the distinguishing characteristic of all great statesmen. He never attempted ends which were beyond his resources, and obtaining what he needed for his purpose, he never risked it in the hope of gaining more." Taylor, *Life and Letters*, II, 744ff., and "Prince Bismarck, A Character Sketch," in Lord, *Two German Giants*, 115ff. Kasson, "Otto von Bismarck, Man and Minister," in *North American Review*, CXLIII, 105-118. A. D. White, *Diplomatenleben*, 114ff., and *Seven Great Statesmen*, 399ff. For other statements of American opinion, cf. Poschinger, *Fürst Bismarck und die Diplomaten*, 399f., and *Fürst Bismarck, neue Tischgespräche*, II, 122. For Bismarck's relations with Americans, see the author's article in the *Virginia Quarterly Review* (July 1929), 397ff., and Snyder, *Die persönlichen und politischen Beziehungen Bismarcks zu Amerikanern*, 39ff.

[12] See the closing chapter of this book, "Outlook."

the British politicians betrayed their uneasiness in knowing that a strong hand controlled the Continent. The attitude of the German-Americans naturally was of considerable importance in American public opinion. Americans of German descent in turn were more or less dependent on influences received in the fatherland and on connections established later. Since immigrants in the nineteenth century came largely from the regions where liberalism flourished, Bismarck's struggle in Prussia was no less unfavorably viewed by them than by the Prussian opposition.[13] Apparently the first article on Bismarck ever published by an American periodical has for its author the German-American Henry Villard (originally Hillgard). He absolutely condemned Bismarck as a man. From his first appearance to the crisis of 1866, so Villard writes, Bismarck had been unable to win either respect or sympathy. His aims all too often had been ignoble, his means nearly always objectionable. He possessed more cunning than wisdom, more recklessness than courage.[14] The war of 1866 was a severe disappointment to the German-American supporters of the idea of "Greater Germany." After the battle of Königgrätz, however, opinion changed, for then they realized that national unification would be attained. Nationally-minded German-Americans always gave Bismarck credit for that. Consequently it was with gratifying unanimity that the German-American press paid homage to Bismarck upon his death in 1898. "The man in whose personality the greatness and dignity of the fatherland seemed embodied, especially for the German-Americans, now has passed away," wrote the *Milwaukee Germania* on August 2, 1898, expressing the attitude of many other papers.

When Bismarck took up the fight for monarchy in Prussia, he found very little sympathy. The American Minister in Berlin prophesied his impending fall. As a commentary on the Conference of Princes in Frankfort, the American consul general in Frankfort wrote in the following strain: "This monarch [the Prussian King] is, as is universally known, entirely dependent upon the influence and advice of his Prime Minister, Count Bismarck. The latter, however, knows, not only, that his selfish and authocratic ideas, are completely negatived by the designs of the intended 'Congress of Princes,' but—not to mention the circumstance, that he is the most disliked diplomatist in Germany and would no doubt, very unfavorably be received by the mass of the people— he is also for his own maintenance's sake necessitated to keep his crowned Master as distant as possible from the intercourse and advice of the more

---

[13] Cf. Gazley, *American Opinion of German Unification*, 469ff.

[14] Villard, "Karl Otto von Bismarck-Schönhausen," in *North American Review*, CVIII, 165ff. Villard later had an extended interview with Bismarck; cf. Villard, *Lebenserinnerungen*, 492ff.

liberal Princes, who might infect him by their progressive and timely ideas to his, the Minister's, own ruin." [14a] The New York *Nation* called Bismarck an unscrupulous servant of the Prussian King, admitting, however, that he had displayed courage such as was hitherto unknown in Prussia.[15]

Bismarck himself once said that he had always been attracted by the United States.[16] He admired the rapidity of their economic development, and repeatedly he defended his own tariff policy by citing the American example. The conservative element in the American Constitution appealed to him. When Bismarck, accompanied by Keudell and an army officer, inspected the Düppel entrenchments on April 23, 1864, the conversation turned to America. Bismarck remarked that he understood the Confederates intended to elect Prince Alfred of England as their King. Lieutenant Scheibert, who had spent some time in the United States, denied the accuracy of that report. He would, the lieutenant said, consider it a misfortune. The Americans had become great under the republic, which was their historical form of government; everything, even education, was directed toward that form of government. In his opinion it would require a revolution to graft monarchy on that tree. "The Minister very briskly touched Herr von Keudell's shoulder, saying: 'You see, my old doctrine: only that which has developed historically is conservative. The American Republic is a conservative form of government, Napoleon's empire is a revolution, the British constitution is conservative, ours revolutionary, and so on.' " [17] Similarly, in an article in the *Staatsanzeiger* of January 4, 1866, dealing with the message of President Johnson and largely from Bismarck's own pen, the message is characterized as "eminently conservative in the very spirit of the Government." Emphasis was placed on one sentence in particular where the President declared his determination to resist the power of temporary passions.[18] Thus Bismarck considered the great conflict between the President and Congress which finally led to President Johnson's impeachment as a test of the power of the conservative element in the political structure of the United States. "Would the impeachment of the President," he asked Carl Schurz in January 1868, "and, if he were found guilty, his

---

[14a] Murphy to Seward, Aug. 14, 1863, Dept. State, *Despatches, Frankfort on the Main,* 13, no. 81.

[15] "The conflict has increased in bitterness and animosity since the fall of 1862, when the helm of state passed into the hands of Bismarck, the most reckless political gambler ever at the head of the foreign affairs of a great state." New York *Nation,* 1865, I, 518.

[16] Poschinger, *Fürst Bismarck, neue Tischgespräche,* II, 274.

[17] Bismarck, *Gesammelte Werke,* VII, 86.

[18] For the message of the President, see Richardson, *Messages and Papers of the Presidents,* VI, 356.

deposition from office, lead to any further conflicts dangerous to public peace and order?" Schurz thought it would not.[19]

Bismarck's American policy may be expressed in a few words: it was his desire to maintain as friendly relations as possible. He never deviated from that policy even in times of mutual irritation. He was not willing to burden the overloaded vehicle of European politics by adding American animosity. During the years preceding the establishment of the German Reich, he valued the good will of the United States most highly. He made it a point to use the German element in America as a link. In the article of January 4, 1866, mentioned above, the blood relationship is discussed. Interest in American events had been increased by the fact that "only the German emigrants had settled in the United States in compact groups" and sustained by "the memory of our own blood having been shed for the preservation of the Union . . ." The Chancellor was glad to have an opportunity to discuss the situation with Carl Schurz, who came to Germany in the winter of 1867-68. The old forty-eighter had not been at all certain that he would be allowed to enter Germany. But he was received with the greatest courtesy and invited to Berlin; on Lothar Bucher's recommendation he was soon introduced to the busy Chancellor of the North German Federation. Schurz clearly was of importance to Bismarck both as a leading German-American and as a prominent American general. In a masterly way Bismarck won his sympathy. He opened the conversation by complimenting Schurz on the audacious liberation of Gottfried Kinkel from prison; in this, Bismarck, being a man of action, was no doubt quite sincere. He established a bond of confidence by asking the forty-eighter what the effect would have been "if in such circumstances I should have appealed to the national feeling of the whole people, proclaiming the Frankfort constitution of the German Reich of 1848-49?" When Schurz in return skeptically inquired whether he really had adopted the poor survivor, the orphan of the revolution of 1848, Bismarck replied: "Why not?" That constitution, he said, despite many features displeasing to him, was not so very different from what he was striving for at present. But not until the following day, after a prolonged discussion of American affairs, did Bismarck proceed to his real political objective, namely, getting information as to the attitude of the Union toward Germany. Would the Americans sympathize with Louis Napoleon in the case of a war? Schurz said they would not unless Germany unjustly forced a war on the French.[20] The Chancellor, at any rate, achieved his purpose. Schurz left him, convinced that Bismarck would push forward

[19] Schurz, *Reminiscences*, III, 276.

[20] For conversations of Bismarck and Carl Schurz on January 28 and 29, 1868, see Bismarck, *Gesammelte Werke*, VII, 231, 240ff.; and Schurz, *Reminiscences*, III, 278ff.

his policy of unification and would undermine bureaucracy because it was too petrified and stupid to serve his plans as a sufficiently flexible and effective instrument.[21] Schurz always admired Bismarck as a great statesman. Even at Eduard Lasker's funeral in January 1884, after certain German-Americans had heaped much criticism on Bismarck in connection with the so-called "Lasker resolution," [22] Carl Schurz spoke of Bismarck as the most powerful statesman of the age, whose far-sighted outlook, whose mighty energy and audacious genius had saved the fatherland from barren disunion and grave weakness.[23] He continued to be in personal contact with Bismarck, offering his services to him. Bismarck recognized Schurz's strong personality. "As a German I am proud of Carl Schurz," he said to Andrew D. White when the latter called his attention to Schurz's success in the fight against slavery.[24] On the occasion of Schurz's second visit with Bismarck, in 1888, the two men seemed to harmonize perfectly. In contrast to his usual practice of getting rid of his guests after fifteen minutes, the Chancellor is said to have ordered wine and cigars.[25] However, when the conflict with the political opposition was at its height in the seventies, Bismarck suspected Schurz of maintaining secret relations with the German Lefts. For this reason Schurz was unacceptable to Bismarck as a minister, since the latter thought he would participate in political intrigues.[26]

Bismarck took occasion to indicate publicly the friendly relations between the two countries. On the day of President Grant's inauguration, March 4, 1869, he was Bancroft's guest at dinner. Although he generally refused to accept private invitations at that time because of the state of his health, he attended that banquet and made the principal after-dinner speech. He was pleased to state the fact "that the cordial understanding founded by Washington and Frederick had never suffered the least disturbance. Not only was there never any difficulty between the two countries, but there was not even anything that would have called for as much as an explanation." Bancroft could report to his President that he had rarely ever seen Bismarck so full of "mirth and frolic" before.[27] August von der Heydt, Minister of Finance, on Bismarck's instructions, made similar friendly statements on Thanksgiving Day. But the Chancellor considered it politically unwise to emphasize too greatly the value of American friendship for the North German Federation. "I am

---

[21] Schurz, *Reminiscences,* III, 268.

[22] See *post,* p. 163.

[23] *Kölnische Zeitung,* Jan. 26, 1884.

[24] A. D. White, *Diplomatenleben,* 124.

[25] Fuess, *Schurz,* 314.

[26] Herbert Bismarck to Bülow, Varzin, Nov. 22, 1877.

[27] Poschinger, *Fürst Bismarck, neue Tischgespräche,* II, 41ff.

convinced," he wrote to von der Heydt on November 23, 1868, "that we may rely on American friendship to some extent under certain circumstances, but to mention it officially might hurt the cause." [28] On March 18, 1869, Bancroft reported that Berlin was interested in and desirous of maintaining the friendly relations which had prevailed during the War of Secession.

In view of the great power invested in their President, Americans, too, were in the habit of judging the policy of other countries by the actions of individual men. They preferred to blame emperors or kings for real or alleged errors, holding monarchies to be the source of all evil. Theoretically, a man like Napoleon, the Caesar of his people, was not so very far removed from democratic ideals. As a matter of fact, certain people considered this a mitigating circumstance ever since the days of Napoleon I. Generally speaking, however, usurpation of power was a special object of hatred. Genuine republicans never forgave Napoleon III his "breach of promise," the fact that he had himself proclaimed Emperor after taking the oath as constitutional President of the Republic of France.[29] Ill feeling over the Mexican adventure and France's antagonistic policy during the Civil War were additional reasons for arousing against Napoleon III a hatred strong enough to make even as self-controlled a man as White think of assassinating the tyrant upon seeing him in person.[30] Viewed from a distance, Napoleon still was in the center of European politics; and in all problems, particularly in those that concerned America, he appeared to be a decisive factor. The rising star of Bismarck as yet looked pale in comparison. Because of frequent changes, only very few of the diplomatists representing the United States in Europe were able to grasp the complexity of European politics. They received only the general impression of continuous unrest and uncertainty radiating from French politics during those years. Even those who were far more familiar with events—such as John Bigelow in Paris and Henry S. Sanford in Brussels—could judge the general situation only as did European diplomats (foremost among whom was Bismarck) in the sense that it was less Napoleon's desire for war than the uncertainty of his position and the necessity of coping with internal conditions that gave an element of insecurity to French politics and might be the cause of conflict at any time.[31] Severe criticism of Prussian politics was not lacking, however. In 1864, not only did the American Minister in Copenhagen,

---

[28] Keudell, *Fürst und Fürstin Bismarck*, 401f.

[29] For such statements see Schieber, *Transformation of American Sentiment toward Germany*, 14ff.

[30] A. D. White, *Autobiography*, I, 96. Stillman, the American journalist, felt the same way; see his *Autobiography*, I, 325.

[31] The private letters of Sanford to his friend, the Secretary of State, are of particular interest in that they display an intimate knowledge of European affairs.

B. R. Wood, vehemently oppose Bismarck as being unscrupulous and the Napoleon of the Germans, but George Marsh, the American representative to Italy, likewise had little sympathy for the Germans. On March 21, 1864, he wrote from Turin: "I am happy to say that the Italians almost unanimously sympathize with the Danes in their present heroic struggle against the rapacity of the Germans whose aggressive character, and especially their national ambition to Teutonize the whole world—while at bottom they care nothing for the establishment of national liberty among themselves—is one of the greatest sources of danger to the peace and social progress of this continent." [31a] But aside from the fact that the Danish crisis did not directly concern the interests of the Americans, it meant a decided relief from their own troubles. The opinion of those who were sympathetic to the German struggle for unification prevailed. A country that had only recently been confronted with the same problem which the Germans still had to solve, could not but understand. Leading Republicans sympathized with Prussia in particular. It was more than an exchange of courtesies when E. D. Morgan, former Governor of the State of New York, replied to an invitation from German merchants of New York City with the statement that during the recent war he had thoroughly studied Prussia's military system and found it of great importance for the general education of the people. In a speech at the unveiling of a monument in September 1868 for the dead of the Tenth Regiment of Infantry in the Civil War, General William H. Emory, Commandant of the Washington garrison, called special attention to developments in Germany. That movement, he said, had its roots in that same liberty whose earliest representative, the Prince of Orange, like Lincoln, had, because of his ideals, fallen by the hand of a detestable assassin. Without a strong military organization, liberty could not be preserved nor could just laws be enforced. This point gave the speaker an opportunity as a soldier to praise Frederick the Great for the excellent army which he had formed. In conclusion, he commented favorably upon the value of German immigration to the American Nation.[32] John Fiske, the historian, in an article "Athenian and American Life" (1872) wrote that Prussia was unquestionably the country of the highest civilization.[33]

There were ideological reasons, too, for that sentiment. Americans generally believed that the national revolutions in Europe would bring about an early

[31a] Marsh to Seward, Dept. State, *Despatches, Italy*, 11, no. 87.

[32] Copy of a letter from E. D. Morgan to a committee of German business men, Feb. 16, 1868; undated newspaper report on General Emory's speech, appendix to Gerolt's report of Oct. 27.

[33] Fiske, *Writings*, XVIII, 426.

triumph of democracy. At an earlier period they had celebrated the Hungarian and Italian struggles for independence. Garibaldi was almost an American national hero and was offered a high command in the Union army; only his extravagant ambition thwarted that proposal. Consequently, the German wars for unification were expected to result in political progress. "The fact is," Bigelow wrote in April 1866, "Europe is going to war as people sometimes go to the brandy-bottle to get rid of their own domestic troubles, and with a prospect of about the same success. I cannot say that I should regret a war, much as I deplore the necessity for it. Europe is so much in debt that every war or the means of carrying it on are now purchased by continually increasing concessions to the people. Anything, therefore, that threatens rapidly to increase the financial exigencies of European governments may be regarded as democratic and wholesome in its tendency." [34]

Motley, too, took comfort from that idea. He did not have too much liking for Prussian ways as such. "Prussia is a mild despotism to be sure," he complained in a letter to his wife on November 18, 1848. " 'Tis the homoeopathic tyranny—small doses, constantly administered, and strict diet and regimen. But what annoys you most is this constant dosing, this succession of infinitesimal Government pills which the patient subject bolts every instant." [35] Thus he did not find it so easy to justify the wars of 1864 and 1866 so far as Prussia was concerned. His own sentiments, as well as those of his family, rather favored Austria. Motley took refuge in prophesying a liberal future for Prussia. In an intellectual and industrial sense, he said, Prussia was no doubt the leading power in Germany. While she was for the present ruled by military despotism, he hoped she would become a free nation in the heart of Europe. Then she could counterbalance France as long as France was ruled despotically; both countries might go together when free. "Prussian military despotism, by the grace of God, is perhaps opening the way more rapidly for liberty in Europe than all that the Kossuths, Garibaldis, and Mazzinis could effect in half a century," he wrote his daughter on August 7. [36] Similarly he emphasized his sympathy for the German movement since its spirit combined science, principles of nationality, and enthusiasm of the people. [37] In a lecture before the Historical Society of New York in 1868, he gave the historical background of that idea. A tendency toward new unity developed from German disunion, which reached its climax after the Thirty Years' War. In 1648 there were more than three hundred dynasties, in 1815

[34] John Bigelow, *Retrospections,* III, 395.
[35] Motley, *Correspondence,* I, 70.
[36] *Ibid.,* II, 241.
[37] *Ibid.,* II, 241ff.

only three dozen, and in 1866 there was practically but one sovereign state left, except for the German possessions of Austria. However, one should not believe that the work just being completed in Germany was merely destined to bring another military power into the world.[38] Motley found it easy to have confidence in his great friend, whom he vigorously defended among his liberal British friends. He thought Bismarck was able to read the signs of the times.[39]

The intellectual relations of the two countries, too, were more active than before. Parallel with the advance of the German language in American schools, an interest had developed in the educational system of Germany. The Prussian school system had attracted much attention in America. According to Charles Brooks it caused a new era in public elementary education in the United States and an educational regeneration of New England. To begin with, the organization of teachers' seminaries influenced the public school system. In the struggle for public schools in America an important consideration was the fact that in Prussia the highest schools had been public ones for a long time. A complete adaptation of the Prussian system was of course impossible. The democratic "principles" would have revolted at once against the strict uniformity of the Prussian system.[40] In the middle of the nineteenth century Americans began to attend German institutions of learning in increasing numbers. Especially those Americans who intended to engage in the academic teaching profession went to study at German universities. These institutions became the models for many an American university; Johns Hopkins University, founded in the seventies, was definitely patterned accordingly. There were varied reasons why the Americans attended German universities. German scholars generally enjoyed a greater reputation than the French. Library facilities were considered better. The esthetic and artistic sensibilities of the French were more alien to the Americans than were those of Protestant north Germany. Many parents did not wish to expose their sons to the legendary "ungodliness and immorality" of Paris. The Americans felt that they learned from the Germans assiduity for work and methodical thinking; the German educational ideal of quest for truth for truth's sake appealed to them as exemplary. But being men of practical imagination they

---

[38] Motley, *Historic Progress and American Democracy*, 39ff.

[39] "The great statesman of Prussia is distinguished for courage, insight, breadth of vision, iron will, and a warm and steadfast heart. His genius consists in the instinctive power of governing by conforming to the spirit of the age. No man knows better than Bismarck, to read the signs of the times." Cf. Motley, *Historic Progress and American Democracy*, 44f. "He is a man of great talent, and most undaunted courage. He is the most abused man by the English newspapers I believe just now going, and I like him all the better for that." Motley, *Motley and His Family*, 178.

[40] Cf. Schönemann, *Die Vereinigten Staaten von Amerika*, II, 179.

found fault with the fact that German education tended to emphasize mental training too exclusively.[41]

As has been mentioned before, the best representatives of American literature thought they owed a debt of gratitude to Germany; as they were strict Protestants their admiration for Prussia is not at all strange.

So it was not by mere chance that George Bancroft came to Berlin in 1867 as American Minister, a man who seemed best qualified to cultivate and develop German-American friendship.[42] His appointment alone proved that the United States wished to maintain the best of relations, for Bancroft was one of those Americans who had studied in Göttingen and Berlin between 1815 and 1820, and who, upon their return home, had contributed much toward spreading an appreciation of German civilization. Bancroft was criticized for adjusting himself too readily to an alien atmosphere, and it was said that he had been influenced by the splendor of the Imperial Court at Berlin.[43] Such criticism of Bancroft's love for Germany is not justified. Ever since his student days he had entertained a pronounced sympathy for German or, to be exact, Prussian ways. His reports from Göttingen had not been very enthusiastic, since social life there did not appeal to him. In Berlin, however, he had found an atmosphere most closely corresponding to his own character. The environment in which he had grown up was not exactly puritanical, but, as the son of a clergyman, he had inhaled the rigorous air of Protestantism, which had determined his bent of mind. He had much cause to be happy, he wrote from Berlin on November 5, 1820, to his patron, President John Thornton Kirkland, of Harvard University, for he found the professors in Berlin quite different in character from their Göttingen colleagues. "There an abhorrence is felt for all innovations; here the new, that is good or promises to lead to good, cannot be too soon adopted. At Göttingen the whole tendency of the courses is, to make the students learned, to fill their memories with matters of fact; here the grand aim is to make them think."[44] Upon his return to America Bancroft and Joseph Green Cogswell, his fellow-student, founded the Roundhill School in Massachusetts. The enterprise failed, but it is note-

---

[41] Cf. Faust, *German Element,* II, 201ff.; Thwing, *The American and the German University,* 40ff.; Hohlfeld, *Der Einfluss deutscher Universitätsideale auf Amerika,* II, 242ff. A. D. White repeatedly discussed in his speeches the influence of Germany's educational system on America, for example, at the centennial of the German Society in New York, Oct. 4, 1884, and in Leipzig in 1908. For a very unfavorable comment on Germany's school system by Henry Adams, cf. Bradford, *American Portraits,* 34f.

[42] For an account of Bancroft's general activity in Berlin, cf. Howe, *Bancroft,* II, 166ff.

[43] Bassett, *Middle Group of American Historians,* 199.

[44] Howe, *Bancroft,* I, 89ff.

worthy for the fact that it was the first American school to introduce the study of German in the curriculum. In 1824, Bancroft published a few studies of German literature. We need not again discuss his attitude. It was characteristic of him that in his *History of the United States* he praised Prussia as the greatest Protestant power on the European continent, as the child of the Reformation that had set reason free.[45] When Bancroft came to Berlin he was at the height of his fame. He had filled important political offices, having been Secretary of the Navy in Polk's Cabinet and Minister in London from 1846 to 1849. As a historian he enjoyed so great a reputation that he was commissioned in 1866 to deliver the memorial address before both Houses of Congress on the anniversary of Lincoln's assassination.

Bancroft found it easy to make himself at home in Berlin. His house near the Tiergarten soon became a center of social life. The historians Mommsen, Ranke, and Droysen, who held him in high esteem as a scholar, belonged to the more intimate circle of his acquaintance; Bismarck, Moltke, and Roon frequently were his guests. Indeed, Moltke and Bancroft were practically on terms of friendship. After the death of Moltke's wife, the two men, casually meeting in the Tiergarten, engaged in serious discussions on the meaning of life. Bancroft also had the privilege of being the guest of the busy commander-in-chief in the very opening days of the war of 1870. He was glad to profess his great personal veneration for the aged general.[46]

We may assume that Motley had introduced Bancroft to Bismarck, for it was within an exceptionally brief time that the two men were on terms of familiarity which considerably exceeded the degree of diplomatic convention. As early as the beginning of 1868 Bismarck invited the American Minister to come to see him whenever he had something on his mind. Some time later Bismarck said that in his opinion Bancroft was the ideal American Minister.[47] Not only did Bancroft admire the Chancellor as a statesman but he respected him personally. Despite their difference in age they had much in common; both were equally disturbed by the conflicts between the state and the Catholic Church, for no one understood Bismarck's policy toward the church better than Bancroft. On September 19, 1869, Bismarck wrote to Motley about him: "He practically believes in the same course of evolution in which Moses, the Christian Revelation, and the Reformation are so many stages. Such evolution, however, is being handicapped by ancient and modern Caesarian powers, by the clerical and dynastic exploitation of the peoples, which use all means of obstruction even to the point of slandering as honest and ideal a minister as

[45] Bancroft, *History of the United States*, V, 6.
[46] Howe, *Bancroft*, II, 237ff.
[47] Poschinger, *Fürst Bismarck, neue Tischgespräche*, II, 274.

Bancroft."[48] It frequently happened that Bancroft accompanied Bismarck on horseback rides through the Tiergarten or that they went out driving together. Their conversation would drift to general problems of life. A song bird attacked by birds of prey would cause Bismarck to deplore the cruelty of nature; or he would talk of his estate with its fine old trees which he was sorry to have cut;[49] or of his dangerous illness in St. Petersburg which brought him to the point of death. In his conversations with Bancroft, Bismarck even touched upon music and literature which by that time he rarely mentioned. Bancroft was the only one among all foreign diplomatists who enjoyed the privilege of visiting him in Varzin.[50]

Bancroft's official activity in 1867 and 1868 also brought him into contact with Bismarck frequently. He had finally been commissioned by his Government to conclude an agreement on naturalization; for decades the obscurity of regulations had been the principal subject of diplomatic negotiations. The national laws of the two countries were radically different from each other. Prussia's military law required military service of every single citizen, a duty which was not canceled by prolonged absence from his native country and for the violation of which he was retroactively liable to punishment. In the United States the common law generally prevailed. This declared citizenship as permanent when once acquired even in case of prolonged absence. Disputes consequently arose again and again, since American citizens of German descent, often drafted for service upon their return to Germany, would appeal to their adopted country for diplomatic protection. That question had been particularly pressing at the beginning of the Civil War, but the Secretary of State postponed its settlement for reasons of expediency.[51] Bancroft's predecessor, Joseph A. Wright, was not the man to bring about an agreement. While acknowledging Bismarck's good will, he bitterly complained of the stubbornness of the Prussian military men which he desired his Government to break by means of a strong gesture. That was not the atmosphere to encourage an understanding. Bancroft soon succeeded in creating such an atmosphere. Bismarck, anxious for political reasons to have the dispute settled, met him halfway. After protracted negotiations an agreement was reached on February 22, 1868. It was a compromise. The Government of the North German Federation agreed that only five instead of ten years of uninterrupted

---

[48] Bismarck, *Politische Briefe*, 372f.

[49] For Bismarck's love of his woods, cf. Westphal, *Bismarck*, 19ff.

[50] Howe, *Bancroft*, II, 169ff. and 226ff.; also Bismarck, *Gesammelte Werke*, VII, 222ff. See also the author's "Unbekannte Gespräche mit Bismarck," in *Süddeutsche Monatshefte* (Feb. 1930), 299ff.

[51] Seward to Judd, Apr. 3, 1862, Dept. State, *Instructions, Prussia*, 14: 348.

sojourn in the United States should be required for naturalization. Bismarck, quite optimistic at that time, did not consider that provision objectionable inasmuch as "national feeling, even among Germans living abroad, recently has been asserting itself more strongly than before."[52] The so-called 2-year clause was added in compensation. It said: "If a German naturalized in America renews his residence in North Germany, without the intent to return to America, he shall be held to have renounced his naturalization in the United States."[53] That article IV caused a great deal of misinterpretation. Various speakers in the Reichstag pointed out its obscurity and unfortunate formulation. But Bismarck thought their misgivings had little foundation. In his speech before the Reichstag on April 2, he said: "We do not wish to hinder those who emigrate in good faith; and those who do so emigrate, that is, not merely for a short time in order to escape from their duties to the fatherland, shall not be prevented from becoming American citizens. Good faith is to be assumed in the case of persons who have stayed there five years and have acquired American citizenship. We assume that the sacrifice of political rights at home and the sacrifice of a 5-year absence is not made for the sole purpose of escaping from military service, but that such a sacrifice would be made only by a person resolved to found a new home over there for himself and his family."[54] The treaty was signed on February 22, 1868. Bancroft, in his report, says that Bismarck treated the affair in a most liberal spirit. Highly divergent interpretations developed at once. The Americans held that the 2-year clause could be enforced only in case the respective citizen expressly stated his intentions. Bancroft, for example, in an open letter printed in the *Frankfurter Zeitung* of April 28, 1868, presented that opinion. An effective operation of the treaty was made all the more difficult as Bancroft concluded other treaties with German states. The treaty with Baden, for example, did not contain a 2-year clause. Nevertheless, the treaties improved relations, forming a legal framework which was observed with good will shown on both sides. Progress had to be admitted by both parties, so that severe attacks against prolongation of the treaties, such as Friedrich Kapp published in *Preussische Jahrbücher*, 1875, proved ineffectual (Schlözer to Bülow November 2, 1875). However, the interests and legal conceptions of the two countries differed too greatly to permit complete adjustment.[55]

[52] Bismarck to Roon, Jan. 13, 1868.

[53] Malloy, *Treaties*, II, 1299.

[54] Bismarck, *Gesammelte Werke*, X, 448.

[55] The records, *Police, General Non-European Affairs,* were used for the above paragraph. Cf. *Foreign Relations,* 1868, II, 40ff.; Munde, *Bancroft Naturalization Treaties;* Keim, *German-American Political Relations,* 51ff.; Hatschek and Strupp, *Wörterbuch,* I, 110f.; Moore, *Digest,* III, 297ff.

Bancroft, both as a man and as a historian, witnessed with enthusiasm the formation of the German national state. On December 11, 1867, Bismarck delivered an address to the Prussian Legislature, mentioning the fact that the Germans abroad hailed the foundation of the North German Federation: "Gentlemen, is it not worth something, since we had to assume those burdens, to see the satisfaction felt so deeply by our fellow countrymen throughout the world that we may say German loyalty in America, New South Wales, etc., is more actively expressed, if not more active, than within our own country?" [56] Bancroft, on that occasion, in a private letter, thanked Bismarck for his recognition of the Americans of German descent. "In my country," he said, "five or six million people consider Germany their mother country. They shared your satisfaction with the advancement of their old home in power, prosperity, liberty, and unity. I really think sometimes that people in America, watching those events from a distance, feel more intensely the greatness of the revolution you have brought about." The latter replied very cordially; in his opinion there were few men more capable of judging the events of 1867 as correctly as the author of the pages dealing with the condition of Prussia and the German Reich in 1763. "I hope that both countries will develop in the same way as hitherto, remaining mutually on good terms." [57]

In the same spirit Bancroft reported to his Government. On the first of November he wrote to the Secretary of State: "The interest of a residence at Berlin at this time is immeasurably increased by the opportunity of watching the progress of the greatest European revolution of this century. . . . The present union of German States is the ripened fruit of nineteen generations of continued sufferings and struggles, and is so completely in harmony with natural laws, and so thoroughly the concurrent act of government and people, that it is certain to endure, and is received with the good will, the consent, or the necessary acquiescence of every power in Europe." [58] Bancroft was much interested in the question as to what extent the American Constitution had influenced the Constitution of the North German Federation. He thought it was based on the same principles that had guided the creators of the American Constitution. Either it had followed a very thorough study of the American Constitution, or similar defects of administration had caused both countries to discover and adopt similar political principles. At a dinner he asked Bismarck about it. The latter agreed, saying "a little of everything." [59]

[56] Bismarck, *Gesammelte Werke*, X, 420.

[57] Bancroft to Bismarck, Dec. 11; Bismarck to Bancroft, Dec. 14, 1867.

[58] *Foreign Relations*, 1867, pt. I, 593f.

[59] Cf. the author's article in *Süddeutsche Monatshefte*, 304. As a matter of fact the American Constitution served as one of several models. In the draft constitution of

In Bancroft's opinion the Constitution of the North German Federation was liberal, or at least capable of development along democratic lines. Everywhere else—in London, in Bavaria, in Vienna, in Pest, in the Kingdom of Prussia itself—a veto power on all liberal legislation was more or less in the hands of the nobility through the constitution of the upper house. "In the Constitution of North Germany, not a rook's nest is left; there is not one single office or place in the government or legislature reserved for the nobles. Neither is any nobleman disfranchised; like others he may be appointed to a place in the Council of the Union, or he may be elected to the House of Representatives. According to the principles of the Constitution, he neither gains nor loses by the accident of birth."[60] Bancroft had come to Berlin via Paris, convinced that France did not want war. Although quite distrustful of Napoleon, he considered the Emperor's position so insecure as to make a desire for war unlikely. His belief in this respect was strengthened by a conversation with the French Ambassador Benedetti who, on April 17, 1869, mentioned to him concessions which the Emperor intended to make toward the liberal movement. But Bancroft considered the Prussian policy still more peaceful. On August 29, 1867, he wrote: "This Government pursues its course toward German unity without jealousy and without fear or present apprehension, and though no one can foretell into what relations the uncertain policy of other powers may drift, it plainly appears that the Government of France is now as little disposed to war as that of this country."[61] On September 15, 1868: "The King of Prussia and his ministers are most heartily desirous of preserving the peace of Europe. Their position and their power are such that they have thus far succeeded and seem likely still to succeed, in their wise and humane policy. The King has dismissed the reserves and has postponed the time for calling out the new recruits, thus sparing his treasury while he

---

Sept. 1, 1866 (by Bucher) section 80 bears the marginal note "cf. American constitution" and "Treaties with foreign countries require the consent of the Reichstag." Article VI of the American Constitution of 1787 forms a marginal note to section 3 of the draft. To the extent that the Reich Constitution of 1849 was used, there is an additional suggestion of the American example in that certain points of the 1849 Constitution were influenced by the American Constitution. Cf. Scholl, *Einfluss der nordamerikanischen Unionsverfassung.* The origin of the Constitution of the North German Federation (cf. Bismarck, *Gesammelte Werke,* VI, 187f.) does not show clearly the extent of foreign influences.

[60] Bancroft to Fish, Berlin, Jan. 17, 1870, Dept. State, *Despatches, Prussia,* 16, no. 63, private.

[61] Bancroft to Seward, Berlin, Aug. 29, 1867, Dept. State, *Despatches, Prussia,* 14, no. 2.

proclaims confidence in the continuance of peace and in his own resources in every eventuality."[62]

To Bancroft the evolution of Germany's unification seemed to be founded on natural law. He considered any attempt at disturbing it a moral wrong. "A war undertaken for the avowed purpose of preventing the peaceable improvement of the German constitution by the joint act of the German governments and people, would be a war of revolution; for the principle that it is the right of a people to reform their government so as to advance their safety and happiness is now the received principle of international law, first proclaimed by the United States, next by France, then by Great Britain practically in its several unions of its kingdoms and its reforms in like manner by the Swiss Confederation, and now formally by Italy, Prussia, and Spain, and practically by the Austro-Hungarian Monarchy. A war directed against that principle could not but convulse the world. The claim of right to forbid a government and people to improve their political condition, is in itself an act of hostility to the human race, and therefore must necessarily fail; but a war founded upon it would be attended by incalculable disasters, so that to deprecate such a war is a proof of friendship for France." Besides, Bancroft thought, such a war would greatly endanger American commerce. Trade between the United States and Germany seemed to him immeasurably more important to the United States than its commerce with any other continental power. "Were German emigration from the ports of Bremen and Hamburg alone to be interrupted, it would occasion a loss of that which nourishes the life-blood of the nation."[63] For this reason Bancroft, in a private letter to Seward, November 3, 1867,[63a] suggested that the President, in his annual message, should say something about the progress of Prussia and Germany and assert that from the American point of view the German states had the privilege of revamping their political organization as they saw fit, without foreign interference. A special situation gave Bancroft an opportunity to discuss that point still more fully. In private company he had criticized France's conduct in the Civil War, threatening that America would express her dissatisfaction on a proper occasion.[64] Having heard of it, the French Government endeavored by intrigues to have the troublesome Minister re-

[62] His predecessor had interpreted Prussia's policy in the same sense: "Count Bismarck, I have every reason to believe, desires peace, for he is in the midst of reconstruction and a war at present could easily undo the work of Sadowa." Wright to Seward, Berlin, May 2, 1867, Dept. State, *Despatches, Prussia,* 14, no. 21.

[63] Bancroft to Seward, Berlin, Nov. 20, 1868, *Foreign Relations,* 1868, pt. II, 57f.

[63a] Bancroft to Seward, Dept. State, *Despatches, Prussia,* 14, no. 14, private.

[64] Willson, *America's Ambassadors to France,* 290.

called from Berlin. General John A. Dix, American Minister in Paris, who was known for his French sympathies, was induced to help bring that about. Dix hastened to inform his Government of the case. On December 19 he sent a copy of his official communication to Bancroft. The latter, replying on December 29, 1868, denied the charge of partiality. Turning the tables, he said that the policy of his colleague in France was in error; France should not in any way be encouraged to start a war. Bancroft pointed out the danger to American commerce in the event of a blockade of the mouths of the Elbe and Weser, calculating the property which 150,000 immigrants annually brought to the United States at $75,000,000, the total influx of capital being from $150,000,000 to $200,000,000. A hint as to the vital interests of the United States would therefore act as an inducement for peace and would be the best evidence of real, reasonable friendship for France. "Instead of this you encourage the French government to undertake the war by assurances, as erroneous as they are unauthorized, that the United States would look on as indifferent spectators during the ruin of their prosperity and the violation of their principles without warning, remonstrance, or 'sympathy.'"[65] Bancroft had an interview with Benedetti, who denied having reported Bancroft's private utterances. On that occasion, too, Bancroft mentioned America's great commercial interests which would be disastrously endangered by a naval war between France and North Germany.[66]

Bismarck ardently supported Bancroft when the latter's position seemed menaced. The American President, instead of backing Dix, had him censured for indiscretion. But the French did not cease their attempts to remove so troublesome a man. New attacks came in the summer of 1869 and were taken up by a Democratic newspaper in America.[67] On September 19 Bismarck inquired of Bancroft as to what could be done to keep him. At the same time he asked Motley, then Minister in London, to use his influence on behalf of Bancroft: "I learn from Paris that they want to take Bancroft away from us on the pretense that he does not represent America in a dignified manner. No one in Berlin would support that assertion. Bancroft is most highly esteemed by all intellectuals, especially in the world of scholarship, he is honored by the Court and by the members of the Government, and has their full confidence. Bancroft is one of the most popular personalities

[65] Bancroft to Seward, Berlin, Dec. 31, 1868, enclosure 2, Dept. State, *Despatches, Prussia,* 15.

[66] *Ibid.,* enclosure 3.

[67] Newspaper clipping among German records, without a headline. Bancroft was reported to have said that the Prussian military system was a "happy reproduction of the American system."

105

in Berlin, and if you still have your old liking for this city, which you watched from the windows of the Logier House, please do as much as you can to keep him here with us." On September 27 Motley replied that he had given his letter to Badeau, formerly President Grant's private secretary; and on March 24, 1872, he was able to inform Bismarck that his report to Washington had helped to strengthen Bancroft's position. Renewed attempts to remove Bancroft during the Franco-Prussian War likewise failed, owing to the Chancellor's persistent opposition.[68]

The Chancellor informed Bancroft of his plans for Germany. It was not his intention to control the decisions of the South German States, but he maintained that, on the other hand, it was the undoubted right of the southern branches of the German nation to connect themselves more closely with the North. He considered the Austro-Hungarian union a *fait accompli*. In the East the Prussian Government was supporting Austria's policy; the alliance between Prussia and Russia acted to preserve the peace.[69] It may be assumed that Bancroft, in October 1868, did not conduct his prolonged conversations with Andrassy and Deak, the leading men of Hungary, without the knowledge and approval of the Chancellor. The outward motive, to be sure, was furnished by the treaties of naturalization. But both Andrassy and Deak talked with remarkable frankness to the American Minister about Hungary's policy. Andrassy, for example, declared that Hungary would not oppose a union between North and South Germany; and an alliance between Russia and Germany could be but beneficial to Hungary.[70] Bancroft summed up his impressions of the journey in a report of April 18, 1870. His report was very favorable as regards Hungary, clearly echoing his conversations there. The country, he said, was completely united; there were no difficulties between Germany and Hungary, and the Hungarian foreign policy was peaceful. Southern Germany would rather join North Germany than the Austrian conglomeration of nationalities. A greater Germany would be possible only as a republic, and no one was thinking of a German republic at present. If the Austrian Government consequently introduced a liberal constitution and pursued a constitutional manner of governing, it would become reconciled to a free and united Germany and accept Germany as a friend. Should those conditions fail to materialize, the German-Austrian provinces would more

---

[68] Gerolt to Bismarck, Feb. 7, 1871; Bismarck, *Politische Briefe*, I, 372f.; *Bismarck-Jahrbuch,* IV, 213.

[69] Bancroft to Seward, Berlin, Dec. 24, 1868, Dept. State, *Despatches, Prussia,* 15, no. 87; see also appendix to this book.

[70] Howe, *Bancroft,* II, 208ff.

and more turn against the Slavic parts of Austria.[71] This report was, of course, very interesting to Bismarck, but the only difficulty was that the American Government published it. The American Minister in Vienna protested violently, thinking it was endangering America's friendly relations with Austria.[72]

The general situation resulted in a sympathetic attitude on the part of the United States. According to all indications, American public opinion would favor the Germans in case of a future war. And so it was indeed during the Franco-Prussian War.

[71] *Senate Executive Documents*, 41st Cong., 2d sess., no. 94.

[72] Jay to Fish, Vienna, July 9, 1870, Dept. State, *Despatches, Austria*, 10, no. 131.

CHAPTER VI

THE UNITED STATES AND THE
FRANCO-GERMAN WAR

I T IS widely believed that public opinion toward a country engaged in
war is determined by a more or less clever placing of responsibility. It is
also said that many would not have been convinced so easily of France's
guilt had it not been for Bismarck's editing of the Ems despatch. But the
fact is ignored that the preliminaries of a war are practically unintelligible
to an outsider and that they develop too rapidly for neutrals to form an independent judgment. And what is, in the last analysis, public opinion? It
is one of the evil habits of our times to call a collection of newspaper articles
public opinion. Newspapers are subject to most diversified influences. It
should be ascertained in each particular case by whom and by what groups
of interested parties the respective papers are controlled. Newspapers are of
importance as gauges of sentiment; but they do not in themselves decide
whither the scales incline. Benevolent neutrality is of importance for belligerent states if a majority of the leading men of the neutral country sympa-
thizes with them. In the present case it cannot be doubted that at the outbreak
of the Franco-German War the leading political, economic, and intellectual
groups in America inclined toward Germany. Neither the Ems despatch nor
indeed the complicated Hohenzollern candidacy had any influence whatsoever.[1] The German diplomatic representatives frequently reported from America during the war that the Republicans sympathized more with Germany,
while the Democrats were more in sympathy with France.[2] Apparently
Republican opinion was more in conformity with German ideas. Following
the Civil War the Republican Party was in absolute control, so that the

[1] Bigelow, for example, learned the facts about the Ems despatch during the course
of the war; cf. his *Retrospections,* IV, 462.

[2] Alvensleben to Bismarck, Washington, Sept. 9, 1870.

sentiment of the South, completely beaten as it was, practically did not count. For the reasons mentioned, the sympathies of the leading men in the Union naturally gravitated to Germany, or to Prussia, which had been one of its few friends during the Civil War. American finance, too, was interested in safeguarding American bonds, large amounts of which were circulating in Germany. Generally speaking, American interest in the European war was considerable. For the first time, a few special correspondents were sent to the war zone. After a cable connected Europe and America in 1867, the American newspapers began to organize an independent news service. As early as 1867 the *New York Tribune* had established an office in London. Most of the war correspondents joined the German Army, and Bismarck was annoyed by their numerous visits, which sometimes proved to be rather irksome.[3]

American hatred of Napoleon took particularly vehement forms of expression. The *Independent* of August 20, 1870, wrote: "If there is any man in Europe who has overstayed his days, who does not belong to the present but to the past, who is a charlatan instead of a statesman, a usurper instead of a legitimate prince, that man is Louis Napoleon. Every drop of blood now shed in Europe adds another stain to his name. He, and he alone, is responsible for the outbreak of the war volcano." Many other papers wrote in the same vein.[4] Charles Sumner, chairman of the Committee on Foreign Relations, in an address delivered in Boston on October 26, 1870, called Napoleon's downfall natural. "Had he remained successful to the end, and died peacefully on the throne, his name would have been a perpetual encouragement to dishonesty and crime. By treachery without parallel, breaking repeated promises and his oath of office, he was able to trample on the Republic. . . . Of a fallen man I would say nothing; but for the sake of Humanity, Louis Napoleon should be exposed. He was of evil example, extending with his influence."[5] As we notice, judgment was strongly influenced by sentiment. Objective discussions of the causes of the war were comparatively rare.[6] Owing to the inadequate news service, it was but

[3] See the list in Snyder, *Die persönlichen und politischen Beziehungen Bismarcks zu Amerikanern,* 69, footnote; cf. the author's article, "Die deutschen und die amerikanischen Einigungskämpfe und die Presse," in the *Festschrift* of the *Zeitungsverlag,* 1931, 65ff.

[4] Schieber, *Transformation of American Sentiment toward Germany,* 20; for further statement, see 14ff. in the same work, and Gazley, *American Opinion of German Unification,* 322ff.

[5] Sumner, *Works,* XIV, 40-43.

[6] Schieber, *Transformation of American Sentiment toward Germany,* 22ff.

natural that British influence also played its part.[7] With what vigor Protestant New England at times hailed the cause of Protestant Germany may be illustrated by a poem "America to Germany" by Charles Goethe Baylor, published in the *Boston Daily Journal* of January 6, 1871. It started with the words: "All hail: O Bible land."[8] Louisa M. Alcott wrote to her mother on August 11: "I side with the Prussians, for they sympathized with us in our war. Hooray for old Pruss!"[9] In the house of Bayard Taylor, the translator of *Faust*, sympathies were great and undivided: "Taylor and I are so excited that we can hardly control ourselves. . . . What do you think my husband did last night? He wrote a German poem: *Jubellied eines Amerikaners*, of which I am enclosing a copy . . . ," so Marie Taylor wrote to her mother on September 3.[10] James Russell Lowell, Ralph Waldo Emerson, and George Ticknor were of the same opinion. But Walt Whitman, after the Battle of Sedan, said that he now had more sympathy for the French than he had ever had for the Prussians.[11] Needless to say, many Americans of German descent watched events in their former homeland with impassioned sympathy. After the Battle of Sedan enthusiasm was so general that people

---

[7] Cf. Raymond, *British Policy and Opinion during the Franco-Prussian War.*

[8] Schieber, *Transformation of American Sentiment toward Germany*, 36.

[9] Alcott, *Life*, 244; E. B. White, *American Opinion of France*, 179.

[10] M. H. Taylor, *Aus zwei Weltteilen*, 154f.

[11] James Russell Lowell to Charles Eliot Norton, Aug. 28, 1870: "The war in Europe has interested me profoundly, and if the Prussians don't win, then the laws of the great game have been changed, for a moral enthusiasm always makes battalions heavier than a courage that rises like an exhilaration from heated blood. Moreover, as against the Gaul I believe in the Teuton. And just now I *wish* to believe in him, for he represents civilization. Anything that knocks the nonsense out of Johnny Crapaud will be a blessing to the world." Cf. J. R. Lowell, *Letters*, II, 71. George Ticknor to King Johann of Saxony, Boston, Aug. 21, 1870: "One thing, however, seems probable, if not certain. A change of power amongst the principal countries of Europe seems coming in the near future. In what direction it will occur, we in the United States, may guess and wish, but we cannot distinctly foresee. Most of us, I think, would desire to have more power given to Germany. Certainly I do. It is a more honest, cultivated, and, above all, a more faithful and true race of men, with which to entrust it. But it is a dreadful thing to reflect through what trials, struggles, revolutions and bloodshed this sort of change of base must be reached. Can our civilization stand such convulsions?" Cf. Johann, King of Saxony, *Briefwechsel König Johanns von Sachsen mit George Ticknor*, 168, and Ticknor, *Life*, II, 490 (letter of Sept. 29). Emerson to Herman Grimm, Jan. 5, 1871: "I give you joy, the new year, on these great days of Prussia. You will have seen that our people have taken your part from the first, and have a right to admire the immense exhibition of Prussian power. Of course, we are impatient for peace, were it only to secure Prussia at this height of well-being." Emerson, *Correspondence between Ralph Waldo Emerson and Herman Grimm*, 85f.

embraced one another in the streets. One of the most impressive demonstrations took place in Belleville where old Körner delivered the commemorative address. Regardless of religion or party, everyone rejoiced. The Philadelphia *Press* spoke of a "triumphant procession" the like of which had not been seen in Philadelphia "since that memorable Sunday of 1865 when the news of Lee's surrender thrilled the loyal heart of our goodly city." Not merely with words did the German-Americans support Germany's struggle for unification; they founded relief societies which collected money, food, and clothing for the widows, orphans, and wounded in Germany. About a half million dollars were collected in that way. They overwhelmed Bismarck with telegrams of approval admonishing him not to leave Alsace-Lorraine in the hands of the French.[12] Among the Irish-Americans there was some sympathy for France, for reasons of gratitude such as were expressed by John Mitchel, a prominent Irishman, in a speech at Cooper Institute, New York, on January 7, 1871.[13]

The American Cabinet was largely in favor of the Germans. Assistant Secretary of State Bancroft Davis, on the day of the Battle of Weissenburg, wrote in his diary that no one was more thankful for the news of the French defeat. President Grant, as a veteran of the Civil War, was bitterly opposed to France and commissioned Davis to assure the French Minister on a proper occasion of the strictest neutrality on the part of the American Government, but to point out at the same time, however, that he should not be surprised if the people vigorously sided with Prussia. The people had a good memory; they remembered that the French had not sympathized with the Union in the Civil War, while the Germans did, buying Union bonds without hesitation. The French, on the other hand, had lent money to the rebels and the French Government had sent an expedition to Mexico, an act which the American people regarded as unfriendly.[14]

Bancroft, no doubt, was one of the few American diplomats who were somewhat informed on Spanish affairs. In 1867, before coming to Berlin, he had stopped in Madrid and had reported to his Government from there as to the possibility of the cession of certain islands in the Spanish West Indies.[15] He must have also conversed with Bismarck about Spain, a topic about which

[12] Cf. Gazley, *American Opinion of German Unification*, 485ff.

[13] "But do not forget—Irishmen will not forget—that when France was a Republic before—that is to say in '98—France sent to the shores of Ireland a larger expedition in ships and soldiers than ever she sent to America. And she sent them to aid in the same purpose—to throw off British dominion." Mitchel, *Ireland, France, and Prussia,* 27.

[14] Keim, *German-American Political Relations,* 8.

[15] Bancroft to Seward, Madrid, July 12, 1867, private, Dept. State, *Despatches, Prussia,* 14, unnumbered.

the latter was familiar because of his particular interest in the Catholic question.[16] It is even likely that Bancroft gave Bismarck many a valuable suggestion. Bancroft, at any rate, had formed the opinion that the Hohenzollern candidacy was only a pretext for the policy of France.[17] However, in his first report of July 16, 1870, he did not place the responsibility for the war on the French people, saying that a majority of the French were opposed to the war. In 1866, the Emperor, who had hoped for some kind of compensation for remaining neutral in the Austro-Prussian War, was severely disappointed. Every day that the war was delayed increased the power and unity of Germany. As French political influence was steadily decreasing, France risked a desperate measure.[18] Bancroft's attitude was strongly influenced by his aversion to the Catholic religion. Jesuits and Ultramontanes, so he thought, were supporting Napoleon. He termed France the champion of Catholicism against Protestantism.[19]

At the beginning of the war, Elihu B. Washburne, the American Minister, was not in Paris. The chargé d'affaires, Wickham Hoffman, considered the conflict a personal difference between Napoleon and Bismarck. "The Emperor prides himself, and with reason, upon his ability and statesmanship. . . . But once Mr. Bismarck has appeared prominently upon the scene, the Emperor's star has paled, and his policy has been thwarted in more than one instance." [20] Bismarck, he said, served as a red rag to infuriate the French. Washburne, who, like his predecessors, Dayton and Dix,[21] did not have a bad opinion of Napoleon, thought the Emperor's surroundings were more to blame. He shared the opinion of other Americans then living in Paris, that the Emperor, while not personally in favor of many recent measures, had yielded to public opinion.[22] It seemed quite clear to him that the war might have been avoided

[16] For a conversation with Bismarck about Spain, see Howe, *Bancroft,* II, 169f.; Bismarck, *Gesammelte Werke,* VII, 222f.

[17] "Germany leaves Spain to choose her own government and regulate her own affairs; and for 160 years France has steadily endeavoured to subordinate Spanish interests and policy to her own." Howe, *Bancroft,* II, 246. D. E. Sickles, the American Minister in Madrid, was of the opinion that, had it not been for French impatience, the Cortes would not have approved the election of the Prince of Hohenzollern. Sickles to Fish, Madrid, June 11 and 13, 1870, Dept. State, *Despatches, Spain,* 53, no. 127, and 54, no. 131, respectively; both printed in appendix to this book.

[18] *Foreign Relations,* 1870, 197f. As late as July 14, 1870, Bancroft doubted whether the Emperor would risk a war in view of domestic consequences.

[19] Howe, *Bancroft,* II, 240.

[20] Hoffman to Fish, Paris, July 8, 1870, Dept. State, *Despatches, France,* 67, no. 217.

[21] Dix, *Memoirs of John Adams Dix,* II, 155f.

[22] Washburne to Fish, Paris, July 22, 1870, confidential: "There is no disguising the fact that the current of the sentiment of our countrymen in Paris and in France

had the Emperor been left to himself. Napoleon's heart had never been in the enterprise for he was occupied at the time in perfecting the parliamentary system. Everything pointed toward a real reform.[23] Motley sympathized with Germany. To him the war appeared as a conflict between a personal and aggressive military monarchy and a national democracy which was striving for consolidation in the form of a great German Reich.[24]

Bigelow, who lived in Berlin during the war as a private individual, entered into an interesting correspondence with his friend, the French statesman Laboulaye, concerning the question of guilt. Laboulaye considered the war between Germany and France a misfortune, ascribable primarily to Prussia's ambition. The French, therefore, would treat Germany very leniently, but Prussia very severely. France, he said, wanted a peace of security not conquest; this, however, did not mean that possession of the banks of the Rhine would not be included among the conditions of peace.[24a] In answer to Bigelow's objection that France had started the war, Laboulaye said it was childish to think it possible to live in peace next to a people that was able to mobilize 800,000 men within a fortnight. "Suppose such a power in Canada, what would be your situation in the United States? The war has been foolishly declared by an incompetent government; we have been surprised; but since Sadowa the war has been inevitable."[25] It was mainly in this letter that Bigelow, like Bancroft, found the mentality which had caused the war.[26] Bigelow, to be sure, disliked Napoleon personally. On July 30 he wrote to Hargreaves: "The feeling here universally is that Europe is no longer large enough for the Emperor of the French, and that this war cannot be satisfactorily ended without providing him with a home somewhere else, where he will have more elbow room."[27]

In Vienna John Jay thought differently. His point of view was quite "American." He believed that monarchies never could be right. His French blood probably inclined him toward France, he being a descendant of the Huguenots. Jay was an able man who had made a good name for himself in Vienna within a short time. Lothar Freiherr von Schweinitz, the Prussian

---

runs very strongly against France." Dept. State, *Despatches, France,* 67, no. 230. J. M. Read, the American consul general, was of the same opinion; cf. Keim, *German-American Political Relations,* 8, footnote 3.

[23] Washburne, *Recollections,* I, 33f.

[24] Motley to Fish, London, Aug. 6, 1870, Dept. State, *Despatches, Great Britain,* 105, no. 415.

[24a] Laboulaye to Bigelow, July 19, 1870; cf. John Bigelow, *Retrospections,* III, 388.

[25] *Ibid.,* IV, 387, 398, 416.

[26] Howe, *Bancroft,* II, 237.

[27] John Bigelow, *Retrospections,* IV, 392f.

Minister, who was later to be his son-in-law, thought very highly of him.[28] Jay held that France, of her own accord, would hardly have determined upon a war with a power like Prussia, in view of the small chances of military success. He suggested a plan of mediation to his Government. Without deviating from traditional American policy, he believed mediation was possible because of the great moral influence which the United States had on Europe.[29]

The United States, in case Spain had become involved, might have been drawn into the war on account of Cuba. Relations with Spain, always strained, had come to a head after 1869. Incessant disturbances in Cuba endangered American commerce, which was considerable. In a note of July 16, 1869, the American Government had raised a vigorous protest against the subjection of American citizens to the martial law prevailing in Cuba. In the spring of 1870, secret negotiations were conducted in Madrid with a view to the cession of Cuba to the United States. There was some danger in case of a Franco-Spanish war that the French would occupy the Spanish colonies. General Daniel E. Sickles, American Minister in Madrid, called his Government's attention to that danger, and the American commander-in-chief in Cuban waters, in a public letter to the *New York Tribune,* July 9, sounded the alarm. The United States, he wrote, would be placed in a difficult situation if Havana were occupied by the French. It could not tolerate occupation by another power, and, if need be, the American Government would have to declare that a state of war existed between the patriots and the Spaniards in Cuba. Sickles, too, as early as 1869, asserted that the United States of America, like Great Britain, was essentially governed by public opinion. The Government had no choice but to carry out the will of the people, and public opinion would force the American Government, sooner or later, to recognize the Cuban insurgents as a belligerent power.[30]

Owing to the rapid development of events in Europe, the Department of State did not have to cope with such a problem. However, another more serious possibility had to be faced—interference with American trade in the case of a prolonged and effective blockade of the German seaports. Like his predecessor, Bancroft demanded that in the case of a Franco-German conflict American warships be sent to the mouths of the Weser and Elbe Rivers for

[28] Schweinitz to Bismarck, Vienna, Aug. 11, 1870. Jay's daughter, later Mrs. von Schweinitz, sympathized strongly with Germany; cf. Schweinitz, *Denkwürdigkeiten,* I, 273, footnote.

[29] Jay to Fish, Vienna, July 16, 1870, confidential, Dept. State, *Despatches, Austria,* 10, no. 136.

[30] Bernhardi to Bismarck, Madrid, Dec. 1, 1869. For negotiations regarding the cession of Cuba, cf. Chadwick, *Relations of the United States and Spain, Diplomacy,* 291ff.; Badeau, *Grant in Peace,* 388.

the protection of American commerce.[31] Jay, too, at the beginning of the war, discussed the question with the British Ambassador in Vienna and they both agreed that a blockade of Bremen would be very injurious to the commercial interests of their countries.[32] Bancroft repeated his demand that the mouths of the rivers be protected, thus seeking to demonstrate that the French blockade of the Baltic was ineffectual.[33] As a matter of fact, the American Government gave orders to the commandant of the European squadron to make for Cuxhaven. On November 14, the cruiser *Plymouth* arrived at Kiel. The officials of the German Navy received the American visitors very cordially, giving them every opportunity to inspect the fortifications of the harbor. After Commander Breese had reached the conclusion that there was no effective blockade in the Baltic, at Bancroft's suggestion he sailed for Cuxhaven to ascertain whether a renewal of the blockade was likely. The result being negative, the ship returned to England. In his final report, of November 14, Admiral Glisson called special attention to the fact that the Americans were treated with exceptional kindness and courtesy by the Germans in Kiel and Cuxhaven. The Department of State had at first contemplated protecting maritime trade with Germany by legal measures. A special session of Congress was to be called for that purpose. That plan was dropped, however, and the French Government was requested to surrender the captured German mail steamers. As was to be expected, the French Government refused to do so.[34] The Prussian Government had proclaimed the inviolability of private property on the high seas as early as 1866, but had demanded reciprocal treatment. In April 1868 the North German Reichstag discussed the Aegidi Bill which provided for negotiations with foreign powers concerning protection of private property in case of war.[35] On July 19, 1870, the Government of the North German Federation presented a declaration in Washington by which private property on the high seas was to be exempt from confiscation by German ships, regardless of reciprocity. The Department of State welcomed the declaration, considering it an endorsement of the Marcy amendment.[36] The German Government expressly assured the American Government that

[31] Wright to Seward, Berlin, May 2, 1867, Dept. State, *Despatches, Prussia,* 14, no. 21; Bancroft to Fish, Berlin, July 23, 1870, Dept. State, *Despatches, Prussia,* 17, no. 116.

[32] Jay to Fish, Vienna, July 16, 1870, confidential, Dept. State, *Despatches, Austria,* 10, no. 136.

[33] Bancroft to Fish, Berlin, Aug. 22, 1870, Dept. State, *Despatches, Prussia,* 17, no. 125; *ibid.,* Sept. 1 and 22, 1870, cf. *Foreign Relations,* 1870, 204, 208.

[34] Washburne to Fish, Paris, July 22, 1870, *Foreign Relations,* 1870, 74f.

[35] Cf. *Staatsarchiv,* XIV, 458ff.

[36] Fish to Gerolt, Washington, July 22, 1870, *Foreign Relations,* 1870, 217f.

the inviolability of private property on the high seas would be insisted upon in the forthcoming peace negotiations.[37] But the French Government restricted itself to recognizing the Declaration of Paris of 1856, which exempted enemy property only in case it was protected by a neutral flag and was not contraband of war.[38] During the war, the French took advantage of their naval superiority so that Germany was forced to retaliate. By decree of January 9, 1871, the earlier one of July 18, 1870, was rescinded.[39]

Only once did the United States find reason for direct intervention. The Far East was in a serious state of unrest. In proportion to its increasing trade the interests of the United States had developed considerably since 1850. The American Minister to China, Anson Burlingame, endeavored to cooperate with the representatives of the other powers in a policy of preserving China's territorial integrity. The United States concluded a political treaty with China on July 28, 1868, on the basis of absolute reciprocity. The American Government above all gave assurance of its support of the central government in Peking, and sought to have the European powers cooperate to that end. On September 25, 1869, Bancroft wrote to Bismarck regarding the possibility of cooperation. Two days later, Bismarck invited Bancroft to Varzin for a conference.[40] The Chancellor expressed himself as opposed to a policy of dismembering the Chinese Empire, a step which could lead only to a state of anarchy. The North German Government, he said, had no cause to use methods of aggression and force, methods from which other countries no doubt would profit.[41] He kept his word. When the Burlingame Chinese Mission came to Berlin to arrange for commercial relations between China and Germany, the delegates were received with the greatest courtesy. By a letter of January 19, 1870, the Chancellor expressly assured the mission that the North German Federation was ready to conform its policy to the requirements of that authority "whose loss in area and in intensive power would have incalculable consequences and would certainly have an effect contrary to that which the interests of the western powers demand with regard to the extension of commercial relations and of civilization."[42] Bancroft, as American Minister, felt that Bismarck desired to deal with the Far Eastern problems in cooperation with the United States. Thus, the Chancellor in 1870 asked the

[37] Bancroft to Fish, Berlin, Oct. 5, 1870, *Foreign Relations,* 1870, 215.

[38] *Foreign Relations,* 1871, 375.

[39] Cf. Geisberg, *Bismarck und das Kriegsvölkerrecht,* 143f.

[40] *Bismarck-Jahrbuch,* VI, 207f.

[41] Bancroft to Fish, Berlin, Oct. 4 and 23, 1869, Dept. State, *Despatches, Prussia,* 16, nos. 41 and 46.

[42] Poschinger, *Aktenstücke zur Wirtschaftspolitik des Fürsten Bismarck,* I, 148, footnote 1.

American Government to participate in combatting the growing danger of piracy in Chinese waters, and the American Government agreed, with certain reservations.[43] On February 9, Bismarck wrote to the German Ambassador in Paris that it seemed advantageous to him to maintain the unity of the central government without sacrificing the solidarity of the interests of European civilization. The aftermath of disturbances caused by the assassination of Christian missionaries in China had by no means ceased when the Franco-Prussian War broke out. The Department of State was fearful lest conflicts between French and German ships in Chinese waters would cause further loss of prestige for the white race. It therefore proposed that the war should not be carried on in Chinese waters. Although Bismarck agreed, France rejected the American suggestion, being unwilling to surrender the advantages of her naval superiority. As a matter of fact, however, no fighting occurred in Chinese waters.[44] For a time Berlin thought of acquiring adequate warships in America, but the Ministry of the Navy decided against such purchases since only first-class men-of-war could have been considered and they were not available.[45]

Bismarck consistently pursued his American policy. He bent his efforts toward having public opinion in the United States favor the German cause. All of his important instructions and circular notes went simultaneously to Washington. At the very beginning of the war he succeeded in getting the statement into the American press that Great Britain was observing her neutrality toward Germany just as she had toward America in the *Alabama* case.[46] In view of the favorable news received from Gerolt and of Bancroft's optimism, Bismarck even hoped that America would bring diplomatic counterpressure to bear against other neutral powers. The Chancellor, therefore, wired from Clermont on August 28: "We understand America's neutrality. Other neutrals will presumably try to bring pressure to bear on us. Can we,

---

[43] Bancroft to Fish, Berlin, Jan. 18, Mar. 3, May 23, 1870, Dept. State, *Despatches, Prussia,* 16, nos. 65, 73, and 90, respectively. For American policy in the Far East, cf. Dennett, *Americans in Eastern Asia,* 175ff.; for the Burlingame Mission, cf. Keim, *German-American Political Relations,* 23ff. In later years also it was Bismarck's policy to cooperate with the United States in questions of the Far East, Bancroft to Fish, Berlin, July 19, 1873, Dept. State, *Despatches, Germany,* 3, no. 501; Schlözer to Fish, Mar. 29, 1876, Dept. State, *Notes from German Legation,* 14.

[44] Fish to Bancroft, Nov. 1 and 8, 1870, Dept. State, *Instructions, Prussia,* 15: 169, 171ff.; Washburne to Fish, Paris, Dec. 9, 1870, Dept. State, *Despatches, France,* 68, no. 331. Cf. Bemis, *Secretaries of State,* VII, 154f.

[45] Bismarck to Thile, for Gerolt, Varzin, July 12, 1870; R. H. Lord, *Origins of the War of 1870,* 197; Gerolt to Bismarck, July 14, 1870; protocol on a session of the Ministry of the Navy, July 17, 1870.

[46] Bismarck to Gerolt, July 26, 1870.

in your opinion, count upon American diplomatic counterpressure favorable to us?" On August 30 Gerolt replied that this could not be expected, but the American press would advocate adequate guarantees from France to Germany.[47] But nothing of the sort happened. After the Battle of Sedan Bismarck had reason to fear that the United States would join the common front of the neutrals.

A wave of enthusiasm passed over the United States after the collapse of the French Empire. The Americans could not refrain from considering any kind of republican movement in the Old World as an imitation of American ideals.[48] The President's annual message of December 4 pointed out that America could not remain indifferent to the spread of American political ideals in so great and highly civilized a country as France.[49] With elections approaching, the American Government did not feel inclined in any way to oppose the general trend of public opinion. The Minister to France was instructed to recognize the new French Government as soon as it was actually in power. That happened on September 7. The American people, Washburne wrote in his note, "associate themselves in heart and sympathy with that great movement."[50] Washburne personally went far beyond that. When a demonstration took place in front of the American Legation, Washburne replied to an address to him by congratulating the French people on the winning of a bloodless victory. The American people, he said, could really appreciate the advantages of a republican form of government.[51] At subsequent public demonstrations Washburne likewise did not hesitate to express his satisfaction with the political change in France.

Bismarck, on the other hand, was much concerned over his opponent's moral victory. He had asked the American Legation in Paris to take care of the nationals of the North German Federation. This made a very good impression in the United States. Washburne performed his task with exemplary loyalty. An order of expulsion brought extreme distress to many thou-

[47] As a matter of fact, Bancroft later suggested counterpressure to his Government; cf. Keim, *German-American Political Relations*, 14f.

[48] Alvensleben to Bismarck, Sept. 9, 1870.

[49] For press opinion cf. Gazley, *American Opinion of German Unification*, 383, and Schieber, *Transformation of American Sentiment toward Germany*, 28ff. The latter, as well as E. N. Curtis, in *American Historical Review*, XXIX, 264ff., holds that a radical change of sentiment took place after Sedan. But that is an exaggeration. Newspapers of the importance of the *New York Tribune* and of the semiofficial *Morning Chronicle* did not change their attitude. The enthusiasm for France soon lessened. For similar developments in Mexico, cf. Schlözer, *Amerikanische Briefe*, 84.

[50] Cf. *Foreign Relations*, 1870, 116f.

[51] *Ibid.*, 118.

sands of German nationals, and it was only the personal intervention of the American Minister that mitigated the catastrophe. Likewise, he was the only foreign diplomat who stayed in Paris throughout the siege and the reign of the Commune, not without endangering his own life, and suffered all of the hardships involved for the sake of the Americans and Germans entrusted to his care. Relations with the Government of the North German Federation were not always free from friction. During the siege of Paris, Bismarck, for military reasons, was compelled to control the American Minister's mail that passed through London. The American Government protested vigorously. But Washburne never desisted from his self-sacrificing work. He fully deserved the gratitude of the Germans which found particularly striking expression in ovations given to him by German-Americans upon his return to the United States. In October 1886, the *Norddeutsche Allgemeine Zeitung* asserted in an obituary that his official activity at that time contributed materially to making more intimate the friendly relations between two kindred peoples.[52]

Nevertheless, Bismarck thought it necessary to suggest to the American Government, through Washburne, a strict observance of neutrality. He also inquired of Bancroft whether Washburne's utterances represented the actual sentiment of the American Government, "which would surprise as well as grieve us."[53] No substantial results were obtained, however. While the President congratulated Gerolt on the German victory of Sedan, he did not permit the slightest doubt to exist that he considered recognition of the French Republic justified.[54] Even Bancroft, who did not expect the Republic to last long, confessed to Thile that he would be twice as enthusiastic as Washburne was reported to be, if a real republic were established. Bancroft believed that in such a case all of the so-called Romanic nations would presumably follow suit.[55]

Motley, too, immediately sent word from London, when the *Daily News* reported it was the opinion of His Majesty's Government that, after the occupation of Paris, peace would be concluded with the Senate, the Chamber, and the Regency as the legitimate French Government, and then the Emperor would be released. Motley, greatly agitated, hastened to see Bernstorff, saying that Gladstone, like himself, was very much concerned by that news; he asked Bernstorff to enable him to set the American Government at ease about it. Bernstorff of his own accord added that it could not be denied "that a

[52] For Washburne's activity, cf. Washburne, *Franco-Prussian War;* Hepner, *America's Aid to Germany; Foreign Relations,* 1870, 189ff.

[53] Bismarck to Foreign Office, Meaux, Sept. 17, and Ferrières, Sept. 25, 1870.

[54] Gerolt to Bismarck, Sept. 20, 1870.

[55] Bancroft to Davis, Berlin, Jan. 22, 1871.

potential counterrevolution in Paris by force of arms would not only be considered impossible by London but also viewed with the greatest disfavor." Bismarck, on the following day, wired from Meaux: It was entirely immaterial to Germany who ruled France but it should be first ascertained whether the French Army under Bazaine, now the strongest in France, sided with the Emperor or with the Republic, before effective negotiations could be undertaken. "Even our *stupid* friends will understand that it is not in *our* interest to help the political parties in France form a united front against us. In the occupied Departments we shall preserve the organization of the French Government recognized by us until we shall have recognized a different government." Motley transmitted the sense of that reply to Washington.[56]

Bismarck was somewhat concerned lest the United States join other neutral countries in intervening to end the war. Not wishing Germany to become too powerful a nation, the neutral great powers of Europe, after the Battle of Sedan, were interested in an early termination of the war. Great Britain, in particular, desired a peace which would leave France territorially intact. The neutrals were awaiting their chance to intervene. It is not for us at this time to point out Bismarck's masterly diplomacy in navigating around that dangerous rock. He kept Austria in check by his firmness, played Great Britain against Russia, and, at the critical moment, he diverted Russia through the Black Sea question.

As early as August 1870, Gerolt was instructed to inquire in Washington as to the attitude of the United States in case the European powers should attempt to intervene. Bancroft Davis replied that the United States would strictly adhere to the principle of nonparticipation in political affairs of European powers. Carl Schurz, also, promised to use his influence in that direction.[57] The provisional French Government, pinning its chief hope on intervention by the neutral powers, relied especially on the United States because of its republican sympathies and its former companionship in arms. Jules Favre, on September 7, sought to influence the American Minister toward mediation. On the same day Washburne reported to Washington the request of the French Government. The Department of State wired[58] to Ban-

[56] Bernstorff to Bismarck, Sept. 15, 1870; Bismarck's reply, Sept. 16, drafted by his own hand; Motley to Fish, London, Sept. 16, 1870, Dept. State, *Despatches, Great Britain*, 105, no. 461. Bismarck would have preferred to have Napoleon remain as Emperor; cf. Poschinger, *Fürst Bismarck und die Diplomaten*, 307.

[57] Gerolt to Bismarck, Washington, Aug. 31, 1870.

[58] Washburne to Fish, Paris, Sept. 13, 1870; Fish to Bancroft, Sept. 9, 1870, telegram; and Bancroft to Fish, Berlin, Sept. 11, 1870, telegram, in *Foreign Relations*, 1870, 119f., 193, and 206, respectively. Bismarck to Foreign Office, Sept. 12, 1870, telegram. Cf. Busch, *Tagebuchblätter*, I, 189.

croft for information as to the potential attitude of Berlin regarding the possibility of mediation. It seems that Bancroft did not transmit the inquiry officially, for Bismarck replied with the counterquestion whether an official answer was necessary. For the present, he said, any attempt at mediation would injure Germany and encourage France. Therefore, Bancroft strongly advised his Government against mediation; intervention by the United States might cause embarrassment to the American Government without being of any advantage to other governments.[59] Schurz, too, was opposed to any interference. From the purely American point of view it would be the best policy to avoid meddling in the war. Schurz was quite skeptical regarding the stability of the French Republic.[60] Jay in Vienna advocated measures of intervention with increasing vigor. On August 11 he inquired of Schweinitz as to the possibilities in case a foreign power should intercede for peace after the next German victory. Schweinitz replied that the whole of Germany would turn against a power that would speak of peace before the necessary guarantees were assured. When Jay mentioned "devastations" in France which should be stopped, Schweinitz energetically protested that not they but a permanent and safe peace was the question.[61] At first Jay seemed inclined to agree with Schweinitz, but on September 13 he again requested his Government to mediate, asserting that it was a matter of honor since America owed France a debt of gratitude for her aid in the War for Independence. After the downfall of the guilty dynasty, a Prussian war against the French people could result only in increasing the horrors of the conflict. Jay was especially opposed to a siege of Paris.[62] However, before all of those reports arrived in Washington, a Cabinet meeting had already decided that mediation would be undertaken only in case both parties requested it. An article in the *Morning Chronicle,* which Alvensleben sent on September 9, essentially expressed the

[59] Bancroft to Fish, Berlin, Sept. 12, 1870, Dept. State, *Despatches, Prussia,* 17, no. 133; cf. Keim, *German-American Political Relations,* 26f., footnote 35.

[60] Schurz to Fish, St. Louis, Sept. 10, 1870; cf. Schurz, *Speeches, Correspondence, and Political Papers,* I, 519f.

[61] Schweinitz to Bismarck, Aug. 11, 1870; cf. Schweinitz, *Denkwürdigkeiten,* I, 269.

[62] Jay to Fish, Vienna, Sept. 13, 1870: "The unpaid debt, which we owe to France, may perhaps be repaid by a word, and even though that word should be ineffectual, the question remains, whether justice, gratitude, and honour do not require that it should be spoken; especially at a moment, when the overthrow of an Empire and the adoption of a Republic, chilling the sympathies of the Courts of Europe, have given to France new claim to those of America. It is the opinion of many that a continuation of the Prussian war against the people of France, now, that it has accomplished the fall of the offending Dynasty, will tend to aggravate, instead of mitigating the horrors of the war; and that a siege of Paris might involve cruelties and barbarities that would disgrace the age in which we live." Dept. State, *Despatches, Austria,* 10, no. 153, 34f.

official attitude: France must not hope for support in the present war; American sympathies for Germany were based on firm foundations.[63]

During the war Bismarck consistently clung to the idea that any attempt at intervention would prolong the war since it would encourage the French to continue the hopeless struggle. On the other hand, he did not refuse foreign help in negotiating an armistice. Certainly it was not merely by accident that General Ambrose E. Burnside, of American Civil War fame, was chosen as mediator. This was a courteous gesture toward the Americans. For this reason Bismarck preferred American mediation to any other.[64] On September 19 and 20, negotiations took place between Bismarck and Jules Favre in Haute Maison and Ferrières for an armistice that would permit elections to be held for the National Assembly. The negotiations failed because Germany demanded the surrender of a few forts. But Bismarck was greatly interested in an armistice, hoping for a French Government that would be empowered to negotiate. It may be presumed that Motley had something to do with causing General Burnside, then in London, to visit the German headquarters. The General's personal ambition was of course another inducement. When Burnside called on Bismarck on September 27, the latter did not seem sufficiently informed regarding his visitor. At any rate he inquired of Moritz Busch who Burnside really was.[65] Burnside came to Paris on October 3 with Paul S. Forbes. He delivered a letter from the Chancellor to Jules Favre, in answer to the latter's complaint concerning the censoring of diplomatic correspondence. Burnside no doubt brought with him suggestions for armistice negotiations. Jules Favre spoke quite frankly. He seemed reconciled to the loss of Alsace but did not wish to decide that question alone. Favre was greatly astonished to hear that the Germans had no intention of preventing the elections in October. Burnside reported the results of the discussions first to the Crown Prince and then to Bismarck, who definitely foretold the entry of German troops in Paris. The Chancellor repeated what he had already said in his official notes, namely, that France would never forgive a defeat, no matter what Germany's conditions might be. For this reason as much territory as possible would need to be wrested from France so as to prevent new disturbances of the general peace. Burnside went to Paris for the second time on October 13. Bismarck requested him to propose a 48-hour armistice for the elections and a 30-day semi-armistice to permit free transit of the delegates to the National Assembly. In military matters the *status quo* was to be main-

[63] Alvensleben to Bismarck, Sept. 10; Fish to Bancroft, Sept. 30, 1870, Dept. State, *Instructions, Prussia,* 15: 161; cf. Keim, *German-American Political Relations,* 28f.

[64] Busch, *Tagebuchblätter,* I, 189.

[65] *Ibid.,* I, 243.

tained on condition that the army of siege would be allowed to increase its artillery. At first it seemed as though Jules Favre would accept that offer. But he wanted time for deliberation, and on the following day discussions were resumed in the presence of Trochu. No agreement was reached, for the French insisted that the Germans give up any territorial claims, while the Americans, of course, could not make such a concession. Burnside, however, not discouraged by his failure, offered his continued services from London. At first Bismarck was very favorably impressed with Burnside's discretion. Later on, however, less favorable reports about him seemed to have reached the Foreign Office, indicating the need for caution.[66]

At an early stage of the war, Bismarck had endeavored to convince public opinion in the neutral countries of Germany's need for security. Bernstorff was instructed to discuss unofficially with British statesmen the conditions which Germany would have to demand. Any feeling of hatred was denied. The Chancellor, in his great circular proclamations of September 13 and 16 had discussed in detail the question of peace. Strongly emphasizing the necessity of protection from future wars, he explained the futility of a policy of confidence in view of the experiences of the past and of the French national traits. Bismarck evidently did not think arguments of racial and linguistic affinity with Alsace-Lorraine would be very effective with the Anglo-Saxon powers.

Both the British and the American press were for the most part opposed to any territorial acquisitions chiefly on idealistic grounds. Liberalism demanded that parts of populations must not be taken away from a given country without the consent of the peoples concerned. While it was generally admitted that the population of Alsace-Lorraine was preponderantly German in language and race, it was thought that the people had become so thoroughly French that annexation would mean actual violation of these prin-

[66] Burnside to Bismarck, Longwy, Sept. 28, 1870, telegram; Washburne to Fish, Paris, Oct. 9, 1870, Dept. State, *Despatches, France,* 68, no. 303; Motley to Fish, London, Nov. 3, 1870, Dept. State, *Despatches, Great Britain,* 106, no. 506; Bernstorff to Bismarck, Oct. 29; Thile to Bismarck, Nov. 13, 1870. Cf. for the discussion with Bismarck, Poore, *Burnside,* 288ff. The conversation with Bismarck reported there is verified by other sources. For Burnside, cf. Russell, *Recollections,* 350ff. The Crown Prince evidently was not informed about Burnside's mission; cf. Kaiser Friedrich III, *Kriegstagebuch,* 149f. For the French point of view, cf. Favre, *Gouvernement de la défense nationale,* I, 276ff., 436ff., concerning the conversation with Burnside. Favre thought that Bismarck had not taken Burnside's mission seriously from the start. In Favre's letter to Burnside, Oct. 10, the proposed 30-day armistice is not mentioned, which surprised Motley; cf. Motley to Fish, Nov. 3. Burnside informed the British press of that omission.

ciples.[67] But there were other reasons as well. When, in its circular note of September 6, the provisional government in Paris declared that it would not cede "an inch of national territory, not one stone of our fortresses," it appeared that in view of the patriotic character of the French people any territorial demands on the part of Germany would prolong the war.[68] Certain business groups, moreover, were afraid that commerce would be severely affected by a continuation of the war. Promising connections with industries in Alsace-Lorraine had been established a few years before. Thus certain quarters loudly clamored for a cessation of the war. Wendell Phillips, a Republican who had distinguished himself in the struggle against slavery, assailed the German demands with extreme vehemence. In a public speech in New York, on March 8, 1871, he declared: "I know what is said of Germany, her metaphysics and her advance in Protestantism; but France has done more for popular rights than a dozen Germanies. . . . Europe congregates against her. There are only three great powers in the world today. England stands third-rate; behind her is the Irish question on the one hand, the *Alabama* claims on the other. Russia, Prussia, and this Government are the only three; and I do not think it becomes the United States to send out congratulations to the blasphemous Emperor of Germany for his cruel conquest in this infamous war."[69]

Naturally, this was not the general opinion. The German need for security was by no means ignored. But because of the lack of knowledge of European affairs, some strange plans for a solution of the problem were proposed. Charles Sumner thought the best guarantee for Germany's safety from future attacks lay in the disarmament of France which would be an economic blessing to that country. On the other hand, he was decidedly opposed to annexation of Alsace-Lorraine. He wished to appeal to Germany "to whom has been opened in rarest degree the whole book of knowledge," not to insist on her brutal policy which belonged to a different age and which did not befit her superior civilization.[70]

The United States Government, too, officially opposed territorial demands. At a private dinner on August 28, Bancroft Davis intimated to Gerolt that Germany might lose American sympathies if she insisted on cession of territory. When Gerolt on the following day took issue with him on that state-

[67] Cf. Gazley, *American Opinion of German Unification*, 400ff.; Schieber, *Transformation of American Sentiment toward Germany*, 30ff.

[68] Assistant Secretary of State Davis also shared that opinion; report of a conversation with the French Minister (Berthémy), Aug. 31, 1870.

[69] Aron, *Alsace-Lorraine*, 35f.

[70] Sumner, *Works*, XIV, 53.

ment, the Assistant Secretary of State replied that he had spoken as one gentleman to another in his own home, but he did not hesitate to repeat his personal view that territorial claims would prolong the war and would therefore not be looked upon with favor by the American people. Officially, he could state only that the United States would not interfere in European affairs just as it would not allow European powers to interfere on the American continent.[71]

It is safe to say that the Department of State expressed that opinion largely for the benefit of the American public. An article in the semiofficial *Morning Chronicle* made considerable concessions. Its author said Alsace-Lorraine could not be neutralized because neutralization would bear the germ of future conflicts in it. Annexation by Germany was undesirable, for the people with their French sympathies would be unreliable citizens despite their relationship of language and descent. The article concluded with the significant statement: "Prussia cannot lay down arms without guarantees for the future; she can generously grant immunity for the past. If, however, Prussia insists on atonement, severity does not exclude justice. Prussia's moral position is still unshaken; she will retain the most sincere friendship of the American people in the future."[72]

Bancroft interpreted the sentiment prevailing in Washington to the effect "that the leading statesmen and public opinion in America consider the present war as chiefly an act of self-defense on the part of Germany with the principal aim, through better demarcation of boundaries, of protecting Germany permanently from renewal by her western neighbor of those wars of aggression which had been so numerous in the history of the past three hundred years. For this and for this alone the proposed reunion of Alsace and German Lorraine is considered necessary in Germany."[73] In vain the French Minister in Washington sought to persuade the Department of State to issue an official declaration regarding the German peace terms. His suggestion was rejected, although conversations with other diplomats gave Gerolt the impression "that nothing had been left undone in order to bring pressure to bear in that sense against the German demands during the peace negotiations in Versailles." The French Minister Berthémy was quite vexed with the attitude of the American Government, remarking, *"ils sont plus Prussiens que les Prussiens."*[74]

---

[71] J. C. B. Davis, *Journal,* Aug. 29, 1877; Gerolt to Bismarck, Aug. 31 and Nov. 17, 1870.

[72] For additional press comment on peace terms, cf. Gazley, *American Opinion of German Unification,* 400ff.

[73] Thile to Gerolt, Oct. 13, 1870, very confidential.

[74] Gerolt to Bismarck, Nov. 9, 1870.

The American Government, in instructions of September 30, expressly refused to influence the German conditions of peace. It merely stated its expectation that the war would not be protracted by excessive demands on the one side nor by excessive sensitiveness on the other. Bancroft was only to express unofficially the hopes and wishes of the President and the American people and to work for such peace conditions as would correspond to the present greatness and power of North Germany without being humiliating and offensive to a great nation that had been America's earliest ally.

Bismarck was effectively supported by Bancroft. Not only for sentimental reasons but in the real interest of his country, Bancroft endeavored to deepen the friendship between the American and German nations. In his report of August 26, 1868, he had explained to his Government the great importance of good political relations with Germany. Now he outlined the vital points of contact between the two countries, mentioning especially Germany's attitude during the Civil War, her fight for the protection of private property on the high seas, and the common policy in the Far East. He spoke also of Germany's system of federation and her struggle with ultramontanism. As for France, on the other hand, there were many differences of opinion. Her foreign policy often ran counter to American interests. France favored the secular power of the Pope. She was a centralized state. America could most easily form a reliable friendship with Germany, because their conditions were similar and because millions of Germans had become American citizens. In the future, Germany would be the strongest power in Europe; her friendship was therefore very important for the United States.[75] Bancroft was not alone in that opinion. Carl Schurz, as early as 1855, had said that together the United States and Germany would have to create the international law of the world since their interests harmonized in all essential matters.[76] At about the same time he wrote in a similar sense to the Secretary of State. Likewise, Sanford, years before, although with a liberal Germany in mind, had advocated a community of interests on the ground that the United States nowhere enjoyed so much sympathy as among the German middle class.[77]

Bancroft incurred the anger of the French when his letter of thanks for Bismarck's felicitations was published at the end of September on the occasion of the fiftieth anniversary of his doctorate. Among other things, he said that he accepted gratefully the good will shown to his age: "old age, which is

[75] Bancroft to Fish, Berlin, Oct. 18, 1870, Howe, *Bancroft,* II, 245ff.

[76] Schurz to Kinkel, Philadelphia, Mar. 25, 1855, cf. Schurz, *Speeches, Correspondence, and Political Papers,* I, 19.

[77] Sanford to Seward, Brussels, Dec. 28, 1863, Dept. State, *Despatches, Belgium,* 7.

always nearest eternity, is, this year, mightiest on earth; this German war is being conducted to its close by the aged. You, to be sure, are young; but Roon must be classed among the venerable; Moltke is within twenty-three days as old as I am, and your king in years and youthfulness excels us all. May I not be proud of my contemporaries?"[78] Bancroft consequently was ready to lend support in Washington to Bismarck's idea of security. The day, he said, would inevitably come when France would annex Belgium. Then the German Rhine provinces would be exposed to the greatest danger. "To guard against it, Germany demands Strasburg, a demand which is now in Europe not censured as extravagant; Germany demands also Metz, and on that the European mind is more divided."[79] It is not unlikely that a few significant articles on the problem of security, published by a leading Republican paper, the *New York Tribune,* were inspired by Bancroft. While the *Tribune* had its own war correspondent, those articles displayed such thorough information and contained such an abundance of facts that their author, Daly, a prominent judge, must have been able to draw from excellent sources. The *Morning Chronicle* actually suspected they were based on an interview with Bismarck by the *Tribune* correspondent. In an article of September 1, "The French Frontier," the historical development of the Franco-German boundaries was outlined. The author came to the conclusion that the population in the Rhineland and Alsace-Lorraine was preponderantly of German origin. It is a debatable question whether victorious Germany did well in demanding the partial or complete cession of French districts inhabited by German-speaking people; but certainly no change of frontiers as intended by Germany would be so flagrantly unjust as the changes incessantly demanded by the French war party ever since 1815. In his final article, "The Basis of a True Peace" (September 15), Daly discussed France's historical Rhine policy, which he considered as continuous from Louis XIV to Napoleon III. "The Germans," he said, "know from the bitter experience of two centuries that France—republican or monarchical—would repeat what had been done thrice before. And all Germans realize that, after they have beaten the armies of the everlasting disturber of European peace by common effort and with a vigor and rapidity practically unexampled in the history of the world, the work will be incomplete, the enormous sacrifices of money and blood in vain, unless they restore Germany's

[78] Howe, *Bancroft,* II, 254f. For Victor Hugo's poems against Grant and Bancroft, see Aron, *Alsace-Lorraine,* 38ff.

[79] Bancroft to Fish, Berlin, Sept. 21 and 24, 1870, *Foreign Relations,* 1870, 207f. and 209ff.; Bancroft to Davis, Oct. 12, 1870, Keim, *German-American Political Relations,* 13, footnote 8.

natural geographic boundaries of which she was originally deprived by French aggression." [80]

Bancroft was displeased with Gerolt, whose indiscreet remarks interfered with his tactics. In Washington, people were somewhat amused to see the old German Minister, through his excessive zeal, spoil the eminent position he had won for himself during the War of Secession. No doubt he was quite right in some of his protests against unneutral conduct of minor American officials; but it was not the official German policy to make an issue of it. In addition, Gerolt was criticized for rather violent statements about Germany's alleged plans for annihilating France.[81] Bancroft therefore took recourse to an unusual step and submitted a complaint to the Foreign Office on October 13. Gerolt, his report said, spoke at variance with his Government's policy. He seemed to take pleasure in describing as the German war objective the complete destruction of the power of France and as great a reduction as possible in her territory. Such remarks he would make with evident gusto, even in a certain tone of irony, which made an unfavorable impression on political circles in Washington and which the French representative very cleverly exploited to Germany's disadvantage.[82] Bismarck acted at once, personally. From headquarters, on October 17, he telegraphed to Washington: "Always emphasize that we are not striving for conquest but only for the necessary protection of our frontiers against France's future attacks. Always speak kindly of France's future."[83] When Bancroft referred to his complaint a few days later, adding another to the effect that Gerolt and Dr. Rösing, consul general in New York, had attempted to enlist American citizens for the German Army (Thile to Bismarck, October 20, confidential), Bismarck took occasion to send detailed instructions to Washington on October 29 explaining the principles of his policy. Gerolt, he said, was sufficiently familiar with the policy of the Royal Government to know that it was one of its principal aims to cultivate friendly relations with the United States and to guard them from disturbances through tactful consideration of American sentiment. Never had it been the desire of Germany's military leaders to destroy France or to reduce her to the status of a minor power. Germany's intended peace conditions were based only on strategic protection of the German boundaries against future wars of aggression. "This will be recognized in the United States as an

[80] The New York Tribune, the Philadelphia Press, the Nation, and Leslie's Weekly supported German claims to Alsace-Lorraine; cf. Gazley, American Opinion of German Unification, 409ff.

[81] Cf. Keim, German-American Political Relations, 19ff.

[82] Thile to Gerolt, Oct. 13, 1870, very confidential.

[83] Bismarck, Gesammelte Werke, VI, 550f.

absolutely justified claim. On the other hand, it may be readily understood that the Americans will condemn a policy of conquest and plans that seem to originate in hatred and passion rather than in a desire for security, and consequently statements such as are ascribed to Your Excellency and to Consul General Rösing not only give offence but may even serve to turn the sympathies of America away from us and to a France allegedly victimized by our ambitions." The Chancellor asked Gerolt to bring his conduct into accord with the policy of his Government.

Although both Gerolt and Rösing, on October 29, very emphatically defended themselves against those charges, Bismarck found it advisable to recall Gerolt when a suitable opportunity presented itself; his services no longer furthered good relations.[84] Gerolt's successor was Kurd von Schlözer. At the same time, Bismarck knew perfectly well that American neutrality had been violated at least once to Germany's disadvantage. Remington, as an agent of the French Government, had made extensive purchases of war materials from American Government arsenals since September 1870. Bismarck, upon the advice of Bancroft, did not officially take up that breach of neutrality, as he had in cases of British violation.[85] Undoubtedly a breach of neutrality had occurred. While private individuals in a neutral country may sell contraband of war to a belligerent party, international law forbids such sales by a neutral government. Even before the end of the war the matter was discussed by American Government officials. Secretary of State Hamilton Fish, in a letter of November 12, 1870, to Davis, offered the excuse that the American Government had not been aware of the fact that the Remington firm had been commissioned by the French Government. The whole affair was made public in 1872, as a result of a scandal in the French Chamber. It aided Carl Schurz in his election campaign against President Grant. The Senate Investigating Committee, however, did not feel inclined to admit the wrong done. On the contrary, it held that the sales had been legitimate and ascribed selfish motives to Schurz for his procedure.[86] Motley, too, sent a word of warning from London with regard to the peace question. His private letter to Bismarck, however, did not express the opinion of the American Minister so much as it did the opinion of Bismarck's friend and a man who had many connections

[84] Bismarck to Kaiser Wilhelm, Versailles, Feb. 11, 1871.
[85] *Foreign Relations*, 1874, 448.
[86] For supplying contraband of war, cf. Hatschek and Strupp, *Wörterbuch*, I, 749f.; Moore, *Digest*, VII, 973f.; Koerner, *Memoirs*, II, 523, raised serious charges of bribery against lesser officials. The sales, he said, were not stopped until a number of German-Americans had remonstrated. For the discussions of 1872, cf. *Congressional Globe*, 42d Cong., 2d sess., XLV, pt. 2, 953, and *Senate Reports*, 42d Cong., 2d sess., no. 183, "Select Committee to Inquire into the Sale of Arms."

in the leading circles of London. His letter of September 9 reflected British rather than American apprehensions. Bismarck, he wrote, should not misunderstand him; no one could be more pleased with the Chancellor's successes than he. But he was pleading for moderate peace terms which would make France a friend of Germany's, as the more modest the demands the more hopeful would be the future. The writer also alluded to possible intervention by Great Britain. Bismarck had Motley informed that he would answer him as soon as he had time to spare, and then he confidentially sent him his circular notes of September 13 and 16. "Damn confidence," his marginal note written on Motley's letter, sufficiently proves that he rejected his friend's theory of confidence and that, if he replied at all, he answered him in that sense.[87]

The dispute over peace terms, of course, had little bearing on the relations between the two countries. The nearer peace approached, the less the Americans were interested in it. Bigelow did not even find the war indemnity very high. He compared the billion that Napoleon I had extracted from Prussia, when she was completely exhausted, with the five billion to be paid by a nation with thirty-six million inhabitants, inexhaustible natural resources, and an unshaken credit.[88] He was also optimistic about the future of a German Alsace-Lorraine and therefore welcomed Roggenbach's appointment as president of the University of Strassburg.[89] William P. Webster, the American consul general in Frankfort, also prophesied in his reports that Alsace-Lorraine, benefiting economically from reunion with the Reich, would gradually adjust herself to the German rule.[90] Respect for the Germans had decidedly increased at any rate. There were prophecies of their hegemony in Europe. According to Bigelow, the Germanic race was destined to rule the Latin race, just as the Northern States of the Union had dominated the Southern States.[91] An essay in the *North American Review* for January 1871 characterized Germany as the leading intellectual power and asserted that the problem of the age consisted of effective union of knowledge and faith. The German quest of truth, it said, was more profound than French thought.[92] In foreign affairs, too, Germany's position seemed changed. With reference to diplomatic representation, the United States declared the newly founded Reich a "first-class power." Instructions to the American Minister in Berlin,

[87] Motley, *Motley and His Family*, 291f.
[88] John Bigelow, *Retrospections*, IV, 458ff.
[89] *Ibid.*, IV, 551f.
[90] *Commercial Relations*, 1871, 369.
[91] John Bigelow, *Retrospections*, IV, 408.
[92] Hemans, "Prussia and Germany," in *North American Review*, CXII, 113f. (1871).

January 31, 1871, heralded the new era. They expressed the hope that the new power would become a milestone for liberty and democracy and an assurance of peace for Europe.[93]

[93] For a connection between the German and American struggles for unification, cf. the article by Oncken, "Der Kampf um die Einheit in Deutschland und in den Vereinigten Staaten von Amerika," in *Die Glocke* (Chicago), I, 1906.

PART II

A WORLD POWER IN THE MAKING

CHAPTER I

THE BEGINNING OF ECONOMIC
CONFLICTS

WITH the end of the Franco-German War struggles for unification came to a close in both Europe and America. A changed world looked at the reconquered unity of the German and American Nations. The German Reich at once stood forth as a world power, elevated above its normal status by the unique greatness of its Chancellor. To speak of Germany's power was now as natural as it had been only a few decades before to declare the Germans incapable of ever attaining national unity. Americans did not hesitate to express their admiration. From the viewpoint of the American merchant the greatest advantage for Germany was her economic unification; others regarded the young Reich as an invulnerable Siegfried. John Russell Young, who accompanied ex-President Grant on his trip around the world in 1878, was convinced, after he had visited Berlin, that Prussia's military power was invincible. As mistress of Europe he thought that she combined the highest intellectual culture with the greatest physical strength.[1] Germany had little to fear from outside enemies, averred Herbert Tuttle in an article entitled, "The German Empire," so long as she kept her standing army on its present standard, save perhaps in the case of the formation of a general coalition against her, which possibility could be prevented by clever diplomacy.[2]

Successive American ministers in Berlin generally recognized the peaceful intentions of Germany's policy. In 1875, the "war-in-sight" year, the American Minister in Berlin occasionally heard it said that it would be more economical to wage a war soon, if it were to come at all, rather than to exhaust the resources by waiting. But such was not the opinion of the Government.

[1] Young, *Around the World with General Grant*, 404.
[2] *Harper's New Monthly Magazine*, LXIII, 591ff.

Peace was desired as much as in France. Germany wanted to preserve the peace and believed that it was possible.[3] On the other hand certain journalists asserted that Germany was the only European country that could profit from a war. John Kasson, Minister in Vienna, reported on January 31, 1878, that Bismarck intended annexing Holland and Belgium to Germany. Nevertheless the Germany Army was praised as a model institution, and the German Navy was even an object of special envy.[4] For her victory Germany was admired—nay loved—by the Americans who were to be among her bitterest enemies during the World War. Walter Hines Page, later Ambassador in London, as a student, took a summer trip through Germany in the seventies with some of his friends. His letters, while not uncritical, indicate full appreciation of Germany's great achievements, particularly in the sciences. He advises his fellow countrymen to realize more clearly than before that the Germans were then leading.[5] Theodore Roosevelt was even more enthusiastic in recording his impressions of Germany during the same period.[6]

The conflict between the State and the Church in Germany had considerable influence on the Catholics in the United States, more so than might be expected. They tried to smuggle propaganda material into Germany by devious means.[7] The German Minister, Kurd von Schlözer, was under the impression that because of the Arnim case, the *New York Herald* for some time was the "focus of all tendencies aiming at the destruction of Germany." However, in many of his reports Schlözer took a more gloomy view of the menace of Catholicism in the United States than was warranted by the facts.

[3] Davis to Fish, Berlin, Apr. 13, 1875; the same, Oct. 11, 1875: "While the triple alliance endures, the peace of Europe is reasonably assured . . ." Dept. State, *Despatches, Germany*, 7, no. 98, and 9, no. 184, 3, respectively. Likewise Aaron A. Sargent, Minister to Germany, reported to Frelinghuysen, May 7, 1883, on the undoubtedly peaceful policy of the triple alliance, Dept. State, *Despatches, Germany*, 33, no. 148.

[4] Schlözer to Bülow, Jan. 21, 1875.

[5] Hendrick, *Page*, 92ff.

[6] "Above all I gained an impression of the German people which I never got over. From that time to this it would have been quite impossible to make me feel that the Germans were really foreigners. The affection, the Gemüthlichkeit (a quality which cannot be exactly expressed by any single English word), the capacity for hard work, the sense of duty, the delight in studying literature and science, the pride in the new Germany, the more than kind and friendly interest in three strange children—all these manifestations of the German character and of German family life made a subconscious impression upon me which I did not in the least define at the time, but which is very vivid still forty years later." Roosevelt, *Autobiography*, 26.

[7] For instance, the *Katholische Volkszeitung* in Baltimore, which published a sensational article, "Glimpses of Berlin Court Life," on Apr. 24, 1875.

Nevertheless, it must be admitted that much subsequent unfriendly criticism of Bismarck and Germany in the Catholic press had its origin in the ecclesiastical conflict. It is significant that the Catholic German-language papers in America generally had very little to say in favor of Bismarck on the occasion of his death in 1898.

The German conception of the United States was different. For some time to come the United States was not to participate in the great political problems that kept Europe astir. Neither did it attempt in any way to build up an armament comparable to the great powers. Europe, therefore, accustomed to military standards, did not number the Union among the great powers. In 1878, in an article of the *Deutsche Revue*, Zorn said of the United States: "Neither the North American Union nor France are good examples. The former certainly is a republic but not a great power; the latter is a great power but not a republic." The United States, as a result of historical traditions and domestic political institutions, no doubt has a republican form of government; in its foreign relations it has never claimed, nor, in fact, occupied a position analogous to a great power of Europe. On the contrary, it is the well-known and governing principle of the foreign policy of the Union to abstain absolutely from interfering in European controversies. In its foreign relations, therefore, the Union does not desire the status of a great power nor does it, in fact, possess such a position. Once in its history, however, the Union was forced by circumstances to exercise a concentrated application of power in a national conflict: the War of Secession.[8] To be sure, this opinion was more current during the first decade of the Reich. On February 13, 1889, the German Minister in Washington, von Alvensleben, wrote to Berlin that the Union with its increasing growth of power might become a very unwelcome factor in the foreign relations of the future. Because of the weakness of its neighbors, the Union might occasionally be tempted to try its excess power against a European opponent.

Before their unification, the Germans had frequently considered the United States a political El Dorado. This idea, however, was gradually discarded; it remained a tradition of democratic clubs which, on more or less fitting occasions, eulogized the allegedly greater political liberty in America. The interest of the German public in the economic situation of the United States, however, became all the stronger; during periods of general business depression many people looked forward to better living conditions in the New World.

Intellectually, Germany at this time gave more than she received. Many

[8] Zorn, "Zur Frage der 'besten Staatsform,'" in *Deutsche Revue*, Apr.-June 1878, 222.

American students attended German universities in the seventies and eighties. As was once the case with the elementary schools, so now the German universities were considered as models for American institutions of learning. Many instructors, trained at German universities, taught at Johns Hopkins University, which had been founded in 1876 on the German system. Harvard and Cornell Universities were also closely connected with the intellectual life and civilization of Germany. Andrew D. White, at one time president of Cornell University, and twice accredited to Germany, first as minister and later as ambassador, was an enthusiastic believer in German ideas on education.[9] Consequently, the German language was given a place of honor in the American schools and universities. The extent to which its significance was realized is shown by a bill introduced in Congress on February 26, 1872, but not passed, to add to the French and Spanish languages the German language as a required subject in the Military Academy at West Point.[10] Generally speaking, however, it must be admitted that the cultural influence of Germany on the United States did not correspond to the former's newly acquired political power. The law of inertia asserted itself. A glance at the American periodicals of the day shows that the political and cultural life of England and France was much more closely followed than that of Germany. France very cleverly took pains to renew its early friendship. The quiet activity in the early eighties of the "Franco-American Alliance" (and later of the Alliance Française) bore rich fruit in the course of time. The Statue of Liberty, France's gift of honor to the American people, made a more enduring impression than could have been obtained by the most skillful diplomacy.

In the decade from 1870 to 1880 political relations between Germany and the United States were rather stagnant. This was but natural. The Americans, after their experiences in the late war, were more anxious than ever to heed Washington's advice to interfere as little as possible in European affairs. Reconstruction of their own political system kept them sufficiently busy. As Germany's policy likewise was limited to domestic interests, the political spheres of the two countries could hardly touch, much less cross each other. Schlözer, in a conversation with Carl Schurz in March 1872, was certainly correct in stating that America was far more distant from Europe than people generally realized. Of the European powers only Great Britain and Spain had interests in common with the United States.[11]

Such statements, however, do not permit us to ignore their economic development during those particular years. In this respect the two states emerged

[9] Cf. Faust, *German Element*, II, 473.
[10] *Congressional Globe*, 42d Cong., 2d sess., XLV, pt. 2, 1217.
[11] Schlözer, *Amerikanische Briefe*, 172.

from the upheavals in their recent past with different results: the United States with a burden of debts and a great loss of people; the German Reich with a surplus of capital and hardly affected as to the size of her population. But both countries were shaken up and transformed socially. It was a long-foreshadowed change that now took its full effect. All things were changing. As to the United States a few figures will serve as an illustration. Between 1870 and 1880 the population increased by eleven and a half million.[12] By the middle of the eighties several million immigrants entered the country. The population, thirty-one million in 1860, had more than doubled by 1890. When Lincoln was first elected in 1860, no more than one-sixtieth of the population lived in towns of eight thousand inhabitants and over; toward the end of the century one-third of the total population had settled in such towns.[13] Economic supremacy, the real war aim of the North and West, had been attained completely. The South was unable to regain its old place, although the development of a textile industry in the old slave States healed the external wounds more rapidly than was expected. Unquestionably the country had been radically changed. In 1890 the population of the North was double that of the South.[14] But there was a shifting of population in the North as well. The westward trend depopulated States that formerly had been extremely important. Railways united the immense territory into an economic unit. In 1890 the Union possessed 163,562 miles of railroads, more than all of Europe combined.[15] The railways were followed by transoceanic cables that narrowed the distance between continents. The irresistible advance of colonization in the West gave continued impetus to diversified industry. Trusts began to dominate the business world. The Standard Oil Company was founded in 1871, and was soon followed by combines of the iron, coal, copper, and leather industries. The rapidity of that development may be illustrated by a forecast made in 1820 by Secretary of State John Quincy Adams, to the effect that the complete colonization of the country might take five hundred years. What happened was quite different. By 1890 free land was no longer available. These changes did not occur without serious disturbances, however. The country suffered for a long period from the aftereffects of the war and especially from the panic of 1874. But when the world business depression of the seventies drew to a close, the country was economically prepared. The United States owed its unique position in world trade to

[12] Jennings, *History of Economic Progress*, 377.
[13] Beard, *Rise of American Civilization*, II, 206ff.
[14] Sartorius von Waltershausen, *Deutschland und die Handelspolitik der Vereinigten Staaten*, 10.
[15] Beard, *Rise of American Civilization*, II, 192.

the fact that it was at one and the same time a wholesale producing and exporting as well as an industrial and commercial country. The European powers, consequently, were faced with the growing pressure of American competition.

The increase of population in Germany was proportionately as large as in the United States; as early as 1880 the Reich had a net gain of 700,000 births a year. The rapid development of an industrial center in the West attracted so many people from the East, because of higher wages, that an actual depopulation resulted in the East. Population shifted to the cities, particularly the large cities. Simultaneously with the United States, Germany passed through a serious economic crisis, having exceeded her strength. The sudden influx of considerable capital abnormally inflated business. The collapse of the so-called period of speculation had its origin in more than one cause. The business depression, after all, was international. There was a great deal of explosive material at hand. Risky investments in the money markets were induced by countless new enterprises. Immediately after the war, for instance, Germany was flooded with American railroad securities that soon were in default. But, above all, Germany could not, for any length of time, afford unlimited individualism in commerce. The policy of *laissez faire* was no doubt possible, or even advantageous, in a country like the United States so long as the extent of the available territory permitted unrestricted employment of human labor. But even there in the seventies the Granger movement was organized in opposition to the arbitrary rule of powerful industrial concerns. Germany could not possibly prosper along individualistic lines in the future. Those evil consequences of excessive business egotism—unreliability and, above all, corruption—are certain to be essentially more dangerous for a country whose chief difficulty was and always had been lack of space, than for countries of unlimited territory like America and Russia where such evils, although serious, are surmountable. Germany was forced to reestablish herself on a substantial basis. Government control of business, a cooperative spirit, and high quality of production were the principles on which Germany's new commercial system had to be constructed.[16] Fortunately for the nation, Bismarck, in time, led it back to its inherent possibilities through drastic reform, for Bismarck's new economic policy of 1879 indeed meant more than simply a change of methods, the value of which will always be a subject of discussion. He needed the aid of conservative elements of the country in order to solve the domestic problems of the Reich as much as he had needed the

[16] At the Philadelphia Centennial Exposition of 1876, Reuleaux, the Reich Commissar, passed the following severe but just judgment on the German exhibit: "Cheap but poor." Langenbeck, *Geschichte des deutschen Handels,* 160.

liberal traditions of an earlier epoch for his work of unification. The new policy simultaneously meant a frank devotion of interests to Central Europe. Prussia's inclination toward a policy of free trade in the fifties and sixties of the nineteenth century was intended to break Austria's dominating influence in southern Germany,[17] and the adoption of a protective tariff policy at this time did not coincide merely by chance with the conclusion of a German-Austrian alliance. More than likely Bismarck was influenced by the success of the American policy of protective tariff. In economic discussions he frequently referred to the United States, and his assistant, Kusserow, while in America, had been won over to the principle of protective tariff and had so reported.[18] Thenceforward Germany's foreign policy had to develop from conservative middle Europe. Those same years are also profoundly significant in world politics. The Congress of Berlin in a certain sense brought to a close the struggles of European powers in the Near East. "From that date the relations between European nations were less affected by questions arising in Europe itself than by the struggle carried on outside of Europe for the possession of colonies and markets."[19] It certainly is not by accidental coincidence that the United States, almost unnoticed, simultaneously set out on its colonial policy: in 1878 it concluded a treaty with the Samoans for the seaport of Pagopago.

The Americans had more understanding than the British of Germany's transition to neo-mercantilism. A British consular report of 1882 forecast paralyzed commerce, rising prices of foodstuffs, and decreased prosperity of the working population as the evil consequences of the new economic policy.[20] The American consul in Düsseldorf on June 7, 1884, reported that wages were increasing as a consequence of the new policy.[21] High-tariff America, naturally, took an entirely different attitude toward the reform than did free-trade England, which considered itself seriously injured. The Americans well understood that Germany, because of her large surplus population, was forced to seek new methods of employment so as to prevent general discontent.[22]

Commercial relations between Germany and the United States developed steadily. Since the sixties the trade between North America and Europe had

[17] Zeitlin, *Fürst Bismarcks sozial-, wirtschafts- und steuerpolitische Anschauungen,* 148ff.; Schmoller, "Vier Briefe über Bismarcks sozialpolitische und volkswirtschaftliche Bedeutung," in Schmoller, Lenz, and Marcks, *Zu Bismarcks Gedächtnis,* 51; Sartorius von Waltershausen, *Deutsche Wirtschaftgeschichte,* 293ff.

[18] Poschinger, *Bismarck-Portefeuille,* V, 113.

[19] Nearing and Freeman, *Dollar Diplomacy,* 244.

[20] *British State Papers,* LXXII, *Commercial Reports,* 1882, Appendix I, 455.

[21] *Consular Reports,* 1884, XIII, no. 42, 15.

[22] Annual report of Consul General Brewer in Berlin, Nov. 12, 1881, Dept. State, *Despatches, Berlin,* 10, no. 14, 4.

far exceeded European trade with the tropical regions of America. The value of Hamburg's transatlantic commerce rose from 56 million marks in 1851 to 256 million in 1877. Before 1860 the lion's share of German exports had gone to South America. Then the tide turned. Between 1874 and 1901 the North American quota of trade trebled. On the other hand, Europe now occupied the first place among the foreign markets of the Union. Great Britain naturally remained at the top, but Germany, in 1890, displaced France and took second place with 11.20 percent of the total European trade of the United States.[23] After 1874 the balance of trade between Germany and the United States was in favor of the latter. Thus the relation that existed before 1840 was restored, for not until that year had German exports exceeded imports from America.[24] In 1873 imports from America amounted to 60,124,000 marks, the German exports to 61,402,000; in 1874 the relation was reversed, with imports worth 61,668,000 marks against exports worth 43,110,000 marks. However, Germany's growing dependence on the American supply of raw materials and foodstuffs was to become still greater. Herein lies the real cause of the Reich's inability to attain commercial reciprocity with the United States. It was but natural, therefore, that American business watched the German market with increasing interest. Owing to its extensive industrial population Germany was particularly receptive to the importation of cheap products, the laborers being dependent on reasonably priced foodstuffs and articles made by mass production. The friendly relations existing between the two countries after the Civil War influenced their mutual trade. At the beginning, however, American trade with Germany was handicapped by the tariff policy and the instability of American exchange. Despite most vehement opposition, the protective tariff gained ground in America after the victory of the North. Not until 1883, however, did it reach a new and more severe phase, but since the German Reich followed a free-trade policy until 1879, the mutual exchange of merchandise necessarily suffered severely.

The instability of American currency was a still more vital factor. The long war had completely ruined the currency and the "greenbacks" dominated. Returning to a stable currency became one of the chief problems of American commercial policy. By virtue of a sort of surprise attack, the Congress of 1873 decided to accept the gold standard.[25] But the decided slump in the silver prices in 1875 deeply troubled influential concerns interested in the production of silver, since America supplied one-half of the world's silver. The struggle for a dual monetary standard was promoted by all imaginable means.

[23] *Quarterly Report of Bureau of Statistics,* 1889-90, 708.
[24] Fisk, *Die handelspolitischen und sonstigen völkerrechtlichen Beziehungen,* 75.
[25] For a discussion of bimetallism, cf. *The Americana,* II.

It was hoped that ultimately gold would be replaced entirely by silver. The Bland Bill of 1878 emerged from those struggles. It provided for a strange mixture of gold, silver, and paper currency. Only a country as favored as the United States could have withstood a law of such contradictions without greater disturbances. Although the gold standard was maintained, it was weak. The Government was authorized to buy up sizable amounts of silver from time to time. After their partial success, the bimetallists naturally were interested in converting Europe to the double standard. Ever since the Paris Conference of 1868 the European states had been on the gold standard. Prussia, although purely a silver-standard country, voiced no opposition. The German laws of 1871 and 1873 for currency reform introduced the gold standard. During a period of transition, however, the taler remained at par. When the Reich began to withdraw the taler more and more and to sell considerable quantities of silver, the price of silver, because of American overproduction, dropped to such an extent as to cause serious losses to the Reich. In 1879 the President of the Reichsbank was forced to admit publicly his error of judgment in the matter of the sales of silver. Bismarck declared that he would no longer assume responsibility for them, and thus they were stopped. As a result there developed a vigorous campaign for the double standard in Germany, which greatly encouraged the American bimetallists. In 1878 an unsuccessful currency conference took place in Paris; Germany was not represented. In 1879 the American Government sent a financial expert to Berlin to get in touch with Bismarck. Prior to his arrival, William D. Kelley, Member of Congress from Pennsylvania, reached Berlin. A report on the conversations which took place between Kelley and Bismarck are given to us by the former Minister in Berlin, Andrew D. White, in his autobiography. They are less interesting for their discussion of the silver problem than for Bismarck's confidential remarks about his ministerial colleagues, which Kelley hastened to publish in the papers. The Chancellor admitted that he had made a mistake in selling silver, an opinion expressed to White by Bleichröder, as well as by the President of the Reichsbank. However, the conversations did not result in anything of importance. The gold standard was not disturbed in any country. Various conferences held on the subject failed because of the opposition of Great Britain.[26]

Despite the temporary currency difficulties and the protective tariff, the American representatives in Germany were hopeful for better trade prospects as a result of high-class products and low prices. Beginning in the eighties,

[26] White to Evarts, Berlin, July 8, 1879, Feb. 7, 1880, private, and Mar. 22, 1880, confidential, Dept. State, *Despatches, Germany,* 25, no. 22, and 26, nos. 88 and 101, respectively; A. D. White, *Autobiography,* I, 581ff.

a number of American products actually captured the German market.[27] The German Reich took over the commercial treaties that the Union had concluded with the Hanse towns (1827) and with Prussia (1828). There followed a continuous dispute between Germany and the United States concerning definitions of reciprocity and most-favored-nation treatment, the latter country refusing to recognize or conclude unlimited most-favored-nation agreements. The American attitude may be explained by the history and geographic situation of the country. American trade had suffered severe losses during the Napoleonic wars. For a time the United States had entirely withdrawn from the seas. The Nonintercourse Act of 1809 declared that the United States would waive the right of confiscation in respect of that country which first canceled measures interfering with American trade.[28] Thus the idea of reciprocity became a principle of American commercial policy. When the policy of protective tariffs had been adopted, the United States could afford still less to concede, through unconditional most-favored-nation agreements, advantages that could be obtained by individual treaties, particularly with Central and South America. That calculation was perfectly simple. In many cases most-favored-nation agreements could not equalize the advantages obtained by independent treaties and tariff regulations, in view of the fact that the country occupied an unusually favorable commercial position as a purveyor of raw materials to the whole world. The fact that the United States abandoned that policy in principle in its commercial treaty with Germany of 1923, merely indicates the changed conditions. At that time the Union depended on most-favored-nation agreements, not as a purveyor of raw materials but as a wholesale manufacturer of finished goods.

The Americans included the most-favored-nation clause in their various treaties only conditionally; they were ready to grant it, provided corresponding concessions were offered by the other party. To be sure, the form of the clause varied. Characteristic reservations, for instance, were contained in the treaties with Prussia (1828) and with Austria (1829). In the so-called "no higher duties" treaties the most-favored-nation clause likewise was only conditional. The treaty with the Netherlands (1782) belongs to that group. The objection raised by the Dutch Government in 1787 against duty on Dutch

[27] "It may be said, indeed, that as our country is the favorite resort of the German emigrant and our securities the favorite investment of the German capitalist, so our products are, of all foreign kinds, preeminently the favorites in the German market." Lee to Seward, Frankfort, Nov. 26, 1877, Dept. State, *Despatches, Frankfort on the Main,* 21, no. 56, 14.

[28] Fisk, *Die handelspolitischen und sonstigen völkerrechtlichen Beziehungen,* 47. For the development of the American tariff legislation, cf. Jennings, *History of Economic Progress,* 452ff.

liquors, while French liquors were exempt, was rejected as incompatible with the principle of justice. France, it was claimed, was paying a high price for that privilege.[29] There was considerable protest in Europe against the commercial policy adopted by the United States. In Europe an unlimited most-favored-nation clause was regarded as the core of any commercial treaty. Great Britain spoke for the other nations. In instructions to the British Minister in Washington in 1885, Lord Granville protested against the American interpretation. The most-favored-nation clause, he said, had now become the most valuable feature of the prevailing system of commercial treaties in force among nearly all nations of the world. More than any other regulation it made for a simplification of tariffs and for an ever-increasing freedom of trade, while the system proposed by the United States would induce the various countries to shut off their markets from the world, thus fettering instead of liberating commerce.[30]

This explains the fact that Germany never was able to obtain unconditional recognition as a most-favored nation on the basis of her old treaties with the United States. The Reich, however, insisted on the principle. In his address to the Reichstag on February 10, 1885, Bismarck mentioned the Union among the most-favored nations: "Not in consequence of Reich treaties, but in consequence of treaties with Prussia and several other German states which are integral parts of the Reich."[31] When the United States demanded most-favored-nation treatment on petroleum tariffs on German railroads, Bismarck expressly endorsed their claim in instructions to Alvensleben, April 3, 1885. Most-favored-nation treatment, he said, was not only guaranteed to them by a treaty with Prussia, the most powerful German state, but similarly by treaties with other German states. "To establish that right it would have been sufficient if even a small fraction of the German Reich territory, before the foundation of the Reich proper, had been by treaty in a most-favored-nation relation with the United States. We always gladly recognize our obligation toward most-favored-nation agreements and accede to the corresponding claims of the United States." Germany, he continued, hoped for a similar courtesy on the part of the United States. This expectation, however, was disappointed. As early as March 27, 1885, the Secretary of State had given a rather evasive answer when the Imperial Minister referred to Germany's most-favored-nation rights in connection with concessions for trade with Cuba and Puerto Rico in the draft of the Spanish-American peace treaty. An American tariff law of June 26, 1884, reduced the tonnage tax to three cents per ton for

[29] Williams, *Economic Foreign Policy of the United States*, 295f.
[30] *Ibid.*, 298.
[31] Bismarck, *Gesammelte Werke*, XII, 591.

145

ships sailing from any harbor in North or Central America, the West Indies, the Bahamas, Bermuda, and the Sandwich Islands to a seaport of the United States. On August 3, 1885, Alvensleben demanded the same privilege for German ships but received an unfavorable answer on November 7. The privilege referred to, he was told, was geographically limited.[32] The dispute did not assume serious proportions until the Dingley tariff frankly abolishing the most-favored-nation principle was put into operation (1897). From that moment on the German Reich faced the question as to whether the former treaties should not be denounced entirely.[33]

Would it not have been possible to end such disagreements by a new commercial treaty? There were indeed several attempts in that direction. Negotiations did take place,[34] but the difficulties were too great. While Germany was still a free-trade country, conclusion of a new treaty was prevented by the American protective tariff, and later on it was blocked by the commercial superiority of the United States. America found it less and less expedient to enter into new agreements, as an arbitrary application of former treaties yielded considerable profits. The question of landed property also presented an obstacle. German nationals did not enjoy the unconditional right of buying or selling real estate in the United States. For this reason, Friedrich Kapp moved in the Reichstag session of May 8, 1883, to demand this concession in the case of future commercial treaties with the United States of America. His motion was carried. The Americans could well afford an independent tariff policy which would tend toward self-sufficiency and the maintenance of

[32] Alvensleben to Bayard, Aug. 3, 1885, *Foreign Relations,* 1885, 443f.

[33] Opinions differ as to whether or not most-favored-nation agreements had existed at all between Germany and the United States. Calwer, *Die Meistbegünstigung der Vereinigten Staaten,* 17, 19, thinks that the treaty of 1828 with Prussia was a pronounced reciprocity treaty, and that Germany had been inconsistent in applying the most-favored-nation clause; for example, the Saratoga Agreement of 1890 was not based on the most-favored-nation clause since privileges were limited to agricultural products. Similarly, Prager, *Handelsbeziehungen des Deutschen Reiches mit den Vereinigten Staaten,* 22, holds that the Reich could not simply take over the former treaties with Prussia and the Hanse towns. Since the resolution of the Federal Council of Oct. 24, 1883, did not mention the United States among the most-favored nations, the Reich originally does not seem to have recognized a most-favored-nation relationship. Bismarck, indeed, from the very beginning recognized the existence of most-favored-nation treaties, but the United States intentionally left the question open so as to be able to settle each case as it arose.

[34] Memorandum of an interview between Bancroft Davis and Secretary of State von Bülow, Sept. 14, 1877; Bülow to Reich Minister Hofmann, Berlin, Sept. 29, 1877; Schlözer to Bülow, Washington, Oct. 2, 1877.

a high standard of living rather than the protection of their products. On the other hand, the Reich was compelled to protect itself from an all too arbitrary American tariff policy through a number of separate agreements.[35]

The second half of 1878 begins a new chapter in the commercial policy of the United States. World depression was approaching its end. Until that time the domestic market had been the great field of activity for American business; now attention was paid to foreign trade. On December 30, 1878, the German consul in St. Louis wrote: "While last year there were yet but a few scattered voices to be heard that called attention to the advantages of an expanded foreign trade and treated the matter more or less as a new idea, interest in that trade has now become general. Almost daily the same cry is emphatically raised in the papers as well as in special commercial conferences which of late have frequently been held in the big cities." The writer called attention to the great dangers that might ensue for German commerce from that new threatening competition. Similarly, the British consul general in Washington reported the tremendous progress of America during the period between 1878 and 1880.[36] At the moment that America started to turn her economic power to the outside world, Europe was confronted with the menacing specter of underselling. America had an additional advantage in that a series of poor crops in Europe and the increased purchasing power of the masses after the end of the world depression prepared the way for an invasion of American grain into the European system of supplies. For instance, while in 1878 the export of wheat to France had been only 4,337,091 bushels, the figure rose to 42,147,558 bushels in the following year, and reached the highest level with 43,601,291 bushels in 1880. In the case of Great Britain the difference was not so great, but after all was considerable:

1878	54,664,732 bushels
1879	57,419,292 "
1880	79,068,075 "
1881	82,550,921 "

Such figures of course were not duplicated in Germany. Then, as before, rye bread dominated consumption. Here also, however, the upward trend was extraordinary.

[35] For Germany's unfavorable commercial position as compared to the United States, cf. enlightening remarks in Tansill, *Purchase of the Danish West Indies,* 383ff.

[36] *British State Papers,* LXXII, *Commercial Reports,* 1880, 159.

Wheat imports for Germany:[37]

1879 .... 422,242 bushels
1880 .... 1,223,279 "
1881 .... 3,029,232 "

This inundation affected Germany all the more seriously as, beginning in 1875, the agricultural depression materially decreased the hitherto high prices for agrarian products. Small farm property became increasingly indebted. It is no wonder that mass imports from America were viewed with mounting anxiety. The German consuls in the United States had little encouragement to offer their Government. The German consulate in St. Louis held that Europe was largely to blame for the situation. While American agriculture had to supply both the American and the European markets, it quietly reserved to itself the advantage of developing its own market. Poor crops in Europe resulted in rising grain prices. Agriculture became more lucrative. "And yet it was Europe whose demand produced corresponding business in America, who contented herself with slight compensation in the form of a few orders at the beginning of America's economic prosperity, orders that have been declining for some time. This advantage of America's development, particularly in agriculture, will continue as long as Europe tolerates the prohibitionist treatment by America and unconditionally turns her trade and gold over to the latter, instead of organizing an independent customs and tariff policy to favor countries that would grant trade for trade and open their markets to industrial products in return for raw materials." The writer thought that better European crops might easily bring about a change, and proposed as a counter-measure the connection of the East with Central Europe through a sort of customs union (May 4, 1881). The consulate in Savannah on July 4, 1881, reported a surplus of American products that were forced to seek an outlet in the European markets. As causes of the large supply he mentioned the vastness and fertility of the country, improved machinery, excellent means of transportation, and the rapid growth in population. Current publications likewise examined the causes of American competition. Max Sering, who studied the situation on a semiofficial mission, came to the conclusion that an excessive supply of grain was the root of the evil. "The war [Civil War] had created a permanent superiority of the Northern States over the Southern States. The protective tariffs, which the industrial interests of the North had now made a permanent institution, were supplemented by the passage of long-sought-for liberal laws for free assignment of public land to settlers. Thereby the North American West became a place of refuge for millions of

[37] U. S. Treasury Dept., Bureau of Statistics, *Statistical Abstract,* 1889, 171.

immigrants who came during the last two decades. Colonization proceeded with extraordinary rapidity in that period because it no longer took place in primeval forests but on the prairies which were easy to cultivate and extremely easy to traverse, and because it was promoted by an unexampled development of railroads as a result of government land grants." [38]

Others thought the trouble was caused by lack of organization and cooperation. They deplored the fact that land in Germany was inadequately exploited. But optimists were also heard; they believed that the decline of Europe was not inevitable. The high quality of its products and the intensity of its industry, agriculture, and animal husbandry gave it a place of advantage. Attention was called to the fact that competition was restricted as a result of the high wages paid American labor. [39] An agreement for a joint policy of protective tariffs was suggested. Among the chorus of voices those, of course, were not missing that paid homage to America in principle. After his return from a journey with an Austrian committee of investigation in the United States, Richard Meyer called the American Union "the extant protest of humanity and Christianity against the European State of bureaucrats and militarists. . . . The peace-loving Union stands sky-high above Europe which is being submerged in barbarism. . . . But I wish to convey the impression that the Union, within the vast extent of its territory, allows man to fulfill his divine purpose in this world better than any great power of Europe." [40]

Comparatively soon the European countries were in a position to meet the grain crisis with tariffs. Bismarck expressly demanded that American competition be checked by means of protective duties. [41] Moreover, by 1884 the production of wheat in America had reached its highest level. But grain was not the only product of American agriculture that perceptibly lowered European market prices. American exports of livestock, chiefly pork and pork products of every kind, had to be considered most seriously, as European agriculture could not possibly keep apace of that wholesale production. In this case, moreover, a constant increase had to be expected. American pressure in this respect affected the whole world. Great Britain was first to protect herself from importation of livestock by prohibiting imports into Canada of livestock from the United States and by requiring by an Order in Council of February 10, 1879, the compulsory butchering of all animals imported into the British Isles. A cattle plague in Texas served as a pretext, but the real motive no doubt was the apprehension of many British and Canadian farmers

[38] Sering, *Die landwirtschaftliche Konkurrenz Nordamerikas*, 532.
[39] Wirth, *Die Krisis in der Landwirtschaft*, 153ff.
[40] Richard Meyer, *Ursachen der amerikanischen Konkurrenz*, 9ff.
[41] Schlözer to Bülow, Washington, Feb. 24, 1874.

over the likelihood of suffering severe damage from the American cattle trade.[42]

France, Austria, Italy, Turkey, Greece, and Germany successively prohibited importation of American pork and pork products.[43] A report of the British consul in Philadelphia seems to have provided the basis for those prohibitions. The consul mistook for trichinosis an epidemic of cholera in the State of Illinois. Thereupon the French Chamber on February 18, 1881, prohibited the importation of American hogs.[44] Undoubtedly these prohibitions were influenced by the desire to restrict menacing imports in the interest of home production. But there can also be no doubt that inadequate meat inspection in America had given cause for complaint for some time. Only microscopic inspection was considered by European experts as a sufficient guarantee against trichinosis, and such inspection was not compulsory in the United States. The Americans explained that their cases of trichinosis had been few, certainly no more numerous than in Europe, and that the salting of exported meat products infallibly killed trichinae. European experts were not prepared to accept this explanation. The European practice of eating pork unboiled would increase the danger of infection. The salting theory was also distrusted. Paul Bert, the French expert, assured the American Minister that he had no personal interest in the maintenance of the prohibition but asserted that with his own eyes he had seen trichinae in American pork and that salting and boiling did not always kill the trichinae.[45] The Americans, themselves, were not nearly so firmly convinced of the unfairness of the criticism raised as they pretended to be. A consular report from Germany on August 27, 1878, frankly admitted that trichinae had been found in American pork. Many reports, it said, had no basis; others, however, were true to fact. Only high quality products could make possible a profitable trade.[46] It is therefore difficult to understand why the American Government would not conform to the regulations in force in Europe. Stubborn denial of American mistakes resulted in a controversy with Germany which was by no means negligible.

The preparatory discussions preceding the German prohibition indicate that apprehensions for national health were not merely a pretense. Nor was there really any cause for an attitude of rivalry, as American imports to Ger-

---

[42] Poschinger, *Fürst Bismarck und die Parlamentarier*, I, 132, and *Aktenstücke zur Wirtschaftspolitik*, I, 339.

[43] For prohibitions on importation of pork and pork products, cf. Sartorius von Waltershausen, *Das deutsche Einfuhrverbot amerikanischen Schweinefleisches;* Keim, *German-American Political Relations*, 67ff.; A. F. Tyler, *Blaine*, 292ff.

[44] A. F. Tyler, *Blaine*, 293f.

[45] *Foreign Relations*, 1884, 138f.

[46] *House Executive Documents*, 46th Cong., 3d sess., no. 9.

many had not assumed the dimensions frequently supposed. By 1873 imports of ham and bacon had reached their highest level of 65.7 million pounds, which amounted to approximately one-fifth of similar exports from America to Great Britain in 1885.[47] Not until after negotiations with the Ministry of Ecclesiastical and Medicinal Affairs, which had begun in 1873 and had been resumed in 1879, was the importation forbidden on June 25, 1880, of all sorts of pork except ham and bacon. When a further number of cases of infection were reported, the prohibition was made complete (March 6, 1883). Bremen and Hamburg, while opposed to the prohibition, joined the majority.[48] The memorandum which Bismarck transmitted together with the bill to the Federal Council on November 21, 1882, characterized meat inspection in America as unsatisfactory. Careful investigations had proved that in America hogs were more frequently infected with trichinae than in Germany.

The German opposition parties violently attacked the law. Their speakers, in the session of the Reichstag of January 9, 1883, argued that the complaints against American pork had not been investigated carefully and that German meat inspection also left much to be desired. They called attention to the seriousness for the consumer of the rise of prices. Bismarck's reply was as brief as it was sarcastic: It was for the commissioners to testify that the matter concerned problems of public health and that the "Federal Council could not take the trichinae of the poor under their special protection."[49]

The German prohibition on imports gave much more offense in America than the earlier prohibitions of other countries. American pork and fats controlled the world market and about 60 percent of these products were exported.[50] American business therefore had reason to expect increased exports to Germany in the coming years. In 1880 the value of German imports of butchered animals from America amounted to RM 7,743,000, jumping to RM 12,497,000 in the following year, while in 1882 the prohibition slashed the figure to RM 861,000. Not until 1887 did the figures begin to rise again.[51] Groups of German-Americans in particular conducted a vehement campaign against Germany's prohibition of imports. Many Germans had settled in the pork centers of the Middle West, and they made no secret of their anger because of lost business. At the same time they were glad to use occasions like the pork dispute to demonstrate their sympathy for the opposition parties in

[47] Sering, *Die landwirtschaftliche Konkurrenz Nordamerikas,* 602.

[48] For transactions of the Federal Council, cf. Poschinger, *Fürst Bismarck und der Bundesrat,* V, 88ff.

[49] *Sten. Berichte,* 1882-83, 29th sess., II, 819.

[50] Peetz, *Die amerikanische Konkurrenz,* 36.

[51] *Die Handelspolitik Nordamerikas . . . sowie die Deutsche Handelsstatistik von 1880-1890,* 683f.

Germany.[52] Indeed, there existed a certain community of interests between those groups and German free traders, and they joined hands in fighting Bismarck's new economic policy. The criticism by Bismarck's opponents that his economic policy had raised prices and was therefore unsocial, was taken up all too eagerly by such German-Americans as were interested in the export business.

The American Government applied different standards of policy to the principal importing countries, France and Germany. The French Government itself was opposed to prohibition but was unable to cancel it because of strong sentiment for it in the Chamber. The Department of State, therefore, hoped to attain its end in Paris through direct negotiations. On the other hand, the German Government was requested to join a commission to examine the justification of the criticism raised against American pork.[53] It was an unfortunate coincidence that Aaron A. Sargent, who had been American Minister in Berlin since 1882, entertained different ideas concerning his mission than had his predecessor. In contrast to previous practice his appointment was due exclusively to reasons of domestic policy and he conducted his Berlin office more or less in the spirit of American party politics.[54] By placing excessive emphasis on the American point of view, he hoped for approval of the public in his own country, especially of the German-Americans. From the beginning he had broken with the habits of his predecessors inasmuch as he made no effort to get into friendly contact with Bismarck. On the contrary, he obtained his political information largely from Bismarck's opponents, a fact that greatly annoyed the Chancellor. Consequently, the atmosphere was already somewhat strained when the Minister chose to add a hidden threat to the not unfriendly invitation of his Government to form a commission. It might happen, he said, that the American Congress would be forced to measures of retaliation and would bar importation of German products (February 23, 1883). The Minister had suggested to his Government, as early as December 1882, increased import duties against Germany. Bismarck's reaction to such an attempt at intimidation may well be imagined. At first he made no reply but inquired in Washington whether Sargent had acted upon instructions from his Government. He considered the note, he said, a case of interference in the internal affairs of Germany. Germany had accepted the rising tariffs without protest, "because we recognize it to be an indisputable right of any Government to

[52] Schlözer to Foreign Office, confidential, Feb. 9, 1884.

[53] Frelinghuysen to Sargent, Washington, Feb. 16, 1883, *Foreign Relations*, 1883, 335f.

[54] Sargent had hitherto had only the experiences of a journalist and a Representative in Congress.

regulate its legislation, and particularly customs, border control, and sanitary measures, according to its own judgment. . . . It is difficult to assume that Mr. Sargent should be so little informed as to the nature of a ministerial position and the limitations of his official competence, as to present to a foreign power a note like the one enclosed. The tenor of its argumentation suggests that he did not take his step without assistance from the opposition in Parliament. If such be the case, it will, much to my regret, be very difficult for Mr. Sargent to acquire that position of confidence with us which his predecessor enjoyed and which corresponds to the continued friendly relations between the two Governments." The Chancellor wished definite information as to "whether the Government of the United States approved and intended to sustain the interference of its representative in the internal affairs and party struggles of the German Reich" (to Eisendecher, Berlin, March 3, 1883). On March 22 Eisendecher replied that the content of the note presented by Sargent was not based on instructions. On March 14 Sargent received from his Government a somewhat veiled reprimand: "So far as your intimation touches the operation of the laws of international trade, it is unexceptionable. Those laws control themselves, and commerce must perforce work its own channels in the most natural directions; but when you go further and indicate the possibility that this Government may resort to retaliation if its views be not assented to by Germany, you introduce an element which it was not intended to present." [55] On July 11 the German Government declined the American invitation for a commission of investigation on the ground that the import prohibitions in question affected far more valuable interests of the German nation than tariff laws, namely, protection of the people from dangers to their health. "German legislation applies and enforces with great rigor the same protection in the case of cattle breeding within Germany, and it is impossible to treat foreign production more favorably than domestic production." Trade with Great Britain is cited as an instance where such unavoidable consideration of the health of the national population was quite compatible with friendly relations. Instructions to Washington January 2, 1884, say: "We had in mind only the protection of the German people from dangers to their health. Any intention of taking measures apt to influence our relations to America was far from our thoughts since analogous prohibitions of imports of American pork had been existing for a long time in other countries—Austria-Hungary, France, Italy, Greece—without ever resulting in similar steps on the part of the American representatives in Paris or Rome. This differentiation is the more conspicuous inasmuch as the political opposition in Germany seized upon that question and found support in the American claim. . . . The decree concerns a measure

[55] Keim, *German-American Political Relations,* 69, footnote 17.

for the continuation of a system applied almost uninterruptedly against one or another of the countries in Europe with whom we are associating, for reasons of sanitary and veterinary regulations." As examples there were import prohibitions on cattle from Russia and Austria which did not affect the friendliness of relations. "How far we have always kept away from such tendencies is shown by the fact that the much discussed duty on grains (one mark per 100 kg.) amounts to but one-third of the duty of one shilling per quarter of grain which Great Britain has been collecting since turning to and adopting the system of free trade. The situation in the present case is simply that the prohibition exclusively affects products for human consumption, while other products, particularly pork lard which is used more for machinery and industrial purposes, are not subject to prohibition, although lard, for example, is imported into Germany to a far greater extent than other meat products."

The American investigating committee in October 1883 summed up its results in a report which called inspection in the packing houses adequate but admitted the possibility of exportations of diseased meat and recommended the use of the microscope, which might easily be added to the present equipment.[56] However, neither the Government nor the public could be interested in the last-mentioned measure. On the contrary, any argument that seemed to justify the American point of view was eagerly hailed. An epidemic of trichinosis in Ermsleben in the fall of 1883 was held to be a striking proof that the German hog and not the American hog was afflicted with trichinosis. Even the American Secretary of State tried to ridicule the matter: Bismarck, he said, might easily let the poor American hogs return to Germany, because, after all, they were not much worse than their German brethren. In the course of this conversation the German Minister remarked that he believed he could promise readmission (October 30, 1883). The Chancellor, however, was not pleased with that answer of his Minister, for the latter should have called attention to the high American duty. The Americans, he said, "want to wage a sort of opium war with the hog, seeking to force us to eat something we do not care to eat. The American reports give evidence of the manner in which the slaughtering houses were managed in many places" (Rantzau, Friedrichsruh, November 17, 1883). The *Norddeutsche Allgemeine Zeitung* of April 27 similarly used the opium war for comparison in this connection.

However, interest in the matter would probably have subsided soon. As Eisendecher reported on May 3, the American press was not greatly interested. Carl Schurz, in the *Evening Post* of April 23, 1883, emphatically stated that no one in America wanted a conflict with Germany. The Americans did not, he said, receive favorably the German prohibition on American pork products.

[56] *House Executive Documents*, 48th Cong., 1st sess., no. 106.

but they were calm about it. For some time, however, things did not quiet down. Sargent's activity in particular proved a troublesome factor. Taking the affair seriously from a political angle, he recommended to his Government on May 4 that an agreement be concluded with France. Aside from the sympathies of her fifty million people, France, he said, had no friends left. In gratitude for French cancellation of the prohibition, the French might be freed from potential measures of retaliation. In a report of March 19 the Minister asserted the Germans had acted only to please the big landowners upon whose support the Government relied. The overwhelming majority of the people were opposed to the prohibition. One of his indiscretions made a very unpleasant impression. The *New Yorker Handels-Zeitung* of March 10, 1883, published an official report by Sargent, dated January 1, 1883, wherein the Minister identified himself with the opinion of the German opposition press, saying it was not reasons of public health but the interests of the hog breeders that had caused the prohibition.[57] The *Norddeutsche Allgemeine Zeitung* of April 24 and May 1, 1883, vehemently attacked that article. Sargent, in his own defense, spoke of distortions,[58] but had he been better informed of the principles of German administration, he would not have been astonished at Berlin's anger at his reproach that the German Government had confused personal interests with the common weal. Moreover, it was not customary in Europe to publish official reports containing criticisms of foreign governments. But that was not the sole difficulty. In his report on the results of the investigating committee, the Secretary of State recommended that the President be authorized "to adopt at his discretion measures compensating for and counteracting such misuses of the incidents of commerce."[59] In January 1884, Representative Townshend submitted a bill to Congress, providing for prohibition of imports from such countries as had prohibited importation from America of certain goods for sanitary considerations. The German Foreign Office very acrimoniously wrote concerning that bill: "Such a limitation simply means that any justification at all is denied to sanitary measures of other countries. The provisions of the bill consequently may be characterized as an unjustifiably hostile onslaught against Germany that we are not in a position to accept without protest." The German Minister was advised at his discretion to call the attention of the American Government in proper and for the present confidential form, to the fact "that Germany by no means defenselessly faces the proposed attack of the United States, possessing the means, by laws concerning importation of grain, cattle, lard, flour, meat of

[57] Cf. *Foreign Relations,* 1883, 324ff.
[58] Sargent to Frelinghuysen, Berlin, Apr. 28, 1883, *ibid.,* 377f. and 381.
[59] *Senate Reports,* 48th Cong., 1st sess., no. 345.

all kinds, as well as by other acts of legislation in the sphere of foreign relations, to ward off treatment which would conflict with the friendly relations of the two countries." Bismarck added in his own handwriting that a customs war, if forced upon Germany, would be accepted. "I am inclined to think that we should not deem it necessary to introduce tariff-war rates against a power like the United States with whom we entertain friendly political relations."[60] From Friedrichsruh Bismarck sent word through Rantzau that Germany could not yield at the moment, for in addition to retaining good relations with the United States, national dignity had to be preserved. The Chancellor could not assume responsibility for a policy of weakness and extreme pacifism that would let evils grow until they were incurable.[61] The Chancellor wrote to the German representatives abroad, in a cautious tone, however. Instructions of February 2, 1884, to the German consuls in America expressed the hope that, upon calm deliberation and consideration of all questions involved, the reasonable, interested, and competent groups of American people would not lend their hands to measures that might trouble for a long time to come the intimate relations between Germany and the United States to the detriment of both countries. In addition the consuls were expected "to avoid any polemics or public demonstration, and everything in general that might impair or disturb our friendly relations with the United States."[62]

Berlin at that time seriously contemplated the possibility of a customs war. American competition was no longer considered very dangerous. It had already receded from its high level. A memorandum of March 6 raises the question as to what could be done to meet American measures of retaliation. First, a fifty-percent increase of the duties on all American goods was considered on the basis of section 6 of the tariff of July 15, 1879. America, it was thought, was not to be regarded as the stronger country. While the American market was desirable, Germany, with her well-developed merchant fleet and diversified industrial products, could find compensation in other markets. The writer of this report demanded restriction of German emigration "for in that way those arteries that conveyed ever new blood to America's economic system would be stopped quite directly." For that purpose a new and more rigid emigration law (Bismarck's note: "that would be useful anyway"), or discontinuance of licenses for emigration agents, and severe penal prosecution of all nonlicensed agents might be considered. Germany's export to America was indeed quite considerable in certain articles. But sales would not stop

[60] Hatzfeldt to Eisendecher, Berlin, Jan. 22, 1884.
[61] Rantzau to Krauel, Friedrichsruh, Mar. 2, 1884.
[62] To the consulate general in New York, Feb. 2, 1884; Poschinger, *Fürst Bismarck als Volkswirt*, II, 162.

immediately even in the event of increased duties. Nevertheless, Germany might suffer serious losses from being crowded out of the American market.[63] An article of the *Norddeutsche Allgemeine Zeitung* of March 1, no doubt inspired by the Foreign Office, spoke of the greater dependence of the United States on Europe than the reverse. The wheat-growing States of the Union owed their importance solely to the work of German farmers. On March 13, word was sent to St. Petersburg that Germany no longer wished to depend exclusively on the United States for petroleum; on certain conditions Germany was ready to grant Russia reduced customs rates in return for supplying petroleum. Possibilities of a commercial treaty were especially held out. On the same day, the Foreign Office inquired in London "whether East India or other British colonies could be developed as regards cotton and whether those countries might be considered for Germany's cotton supply." From London came the reply that North American cotton was preferred to Indian cotton.[64]

The Department of State, of course, was willing to make concessions. Frelinghuysen even admitted the tactical blunders of the American Minister in Berlin. It was impossible, he said, to compel great nations like Germany and the United States to yield through strong words; that was useless. Matters should be viewed calmly and deliberately. The *Washington Post* of February 16, 1884, also declared against retaliation. There was no reason why the two countries should not continue in the best of harmony.

But in the meantime a painful incident had aroused considerable popular feeling in both countries. Bismarck had always found an opponent of his policy in Eduard Lasker, the leader of the left wing of the National Liberal Party. In an address to the Reichstag on March 13, 1884, Bismarck said that Lasker weakened and impaired, as much as possible, any support that the Government and he as Chancellor might have expected from the National Liberal faction; he spoiled the broth as it were, and, if Lasker did give his support, he diverted it into channels where it was less useful and less acceptable. During the discussion of the constitution, no Government bill could be

[63] Poschinger, *Fürst Bismarck als Volkswirt,* I, 162.

[64] German publicists on the whole did not consider a customs war very favorably. Germany depended on American cotton, copper, petroleum, and foodstuffs, according to Sartorius von Waltershausen, *Deutsche Wirtschaftsgeschichte,* 413ff., and *Deutschland und die Handelspolitik der Vereinigten Staaten,* 75f. Prager, too, in *Die Handelsbeziehungen des Deutschen Reiches mit den Vereinigten Staaten,* 19, points out the great difference in value between American imports and German exports. Calwer, on the other hand, in *Die Meistbegünstigung der Vereinigten Staaten,* 122ff. (published, however, in 1902), does not judge the situation to have been unfavorable for Germany, since Russian imports, even by that time, had made Germany largely independent of American petroleum.

approved unless it bore the stamp of Lasker, and that could be obtained only on conditions which, in Bismarck's opinion, made the matter worse. In particular, the Chancellor blamed him for splitting the National Liberal Party, "the only one that ever endeavored to become a majority party." Bismarck said in 1878 that Lasker's activity, more than anything else, put obstacles in his way.[65] When Lasker took charge of the seceding element after the schism of the National Liberal Party, his opposition to Bismarck increased even more. They often clashed seriously in the parliamentary controversies over the new tariff policy. In the winter of 1883-84, Lasker made a lecture trip to the United States. Because of the existing tension it was natural for Bismarck to be displeased with the excursion of his opponent to the New World. He charged the German Minister to keep him well informed about Lasker's statements. Several times Lasker criticized Germany's domestic policy before American audiences. The *Washington Post* of December 10 reported Lasker to have said that American civilization was superior. In an interview in Galveston he spoke of the necessity of organizing a more determined and general opposition against Bismarck.[66] Nor did Lasker fail in his lectures to attack Germany's new economic policy. During his tour of the United States Lasker suddenly died of a heart attack on January 5, 1884. On January 9 Representative Ochiltree, a close friend of his family, submitted to the House a resolution expressing to the brother of the deceased and to the German Reichstag the sympathy of the House upon the death of the great German statesman whose "firm and constant exposition of and devotion to free and liberal ideas have materially advanced the social, political, and economic conditions of those people."[67] The resolution was passed by a nearly empty House and was transmitted to the American Legation in Berlin, which delivered it on February 9. The Chancellor refused to accept the resolution, however, because it contained a eulogy of his political adversary. On such occasions the Chancellor's self-control seems particularly admirable. In his first handwritten drafts of his instructions to Eisendecher on February 9 he was still exceedingly irritated by the imposition of being forced, as it were, to endorse personally an extravagant eulogy of his political antagonist. Statements similar to those just mentioned accumulated concerning Lasker, reaching a climax in the statement that Lasker's activity had been more harmful than beneficial to the development of the Reich. The final text, however, was written by a diplomat's hand: "Any recognition of the personal qualities of a

[65] Bismarck, *Gesammelte Werke*, XII, 412; Poschinger, *Fürst Bismarck, neue Tischgespräche*, II, 91.

[66] Bismarck, *Gesammelte Werke*, XII, 410.

[67] *Ibid.*, 411; Poschinger, *Fürst Bismarck und die Parlamentarier*, III, 117, footnote 2.

German abroad can only be gratifying for our national pride, particularly when it comes from so eminent a body as the American House of Representatives. I should therefore have gratefully received the communication from Mr. Sargent and asked His Majesty the Emperor's permission to present it to the Reichstag if the resolution of the ninth of this month did not simultaneously contain an expression of opinion on the tendency and effects of the political activity of Deputy Lasker that is contradictory to my conviction. According to my knowledge of the actual development, political and economic, of the German people, I cannot admit that opinion to correspond to the facts as experienced by me. I should not dare oppose my personal opinion to that of so august a body as the House of Representatives of the United States, had I not, in consequence of more than thirty years of participation in the domestic politics of Germany, acquired experience enough to encourage me to attach a certain competence to my own judgment within that sphere. I cannot make up my mind to submit to His Majesty a request for an authorization to communicate the resolution of the House of Representatives of the United States to the Reichstag, because in this case I should have to identify myself officially with, and ask His Majesty's approval of, an opinion the correctness of which I am unable to acknowledge." [68] In connection with a telegram from Eisendecher on February 20, Bismarck remarked that the presumption of an official governmental glorification of Lasker was disgraceful and humiliating to the German Government.

Despite his personal chagrin, it is surprising that Bismarck should have acted in such a serious fashion over a comparatively insignificant matter. Personal grudge certainly was not the determining factor. The Chancellor evidently wanted to seize the opportunity to rid himself of the American Minister, who was discomfiting to him. He therefore criticized Sargent for not having informed his Government in time that the procedure was not feasible. Eisendecher was asked to collect material against Mr. Sargent, for "as long as we have Mr. Sargent as American Minister, we cannot maintain the former good relations." Eisendecher was instructed to consider it his foremost mission to bring about a change in American representation (Rantzau for Foreign Office, Friedrichsruh, March 1). Thus the official statements of the Chancellor display a very personal animosity against the American Minister: "The pork retaliations and their exclusively anti-German motivation, while ignoring the same or even far more rigorous measures of other countries; the appointment and continued service of a Minister in Berlin who is hostile to the German Government and conspires with its opponents; toleration of Mr. Sargent's journalistic agitation and of his rela-

[68] Bismarck, *Gesammelte Werke*, XII, 411f.

tions with the leaders of the Progressive Party; the impertinent affront to the Reich Government by the German Progressive Party . . . all those facts could leave us indifferent only if we were indifferent to our own national dignity and to the disrespect shown for it by foreign countries" (to Eisendecher, Friedrichsruh, March 7). On March 8, Eisendecher was informed that the German Government, had it not been for the malicious anti-German pork policy, might have been contented with commissioning the Minister to say orally that it was not feasible to transmit the resolution, or with telling Mr. Sargent personally that transmission was impossible because he would only injure himself. The *Deutsche Tageblatt* was soon to publish an article, inspired by Bismarck, on the exceptional position of the American Minister which made its transmittal impossible. From the very beginning, the German Legation in Washington expected the Lasker resolution to make an unfavorable impression in Berlin. It is likely that Eisendecher had already discussed the matter with the Secretary of State. The situation became somewhat critical because the Department of State, for reasons of prestige, refused to withdraw the resolution. The American Government realized that it had made a mistake but requested the German Minister to prevent official rejection of the resolution. Eisendecher therefore cabled for permission to interpret Bismarck's note regarding rejection of the resolution in the sense that it would be returned only if the American Government so desired. Permission was granted. When Eisendecher officially called on the Secretary of State, an almost farcical incident occurred. Fearing an official return of the resolution, Frelinghuysen received him with a long face. They conversed about all sorts of other things, but still the resolution was not returned. After the Minister and Count Leyden, secretary of legation, had left the office of the Secretary of State they were dismayed to find that by mistake they had left the document on the table. Leyden thereupon returned at once and succeeded in obtaining the resolution before anyone had noticed it.[69] After the issue regarding the return of the resolution had thus been surmounted, the American Government found a way out of the difficulty by officially declaring that it was not interested in differences among the various organs of government in Germany. Bismarck sought no quarrel with the United States, but he faced the question as to whether there was not some plot in America to extend the front of his political opponents as far as the other side of the ocean. His experiences in the contest between church and state may have aroused his suspicion. In the Lasker case Bismarck had all the more reason to suspect the international origin of such an intrigue, as Lasker, because of his Jewish birth, had been

[69] Oral report of Count Leyden, the former Minister, who kindly consented to its publication.

highly feted by the strong Jewish element in the large American cities. Bismarck's point of view no doubt is reflected in a contemporary Foreign Office memorandum of the events leading up to the Lasker resolution. The memorandum centered about Lasker's Jewish affiliations. Likewise, Carl Schurz was not spared, being criticized for using the occasion to put himself in the limelight, and the question was raised as to possible ties between him and the liberal opposition in Germany.[70] In this respect the Chancellor never quite trusted Carl Schurz. When there was a chance for Schurz to be appointed Minister to Berlin in 1877, Bismarck objected because Schurz might form a political center as a result of his connections with liberalism.[71] Of course he did not wish to wound American sensibilities. On March 5 he confidentially wrote to Eisendecher that he did not think there were any ulterior motives in the resolution; he would not even call it tactless. Congress had been absolutely uninformed as to actual conditions. The House of Representatives merely intended to give general expression to America's friendly feelings for Germany which Bismarck had not unsuccessfully cultivated for more than twenty years. How interested Bismarck was in getting his opinion before the public is demonstrated by his acknowledgment of a message from the city of Marggrabowa. In his answer he warned them not to spread the misunderstanding, "just as if the resolution of the American House of Representatives had not been motivated solely by the desire to express America's good will for Germany."[72] In his speech of March 13, replying to an interpellation on the Lasker resolution, Bismarck discussed the friendly relations with the United States. Never had he spoken so eloquently on the friendship inherited from Frederick the Great. "I dare say that from the beginning of my Ministry until the present day nothing has happened to trouble the mutual relations, that I ascribe the same force and warmth to them today as I found when I took office, and that the events of which I am speaking at the moment are without influence upon them and will remain so." He in no way found fault with the Americans for the resolution and "never thought that any attack or malice against me and the Imperial policy or any implied criticism contained therein of the Emperor and his policy had ever been intended by any American; they simply did not know what sort of a man Mr. Lasker was."[73] Thus he considered the affair completely settled when he received another letter from Eisendecher on March 28. The report contained this statement: "The

[70] *Promemoria über Veranlassung, Entstehung und Übermittlung der Lasker-Resolution*, Mar. 13, 1884.
[71] Herbert Bismarck to Bülow, Varzin, Nov. 22, 1877.
[72] Poschinger, *Fürst Bismarck und die Parlamentarier*, III, 119f.
[73] Bismarck, *Gesammelte Werke*, XII, 408, 409.

matter may consequently be regarded as settled"; Bismarck commented on the margin: "Long ago."

The Chancellor now turned against his political adversaries with increased vigor. In the *Norddeutsche Allgemeine Zeitung* he complained that so little indignation had been aroused by the fact that a foreign body had attempted to meddle in internal affairs of the Reich. For the most part he personally conducted the press campaign.[74] Certain newspapers, he permitted the *Norddeutsche Allgemeine Zeitung* to state on February 23, did not allow the opportunity to pass without again demonstrating the meanness of their character. It was not among American Representatives but only among German party members of a Secessionist Progressive complexion that one would have to look for a conscious intention to glorify German tendencies and partisans that were antagonistic to the Government. "In this case we are really convinced of an intrigue carefully planned long ago, all the more so since there are men among the leaders of the Secessionist faction whose intimate connection with American partisans must have considerably facilitated the execution of their intention. They evidently arranged the scheme so as by devious means to hitch the Prussian Government, against its will, to the wagon of the Secessionist Party. They are heirs to the political legacy Deputy Lasker may have left. To seek to increase that even after Lasker's death by a sort of speculative venture is an effort which, to use an American expression, one might call 'smart'; but they should not have taken it for granted that the Chancellor would readily play the part assigned to him." For purposes of comparison, the *Magdeburger Zeitung* had referred to the assassination of Czar Alexander: "To express to the Russian people Germany's sympathy because of the assassination of the Czar did not mean meddling with Russian national affairs. No Russian paper, however mad, would have dreamed of saying such a thing." The *Norddeutsche Allgemeine Zeitung* of February 25 remarked in reply that the Chancellor by no means rejected the expression of sympathy on the part of the American House of Representatives at Lasker's death, but merely refused to transmit officially an expression of opinion to the effect that Mr. Lasker's Liberalist policy had promoted the political and material welfare of Germany. "In order to consider our expression of sympathy for the death of the Czar of Russia as analogous, one would have to descend to the level of the logical capacity of the *Magdeburger Zeitung* and its readers. For both of them we beg to offer another example which may conform to the range of

---

[74] The articles in the *Norddeutsche Allgemeine Zeitung* on the Lasker case were mostly written by Bismarck himself, as shown by their style and the handwritten drafts.

their minds: If the Imperial Ambassador in London expected the British Minister of Foreign Affairs, Lord Granville, to present an official declaration to Parliament saying that Sir Stafford Northcote, by manifesting his conservative mind, had rendered important services to the 'social, political, and economic conditions not only of the British but of all nations of the world'— in that case the analogy would be complete. Sir Stafford Northcote is the leader of the present opposition against the British Government, just as Mr. Lasker was at least one of the leaders of the Progressive-Secessionist opposition against the Government of the Emperor. To expect the Chancellor to inform the Reichstag that Lasker's opposition was meritorious and beneficial or, in other words, that his own policy as opposed by Lasker was injurious, is exactly equivalent to expecting Mr. Gladstone to acknowledge publicly and officially that Sir Stafford Northcote had deserved well of his country by moving a vote of no confidence." The *Nationalzeitung* mockingly asked the Government for more information as to whether they took the affair seriously or lightly, for otherwise it might become tragicomical. The reply of the *Norddeutsche Allgemeine Zeitung* of March 1 was: "We record with gratification the attempt of the *Nationalzeitung* at leading us *ad absurdum* in dialectics. We set a different antithesis against the antithesis of the Secessionist sheet: either its attempt was made '*mala fide*' or the scholars of the *Nationalzeitung, quoad artem logicam*, are still in a stage of pitiful lack of breeding."

The Reichstag originally intended to reply to the resolution from the floor. Bismarck threatened to dissolve the Reichstag if that occurred because of interference with the prerogatives of the Emperor.[75] He was quite right in stating that the most vehement attacks against him came from the German-American press. The Indianapolis *Tägliche Telegraph* of February 23 stated: "The caricature that is presented by the alleged parliamentary system of government over there stares at us from every line. Every word testifies that the Germans are languishing under the guardianship of a dictator who received his training in Russia." The former "Forty-Eighter Democrats" also wanted to be heard: "All German-Americans no doubt are of the opinion that a republican system would stand the test in Germany as well as in the United States. If it were ours to say, Germany would be a republic," wrote the Philadelphia *Neue Presse* on February 21. But the Chancellor had his partisans too. A number of Anglo-American papers in particular sided with him. The *San Francisco Chronicle* of February 23, comparing the controversy between Lasker's party and Bismarck with the quarrel between the Confederates and

---

[75] Rantzau to Foreign Office, Friedrichsruh, Mar. 4; *Norddeutsche Allgemeine Zeitung*, Mar. 8, 1884.

Lincoln's absolutism during the crisis of 1861 to 1865, severely attacked the American Minister in Berlin for describing Germany's prohibition of pork imports as a measure inimical to the United States. In the *St. Louis Post-Dispatch* of February 15, W. C. Gibson declared that the prohibition of pork imports was a European affair: "The two nations are too great to be jealous or envious of each other. Each wishes to promote its own civilization in its own individual way. The happiness of the peoples of both countries can be greatly advanced by mutual good will and respect." At this time the military preparedness of the Union was publicly criticized. The *Evening Star* of February 16 characterized Germany as "the most extreme and arrogant despotism of the civilized world," telling its readers that America's military establishment was woefully neglected. Sargent, on his return to the United States, told a reporter of the *New York Herald,* according to an interview published on July 6, that Bismarck merely smiled at an intimation of war since the many Germans living in America would never let things go that far. Moreover, New York was absolutely defenseless against an attack.

Continued criticism by the German Government press made Sargent's position untenable. For a time he hoped for a strong gesture from his Government. To an inquiry from the Department of State as to whether something could be done about the press campaign against him, he replied that his situation was intolerable; Bismarck had misrepresented matters to the Reichstag; none of Lasker's friends were personally known to him. He put his fate in the hands of the President. ". . . I think closing the Legation the only adequate return for such an invasion of the sanctity of a diplomatic representative. But I make that suggestion with extreme diffidence from its gravity and hope its bearings will be fully weighed." Sargent requested that the German Minister be told that he had acted in accord with the Department of State, and that information to the same effect be published in the papers. That would help considerably. Sargent defended himself against the charge that by delivering the resolution he had embarrassed his Government. Refusal to do so would have meant insubordination, he explained, and yet the German Foreign Office had turned him down like a lackey.[76] On March 16 Sargent again requested that he not be recalled, for if he were, independent service in the future would be impossible. Bismarck's point of view was this, he pointed out: We want good relations with America as long as she lets conditions be dictated to her. But the Department of State was loath to adopt such violent tactics. It offered Sargent another post as Minister to Russia, but this he

[76] Sargent was no longer received in the Foreign Office after he had delivered the resolution.

declined, taking instead a prolonged leave from which he returned to Berlin only to present his letter of recall.[77]

The Minister's departure from Berlin relieved the tension. That Bismarck in his speech to the Reichstag on March 13 had been very considerate of American pride, has been mentioned. The discussion in Congress was likewise less stormy than had been expected. On February 28 Representative Deuster read to Congress the reply of the German liberal union to the resolution, in which there was mentioned the desirability of deepening friendly relations. That reply, said Deuster, reflected the true sentiments of the German people. The following speaker, Gunter, shared this opinion. The overwhelming majority of the German people, he said, felt very friendly toward America. Kasson objected to further discussion. "When we are informed that our rights or our interests or our honor have in any way been affected I have no doubt there will be perfect accord on both sides of this House in respect to the proper action to be taken." On March 10 Representative Hiscock offered a resolution "That this House can not but express its surprise and regret that it should be even temporarily within the power of a single too-powerful subject to interfere with such a simple, natural, and spontaneous expression of kindly feeling between two great nations, and thus to detract from the position and prestige of the crown on the one hand, and from the rights of the mandatories of the people on the other." However, the Committee on Foreign Affairs was wise enough to reject that resolution on the ground that it was not a question of relations between two organs of the two Governments. Ochiltree, in a lengthy speech on March 19, lauded the merits of the deceased in whose memory he hoped the German people would sometime erect a monument. Hiscock spoke of the antisemitic background of the matter. Phelps closed the discussion with a very conciliatory speech in which he said that nothing remained for the House to do after Bismarck and Frelinghuysen had settled the case.[78]

Sargent was replaced by the level-headed John A. Kasson, a former Minister to Austria, and a great admirer of Bismarck. At the outset, he avoided a discussion of the pork problem. Instead, he strove to create a better atmosphere, in which he was soon successful. To be sure, the prohibition of pork imports remained; the American tariff policy made it difficult for the

[77] Sargent to Frelinghuysen, Berlin, Mar. 15, 1884, and telegrams Mar. 27 and 29, 1884, Dept. State, *Despatches, Germany,* 35. For an unfavorable comment on Bismarck's conduct in the Lasker conflict, cf. A. D. White, *Autobiography,* I, 588f.
[78] Feb. 28, Mar. 10 and 19, 1884; *Congressional Record,* XV, pt. II, 1463ff., 1766, and pt. III, 2073ff.

Reich to make concessions. President Grover Cleveland threatened in 1888 to impose higher duties on German goods, but nothing was actually done. James G. Blaine, Secretary of State for the second time, in 1889, proceeded with renewed vigor to settle the pork problem. He first turned to France. In a note of July 11, 1889, he expressed his regret at the failure of the French Cabinets to have the Chamber cancel the prohibition of pork imports. It was, he said, an unfair and unnecessary discrimination against the United States. No case of illness due to American pork had ever been proved. He intimated the possibility that Congress might take measures of retaliation. The French Minister in Washington admitted that the prohibition no longer was based on grounds of public health, but his Government was unable to have the law rescinded in view of the strong opposition in the Chamber.[79] In August 1890 came the long-awaited act of Congress, not in the form of retaliation, however, but in the form of a law for meat inspection that one year later, with some amendments, at last satisfied European demands. The Americans had forsaken their stubborn self-righteousness. A minority report submitted to the Committee on Foreign Relations stated that the desire of the European Governments to protect their domestic production was the real reason for the prohibition of imports. The American people had no cause for complaint. "After surrounding ourselves," the report said, "for more than twenty years with a protective tariff wall so high as to exclude virtually all the products of Germany which compete with ours, it is rather late for us to advocate retaliation against a Government which merely follows our example. In fact Germany's action is retaliation, and the cry of 'Stop thief' cannot change the true condition of things. We have got to learn that we are not so great and independent as to enable us to defy the laws of political economy and the amenities of international trade with impunity. We have been told again and again that our true policy was to shut up our manufactures from the competition of the world, and that all the nations thus excluded would be compelled, nevertheless, to buy our breadstuffs and provisions—that they could not do without them. We are greatly surprised and indignant when one important customer says he can get along without our hog products, and forbids their coming in; and we propose to retaliate! For what? For simply and frankly forbidding them to be imported. Suppose, instead of doing this, Germany had imposed a duty of 100 per cent. on them, which as effectually prohibited their importation, what then? Where would be our so-called retaliation? The undersigned can see no difference whatever in the two methods of prohibition, so far as

[79] A. F. Tyler, *Blaine*, 299f.

results are concerned, only that one is manly and direct, while the other is indirect and based on false pretenses." [80]

The President recommended, in the event of a continued embargo, that German and French products be shut out for the same sanitary reasons. Germany, of course, did not agree with that point of view. An article in the *Nationalzeitung* of March 28 stated that imports of German pork products into the United States consisted only of high quality sausages, the manufacture of which was carried out with particular care.[81] The correct method for having the import prohibition rescinded would be to effect a reform of the American packing houses. In the Reichstag sessions of January 22-23, 1891, a motion of Barth and Associates for cancellation of the import prohibition of March 6, 1883, was acted upon. Again the same arguments were advanced and again the Government replied that the problem of public health was still urgent. The representative of the Government conceded, however, that there was no intention of indefinitely prolonging the prohibition. But the present American meat-inspection law was declared unsatisfactory inasmuch as the control provided for was not compulsory and was not carried out until after the meat was already packed.[82]

The quarrel about the import prohibition on pork was finally settled within the framework of general tariff negotiations. Harrison's victory over Cleveland in the Presidential elections of 1888 once more gave the protective tariff party the upper hand. It began at once working out a new tariff. Many in the Republican Party wanted to have sugar placed on the free list, while others, led by Secretary of State Blaine, favored resumption of negotiations for most-favored-nation treaties. The result was a compromise. Sugar and other tropical products were put on the free list, while the President was authorized to impose by proclamation duties on otherwise duty-free importations of sugar, molasses, tea, coffee, and hides as soon as any country exporting such articles to the Union placed "unjust and unreasonable" duties on the same articles of the Union. Germany at that time exported much beet sugar to the United States. Consequently, she was vitally interested in not having the reciprocity clause of the McKinley Tariff of October 1, 1890, applied to her sugar. When the United States negotiated with countries producing cane sugar, on the basis of the reciprocity clause, Germany wished to participate. On account of the illness of Count Arco-Valley, the German Minister, the chargé d'affaires, Mumm von Schwarzenstein, conducted the negotiations for Germany, while

[80] *Senate Reports*, 48th Cong., 1st sess., no. 345, pt. 2. Keim, *German-American Political Relations*, 71f., footnote 22.

[81] *Foreign Relations*, 1888, pt. I, 629f.

[82] *Sten. Berichte*, VIII, 1, 1890-91, 49th and 50th sess., II, 1096ff.

the United States was represented by John W. Foster. Mumm declared his Government was ready to cancel the prohibition on the import of American pork on the basis of the new meat-inspection law, with the understanding that the reciprocity clause would not be applied to German sugar. In his reply, the President could not refrain from a little sarcasm: Germany should not confuse cancellation of the import prohibition with an unrelated question, since Germany had shut out American pork because of its danger to health. On the other hand, he declared himself to be willing to negotiate with the German Government for commercial reciprocity "with the greatest spirit of liberality, and the prompt action of that government regarding the pork inspection will have its due weight in determining the terms of the reciprocity arrangement."[83] Thus the Saratoga Agreement was concluded. It took the form of an exchange of declarations between John W. Foster and the German chargé d'affaires. The German Government, on August 22, 1891, promised readmission of American pork and pork products to Germany, and declared its readiness to grant the United States such reductions of customs duties on agricultural products as had been granted or were going to be granted to Germany by the United States in the course of the pending negotiations for a commercial treaty. In return, the American Government agreed not to enforce the reciprocity clause of the McKinley Tariff against German prod-ucts. The Saratoga Agreement greatly aided in clearing the atmosphere between the two countries.[84] Bismarck did not favor this particular solution of the problem. As a matter of fact he permitted the *Hamburger Nachrichten* of November 11, 1891, to say that in the American-German case the aim of the concession consisted in "attaching officially the same trustworthiness to a foreign certificate as to that heretofore only enjoyed by a domestic official certificate. This is a very considerable concession and an expression of confidence in the reliability of foreign statements that other countries as a rule do not grant and that we have not hitherto had with regard to all peoples and all foreign Governments."[85] In the series of commercial struggles, the Saratoga Agreement as a matter of fact was but an armistice. By the Dingley Tariff of 1897 the American Government violated the principal idea of the agreement. But the controversy about prohibition of pork imports is an im-

[83] Cf. Keim, *German-American Political Relations,* 74.

[84] For the Saratoga Agreement, cf. Poschinger, *Die deutschen Handels-und Schiffahrtsverträge,* 443ff.; Keim, *German-American Political Relations,* 74ff.; Bemis, *Secretaries of State,* VIII, 191; Foster, *Memoirs,* II, 12ff.; *Senate Executive Documents,* 52d Cong., 1st sess., no. 119, Exhibit K.

[85] Penzler, *Bismarck und die Hamburger Nachrichten,* I, 312f.

portant indication of the fact that business between the two countries was intimately interrelated and that points of friction had developed.

However, it would be too early to speak of sharp competition in the world markets. At that time, the foreign trade of the United States was still in its infancy. It lacked adaptability to the demands of other countries. Occasionally, the superiority of German and British merchants was frankly admitted. Americans thought it disgraceful that Germany should have so large a share of Central American commerce.[86] The American commission which investigated the opportunities for United States trade in Central and South America at the beginning of the eighties, in its reports complained of the lack of an American spirit of enterprise. For instance, a report from New Orleans dated December 31, 1884: "It has been said that for forty years the people of the United States have paid little attention to the foreign trade, and what our fathers knew about the subject has never been learned by their children. We have been so busily engaged in the development of domestic resources, so absorbed in stretching a net-work of railroads between every city and hamlet of our States, in connecting our great agricultural regions with the sea-board, that our foreign commerce has been comparatively forgotten."[87] This self-evaluation may be supplemented by a German opinion: The North American industrialist generally faced the demands of international trade relations without understanding or perhaps even with aversion. According to his own admission he was too much favored by the existing chances for quick profits at home to endeavor to adjust himself to the demands of a foreign market that would force alien conditions upon him in the manufacture of his products.[88] As late as 1878 the German consul in St. Louis advised German trade organizations to start business in Central America, the countries of which were then still considered as open to exploitation commercially (to the Imperial Chancery February 16). Nevertheless, United States trade was also constantly increasing in Latin America. The German merchant gained ground in Central and South America. Between 1874 and 1885 total exports from the Central American countries to Hamburg rose from RM 3,094,190 to RM 13,838,890, exports from Mexico alone from RM 4,869,380 to RM 10,-228,780.[89] German business houses controlled a large part of the exports from Brazil and German capital was active in Venezuela. But if the Union looked with displeasure upon German success in Central and South America,

---

[86] *Consular Reports,* 1886, XX, no. 70, 373.

[87] *House Executive Documents,* 48th Cong., 2d sess., no. 226, "Report from the Central and South American Commissioners."

[88] *Deutsches Handelsarchiv,* 1886, pt. II, 55.

[89] *Ibid.,* 1887, II, 24.

there may have been political as well as commercial considerations involved.

Long before its completion, an interoceanic canal occupied considerable prominence in the political discussions of the United States. Originally, the idea of a canal had been hailed in many fine words as an admirable means of conciliating and binding nations to each other. Later, however, the Americans seemed to think it would be a great advantage to have the canal at least built by an American company. It was only a short jump from there to the conviction that the canal would have to come exclusively under American control and to serve American commerce alone. The Presidential message of March 8, 1880, expressed the case bluntly and briefly: The policy of the United States was directed to the control of the canal.[90] American nervousness was increased by the fact that for a long time the location of the canal remained uncertain. Directly or indirectly, it was certain to affect the policy of the United States toward the Latin American countries. Enforcement of the Monroe Doctrine was an object of special concern for American politicians. President Grant's message of December 4, 1871, had extended the scope of the Doctrine: In the natural course of events the political ties of Europe with the American continent would end completely.[91] Thus all events in any way connected with the problem of the canal, politically or economically, were watched with particular care. For comprehensible reasons the Americans did not wish to concede to any European power the privilege of possessing parts of the canal, much less of controlling it. Any possibilities that might in future have some bearing on American security or American trade were taken into account. Thus everywhere we see excessive anxiety, and even suspicion, of harmless German trade relations in Latin American countries.[92]

Bismarck had a theoretical opinion of his own on the Monroe Doctrine. We find it expressed in an article of the *Hamburger Nachrichten* of February 9, 1896. He called it an impudence: "It is our impression that the great wealth that the American soil furnishes to its inhabitants causes some American legislators to overestimate their own rights and to underestimate the independence of other American and European powers."[93] Nevertheless, Bismarck as a practical politician was always considerate of American sensibilities.

---

[90] *Senate Executive Documents,* 46th Cong., 2d sess., no. 112, "Proposed Interoceanic Canal."

[91] *Cambridge Modern History,* III, 22.

[92] For the development of the Panama policy of the United States, cf. E. E. Sparks, *National Development, 1877-85,* in *American Nation Series,* XXIII, 202ff. and Coolidge, *United States as a World Power,* 267ff.

[93] Hofmann, *Fürst Bismarck,* II, 357.

This consideration was particularly evident during the war between Peru and Chile in 1879. A few European powers were planning joint intervention for the protection of their commerce, and for general political reasons Bismarck did not wish to stay out. But in view of the fact that the Americans were jealously watching any development of European power in their hemisphere, he advised the British Government to have the United States participate in the negotiations. Without American cooperation, the Chancellor would be opposed to armed intervention. On the other hand, mère diplomatic intervention would have possibility of success only in case the party dissatisfied with the settlement knew for certain that the American Government would not support it.[94] Bucher, on Bismarck's behalf, subsequently discussed American participation in the intervention with Andrew D. White, the American Minister in Berlin. White, however, referred to the Monroe Doctrine and declined to participate.[95] Bismarck fully realized the practical value of the Monroe Doctrine for American policy. In instructions to Schlözer dated December 18, 1871, Bismarck discussed in detail an alleged statement made by the German Minister in Washington concerning the Monroe Doctrine: "It is not for us, in our relations with the American Government, to take official notice of a doctrine upheld by a number of American statesmen, although we are conscious of it and have to take it into consideration. To mention it would be the more regrettable as the matter in question did not even call for it. The passage in President Monroe's message of 1823 from which the doctrine evolved was caused by the apprehension prevailing at the time lest European powers support Spain in her fight against the rebellious colonies. Monroe declared it impossible for the Allied Powers (Holy Alliance) to extend their political system to any part of the American Continent without endangering the happiness and peace of the United States, and he did not wish the American Continent to be regarded as an object of future colonization by European powers. Neither of these points was involved in our suggestion; and if the American Government suspects such ulterior purposes in any of the other powers, there would be no better method for preventing their realization than joint action by Germany and the United States as we proposed. . . ."

Germany's policy in Venezuela clearly proved that the Chancellor was absolutely sincere in his intention to respect the Monroe Doctrine. Some time before, the North German Federation had tried to collect claims in Venezuela of certain North German citizens. But revolutionary events there in 1869 and 1870 made the Venezuelan Government unwilling, if not unable, to meet its

[94] Herbert Bismarck to Bülow, Varzin, June 2, 1879.
[95] A. D. White, *Autobiography*, I, 596ff.

financial obligations. A few European states considered the idea of joint action since they had more or less money involved. The German Minister thought collective action was the only way to accomplish anything at all. Latin American respect for Europe had greatly declined since the execution of Emperor Maximilian. The German Reich entertained no ambitious plans, but merely wanted payment of debts estimated at approximately $56,000, and protection of its nationals from treatment by the Venezuelan Government in violation of international law. As to chances for trade in the West Indies, the German Minister in Caracas was not very optimistic: Venezuela could develop only under the control of a great power, but the Americans objected to this. The Minister regretted this; he thought—and this is the remarkable point—that American control of the West Indies would be to the interest of Germany (April 18, 1872, confidential).

Berlin was strongly desirous of reaching an agreement with the United States regarding the joint procedure planned. On June 1, 1871, Gerolt inquired at the Department of State regarding it. The Department, obviously surprised to see Germany among Venezuela's creditors, "had a very vivid recollection of joint European action in Mexico" and wished to be informed of the real purpose of the undertaking proposed. In general the Department of State was ready to adopt similar measures if they would compel Venezuela to adhere more strictly to her obligations. However, in case of forcible proceedings against Venezuela, the United States could not remain an indifferent observer. Bancroft very calmly wrote from Berlin on July 6, 1871: "The German Government knows very well that the days of the colonial system have passed long since. It will not try to restore a system that certainly belongs to the past and cannot be revived." The American plan was essentially this: The United States would seize the Venezuelan customs houses and distribute the revenues among the creditor countries in proportion to the amounts of debt. Since American claims were by far the largest, this plan was justified. Indeed, Bismarck announced his approval at once. He advised the European creditor countries to accept the American suggestion. Thus the American Government was informed that the warship *Gazelle* would be sent to Venezuela, and it was stated that the Reich had only commercial and no political interests to protect. "We owe it to the personal interests of our national and of our stately dignity to adhere to a just and lawful treatment of the same, and believe, in order to attain that purpose, we shall have to accustom the Governments and people of South America to the idea, hitherto strange to them, that the German flag represents a Navy, which is determined to carefully respect the law of nations on its part, but at the same time, if need be, will not be restrained, by its limited power, from exacting of others to accord the same rights to Germans." [96]

[96] For Germany's Venezuelan policy, cf. Bismarck to the missions in Paris, Rome, London, The Hague, Copenhagen, Madrid, Feb. 20, 1872; reports from Caracas, July 21 and Nov. 17, 1871; Schlözer to Fish, Jan. 20, 1872, confidential, Dept. State, *Notes from German Legation*, 11.

CHAPTER II

GERMAN EMIGRATION AND EMIGRATION
POLICY AFTER THE ESTABLISHMENT
OF THE REICH

I T IS impossible to discuss commercial relations between Germany and the
United States without considering emigration. It was one of the primary
factors in the commercial relations between the two countries. Of what importance is the turnover of goods as compared to the capital which the German
emigrant brought to America in his person and in his labor? This capital
cannot be expressed by figures alone. The emigrants caused new connections
to be established and new markets to be opened. From a general point of view,
German emigration, particularly emigration in the seventies and eighties,
resulted in a great advantage to American business and a great loss to German
business.

It had been hoped that German emigration would decline considerably
after the establishment of the Reich. This hope was in vain. The total number
of emigrants in 1871 was only 76,224; it jumped to 128,152 in the following
year, but dropped again after 1874 because of the beginning of a world-wide
business depression. In 1878 another rise set in, which in 1881 reached the
maximum of 220,902. The year 1891 may be called a turning point in German emigration, for the curve steadily, although in a zigzag course, declined
thereafter.[1] The figures are as follows:

836,970 between 1871 and 1881
1,241,610   "   1882 " 1891
431,859   "   1892 " 1901[2]

[1] Department of Commerce and Labor, Bureau of Statistics, *Statistical Abstract*,
XXX, 65-69.
[2] Joseephy, *Die deutsche überseeische Auswanderung*, 33f.

174

The causes were various. It will be recalled that the emigrants of the eighteenth and the second half of the nineteenth centuries were driven from their homes chiefly by religious and social and later by political troubles. Since the sixties economic causes increasingly predominated. The paths of the European countries and the United States had parted. In some of the industrial countries of Europe, especially Great Britain and Germany, the spread of industrialization and the resulting overpopulation tended to decrease the available land and deprive the rural workers and farmers of their chances for making a living or for acquiring property. At the same time, in the United States great possibilities for rural settlements still existed. As a result, emigration to the United States, particularly from rural districts, greatly increased. But this was by no means an exclusively materialistic movement. The main wave passed over the Nordic countries or countries of Nordic origin—Great Britain, Scandinavia, and Germany. It was a final revolt of agrarian man against mechanization and uprooting. These emigrants were driven abroad by their longing for land of their own.

German emigration was stimulated by the great shifts of population. As late as 1882, some 42.51 percent of the total population engaged in agriculture, but only 28.65 percent did so in 1907; industry employed 35.51 percent in 1882 and 42.75 percent in 1907.[3] So huge a shifting of population within the national boundaries necessarily resulted in hardships for the individual. Industry was unable to absorb so many people in so short a time. External impetus came from the agrarian crisis that had been steadily increasing since the middle of the seventies. A slump in agricultural prices was paralleled by a rise in wages. The cost of agricultural production increased in proportion. Farms dependent on labor not infrequently got into debt, which resulted in forced sales. Industry being able to pay higher wages, the rural regions suffered from an appreciable scarcity of labor that made intensive farming impossible. Agriculture lost its most efficient forces; it often had to resort to seasonal workers. Local home industries disappeared. Many people who had turned to agriculture when the situation was favorable were crowded out again when prices dropped. They consequently looked for new opportunities to make a living in other lands. West Prussia and Pomerania were particularly hard hit by the agrarian depression. From those states, therefore, emigration was the greatest. From regions where big estates prevailed, rural workers and descendants of those owning small farms generally emigrated. In areas where the land was divided into small parcels, the emigrants came from independent owners of small tracts of land. For this period Germany

[3] *Ibid.,* 54. The following account is based largely on this work, 72ff.

has no accurate statistics that classify emigration on the basis of vocations. American records, however, show rather clearly how it was distributed. Needless to say, other professions were also affected by the depression. Emigration to the United States was very advantageous in that but little capital was needed to start a business. American wages remained comparatively high because of a steady demand for skilled labor. Many immigrants had their traveling expenses paid by their American relatives. Emigration always increased in the wake of poor crops. When American friends and relatives told German country people of the fabulous wages over there—two or three dollars a day—the latter were of course only too glad to pull up stakes and try their luck in America. In the southwestern part of Germany emigration was chiefly stimulated by a rapid increase in population that assumed serious proportions wherever no industries had developed to absorb labor.[4] Additional reasons, of course, might be mentioned. It is safe to say that no cause can possibly be imagined that influences human affairs and that does not at the same time affect emigration.[5] General conscription has been mentioned as among the principal causes. In so large a group of emigrants, there were no doubt many young men who wished to escape military service. But in most cases that was not the decisive motive. Great Britain, without general conscription, sent abroad just as large a stream of emigrants. Some of the American consuls in Germany did not consider military service a principal cause of emigration. Consul George L. Catlin in Stuttgart, for example, in a report of March 8, 1881, pointed out that the Prussian military law of 1867 did not influence emigration.[6] On the contrary, it was said that military service was popular as a part of the national traditions. Moreover, the Americans acknowledged the high educational value of military training. They found in it an explanation of the self-discipline and efficiency of the Germans. Next after the enticing economic prospects in the United States, the general human urge "to get on" may be considered the chief cause of emigration, if a definite formula must be attached to the movement.

Emigration to the United States from Great Britain and the Scandinavian countries developed under very similar conditions. It was largely brought about by the world business depression. British emigration reached the peak in 1883 as a result of the great crisis in Ireland. Most of the British emigrants also went to the United States, averaging at least 100,000 people annually for the decade from 1880 to 1890. The Irish did not, of course, care to live again in a country under the British flag, while the British laborers did not possess

---

[4] Sering, *Die landwirtschaftliche Konkurrenz Nordamerikas,* 98ff.
[5] Joseephy, *Die deutsche überseeische Auswanderung,* 37.
[6] *Consular Reports,* 1881, II, no. 6, 564.

a highly developed national spirit. In the case of Great Britain emigration was likewise connected with the problem of distribution of land. Elimination of the duty on grain resulted in a shift from grain raising to grazing and dairying, and the country no longer was able to produce its own food supply.[7]

The Americans realized the difficulty caused by overpopulation in Germany. The Bureau of Statistics in Washington, in a report of February 9, 1887, described the situation correctly: "The position of Germany is peculiar, in that it has a rapidly increasing population, that is continually crowding upon the limited areas, as yet unoccupied or uncultivated, and upon the opportunities for profitable employment. There is no outlet, such as the vast plains of Russia offer, to the increasing population of that country for colonizing from within—if I may use the term—a process that has prevailed in the United States. Prussia was long the 'colony' of the other parts of Germany, the tide of migration flowing from the rural districts into towns, from towns into cities, and from the cities to the capital, wherever the highest returns were offered to labor."[8]

Americans generally regarded German immigration with favor until the eighties, although there was a tendency to look condescendingly upon those who were not one hundred percent American. The capital brought in by an individual person was estimated at $100; his labor was calculated at $1,000.[9] Immigration was good business for the country receiving it. A bill for restricting immigration was submitted to Congress in 1872, but a radical change in immigration policy did not take place until very much later. Save for individual complaints, the American representatives abroad considered the German settler as a valuable addition for their country. It was generally hoped that the monopoly of German immigration would be retained for the United States in the future, inasmuch as it had contributed so much toward the development of the country.[10] The conservative basis of German character was especially praised. A consular report of 1890 says: "No one who has

[7] Cf. Rathgen, *Englische Auswanderung und Auswanderungspolitik,* 156ff.

[8] *House Executive Documents,* 49th Cong., 2d sess., no. 157.

[9] "Concerning German emigration American economists have two different points of view, on the one hand the advantage accruing to the country from the labor of the immigrant in general, and on the other hand the amount of cash he brings with him. Some of the Germans arrive here almost penniless, but many of them have larger or smaller sums of money with them. The average amount of capital immigrating in this way is estimated at $100 a head, and the labor value of each German immigrant at $1,000 at least." Schlözer to Bülow, Washington, Nov. 2, 1875.

[10] Sargent to Frelinghuysen, Berlin, Mar. 13, 1883: "Our relations with Germany, a country which contributes to our own one of the best elements of the citizenship, continue to be cordial."

lived awhile in the German countryside but feels anew the conviction that in patient and painstaking industry, thrift, and the serious character which is antirevolutionary and truly civic, the Germans are the most admirable people on the continent of Europe. The Socialist movement in Germany is a rationalist movement in politics. There is no large revolutionary or anarchistic sentiment in Germany. The Germans expound the most daring theories but leave others to exploit them. They respect authority, love institutions, and take a good slice of a century to hunt up a constitution for a constitutional government after they have decided to have one. The German influence in the United States, on the whole, is, and will continue to be, conservative."[11] Such opinions partly explain the fact that an influx of socialist ideas from Germany was not feared so much as might otherwise have been the case.[12] For a long time the Americans believed themselves entirely immune from socialism. As late as the beginning of the eighties, they did not reckon on labor strikes and considered that therein they had a great advantage over Europe. But the subsequent big strikes and anarchist plots opened their eyes. From the very beginning, the Germans played a leading part in the socialist movement in the United States. When the socialist question temporarily came to the fore, Americans of German descent had to listen to much unfriendly criticism. But that did not materially change the immigration policy. The opening up of new free land reduced the socialist movement in the United States to absolute insignificance.[13] Not until colonization gradually stopped and the influx began of immigrants of the Latin and Slavic races, whose low standard of living unfavorably influenced wages, did a change occur in American immigration policy. Europe was blamed for seeking an easy way to rid itself of its paupers and criminals.[14] Immigration of contract labor was prohibited in 1886. A report of the German Minister in Washington dated August 2, 1888, mentioned new bills for the restriction of immigration, aimed in particular at the Italians. Primarily, attempts to bring discharged convicts to America were severely criticized. The editor of the *New Yorker Staats-Zeitung* told of various European organizations whose purpose was to send discharged convicts to the United States. Similarly, the German consulate in Chicago on July 21, 1888,

---

[11] *Special Consular Reports,* II, 247f.

[12] An anonymous article in the *North American Review,* CXXVIII, no. 269 (Apr. 1879), dealt in detail with German socialism.

[13] In 1892 the Socialist Party managed to poll only 20,000 votes in the Presidential elections, Beard, *Rise of American Civilization,* II, 252.

[14] This sort of criticism was, of course, exaggerated. Richmond Mayo-Smith, *Die Einwanderung in die Vereinigten Staaten,* 269ff., proves that mental diseases and criminality were comparatively no more numerous among the immigrants than among the native-born population.

described the growing objection to immigration: The industrial workers, belonging to one of the most numerous and powerful groups of interests, believed that the number of laborers in the United States fully met the demands of domestic industry, and that newly immigrated laborers, by selling their labor for a pittance, were forcing American workmen from their jobs. As the employers were enjoying tariff protection from the competition of cheap goods, so labor was entitled to protection by law from the competition of cheap immigrant labor. The second group of opponents of immigration advanced political arguments. It charged that many immigrants were infected by socialist and communist tendencies, and that recent immigrants were largely responsible for the bombing plots of 1886. The third group, finally, was interested in the preservation of American traditions. The author of this report added "this tradition may be characterized as a remnant of puritan religious institutions, morals, and thought, which hitherto have contributed so essentially to the moulding of the national mind."

An article in the *New York Times* of April 15, 1887, illustrates very clearly the change in public opinion. The paper stated that a questionnaire of the Commissioner of the Wisconsin Labor Bureau had demonstrated a strong aversion to any further Government encouragement of immigration. "We do not want criminals, and there is a law for their exclusion. We do not want insane persons or paupers, but they come in spite of the law. . . . We do not want the thousands of laborers who are coming in with the intention of living here for a few years upon food that the native laborer rejects, of working for very low wages, and of then returning to Europe to spend the remainder of their days. We do not need them. We are better off without them. They are willing to live on food that is little better than garbage, their habitations are nests of filth and disease, and their competition tends to degrade the native workmen. Colonies of such immigrants in this city are a standing menace to the city's health. The country would gain by excluding them." Thus the immigrant had ceased to be regarded merely as an advantage for the country, although such criticism applied least of all to the Germans. Prosperity of the masses was the gospel of the country. As soon as prosperity was threatened, legislation sought to stem the tide of immigration.

The establishment of the Reich gave American citizens of German descent new pride. Even the formation of the North German Federation had made a strong impression: ". . . Your Excellency may permit me to add," von Brause, the German chargé d'affaires, wrote on July 15, 1869, "that, although we must not entertain any illusions about the Germans in America exercising a decisive influence on the national policy of the United States now or in the near future, there is no question but that the pride of our fellow countrymen has risen immensely since the victory of 1866 and the introduction of a common flag, and that the name of Your Excellency meets with veneration among the people throughout the country. . . . Even societies of South Germans are using more and more the colors of the North German Federation as national emblems for public parades and the like." Schlözer reported on March 24, 1872: "Nearly every day the former German is reminded that his political and social position throughout America has become a different and powerful one since the tremendous victories of the home country and since the establishment of the Empire, while formerly he occupied a subordinate position. The local Germans now boast with satisfaction of that great achievement at every meeting and in their whole press."

Nevertheless, it cannot be said that the Germans were less rapidly Americanized than before. American education endeavored to make a good American citizen of every single immigrant as quickly as possible. Mastery of the English language and adaptation to the manners and customs of the country were required for success. At that time there was less self-deception in Germany as to a potential support by German-Americans in case of a serious conflict between the two nations. During the Samoa conflict of 1889 the German consul in Cincinnati was convinced that the Americans of German descent would fight against the fatherland. "Many immigrants and their children often become our most embittered enemies," he said. Herbert Bismarck, the son of the Chancellor, commented on this statement with the marginal note "known." [15]

The German public therefore took more and more interest in the question as to whether a one-sided emigration to the United States was not a loss rather than a gain. The emigrants increased trade relations with the Union; it was due to them that new connections could be continuously established. On the other hand, emigration was largely responsible for increasing American competition. German immigration supplied the demand of the United States for skilled labor and trained artisans. Turning emigration into other channels was not a new idea. As early as the fifties there were societies in Germany whose object was to obtain suitable land where Germans might settle without having to give up their national traditions. But in a period of political weakness that movement did not possess sufficient vigor. For centuries it had been traditional for the German to work for other nations. He seemed to need no land for his own development. Now things changed. The newly won political position sharpened the national consciousness. The Germans were no longer to be "cultural fertilizer" for other peoples. They were to preserve their own characteristics in closed settlements. This idea played an important part in the

[15] German consulate in Cincinnati to Bismarck, Feb. 12, 1889, secret.

colonial movement. However, one thing was frequently ignored, namely, that only certain territories were suitable for colonization on a large scale; tropical climate makes demands on inhabitants of the temperate zone that only a comparatively small number of people are able to meet. In other countries, like South Africa, Asia Minor, Syria, and Mesopotamia, German colonization would have encountered political difficulties, particularly because of British claims.[16]

To be sure, there were determined opponents of an official emigration policy. Deputy Bamberger, in a speech before the Reichstag on April 22, 1880, expressed doubts as to the possibility of directing emigration into other channels. Emigrants, he said, would go to America because relatives living there had written them about good opportunities.[17] The Prussian Government had long been concerned about the fate of its emigrants. A memorandum of the Minister of Education, Eichhorn, dated February 17, 1845, on the attitude of Prussia toward German emigration, especially to North America, vigorously complains of the unfortunate results of one-sided emigration to the United States. "America receives a contingent of industrious and easily satisfied citizens who quickly adjust themselves to the peculiar conditions of the country and are politically of considerable importance in that they, naturally differing from the native Americans, join the ranks of Democrats and Locofocos, who in that way gain in power." Germany was losing so many of her industrious people, and those who returned were good-for-nothings as a rule. German emigrants should be encouraged to maintain a national consciousness and realization of their ties with their former countrymen so as to secure, on the one hand, influence of German national life on the political life of foreign continents and, on the other hand, to acquire points of contact for national trade and navigation. Nevertheless, the Prussian Government refrained from any interference on behalf of emigrants. To an inquiry of the consulate general in Rio de Janeiro, December 15, 1845, the Ministry replied that official support of emigrants was out of the question. "According to our law, the certificate of discharge which replaces the old emigration law, completely severs the tie between the Prussian State and its former subject. A discharged Prussian subject not only loses the right to demand readmission to Prussia or support from his former native town, but he ceases to be a Prussian and must therefore be treated like any other foreigner." And a letter of the Minister of Commerce and Industry to Bismarck on February 21, 1863, is quite noncommittal with reference to the extent to which German emigration should be either officially organized or, when organized by private

---

[16] Cf. Joseephy, *Die deutsche überseeische Auswanderung,* 140.
[17] *Sten. Berichte,* 1880-82, II, 867ff.

companies, promoted and supported. In his emigration policy Bismarck on the whole followed the principles of the Prussian Government. More and more he considered emigrants as German citizens who had left their home country in order to escape from certain obligations to their native state. The emigrant, he said, aside from the costs of emigrating, took away from his native country considerable capital in the form of education. For this reason he had no further claim on Government protection. "I am not in favor of emigration in general," he said in a speech before the Reichstag on June 26, 1884, "and particularly not of the morbid promotion of emigration we indulged in during the first years of the German Reich—with my endorsement, I admit; but I paid no attention to the matter at that time. I am fighting against promotion of emigration; a German who discards his fatherland like an old coat is for me no longer a German; I take no further interest in him from a national standpoint."[18] After all, Bismarck did not feel any responsibility for Germans who had forsaken their original citizenship. In his negative attitude he went so far as to refuse to participate in an international agreement for the protection of overseas passengers, because "emigration is encouraged by such governmental solicitude for emigrants in excess of an indispensable degree of humanitarianism."[19] Bismarck's feeling of German nationalism was a natural pride, not a racial experience. For him Germans living abroad were not members of a large family, but citizens of a foreign state. "Emigrants who left Germany," he said in 1873, "are objects of governmental care no more than any foreigner, that is to say, within the limits of Christian charity like any stranger."[20] In 1879 he complained to a Russian diplomat that the Russians called their Baltic provinces German. Only the nobles were of German origin; the Emperor of Russia did not possess more loyal subjects. When in April 1875 Austrian students wanted to congratulate him on the occasion of his sixtieth birthday he let them know that Germany would count on them, yet that they were needed in Austria. A powerful German-Austria was indispensable for Germany.[21] This opinion did not prevent him from using kindly expressions occasionally about the Germans living in America. He called them a connecting link between two nations, a more tractable group than their brothers at home. In America revolutionary opinions were mitigated and radicals turned conservative. The word "unity" cast a spell over them, showing its beneficial influence in two ways: the United States taught the German-Americans to appreciate unified Germany; on the other hand, the

[18] Bismarck, *Gesammelte Werke*, XII, 486.
[19] Marginal note in a report from Washington, Mar. 13, 1883.
[20] Poschinger, *Neues Bismarck-Jahrbuch*, I, 220.
[21] Franz, *Bismarcks Nationalgefühl*, 96ff.

former lack of unity in Germany, which they had so long deplored, caused them to regard as pernicious any element of disunion in their new country. On July 8, 1890, he told a delegation of New York Independent Marksmen that there had been times when one man boasted of being a Saxon, another of being a Prussian, a third one a Hessian, while only those coming from the petty states bashfully said that they came from Germany. "But now all of them say they are Germans, and if the former feeling of a certain bashfulness in admitting German origin still existed, you gentlemen would not have come over to Berlin."[22] He appraised Germans living abroad with the eyes of a politician. For him they were pioneers in promoting good relations. Schlözer, after the Franco-German War, complained of lack of generosity on the part of the German-Americans in connection with a collection for the Niederwald Monument. Bismarck was of a different opinion. ". . . As regards your opinion of the Germans in America . . . it seems to me that Your Excellency expects more than is fair. However many ties may join the German-Americans with Germany, they are after all Americans. We must not judge their present conduct by the idealist conceptions aroused in us by the tone of American telegrams and resolutions in the summer of 1870, and we must not bespeak the same devotion from the German-Americans as from the better and intellectual elements in Germany. The enthusiasm of those war days, politically valuable as it was, stood the test to a degree far beyond my boldest expectations. I confess that I should not have been surprised if only the tenth part of the million actually raised had been collected. . . . It is politically expedient for us to maintain at least the fiction, and it is indeed more than a fiction, that the Germans there take a vivid interest in their native country that continues permanently, regardless of the combinations of American domestic politics to which the Germans are subjected. It will consequently be of advantage, if you will have an attentive eye and a kind word for any symptom of such interest, overlooking the unpleasant things and, when conspicuous, make *bonne mine à mauvais jeu.*"[23]

As to the causes of emigration, Bismarck expressed different ideas, suiting them to his purposes in domestic controversies, according to his temperament. Emigration served him as a means of justifying his protective tariff policy. His utterances on the causes of emigration almost invariably occurred in connection with great economic debates. It was inevitable that facts should sometimes be slightly distorted. Such was the case in his speech of January 8, 1885.

[22] A. D. White, *Diplomatenleben,* 115; Bismarck, *Gesammelte Werke,* XIII, 14.
[23] To Schlözer, Apr. 16, 1872. Concerning the position of the Germans in the Union, Bismarck once suggested that unfortunately they served as "fertilizer" for the Yankee. Cf. his marginal note on a report from Washington, Feb. 13, 1889.

Deputy Richter had cited the unrest in the tobacco industry as an explanation of the emigration of tobacco workers, adding that Germany's economic policy since 1879 had encouraged emigration generally. In his rebuttal the Chancellor used somewhat dubious arguments. The well-to-do workers, he said, were particularly inclined to emigrate, but would not do so if they had a tariff to protect them. It was most important that agriculture and industry should join hands. "Wherever industry and agriculture cooperate, as they do in Westphalia and on the Rhine, where grain yields higher prices, of which you are always afraid, people are sufficiently prosperous to get along without emigrating; there they live peacefully and contentedly." Industry should be developed in agricultural regions. Similarly, on June 26, 1884, he advanced the idea that exports prevented emigration.

Bismarck's theory of the causes of emigration may best be learned from his speech of June 14, 1882. There he emphasized most strongly the point that lack of industry in agricultural districts was the chief cause of emigration. The state of affairs prevailing at that time justified his stressing the emigration of farmers. Why does emigration from agricultural regions predominate? The Chancellor answered this question with the statement that those people had no industry and that industry had been suppressed and smothered by free trade. He mentioned the advantages industrial workers enjoyed and the hopelessness of the agrarian workers. "I think that the lack of industry, in other words, the lack of protection for national labor through a protective tariff, no less than the pressure of direct taxes, is the principal cause of the fact that the least populated provinces show the largest number of emigrants. Man's hopelessness impels him to emigrate. The *terra incognita* of foreign lands holds out all sorts of promises to him that he might there achieve what he never could at home. This, then, is the reason why rural workers emigrate, because they have no industry near them, and because they cannot utilize the products of their labor. . . ." Except for Bismarck's argument that an industrialization of the agrarian east would improve conditions (an assertion which explains his struggle for a protective tariff), his analysis of the case no doubt is correct. But in his statements we fail to find any positive suggestion as to how the great question of emigration could be remedied, or any attempt to regard the problem as anything but a temporary economic evil.[24] As long as it seemed impossible to improve the situation of agriculture, it was necessary to control emigration or at least to dismiss the individual emigrant with the good will of the Reich. Bismarck did not take sufficiently into account the

[24] Bismarck's speeches on emigration, Mar. 8, 1879, June 14, 1882, June 26, 1884, and Jan. 8, 1885; *Gesammelte Werke*, XII, 41f., 373ff., 486, 542ff. Cf. Hagen, *Bismarcks Kolonialpolitik*, 218ff.

emigration caused by an all too rapid increase of population.[25] The emigration policy of his age failed to appreciate the imponderable but very real values of the idea of nationality.[26] Bismarck thought he could prevent excessive emigration by making it more difficult and by increased propaganda against it. Upon his orders the press published unfavorable news about America; he even was not disinclined to accept an offer from a German-American who suggested anti-emigration propaganda in Germany. The Chancellor argued that emigration had to be fought with the same means used to promote it.[27] Two decrees, October 15, 1879, and May 20, 1881, forbade Government organs to assist emigrating Germans; emigration was to be made more difficult, though no pressure was to be exercised, and at any rate, any Government expenditures were to be avoided.[28]

First the Chancellor insisted on strict supervision of those subject to military service. The optimism he displayed when the Bancroft treaties were concluded had disappeared entirely.[29] Increasingly irritated by slackers, he demanded rigorous enforcement of the military laws. Persons under the age of twenty-five and subject to military service were forbidden to emigrate by a law of June 7, 1871. Ever since 1868 the emigration ships in Hamburg and Bremen had been controlled by special agents. The Chancellor personally investigated the measures of control taken in those cities. Reports set his mind at rest. Before the departure of any emigrant ship, the inns and ships were inspected and all men subject to military service detained until counter orders were issued. Nevertheless, many succeeded in escaping to America since Dutch steamship companies took advantage of the situation to attract those people by means of particularly favorable offers.[30]

The Bancroft naturalization treaties of 1868 remained in force.[31] It was too difficult to modify existing agreements despite their imperfections, which mainly consisted in an obscure interpretation of the two-year clause and in the special treatment of residents of Alsace-Lorraine. In view of the increasing

[25] Zeitlin, *Fürst Bismarcks sozial-, wirtschafts- und steuerpolitische Anschauungen,* 174.

[26] On the whole, Hagen's interpretation of Bismarck's colonial policy seems plausible, but he exaggerates contradictions in Bismarck's attitude, *Bismarcks Kolonialpolitik,* 220ff.

[27] Bismarck to Schlözer, Sept. 24, 1873, confidential.

[28] Hagen, *Bismarcks Kolonialpolitik,* 221; for emigration legislation, cf. Poschinger, *Fürst Bismarck und der Bundesrat,* I, 150ff.

[29] See *ante,* p. 101.

[30] Schlözer to Bülow, June 13, 1874. The Chancellor to the Hamburg Senate, Mar. 14, 1882. Senate Commission in Bremen to the Chancellor, Apr. 4, 1882. Ministry for Commerce and Industry, Sept. 21, 1883.

[31] See *ante,* p. 100f.

numbers of emigrants, the German Reich was particularly interested in the two-year clause. Under its provisions no American who had formerly been a German citizen could stay in Germany longer than two years without becoming again subject to the German military laws. Such rigorous terms were necessary principally for their effect on Germans liable to service. The Americans argued that citizens, once naturalized, could not lose rights acquired in their adopted country, unless they intended to live permanently in their native country.[32] Far more serious was the friction caused by citizens of Alsace-Lorraine. The German Government did not wish to have them included in the Bancroft treaties since they had not become German subjects until 1871.[33] That could be easily understood. Heavy emigration from Alsace-Lorraine called for caution. It was mainly attributable to the excellent personal relations existing between most of the American Ministers in Berlin on the one hand and Bismarck and prominent members of the German foreign service on the other that, despite radical differences of opinion and countless individual cases of controversy, an agreement was usually reached. Some of the American Ministers were sufficiently unprejudiced to appreciate the difficulties of Germany's political situation which necessitated a strict enforcement of the military laws.[34] At the same time, American Government officials were increasingly vexed at the all too many naturalized persons who considered their American citizenship merely a convenience, lived abroad continually, and remembered their American allegiance only if they wished to get out of some difficulty. Sargent really rejoiced to see such "Americans" subjected to the German law; the German law, he said, was good for such people, for it taught them how to appreciate American democracy again.[35]

The German public was definitely alarmed by the rising tide of emigration in 1876. An American consular report from Aix-la-Chapelle March 30, 1881, observed that people in certain regions were actually excited over the question of emigration. It was the main topic of conversation in political and business circles.[36] More than ever it seemed urgent to take measures to divert emigration from North America. Everybody agreed that emigrants to the United States would inevitably forego their allegiance to Germany. Moreover, a large number of the emigrants were of a particularly valuable element, artisans and farmers' sons who would become a great asset to alien commerce at the expense of their native country. Prince Hohenlohe-Langenburg, during the

[32] Fish to Bancroft, Jan. 21, 1875, Dept. State, *Instructions, Germany,* 16: 14f.; Davis to Fish, Berlin, Feb. 12, 1875, Dept. State, *Despatches, Germany,* 6, no. 73.
[33] Cf. *Foreign Relations,* 1881, 448ff.
[34] A. D. White in particular; cf. his *Diplomatenleben,* 78f.
[35] Sargent to Frelinghuysen, Berlin, Jan. 22, 1883, *Foreign Relations,* 1883, 330f.
[36] *Consular Reports,* 1881, II, no. 7, 701f.

discussions in the Reichstag on the Samoa Bill, April 22, 1880, declared that the emigrants were made of excellent stuff. "Young, strong men with possessions not inconsiderable move away, while the old and unfit are frequently left behind, a burden to their communities." [37] The German consul general in Savannah wrote on July 20, 1878: "The immigrated elements are for the most part of a very efficient kind; following the steps of predecessors already settled in the country, and with sufficient means and well-calculated plans, all of them primarily represent a loss for their native country; they include five thousand Prussians, who recently arrived with their families." A report of the consulate general in New York, March 26, 1881, asserted: "Young couples with babies come here in numbers never seen before, most of them after previous consultation and provided with some funds, the proceeds of the sale of former property. Adventurers who wish to go out into the world to try their luck have become quite rare." During that period the Americans had an equally good opinion of the German immigrants. They were, without exception, so it was said, of the best agricultural class; they brought money with them, the savings of years or the proceeds from the sale of some property. The German newspapers were correct in asserting that Germany had never before lost so many valuable and industrious people as had emigrated to the United States in recent years, the American Consulate reported from Bremen on April 12, 1881. In the east the loss to agriculture was so noticeable that German farmers and landowners complained of being unable to get good help. Whole families had left for America while those remaining were worthless. [38]

Thus the question again arose as to whether it might not be possible to settle at least a part of the emigrants in countries where, in contrast to the United States, they need not renounce their German nationality. And again the same suggestions were made which had been discussed for decades and included in the program of the Central Society for Commercial Geography and Promotion of German Interests Abroad. Among the countries suitable for German agricultural colonies, Central and South America were mentioned, particularly southern Chile, southern Brazil, Argentina, and Uruguay. Southern Brazil appeared to be the most favorable of all, because many Germans had settled there since the first half of the nineteenth century. In 1824 Emperor Pedro I, with the assistance of Germans, founded São Leopoldo in the province of Rio Grande do Sul. Major Koeler, financed by the Brazilian Government, in 1843 laid out the settlement of Petropolis. In 1851 the Hamburg Society for Colonization founded the colony of Doña Francisca with

---

[37] *Sten. Berichte* (Reichstag), VI, 3, vol. II, 860.
[38] According to an undated German press notice.

Joinville in the province of Santa Catharina. Blumenau was established at about the same time. After that, German colonization spread over the provinces of Rio Grande do Sul, Santa Catharina, and Paraná, the colonies in the province of Rio Grande do Sul being the most flourishing.[39] The number of Germans living in Brazil at that time was estimated at approximately 200,000. As a few German companies controlled a large part of the Brazilian export trade, the prospects for settlement on a large scale seemed auspicious. The Brazilian Government wanted immigration, particularly after the seventies. The struggle for abolition of slavery had caused release of slaves here and there. Many landowners wished to secure free labor in time so as not to be caught unawares by the forthcoming general law for emancipation. Since 1847 the Brazilian Government had spent more than one hundred million dollars to increase immigration. The German immigrants were well received, being considered especially industrious and reliable. Great profits seemed to be in store for German immigrants of sufficient industriousness. Experts described the favorable climate of southern Brazil, where Central Europeans could be assimilated, and the possibility of raising both tropical and European plants at a good profit. People emigrating to the United States injured the commerce of their native country, while such was not the case in Brazil. The immigrant seemed to anticipate the production of raw materials for hundreds of years to come. Southern Brazil was just passing from the stage of cattle breeding to that of agriculture. The settler used German goods almost exclusively, *i.e.,* he remained a purveyor and a customer of the old country without coming into conflict with his obligations to the Brazilian State. Other experts mentioned the fact that the Germans could preserve their culture, language, and habits far more easily in Brazil than in the United States. The province of Rio Grande do Sul was said to have its special advantages, being half the size of Germany and capable of easily accommodating another million people. The climate resembled central Italy; even in the hottest months the temperature did not rise above the average of midsummer days in Central Europe. There were some objections, however. Many German colonists had had unfortunate experiences in the past. They had been reduced to a slavelike dependence on the landowners. For this reason Prussia, in 1859, had forbidden any propaganda for emigration to Brazil, and, a few years later, prohibited any emigration there at all. No doubt even at that time there were some dangers. The country did not possess a strong government; security under the law was very imperfect; the system of hereditary tenancy might menace the personal liberty of the settler. Nevertheless, times had changed considerably. The Brazilian Government sincerely endeavored to protect the immigrants. The

[39] *Brockhaus Encyclopedia,* III, 252.

many Germans constituted a stronger support for the newcomers. Cancellation of the decree of 1859 was demanded. It did not achieve its purpose because licensed emigration agencies were being replaced by others that were doing business without any license and without corresponding guarantees.[40]

The Society for Commercial Geography and Promotion of German Interests Abroad energetically advocated government control of emigration to Brazil; the Germans living in Brazil likewise repeatedly submitted requests for cancellation of the decree of 1859. Le Maistre, the German Minister in Rio de Janeiro, strongly advised that prohibition of emigration be not limited to Brazil alone because of Brazilian sentiment. He consequently proposed cancellation of the decree, suggesting a form of general regulation instead. It was his opinion that the only disadvantages of emigration to Brazil were the tropical climate, the foreign civilization in the northern parts of the country, the competition of slavery, low fertility of the land, legal insecurity, and lack of good communications. As for arbitrary rule by officials in the interior of the country, inefficient administration of justice, lack of schools and intellectual institutions, such disadvantages as these Brazil had in common with all other countries to which European emigration turned. On the other hand, Le Maistre was rather skeptical regarding the question as to whether the Germans would be able to maintain their national character in Brazil. He said that the Germans of the second generation gave up their nationality; they were no longer Germans but Brazilians.[41]

The Foreign Office could not avoid giving some attention to such suggestions. When the German Minister in Rio de Janeiro inquired whether the decree of 1859 had not better be restricted to northern Brazil, the Foreign Office replied, on November 15, 1880, that it was intended to issue a uniform emigration decree for Germany. "The German Government hitherto has not taken action with regard to the agitation of the Central Society for Commercial Geography for a uniform emigration policy. That agitation, intended first of all to turn emigration to southern Brazil and other South American countries, suggests the danger of inducing people to emigrate inasmuch as it is apt to influence a larger group of persons than those who have already of their own accord decided to leave their country. If such be the case, the Government could not help considering the restriction of the work of the Society to proper limits. The efforts of the Society may succeed, however, in bringing about a reliable German enterprise for the purpose of settling emi-

---

[40] Report of Judge D. Dilthey to Foreign Office on the condition of German emigration to southern Brazil, Uruguay, and Argentina, on the basis of personal observations in 1880-1881.

[41] Reports of Le Maistre, Rio de Janeiro, Sept. 26, 1880, Nov. 1 and Dec. 9, 1884.

grants in a suitable part of southern Brazil under admittedly acceptable conditions. In this case it would still be an open question whether this Government might see fit to consider the tentative authorization of such enterprises" (for the Chancellor, Thile to Le Maistre, November 15, 1880, confidential). A memorandum of Count Beust, secretary of legation in Washington, who had traveled extensively in southern Brazil, gave Bismarck an opportunity to express his personal opinion. After describing the dangers of emigration to the United States, Count Beust continued: "The Germans who turn to the United States are forever lost to the fatherland with all they are and possess. They become our competitors there, in many branches teaching the Americans and founding new industries. Often they are our political opponents, playing a part that does not correspond either to their mental faculties or to the position of Germany among civilized nations." Since acquisition of agricultural colonies was not feasible, emigration should be turned into directions more advantageous for the emigrants than those hitherto taken. Emigration should not be encouraged. However, the German Government should endeavor to have the emigrants concentrated in countries of subtropical and temperate zones where, essentially dependent on agriculture, they would be customers for German industrial products while supplying their raw materials in return and where they would remain Germans and could develop States of their own [and then? cf. North America and England].[42] In the United States the emigrants were confronted with a plucky, energetic Anglo-Saxon population, in many ways unscrupulous and for the most part of superior training and experience, making success in all branches of business extremely difficult [What is that to us? If it were different, still more people would go]. "On the other hand, southern Brazil offers such advantages as are termed *desirable*[43] [?] for Germany and her emigrants. It has a temperate climate but raises products both of the tropical and the temperate zones, and in its extended and uncultivated territories, lacking industry, could accommodate many more millions of consumers of foreign industrial products. Rio Grande do Sul, in particular, may be recommended as a goal of voluntary German emigration, this province being suitable as a point of crystallization for establishing a *German State*[43] in South America" [What would *that*[43] mean to us? Hostility rather than anything else].

Count Beust recommended *official intervention*[43] of the Imperial Legation in Rio de Janeiro on behalf of the colonists, asserting that it would be easier and more fruitful to influence people in power there than in the United States. [For people no longer German subjects? This is legally improper and politi-

[42] Bismarck's marginal notes are printed in brackets.
[43] Bismarck's underscoring is indicated by italics.

cally it would promote emigration]. "Once before in this century it happened that São Paulo and Rio Grande do Sul tried to secede from the Empire, and in common with Santa Catharina and Paraná they will repeat that attempt and probably with success. If by that time the German element is so strong that it has numerically greater importance than today, it will assume political control of the secessionist States, and from the relations with them the German Reich will derive those advantages that are generally connected with the possession of agricultural colonies" [Those people will be progressive republicans. No more friendly toward their fatherland than the Yankees are toward England]. In conclusion the author offered the following suggestions: Establishment of official consulates in southern Brazil [for promotion of emigration?]; Secretary of Legation Count Monts in Rio de Janeiro to be commissioned to inspect the region and report [I am not anxious to know how people fare who cast off the dust of their country]; the German consuls in Brazil to report Government offers of private land [I certainly shall beware of becoming an emigration agent]; *cancellation* [43] of decrees still in force in Prussia and other German states for rendering emigration to Brazil more difficult [extension to all emigrants]; official support of the work of the Central Society for Commercial Geography and Promotion of German Interests Abroad [no longer].[44]

Bismarck's marginal notes show that in principle he was opposed to Beust's opinion. That was clearly expressed in his reply to Beust on March 18, 1881. He objected to any form of Government support, no matter whither emigration was turning. On the contrary, the regulations regarding emigration were to be extended. The emigrants, he said, left their country, either giving up their German citizenship or intending to sever that relationship sooner or later. Intervention in favor of the colonists through the legation or consulates was out of the question, legally in the former case, politically inexpedient in the latter because it would stimulate emigration. Promotion of the Central Society could not be contemplated. "As to the possibility of creating states, which some people expect of German immigration in southern Brazil, the Chancellor cares little, being of the opinion that the German element there would under certain circumstances pursue political tendencies running counter to Germany's interests, and would likewise, in other respects, hardly go beyond that degree of practical good will for the fatherland which the Yankee has entertained for England since the Declaration of Independence." On April 7, the Foreign Office termed the idea of diverting emigration to South America a theory that the Government should rather fight than encourage, because of its serious consequences. "Aside from the above points of view, emigration

[44] Memorandum of Count Beust, secretary of legation, Berlin, Mar. 4, 1881.

to Brazil, even if the intended purpose were achieved, runs counter to the interests of the Reich; it is apt to trouble international relations abroad, and people determined to leave their country permanently have no claim on Government protection at such a price." At any rate the Government could not consider as its mission the promotion of emigration in any manner or the assumption of responsibility for the future of the emigrants by aiding them along a definite line. A memorandum of October 3, 1881, arrived at the same conclusions. "Recent tendencies toward diverting German emigration to certain other points cannot be considered to conform to the interests of the Reich, because experience shows that practical operation of such intervention affects people other than those already determined to emigrate to America and consequently promotes emigration." The Chancellor wrote on the margin of a memorandum by his son Herbert, January 4, 1886, that promotion of emigration was not one of the functions of the federated governments. By encouraging emigration in definite directions, as opposed to the *status quo,* the Government would assume a certain degree of responsibility for the future of the respective emigrants. There was neither a duty nor an occasion to do that, hence the negative attitude.

The North Americans, however, did not think that Government promotion of German emigration to Brazil would meet with much success. They considered conditions in Brazil too unsafe; they regarded advantages of their own country far too highly not to consider the United States as the enticing goal of German emigration in the future.[45] Not until later did Americans pay more serious attention to German plans of colonization. In 1900 the American Minister in Petropolis reported: "It is true that the German Minister here, Count D'Arco-Valley, to whom his Emperor has repeatedly confided delicate missions, recently made a trip through the States of Rio Grande do Sul, Santa Catharina, and Paraná, traveling incognito under the pseudonym of P. Valley. He seemed to have been rather depressed than elated by his trip, thus confirming the impression existing among those who, like myself, have been brought in contact with men from southern Brazil, that there exists among the German colonists absolute loyalty to their adopted country."[46]

Bismarck's attitude was strongly influenced by considerations of foreign

---

[45] ". . . they have not the impetuous Yankee in the background pressing the immigrant on and on until he astonishes himself and all Europe," consular report from Santa Catharina, Sept. 10, 1882; *House Miscellaneous Documents,* 47th Cong., 2d sess., no. 19, 322. But complaint was made of keen German competition (Vice Consul Preller, Rio Grande do Sul, Brazil, Mar. 31, 1881, Dept. State, *Despatches, Rio Grande do Sul,* 6, no. 10).

[46] C. P. Bryan to the Department of State, Petropolis, June 25, 1900, Dept. State, *Despatches, Brazil,* 65, no. 259.

policy. He did not wish to give unnecessary offense to the United States. After the overthrow of the Brazilian Empire in November 1889, Germany was concerned about the fate of the Germans living in Brazil. Friedrich Fabri, the well-known colonial expert, expressed apprehensions as to the increasing influence on developments in southern Brazil of elements immigrating from the United States. "If by that time the German element has not been sufficiently strengthened and extended, the Yankees would gain the upper hand to the later detriment of the South." [47] The *Kölnische Zeitung* of November 16 discussed the same idea with official encouragement: "In southern Brazil a considerable part of the population, faithfully attached to the fatherland, cultivates its German traditions—as early as 1872, some 45,829 Germans were counted in Brazil—and since it hardly seems possible for a future republic indefinitely to save from chaos the immense territory of the state in its present form, it is especially the future political fate of the south that now claims our interest and sympathy." This article was discussed in the United States, and German intervention in Brazil not considered impossible. As soon as Bismarck heard of the rumor, he had the German chargé d'affaires in Washington officially declare that Germany did not intend in any way to interfere with the course of events in Brazil, particularly in the province of Rio Grande do Sul. The American Government assured the chargé d'affaires that it had never paid attention to the prevalent rumors about German intervention. [48] In instructions of the Foreign Office to Schlözer on March 28, 1880, the governing reasons are mentioned for the Chancellor's opposition to any scheme of colonization in America. It said His Serene Highness had remarked that unfortunately the weakness of the German Navy was to be added to the general reasons against raising the German flag on the other side of the ocean, and particularly on the American continent. [49]

It is evident that the psychologically favorable hour for diverting emigration to Brazil was at the beginning of the eighties. [50] Later on conditions were not so favorable, when Brazil was able to meet its needs for labor through the increasing influx of Italians. Le Maistre observed a growing aversion on the part of the Brazilians to the German immigrants. The preference of the land-

[47] Fabri to Foreign Office, Godesberg, Nov. 19, 1889.

[48] Memorandum of the Department of State on a conversation with the German chargé d'affaires, Dec. 2, 1889, Dept. State, *Notes from German Legation*, 22.

[49] Poschinger, *Neues Bismarck-Jahrbuch*, I, 274.

[50] It seems noteworthy that Coolidge, the American historian, in his *United States as a World Power*, 208ff., thinks it was a serious mistake for the Prussian Government to forbid or impede emigration to Brazil between 1859 and 1893. To be sure, in 1908 when the book appeared, the author thought that German intervention in South American affairs might result in a war between the United States and Germany.

owners for Germans had vanished at the moment when the latter became farmers. The attitude of the Portuguese was increasingly unfriendly (to Bismarck, November 18, 1886, and September 30, 1888). At a later period emigration was no longer a burning question that required an immediate solution. It was stated that German emigration did not hurt the Reich from the standpoint of size of population. The percentage of emigrants in proportion to the total population amounted to only 1.3 percent between 1871 and 1910. Shortage of labor could be supplemented through the Poles.[51] But the final and decisive point is this: Germany wasted her people in an unpardonable manner in the seventies and eighties of the last century. The pessimists were right. The stream of emigration took most valuable forces to foreign countries. But even planned settlement could not possibly have fulfilled the audacious dreams of some Germans. A German state in America would have been certain to cause serious friction with the United States. But even the most pedantic interpretation of the Monroe Doctrine would not have justified the United States in opposing heavy emigration to Brazil. In that respect, the proponents were right. German traditions were preserved far better in Brazil than in the United States. Possibly there is no other non-European country where the Germans clung to their native traditions so faithfully as in Brazil. The history of Brazil during the World War has not been written as yet; perhaps it would demonstrate that the Germans there held their position despite the universal attack of enemy propaganda. At least attacks against the German language in Rio Grande do Sul were unsuccessful. Today Brazil has once more become one of the most important countries for German emigration.[52]

Emigration policy in Bismarck's era was based on the theory that the Government had no responsibility for Germans outside the Reich. Even Great Britain with her colonies was unable to turn the tremendous stream of emigration from the United States. But the British nation was more intensely interested in the welfare of the emigrant. Efforts were made at an early period to assist and advise the individual. The Royal Colonial Institute, founded on January 25, 1868, grappled with the emigration problem at once. A vigorous campaign started about 1882. Societies, politicians, and newspapers advocated protection for the emigrant. In 1886 the National Association for Promoting State-directed Colonization was in a position to present its wishes to Lord Granville. The Colonial Office constantly endeavored to conclude special

[51] Joseephy, *Die deutsche überseeische Auswanderung,* 111.

[52] In Oct. 1901 the American Minister in Berlin wrote of the German settlers in Brazil: ". . . and in South America he still retains, to a considerable extent at least, his German tastes and habits." *Foreign Relations,* 1901, 191.

agreements with the British dominions and colonies in favor of the emigrants. The Emigrants Information Office advised emigrants in every way.[53] And, were the British emigrants in the United States really altogether lost to their native country? Bismarck thought so. But the future proved that Anglo-Saxon solidarity was anything but a mere word. The German emigrant, on the other hand, came into an English-speaking world. Everywhere he had to make his way in an alien and frequently hostile environment. Germany, once it had become a vital factor in the world's history, could no longer afford waste in any form. Emigration, of course, is desirable, and even necessary to a certain degree. It makes possible an animated and fruitful exchange between nations. But Germans should never have emigrated from the Reich under police pressure or in the feeling that they were no more than foreigners to their native land.

[53] Rathgen, *Englische Auswanderung und Auswanderungspolitik,* 125ff.

CHAPTER III

GERMANY AND THE UNITED STATES
IN THE PACIFIC

I. THE COLONIAL POLICY OF GERMANY
AND THE UNITED STATES

W HEN the emigration movement reached its climax, Germany had to
face the question of whether or not she was to acquire colonies as
other great powers long since had done. The connection between the two
problems was quite logical. The rapid increase of population heightened the
demand for overseas possessions. An immediate solution was required because
of the scarcity of food and raw materials. The early colonial enterprises of the
Great Elector failed because there was not sufficient power to maintain them
and because the people were not sufficiently prepared for the colonial idea.
Discussion of the matter, though quite lively since the forties of the nineteenth century, remained purely academic. Realization of any such plans was
out of the question at the time. During the Franco-Prussian War the Government was flooded with suggestions. Saigon on the Indo-Chinese coast was
especially mentioned; it should be acquired from France as a part of the war
indemnities. At that time Bismarck was absolutely opposed to colonies. He
realized better than those who wanted colonies just how difficult it had been
to establish the German Reich without interference from other powers. In the
first decade after the foundation of the Reich his policy was dominated by the
one idea: To have the young national state appear as modest and sympathetic
as possible to the other nations, in order to accustom them to its presence in
the family of nations. Moreover, Germany had no navy.

"As long as I am Chancellor," Bismarck declared to a Reichstag Deputy in
1881, "we shall have no colonial policy. We have a navy that cannot sail;

we must not have any vulnerable points in other continents that would fall prey to the French as soon as war starts."[1] He was likewise convinced that a colonial policy could be successful only if the people were sufficiently interested. Nevertheless, he studied the colonial question rather early. This may be inferred from a conversation in 1876 with two overseas pioneers. They had submitted an elaborate plan, indicating that South Africa and the Boer Republics were suitable for German colonization. Bismarck told them that he had been studying the problem of colonization for a long time, as he was convinced that a nation like Germany could not exist indefinitely without colonies, but, without adequate preparation and without the necessary popular support, he hesitated to tackle the difficult problem, for the Reichstag would not be willing to vote the necessary funds, unless impelled by strong public opinion (which he thought did not exist).[2] Bismarck's policy until about 1875 may well be called "diplomatic guardianship."[3] Acquisition of colonies at that time certainly was not contemplated. But the Government attentively pursued the development of overseas trade, considered establishing coaling stations, and extended the consular service. British annexation of the Fiji Islands brought about a sudden and obvious change. Many German settlers, believing in free trade, hailed the event. When the German consul in Levuka expressed his apprehensions, Bismarck replied on January 17, 1875, that he did not in the least share the consul's fears. On the contrary, he pointed out, British annexation might be of advantage to the German settlers because it gave them security and the protection of a strong government.[4] But the facts proved to be different. German commercial interests suffered seriously. The British administration of the Fiji Islands systematically undermined the influence of German commerce. This convinced Bismarck that the theory of free trade would not function in practice. Parts of the British Empire began to restrict foreign trade. At the same time, certain measures of the American Commissioner in Samoa put the Germans there in a critical position.[5] Thereupon Bismarck altered his course slightly. While as yet nothing like a colonial policy could be contemplated, the Reich exerted greater efforts for the protection of Germany's overseas trade. As a beginning the German Government protested against British and Spanish encroachments. In 1873, the Governor General of the Philippine Islands confiscated on German ships the cargoes destined for trade with the Sulus. Thereafter an attempt was made to protect

[1] Poschinger, *Fürst Bismarck und die Parlamentarier,* III, 54.
[2] Hagen, *Bismarcks Kolonialpolitik,* 52.
[3] Townsend, *Modern German Colonialism,* 55.
[4] *Ibid.,* 57.
[5] See *post,* p. 225ff.

German overseas trade through a series of treaties of friendship and commerce. The treaty with the Tonga Islands in 1876 carefully avoided any allusion to colonial aspirations. Not until the time of the Samoa Bill (1880) did the new element enter. There the neutrality of Germany's commercial settlements overseas was for the first time declared a necessity.[6]

Finally, in 1883, Bismarck determined upon a colonial policy. At first he wished to avoid a bureaucratic-military administration and to give preference to the German merchant. But the necessity of protecting the German colonies with the forces of the Government proved too strong. Bismarck's decision was vitally influenced by the fact that the German public had become more and more familiar with the colonial idea. Since 1878 the Central Society for Commercial Geography and Promotion of German Interests Abroad had made the colonial problem the main point on its program. The Colonial Society was founded in 1882, Hübbe-Schleiden and Fabri starting the campaign.[7] The Chancellor was no longer able to ignore the national aspirations. As time went on, he welcomed the pressure of public opinion as a means of explaining his colonial policy to Great Britain. In his vivacious way he assured the British Ambassador in 1883 that the colonial question had obtained a greater hold on the sentiment of the German people than it should have, but for the moment there was no restraining it. He referred to the French as an example, saying that they were ambitious to excel in horsemanship for which they had never shown great aptitude. Similarly, the Germans now wished to show their prowess on the sea. This sentiment had so entangled itself with domestic politics that it had now to be treated with greater deference and circumspection than had appeared to be necessary at the beginning.[8] This certainly was not Bismarck's final opinion. So keen an observer could not fail to notice the changes that meanwhile had been taking place in the world. There was, first of all, the collapse of the once-dominant theory of free trade. Acquisition of sources of raw materials had proved to be necessary for the preservation of national independence. The Far East and Africa became topics of political discussion. Germany could not possibly afford to remain indifferent. If the Reich supported British policy in Egypt, it was entitled to compensation. If Franco-British disagreement were to serve Germany's foreign policy, Germany needed objectives that permitted cooperation with France under certain circumstances. After the beginning of the eighties colonial questions could no longer be separated from considerations of foreign affairs. For a long time, however, Bismarck clung to the idea that it was undesirable to hold colonies

[6] Cf. Townsend, *Modern German Colonialism,* 118ff.

[7] Hagen, *Bismarcks Kolonialpolitik,* 25ff.

[8] Malet to Granville, Berlin, Oct. 23, 1884, confidential.

by military force as the French had done. An ordinance of November 28, 1885, proclaimed that Germany merely intended to protect its trade wherever it developed.

For Bismarck to amass colonial possessions of so considerable an extent within such a short time was an astonishing achievement. To be sure, compared to the value and extent of Great Britain's colonial empire, Germany's overseas possessions were insignificant. The main point, however, was this: Germany's colonial policy did not necessarily trouble her relations with Great Britain. The Chancellor's deliberate and steady procedure forestalled British suspicion that might have proved detrimental to German interests. Carl Peters criticized the Chancellor for losing the whole of Africa by his hesitation. On the other hand, and probably with more justification, similar negligence was laid at the door of British statesmen who, in the sixties, rejected any further expansion in Africa and who, as late as 1876, failed to accept Stanley's offer to acquire the Congo Basin. At that time British imperialism was not so active as a decade later. Nevertheless, it is quite probable that the launching of a German colonial policy immediately after the foundation of the Reich would have met with serious opposition from Great Britain. British liberals used to explain their inactivity by the fact that colonial plans of other powers did not exist. In order to have obtained their proper share when the world was divided up, the Germans would have had to unite in 1848. In the decade between 1860 and 1870 the British Empire passed through a national crisis, besides being greatly handicapped by the American Civil War.

But the chief obstacles to the German policy did not come so much from England as from the British colonies, primarily South Africa and Australasia. Expressions of good will were not lacking in England. Memories of the past were still alive; the British were not aware of Anglo-German differences, but of Anglo-French differences. The two countries had much in common through descent, language, and religion. Thus there was a certain traditional affinity. The British respected the Germans for their industry; before the foundation of the Reich, Germans not infrequently advanced to leading official positions in British colonies. Widely read magazines like the *Nineteenth Century* or the *Fortnightly Review* described German colonial policy as an advantage to British commercial and colonial policy. The radical-liberal *Pall-Mall* went so far as to insist that friendship with Germany should be declared the supreme principle of British foreign policy (September 2, 1883).[9] Likewise speeches by Cabinet members sometimes overflowed with good will, although they suggested to the Germans that Great Britain might be preordained for the high

---

[9] Hagen, *Bismarcks Kolonialpolitik*, 405f.

mission of colonization while other peoples were likely to lose their political power in undertaking such a task.

The sentiment in the British dominions and colonies was, however, quite different. There democracy was the godfather of the new imperialism. Already the British Empire was undergoing a radical reorganization at a time when official England under Gladstone was still entertaining the ideas of a bygone era. During the last few decades before the foundation of the Reich, colonies had been considered as a burden to be disposed of somehow. But under the influence of trained British theorists and men of practical experience the empire idea asserted itself all the more strongly after the close of the American Civil War. Pointing to their advancing economic development, the British colonies made demands of their own. Frequently their egotism assumed a menacing tone. As a matter of fact, it was they who most strongly championed the idea of a commonwealth of nations since their security was so closely bound up with it. What they wanted was the greatest possible freedom of development within the framework of the British world empire. Following the example of the Canadian Confederacy of 1867, Australasia demanded a similar status. The Australian Government had been granted practical autonomy since 1850. But the discovery of new gold mines stimulated immigration tremendously. Radical-democratic elements gained the upper hand and insisted upon ever greater independence from the motherland. In the course of time, however, it appeared that a union of the Australian colonies was not such a simple thing to accomplish; the interests of the several colonies were too diversified. The British Government cleverly made them realize from time to time that their own forces would not be strong enough for their protection.

The initiative of the British dominions and colonies inspired and deepened the imperialistic idea. They felt most directly the necessity of unity; they constantly forced the mother country to pay attention to the problem of common defense. The commonwealth of nations replaced the old colonial empire. While its various links were loosened, the tie of common advantage and the Anglo-Saxon instinct for power held them together. In her foreign policy England had to consider the interests of her colonies to an ever-increasing degree. The commonwealth was the sworn enemy of any colonial expansion of other powers. The British Government found it useful in political negotiations to refer to the wishes of its colonies. The Government naturally could not afford to obstruct the colonial aspirations of other powers in principle, being a European power and as such too greatly dependent on occasional support. But it entrenched itself behind difficulties created by the colonies so as to yield as slowly and as little as possible. Great Britain's attitude toward

Germany's colonial policy was anything but generous. Wherever the Germans settled, the British established themselves nearby. They acted somewhat like a business house that buys up adjacent land to prevent competing firms from further expansion.

The United States needed no sources for raw materials. The Monroe Doctrine could warn against the acquisition of distant colonies without endangering American interests. Groups of islands close to the American coast, if they seemed to be of value commercially, were declared to belong to the American system. In the first half of the nineteenth century American imperialists thought in terms of Mexico and Canada. But the tendency to hold the key positions on the Atlantic and Pacific coasts, Cuba and the Hawaiian Islands, runs through American history like a red thread. The Ostend Manifesto of October 18, 1854, masked only superficially the intention of annexing Cuba.

The United States of course did not participate in the competition for the Dark Continent. In view of the fact that Africa played such an important part in the foreign policy of the great powers, the policy of the United States might well have appeared to be devoid of intention to expand. Thereto must be added the great indifference of the American population, which after the end of the Civil War was but slightly interested in foreign affairs and refused to follow such far-sighted leaders as Grant and Blaine. This indifference explains why the American press only occasionally dealt with Germany's colonial policy so that there was practically no public opinion regarding German colonial policy during the era of Bismarck.[10] It was that lack of understanding of foreign political aims and that lack of desire for power that gave much concern to Americans devoted to imperialist traditions. John A. Kasson, American Minister to Germany, who in 1884 and 1885 lived in the centers of European imperialism, repeatedly attacked his Government for its weak foreign policy. On April 13, 1885, he wrote to his Secretary of State: "I venture to add an expression of my sorrow, bordering upon a sense of shame, that the blindness, weakness, and timidity of a long continuing so-called American policy has made our flag on the Pacific Ocean insignificant, and has led foreign nations to ask for our views, if asked at all, *after the fait accompli,* instead of before it. The Pacific Ocean should have been an American sea, traversed by American ships not only to Japan and China, but to the new Australian world, touching at numerous islands having American plantations, and covered by the American flag. Instead of this, which would have signified peace, prosperity, and wealth, we have now everywhere the flag of the three embattled nations of Europe, still grasping for the insular fragments left

[10] Mr. Lionel Summers, who was kind enough to examine American publications on that subject for me, shares this view.—The author.

201

unappropriated, and exposing every American interest of the present and the future on the Pacific to embroilment in their wars.

"The system of Protectorate, as now understood, if adopted by us for such islands as Samoa, or for other weak governments where we have special interests, is well adapted to our situation, and would be of special advantage to the beneficiaries of it, as it would give to us the control of their foreign relations.

"It should not occasion surprise if we yet see these European Governments intriguing for the possession of the Sandwich Islands." Kasson concludes with the ironical remark: "Would it not be well to send a Quaker to be Minister there, that Europe may have notice that our rights in such an emergency will be defended in our usual energetic manner?"

In his lengthy report of April 30, 1885, written shortly before his departure from Berlin, Kasson expressed himself still more frankly on the foreign policy of his country. That report is documentary evidence of the high esteem Bismarck was enjoying throughout the world. It is a eulogy of the great statesman, although Kasson, in deference to traditional American ideology, had to describe Bismarck's policy as a purely egotistic and materialistic one.[11] Kasson summed up in the middle of his report the principal point in which he was interested, after fully analyzing the policy of the Chancellor. Beginning with the effects of Bismarck's immense diplomatic success on Germany's position as a world power, Kasson draws certain conclusions for his own country: "Germany, almost unknown in Asia twenty years ago, is now a great moral power there, of which the oldest Asiatic nations stand in awe. At that period equally unknown in Africa, she is now an African colonial power, and one of the dictators in Egyptian affairs. At that date unknown in the Pacific ocean, she is now the proprietor of islands and harbors there for the founding of colonies, and for the extension of her commerce. Then known to the United States only as a sympathetic national and commercial friend, and without a navy, she is now known to us by her calculated hostility to our agricultural and commercial development, by her aggressions in the Samoa Islands, and by one of the ships of her navy which in a distant sea illegally violated one of our unarmed commercial vessels, in the absence of any American navy to resent it.

"It is to be remembered that the first point of Prince Bismarck's policy is the rounding out of the Empire, and the securing of its safety against continental hostilities, especially against France. Next, providing for the external development of German industry, and for the emigration of her surplus population at the same time by the establishment of colonies on other conti-

[11] Cf. appendix, p. 304ff., for the complete text of Kasson's report.

nents and islands, where Germans shall retain their allegiance and lend strength to the mother country, instead of leaving her weaker by their withdrawal to an alien land. In the execution of this second point he was already in accord with France; and by quarreling with England he has now also obtained the consent of the latter. The new German subsidized steamship lines to distant seas are now inviting the colonial extension of Germany in imperial rivalry with England.

"This review, Mr. Secretary, is not written for publication. It is not intended to be a Platonic essay, nor a mere contribution to general literature. It is offered in the hope—not so strong as I could wish it to be—that it may tend to persuade my Government of the *necessity* of foresight, and of energetic action at an early day, in two directions:—First, to obtain a navy strong enough, in presence of new elements of international complication, to secure respect for our flag, and to maintain our asserted rights. Secondly, to anticipate and provide against the coming hostile European action which will be directed to the overthrow of our much vaunted, and newly imperilled 'Monroe Declaration.'

"If it may possibly induce more confidence in my views of European tendencies at this time, I venture to refer to my later Despatches as Minister in Vienna, in which I urged the then Administration to prepare for a coming European reaction against our agricultural interests,—a war of tariffs or prohibitions against our great line of exports. That forecast proved correct, our Government took no decisive measures, and we remain today the victims of that policy, without prospect of relief."

Kasson's criticism overshot the mark. He judged the situation from a one-sided European point of view. To a certain extent the United States could well afford to defer an active policy. The Government, however, kept close watch. The idea of an interoceanic canal was enough to force the leaders of American policy to be on the alert. The Department of State always sponsored American claims whenever American interests were involved. Such was the case even in Africa. Soon after its foundation the Union had had trouble with the three pirate states of Tunis, Algiers, and Tripoli. At first, because of the weakness of its navy it had to pay high tribute for the protection of its merchants; then the arbitrariness of the pirate peoples led to the first armed action of the new American Navy. Later on relations with the Negro republic of Liberia became important.[12] Humanitarian Americans had helped Christian Negroes to establish a place of refuge there and in 1862 the United States recognized Liberia as an independent country. Liberia thereupon became a

[12] For the relations of the United States with the so-called Barbary States and Liberia, cf. Moore, *Digest*, V, 391ff. and 762ff.

foothold for American commerce in Africa. While a protectorate was not officially declared, the annual message of the President of December 6, 1886, stated it to be the moral right and obligation of the United States to support Liberia in the preservation of her independence. The President took occasion to recommend that Liberia be presented with a warship.[13] The American Government was repeatedly forced to protest against French attempts at interference in Liberia, endeavoring to maintain the predominance there of American commercial interests.[14] It was not surprising, therefore, that representatives of the United States took part in the Morocco Conference at Madrid, in June 1880, since the sole subject of discussion was suppression of the slave trade.

The situation had already changed when the West African Conference was held in Berlin in 1884.[15] Stanley's expeditions in the Congo Basin disclosed unheard-of possibilities for commerce. The Americans also paid attention. The New York Chamber of Commerce asked the Government to protect American interests in Africa. Because of the shorter distance by sea, they thought competition with the other powers could be successfully maintained.[16] The Secretary of State informed Morgan, chairman of the Senate Committee on Foreign Relations, on March 13, 1884, that the Government was interested not only because of the trade of American citizens but also for the reason that it considered this an effective means of attacking the slave trade at its roots.[17] As early as 1879 Edward F. Noyes, American Minister in Paris, had been instructed to investigate the commercial conditions along the Mediterranean and the west coast of Africa.[17a] In 1884 Willard Tisdel was sent as a Special Agent to explore the Congo region. In his instructions, it was stated that American policy had logically been to avoid entangling alliances and to steer clear of interference with the affairs of other nations. While there was no intention of deviating from that policy, yet the economic and political rights of American citizens would have to be protected "and in the valley of the Upper Congo we claim those rights to be equal to those of any other nation." Tisdel, after his expedition, warned his fellow countrymen against settling on the West African coast without large capital since they would have to compete there with established Dutch, British, and German companies.[18]

[13] *Foreign Relations*, 1886, vii.

[14] *Ibid.*, 1888, pt. II, 1084ff.

[15] Cf. Moore, *Digest*, I, 117ff.

[16] *Foreign Relations*, 1879, 342ff.

[17] *Senate Reports*, 48th Cong., 1st sess., no. 393, 10.

[17a] Seward to Noyes, Aug. 29, 1879, *Foreign Relations*, 1879, 342ff.

[18] Frelinghuysen to Tisdel, Sept. 8, 1884; Tisdel to Frelinghuysen, London, Nov. 23, 1884; Tisdel to Bayard, Lisbon, Apr. 25 and June 29, 1885; *Foreign Relations*, 1885, 282ff.

Stanley had first offered the Congo Basin to Great Britain. When it declined, King Leopold of Belgium was far-sighted enough to establish, under the guise of humanity and unselfishness, the International African Company, which at once settled in the new land. The Americans were inclined to take the high-sounding phrases of the Belgian King at their face value. Believing that their own interests would be best taken care of by the International Company, they were the first to recognize its flag. When, on February 8, 1884, Great Britain and Portugal concluded a treaty purporting to assign the upper part of the Niger to Portugal, Germany and France began to insist vigorously on their rights. Bismarck seized the opportunity to approach France, since relations with Great Britain had become somewhat strained. Negotiations with the French Ambassador, Baron de Courcel, conducted personally by Bismarck, led to a basic agreement on the West African question. The German Government invited all powers interested in Africa to a conference. Great Britain, although suspicious of the Franco-German rapprochement, after some hesitation decided to accept the invitation. Since Senator John T. Morgan had submitted a resolution to the American Senate on February 26 demanding neutrality of the Congo Basin from the source to the mouth, the German Government first inquired whether or not the American Government would accept an invitation to the Conference (May 4).[19] On May 21 the German Minister reported that the American Government had not entered into negotiations with any other government concerning that matter. Nor had it any intention of doing so; it sought no privileges for itself, but suggested regulation of conditions and commerce on the Congo with due consideration for the interests of all nations involved.[20] Upon advice of Ferry, the French Premier, the invitation to the Berlin Conference was sent to the United States. This seemed all the more proper as Stanley was an American citizen. In its preliminary discussions the German Government had referred to American recognition of the International Company. The American Government at first hesitated to accept the invitation, although agreeing with Germany in rejecting the Anglo-Portuguese treaty. Kasson was asked for his opinion. He urged acceptance, as important commercial interests of the United States were at stake. Moreover, the third point of the agenda affected the rights of the natives in whose protection the United States was particularly interested because of Liberia. If the decision had been left to Kasson, the United States, like the other powers, would have sent warships to the Congo and negotiated with the natives for acquisition of land.[21] On

[19] *Staatsarchiv,* XLV, 11f.
[20] *Ibid.,* XLV, 14.
[21] Kasson to Frelinghuysen, Berlin, Oct. 10, 13, and 15, and Nov. 10, 1884, Dept. State, *Despatches, Germany,* 36, nos. 33, 34, 40, and 60, respectively.

October 17, 1884, the American Government accepted with reservations the invitation to the Conference. The Conference was to deal exclusively with the commercial interests in the Congo Basin and West Africa. The German Legation in Washington assumed "that the reservations were caused partly by consideration for Great Britain, partly by a touch of jealousy of the fact that European Powers had taken the initiative in regulating a matter where the United States claimed priority" (Alvensleben, October 19). The American Government appointed John Kasson, Minister to Germany, and Henry Sanford, former Minister to Belgium, as commissioners. Bismarck treated the American representatives very courteously. During the preliminary discussions he had repeatedly expressed his intention of cooperating with the United States. When Kasson thanked him for his invitation, he amiably replied that only the action of the American Government had made the Conference actually possible. Germany, he said, in recognizing the flag of the Congo company, had followed the American example.[22]

In his opening speech of November 15 Bismarck mentioned the general desire to civilize the natives of Africa.[23] The fundamental object of the Conference was to assure complete freedom of trade in the basin and estuary of the Congo. All nations should have free access without being discriminated against in the matter of customs tariffs. Fees should be collected only for the purpose of covering indispensable administrative expenses incurred in the interests of commerce. The Congress of Vienna had proclaimed freedom of navigation on all rivers flowing through more than one state. This principle had been incorporated in the public laws of Europe and America. The German Government would be glad to receive proposals for regulating navigation on all African rivers, but the program of the Conference was limited to the question of freedom of navigation on the Congo and the Niger. The representative of the British Government declared that it was ready to extend freedom of navigation to all African rivers, in accordance with the principle of the Congress of Vienna. But practical application of the principle was very difficult. While Congo navigation could be regulated by an international commission, the situation on the Niger was entirely different. The development of traffic on that river was due to British influence, and for this reason the case would have to be treated differently. On November 19, Kasson made an elaborate address from which are summarized a few leading

---

[22] Kasson to Frelinghuysen, Berlin, Nov. 17, 1884, confidential, Dept. State, *Despatches, Germany*, 36, no. 70.

[23] Protocols of the West African Conference, cf. *Staatsarchiv*, XLV, 47ff.; *Senate Executive Documents*, 49th Cong., 1st sess., no. 196. Cf. Zimmermann, *Kolonialpolitik*, 131ff.

statements. Immense territories in the heart of Africa had been unknown until 1874. An American citizen, supported by American and British friends, decided to carry the light of civilization into those unknown regions. On his entire trip nowhere did he find state authorities, fortifications, civilized places of asylum, or established governments, except such as native tribes possessed. His discoveries attracted the attention of all nations. It was evident that those regions would soon be exposed to the dangerous rivalry of different nations with conflicting interests. It was the desire of the American Government to have those discoveries used for the civilization of the native races and for the abolition of slavery contracts. The President had recognized the government of the International Company. He thought that he had acted in the common interest of civilized nations in recognizing the only flag symbolizing government in those regions. With due consideration to just territorial claims of other governments, he wished to see the borders of the territory that was to enjoy the advantages of the new regulation extended as far as possible. Wherever the future boundaries of that neutral and peaceful power might extend he saw guarantees for the preservation of peace and for the progress of African civilization, as well as for the development of commerce profitable for all nations.[24] In an exposé of December 10, Kasson pointed out the dangers from the savages to life and property of the whites in the event of war. The signatory powers therefore should undertake to submit any point of dispute to a court of arbitration of civilized nations. In that territory there should be no military action carried out by one belligerent against another, and no contraband of war should be supplied by any state of that free zone to a belligerent party.[25] In the session of January 31, he supplemented his proposals. Modern international law recognized the right of native races to dispose independently of their inherited land. In compliance with that principle the American Government would join in accepting a regulation based on the principle of voluntary consent of the natives whose land is to be occupied in all cases when appropriation of such land was not provoked by attacks from them.[26] The German Government, in the session of December 22, 1884, accepted the American proposal for neutralization of the Congo Basin. The French opposed it. Their counterproposal, namely, that each power should have the privilege of declaring itself neutral within the zone of commerce and of inducing the other powers to respect its neutrality, was recorded by Kasson as his personal success. In particular he welcomed the clause that obliged the powers to accept mediation of a third

[24] *Staatsarchiv*, XLV, 61ff.
[26] *Ibid.*, XLV, 173.
[25] *Ibid.*, XLV, 149f.

party before a conflict in the African zone. That, in his opinion, meant recognition of a modern principle for which American public opinion had always been fighting. It was not yet a court of arbitration, but a station along the way toward it. Thus the American commissioners did not hesitate to sign the General Act of February 26, 1885. They were convinced of having completed a successful piece of work. Without American cooperation outside the Conference sessions proper, Sanford wrote on January 14, 1885, the work of the Conference would have been in vain because it left unsolved the question of territorial boundaries and other serious difficulties. Likewise, Kasson defended his signature: because of American business interests it was necessary to secure the same advantages as the other powers. Omissions might cause conflicts and a possible change of policy on the part of the states interested in Africa. "We were grantees not grantors." It would have been unwise to postpone the day when the privileges were to be put into operation.[27]

Nevertheless, the General Act of the West African Conference was not submitted by the President to the Senate for action. The decision was caused by the fear of entanglement in European conflicts. The Presidential message of December 8, 1885, expressed it clearly enough: to share in the obligation of enforcing neutrality in the remote valley of the Congo meant alliances. It was impossible to assume such a responsibility. However, the Department of State would take a friendly attitude toward the General Act.[28]

The United States observed the beginnings of Germany's colonial policy without concern, nay even with indifference. It realized that Germany's large surplus population necessitated acquisition of overseas possessions. On the other hand, it was thought that the unfavorable geographic situation of Germany precluded a colonial policy on a large scale, if it did not prevent it altogether. Sargent's report of March 12, 1883, on colonial questions and emigration, sounds rather skeptical.

"In conclusion, upon this whole question I may remark that there are peculiar reasons why Germany could not easily hold possessions abroad. Its geographical position forbids it. England, as an island, is secure against invasion, and can therefore send assistance to her colonies without impairing her defensive powers at home. The United States has an enormous sea-coast; its states are not separated by a sea; its peaceable and comparatively feeble

[27] Kasson to Bayard, Berlin, Feb. 23 and Mar. 16, 1885, Dept. State, *Despatches, Germany,* 37, nos. 181 and 183, and 38, no. 205. *House Executive Documents,* 48th Cong., 2d sess., no. 247. *Senate Executive Documents,* 49th Cong., 1st sess., no. 196.

[28] Moore, *Digest,* I, 119; Bayard to Alvensleben, Apr. 16, 1886, Dept. State, *Notes to German Legation,* 10: 429ff.

neighbors give it no uneasiness, and it could support a relation to its colonies if its policy ever dictated it; but Germany has a limited coast; its navy is not calculated for extensive enterprises; its neighbors are dangerous at all times, and require of it occasional exertions and constant expensive military preparations that absorb its means and energies and forbid it to incur the liabilities which its self-respect would impose upon it as a colonizing nation. "I therefore believe that this agitation will be barren of important results, and that the United States will receive, as heretofore, the fertilizing stream of German emigration which has aided in its magnificent development."[29]

But thereafter Germany's aspirations were watched with attention. As mentioned before, the United States had the West Indies very much at heart; American trade continually advanced there and American capital entrenched itself with increasing firmness in the West Indian islands. Cuba, with its wealth of sugar, was foremost; the Americans were particularly sensitive about it. When in 1884 rumors were current to the effect that Cuba was to be ceded to Germany, the American Government saw fit to point out that a permanent foothold by an imperial monarchy possessing a first-class navy, at a point so contiguous to this country, would menace the independence and peace of the United States.[30] A short time after the North German Federation was founded, Americans had become convinced that Germany intended to acquire a naval station in the West Indies. Charles Sumner, chairman of the Committee on Foreign Relations, in a letter to the Secretary of State on May 30, 1868, asked for information on that question. The Presidential message of May 31, 1870, to the Senate alluded to a foreign power that was ready to pay two million dollars for the harbor of Samaná (Santo Domingo). This could have referred only to the North German Federation. The German Minister in Washington ascertained that a letter from a certain man named Hartmann had been read at a secret session of the Senate, the writer informing the President of the Dominican Republic of intentions of the North German Federation with regard to the bay of Samaná. Although Sumner and Schurz called the matter a "humbug"—Schurz thought that it represented Grant's efforts to bring pressure to bear on the Senate—the Assistant Secretary of State had officially taken up the affair for he stated that Berlin was rather surprised by American resistance.[31] As a matter of fact, the Americans had repeatedly thought of incorporating Santo Domingo in the Union. This plan crystallized when the Spaniards definitely withdrew from the island in 1865. President

[29] *Foreign Relations,* 1883, 354f.

[30] Frelinghuysen to Foster, Aug. 29, 1884, confidential, Dept. State, *Instructions, Spain,* 19: 642f.

[31] Gerolt to Bismarck, June 3, 1870.

Grant had determined to crown the political achievements of his Presidency with the acquisition of Santo Domingo. Thwarted by the resistance of the Senate and especially of his opponent Sumner, he could not reconcile himself to his failure. In his annual message of 1876 he again pointed out the advantages of the acquisition of Santo Domingo, saying that the island could raise the same products as Cuba.[32] Despite all denials, the Americans in 1871 actually suspected Germany of planning to acquire Santo Domingo. In the great Senate debate of January 11, 1871, several speakers claimed to be informed of German aspirations concerning Santo Domingo. Senator Morton, especially, alleged that he had definite information about it. Carl Schurz, in an elaborate speech imbued with the spirit of the free-trade policy, attempted to refute this suspicion. No other power in Europe, he said, endeavored so loyally to cultivate good relations with the United States. Germany did not possess one square foot of land outside the Continent except the small islands along her coast. And yet she had the most advantageous colonial system that ever existed. "It will have been noticed that of late years the German commercial marine has developed in a greater proportion, perhaps, than the commercial marine of any of the maritime nations. Germany had no numerous fleet of war vessels to protect her commerce. Germany had no colonies, in the ordinary sense of the term, to nourish that commerce. But Germany had something far better. Instead of keeping up colonial establishments, for which the home Government is politically responsible, and which it is bound to protect and defend with arms, Germany has clusters of mercantile establishments in every commercial town on the globe—in Europe, America, Asia, Africa, and Australia—colonies not political, but colonies commercial, which protect themselves, regulate themselves, and feed German commerce of their own motion, without imposing upon the mother country the remotest political responsibility." [33] However, Schurz did not succeed in dispelling suspicion. As late as 1881 White reported from Berlin the visit of a representative of the Germans living in Santo Domingo. Bismarck, he said, could hardly fail to cast his eyes on Santo Domingo. There were many Germans there. No doubt they would support the Chancellor, while the tradespeople and a large part of the population would gladly welcome annexation by Germany for the same reasons that they requested annexation by the United States and Spain, namely, for the protection of life and property and in the interest of peace. He thought that attempts would soon be made to bring the island under Ger-

[32] For American policy in Santo Domingo, cf. A. D. White, *Autobiography*, 150ff., and Moore, *Digest*, VI, 509ff.

[33] *Congressional Globe*, appendix, 41st Cong., 3d sess., XLIII, pt. 3, 32f.; Schurz, *Speeches, Correspondence, and Political Papers*, II, 111.

man rule. The Chancellor would maintain his present attitude as long as America insisted on a policy that had stood the test of time and was strong enough to enforce it.[34]

Was there an element of truth in all this? Generally speaking, the Reich indeed intended to acquire a coaling station in the West Indies. Bismarck, although at that time opposed to anything like a colonial policy, was impressed by the arguments of naval experts who recommended the establishment of such a coaling station. When the warship *Königin Augusta* sailed in 1868 for an extended voyage, her commander, Captain Kinderling, was commissioned to investigate on the spot the possibilities for such an establishment. Kinderling, however, exceeded his orders. In a letter to the German consul in San José, Costa Rica, he asked the Costa Rican Government for a promise to the effect that it should consider itself obligated, "until December 1, 1868, not to enter into negotiations regarding the port of Limón with any foreign government or private company." The Costa Rican Government denied this request on the ground that concessions could be granted only to private companies. Through an indiscretion this correspondence was published; in the course of time it came to be reprinted in the American press whenever Germany was suspected of violating the Monroe Doctrine.[35] Germany was alleged to have been approached several times for the annexation of Santo Domingo. In 1872, Báez, President of the Dominican Republic, after failing in his negotiations with the United States, declared himself ready to discuss with Germany the cession of large tracts of land. Naval officials wished to follow up these overtures, while Count Bernstorff in London advised first reaching an understanding with the United States. Bismarck was opposed to such plans.[36] Much later, in 1898, Germany was again confronted with that question. The Imperial Minister Resident in Haiti communicated the desire of the Dominican President to enter into negotiations with a European power, preferably Germany, for the acquisition of land. The German Government inquired in Washington how a German military establishment in Santo Domingo would impress the United States. The German Ambassador, while convinced that it would make an unfavorable impression, considered the project very valuable "in the event of being able to speak in a different tone of voice." He therefore favored delayed action on the matter but suggested that all consequences would have to be risked if the project were carried out. However, when the matter was sub-

[34] White to Blaine, Berlin, Apr. 4, 1881, Dept. State, *Despatches, Germany*, 28, no. 196.

[35] Bülow to Kaiser Wilhelm, Berlin, Nov. 7, 1874; see also *post*, p. 222.

[36] Bernstorff to Bismarck, London, Feb. 28, 1872.

mitted to the Emperor, he declared he would have nothing to do with it, for he did not wish a quarrel with the United States.[37]

The Americans already imagined the Germans occupying the island of St. Thomas in the Danish West Indies. As a matter of fact, such plans had existed ever since the days of the Great Elector. The Brandenburg, later Prussian, Government, had tried several times to acquire St. Thomas.[38] On January 31, 1868, both Houses of the Danish Reichstag resolved to sell St. Thomas and St. John to the United States. The treaty, however, was never put into operation. It lapsed on April 14, 1870, without being ratified by the United States Senate. But the idea was not abandoned. When, in the early seventies, it was rumored that Denmark intended to exchange St. Thomas for parts of North Schleswig, the American Government was alarmed. Its foreign representatives in Berlin and Copenhagen were asked for detailed reports on the matter. Bancroft was convinced that the German Government did not plan to acquire St. Thomas. Reports from Copenhagen were also reassuring; the German chargé d'affaires there had officially denied any such intentions on the part of his Government. The Department of State was appeased. It could not have been indifferent to a change of ownership of St. Thomas.[39] It is a matter of surprise in this connection that the United States, in 1878, without protest, allowed the transfer of St. Bartholomew from Sweden to France; probably that island did not seem to be of any value.[40]

The Americans did not fully appreciate the importance of the Pacific Coast until after they had acquired Alaska. Ambitious minds began to dream of the Union dominating the Pacific Ocean. Their eyes turned to the Far East; more and more were the trade routes to China and Japan extended. Thus the Sandwich Islands assumed prime importance to the United States. Like Cuba in the Atlantic, Hawaii in the Pacific became an outpost of American commerce.[41] The United States neither could nor would let the Sandwich Islands

---

[37] *Die Grosse Politik*, XV, 109ff. The Ambassador alluded to the tension caused by the Manila incident.

[38] Cf. Schück, *Brandenburg-Preussens Kolonialpolitik*, I, 176ff.

[39] Cramer to Fish, Copenhagen, Jan. 14, 1874, Dept. State, *Despatches, Denmark*, 12, no. 228; Bancroft to Fish, Berlin, Jan. 9, 1874, and Fish to Bancroft, Feb. 11, 1874, *Foreign Relations*, 1874, 368, 439f.; Fish to Nicholas Fish, Dec. 15, 1875, Dept. State, *Instructions, Prussia*, 16: 131; cf. Tansill, *Purchase of the Danish West Indies*, 173; Hunter to Cramer, Sept. 1, 1879, *Foreign Relations*, 1880, 344; consular report from St. Thomas, Jan. 2, 1874, Dept. State, *Despatches, St. Thomas*, 10, no. 149.

[40] Cf. Coolidge, *United States as a World Power*, 113.

[41] "The position of the Sandwich Islands as an outpost fronting and commanding the whole of our possessions on the Pacific Ocean, gives to the future of those islands a peculiar interest to the Government and people of the United States." Seward to Spalding, July 5, 1868, Moore, *Digest*, I, 484.

pass into the hands or under the influence of a foreign power. In the event of war, it was feared that the United States would be cut off from the main routes to the Australian colonies and the Orient. For this reason the United States had recognized the native Government of Hawaii as early as 1842. Great Britain and France followed suit in November 1843. Annexation came near to being realized under Secretary of State Marcy. The reciprocity treaty of January 30, 1875, obligated the Hawaiian Government not to conclude most-favored-nation treaties with other powers. This practically ended Hawaiian independence. The question of annexation became a pressing matter after the death of King Kalakaua and the accession of Queen Liliukalani, who was averse to foreign influence. Annexation was definitely completed on August 12, 1898, when all other possibilities of establishing a stable government had failed.[42]

German commerce had considerable interests in the Sandwich Islands. A treaty of friendship and commerce with Hawaii of March 25 and September 19, 1879, was one of the first of its kind to be acted upon by the Reichstag.[43] For this reason the Americans were always somewhat suspicious. When a visit to Berlin by the Hawaiian King and Cesar Moreno, his counselor, was contemplated, the American Minister was instructed to inform the Foreign Office that the United States would look with displeasure upon any negotiation and discussion directed toward bringing the islands under European control. The Department of State might be obliged to refuse recognition of transactions for the purchase of land.[44] Although Bismarck regarded the American-Hawaiian reciprocity treaty as unfavorable for German commerce, any plan to establish German colonies on the islands was far from his mind. On the contrary, in a conversation with Bancroft, January 25, 1873, he advised the United States to annex Hawaii. Later on he used the American plans regarding Hawaii as a means of bringing pressure to bear for concessions in the Samoa dispute.[45]

It is far more astonishing that the United States did not clash with the interests of Great Britain regarding the Sandwich Islands. It may not be inappropriate in this connection to say something about Anglo-American relations. Of course, the Sandwich Islands were of great importance to British trade. Great Britain considered the reciprocity treaty between the United States and Hawaii a serious detriment to her own interests, and it would not

---

[42] Cf. Moore, *Digest*, I, 475ff.

[43] Poschinger, *Die deutschen Handels- und Schiffahrtsverträge*, 125ff.

[44] Evarts to White, Oct. 16, 1880, confidential, Dept. State, *Instructions, Germany*, 17: 10ff.

[45] Bancroft to Fish, Berlin, Jan. 25, 1873, Dept. State, *Despatches, Germany*, 3, no. 453; see *post*, p. 248f.

have been surprising if British policy had been more deeply concerned about Hawaii than actually was the case.[46] We shall see later how keenly Hawaii was interested in changes of ownership in Polynesia.[47] When American annexation of Hawaii seemed imminent, the German Government vainly endeavored to discuss the question in London. The British Government felt disinclined to expose itself to new differences with the United States, since all existing disputes between the two countries belonged more or less to the past. Disagreements about fishery rights in Canadian waters and the Bering Straits and controversies in connection with the Clayton-Bulwer Treaty of April 19, 1850, concerning Central America, were unavoidable legacies from earlier times. Neither the transformation of the British Empire nor the encroachment of American spheres of interests in the oceans dominated by Great Britain gave occasion for new quarrels. And yet there were a few questions capable of arousing animosity in public opinion of the two countries. Such a question was the Irish situation. The large Irish element in American cities could not consider the brutal treatment of Ireland by the British Government as anything but a challenge. Nor were relations between Canada and the United States very friendly. After the United States had adopted a strict tariff policy there were constant economic disputes. Many Americans still hoped to see Canada unite with the United States, but Canada itself was absolutely opposed to such a solution, although, from a business point of view, it would have been an advantageous one. Canada was loudest in its demands for British economic retaliation against the protective policy of the United States.[48]

But it must be borne in mind that the United States in its foreign policy was far more free from the pressure of inherited necessities than were the old countries that carried the burden of "given conditions" from one century to another. The Union was a colonial country. The commerce of colonial commonwealths is ever seeking new channels, and at the same time political domination shifts from one section of the country to another with much greater rapidity than is possible in old-established states. As a power bordering the Atlantic Ocean, the United States was far more closely linked to the European system of states than it cared to admit. As an Atlantic colony of Great Britain it fought for its independence. Again and again the arbitrary methods of British naval warfare forced the United States into a community

[46] The reports of the British representative in Honolulu do indicate some concern, and there were occasional discussions between London and Washington about Hawaii, but without political consequences.

[47] Cf. *Die Grosse Politik*, IV, 176.

[48] Cf. *Cambridge History of the British Empire*, VI, 644ff.

of interests with other European states.[49] But in the Pacific the Union encountered the British Empire. That was a tremendous difference. The United States was geographically tied to Canada and the Australian colonies. There the spheres of interests mixed. United States trade with Australasia probably began simultaneously with that of Germany. But communications became far more direct after steamship lines and cables connected the Pacific Coast with Australia. It does not follow that the British colonists generally were very friendly to the Americans. Most of them considered themselves Englishmen with superior civilization and traditions. When the British West Indies came almost completely under the influence of American capital as a result of the cane-sugar crisis, the colonists coined the saying that the Americans were their friends economically but their enemies socially.[50] But that did not prevent surprising similarities of a political and social nature. Did not colonial society have nearly the same needs here as there? They had such problems in common as those resulting from the immigration of colored races. New Zealand and the Union were frequently compared; rapidity of development was as astonishing in one country as in the other. It was not inaccurate to call the New Zealanders the Yankees of the Pacific. "If all the nations of the world were classed according to the number and importance of their points of resemblance," an American author wrote in 1904, "the United States, New Zealand and Australia would stand in a group together, with England, Switzerland and France close by, and Belgium, Denmark, Germany and Scandinavia not far off. . . . The United States in recent years has devoted her superb vitality to the development of machinery, the organization of business for private profit, and the building of giant monopolies, while New Zealand has devoted her superb vitality to the development of just political and industrial institutions."[51] The early emancipation of woman in New Zealand aroused all the more comment in the United States, because the American woman had been conceded a privileged position ever since colonial times.

Anglo-Saxon rapprochement gradually evolved under the influence of political and economic conditions. The two Governments contributed very little, cherishing their old resentments. When their interminable controversies brought them to the verge of war over Venezuela in 1895, the Governments were astonished and dismayed. The transformation came from the periphery, not from the center. It is characteristic that the idea of an entente was achieved

[49] See *ante,* p. 11ff.

[50] Between 1850 and 1900 production of beet sugar increased thirtyfold, while cane sugar production only trebled. Later on, however, the situation was reversed.

[51] Parsons, *New Zealand,* 690f.

in the closest association with the general colonial movement. An ex-governor of New Zealand, in an essay, "German Colonisation: A Review of the Samoan Situation," suggested that there would be one hundred million English-speaking people within fifty years, and inquired what is to prevent them from coming to a permanent understanding.[52] Nor can it seriously be doubted that in the officers' wardrooms on British and American ships Anglo-Saxon friend-ship was occasionally celebrated even at that time with toasts like "blood is thicker than water." [53] The Australian colonies welcomed the outbreak of the Spanish-American War in 1898, with outspoken sympathies for the American cause. Monster demonstrations for the American consul took place in Auck-land. Many New Zealanders reported for voluntary service in the American Army.[54]

The United States lacked the opportunity, as well as the ability, to enter into competition with the British when it began to take a more lively interest in its trade with the Far Eastern powers. Cooperation was the natural thing. At that time the foreign policy of the United States—and that, too, is typical of a colonial country—was primarily a commercial policy. Everywhere it faced the superior political tradition of Great Britain. Quite unconsciously the United States submitted occasionally to British guidance, when their interests did not clash. The more other powers, like Germany and Japan, advanced in the Pacific sphere, the more closely did the Anglo-Saxons draw together for defense.

In the south Pacific the United States in general made no claims. On all island groups it had commercial establishments or missions which amounted to about the same thing. But those islands were not included in the American sphere of interest. The United States watched British and German manœuvers in those regions with complacency. However, the annexation of the Fiji Islands did create some excitement in the United States; it threatened to retaliate by annexing Hawaii, but an official protest did not follow either in

[52] Pamphlet enclosed in American consular report from Auckland, May 20, 1889, Dept. State, *Despatches, Auckland,* 9, no. 11.

[53] Cf. the statement of Kane, the American admiral, after the catastrophe in Apia in 1889, *post,* p. 261.

[54] Newspaper clipping, without headline, in consular report from Auckland, July 28, 1898, Dept. State, *Despatches, Auckland,* 10, no. 28. A consular report of May 13, 1898, from Auckland (Dept. State, *Despatches, Auckland,* 10, no. 21) says: "The excitement runs high throughout Australasia, and particularly in New Zealand. I think it quite safe to say that 99 per cent of the Colonials are friendly to the United States in its present war with the Spanish. I have never listened to more loyal speeches or sermons in any part of America than I have heard in the city of Auckland, during the past few weeks. In fact, nothing is being talked about except the war."

this case or on other occasions.[55] On the contrary, the Department of State went on record as being opposed to unnecessary interference. When the Hawaiian Government urged that the United States protest against further annexations of ownerless islands in Polynesia, the American Government, on December 6, 1883, refused, on the ground that there was no cause for protest since those islands were more closely connected with Australasia than with Polynesia.[56] This noninterference also benefited Germany. The Americans asserted that they had no commercial relations with the Marshall, Gilbert, and Solomon Islands, which were claimed by Germany. They insisted only that trade of American citizens remain unmolested on islands as yet ownerless.[57]

In a certain sense the Caroline Islands were an exception.[58] The United States could not remain indifferent to the ownership of the Caroline Islands because of potential reactions on relations with Spain. Germany's claim to the Caroline Islands was based on an agreement with Great Britain. A joint Anglo-German declaration of April 6, 1876, had stipulated that, in addition to the northern part of New Guinea, between the 141st degree of east longitude and the 8th degree of south latitude, all islands in the north, including the Caroline and Marshall Islands, should be assigned to the German sphere of influence. On the basis of the bull of Pope Alexander VI, of 1493, providing for the division of the territory of the world, Spain included the Caroline Islands in her sphere of interest though she had never exercised rights of sovereignty there. In 1875 the Governor General of the Philippines and Hong Kong claimed customs control over all ships touching the Caroline and Pelew Islands. Great Britain and Germany jointly rejected that claim on March 4, 1875. After that, the Spaniards made no further advance for ten years. Finally it was rumored that Spain intended to claim ownership of the islands. A press notice of March 1885 announced that the Spanish Governor of the Philippines had been commissioned to occupy the islands with military forces. Reports became insistent enough for Robertson & Hermsheim, the com-

[55] Schlözer to Bülow, Dec. 21, 1874, confidential.

[56] "These islands are geographically allied to Australasia rather than to Polynesia. At no time have they so asserted and maintained a separate national life as to entitle them to entrance, by treaty stipulations and established forms of competent self-government, into the family of nations, as Hawaii and Samoa have done. Their material development has been largely due to their intercourse with the great Australian system, near which they lie, and this Government would not feel called upon to view with concern any further strengthening of such intercourse when neither the sympathies of our people are touched nor their direct political or commercial relations with those scattered communities threatened by the proposed change." Moore, *Digest*, I, 491.

[57] Bayard to Pendleton, Feb. 27, 1886, Dept. State, *Instructions, Germany*, 17: 602ff.

[58] For the Caroline Islands dispute, cf. *Staatsarchiv*, XLVI, 159ff.

pany most interested, to urge the German Government to act. Berlin was particularly opposed to the Spanish aspirations, as the Caroline Islands promised to become of particular value to the future of German trade because of the proximity of the Bismarck Archipelago and Kaiser Wilhelm Land. In the event of Spanish occupation German commercial interests would probably be endangered, because Spain generally imposed differential dues and duties in her colonies on foreign imports and exports. However, before deciding on any course of action, the German Government wished to have the backing of London, where at that time important conversations were in progress between Krauel and Thurston on demarcation of spheres of interests in the south Pacific. London discounted the rumors about Spain's intentions but expressly declared that Great Britain did not recognize any rights of Spain, historical or otherwise, to the Pelew and Caroline Islands. The islands were not without importance to the British Navy, so it was stated, if the coal mine discovered on the island of Yap and worked by a British company would yield a good output. British policy in this case could afford to be generous, for the Australian colonies showed little anxiety about the matter of ownership of the Caroline Islands. Berlin therefore decided to anticipate potential action by Spain, and announced Germany's claim to the Caroline Islands on August 6. The Spanish Government protested in a note of August 12, but gave no evidence to support its alleged sovereignty. On August 24, the *Norddeutsche Allgemeine Zeitung* refuted that protest, saying that Germany and Great Britain had remonstrated against Spanish claims of sovereignty as early as 1875 without being contradicted. The conflict was aggravated by the fact that the commander of the German gunboat *Iltis* hoisted the German flag on the island of Yap in the presence of Spanish warships. This incident aroused so much excitement that a mob attacked the German Legation in Madrid and the consulate general in Barcelona.[59]

The Foreign Office had not been prepared for such a violent outburst of Spanish sentiment. From the outset Bismarck took the affair very calmly; at the beginning of the crisis he was not even in Berlin. Bismarck was by no means willing to have the relations between Germany and Spain menaced by that incident. Many people wondered just what Bismarck's intentions had been in the whole affair. The American Minister in Madrid advanced the

[59] Preussische-Hamburger Gesellschaft to Bismarck, Mar. 13; Krauel to Bismarck, London, Apr. 14; Foreign Office to Hatzfeldt and Solms, June 3; Hatzfeldt to Foreign Office, June 7; Solms to Foreign Office, June 9; Herbert to Wilhelm Bismarck, June 23; Foreign Office memorandum, May 29; Robertson & Hermsheim to Bismarck, Hamburg, July 16; Foreign Office to Bülow (in attendance on the Kaiser), July 18, 1885. Cf. Schulthess, *Europäischer Geschichtskalender,* 1885, 122f.

theory that Bismarck intended to overthrow the Spanish King in view of his increasing disappointment because the King had not succeeded in obtaining a decisive influence on the Spanish political situation.[60] But nothing of the sort could have passed through the Chancellor's mind. Indeed, in the course of the dispute, he repeatedly stated that Germany was not interested in the maintenance of a monarchy in Spain. Establishment of republics in Spain and Italy would confirm the unity of monarchies, which at last would realize that they would have more to lose through republican forms of government than they could gain from attacking one another.[61] But the Chancellor wished to have the matter settled in such a way as to protect King Alfonso personally. This is evinced by several ordinances.

Bismarck presumably took very little interest in the matter anyway, and it was no doubt due only to pressure from interested German companies that he gave his consent for action on the part of Germany. No sooner did the dispute assume serious proportions than he stopped it, especially since British support was very weak.[62] Bismarck's disappointment with Great Britain's policy shows clearly in a memorandum of September 7 by Rantzau. "We have made a bothersome mess with the coral reefs in the Pacific," Bismarck said to Raschdau. It was the impression of the Counselor that Bismarck referred to the Foreign Office.[63] After returning to Berlin, Bismarck took the matter in his own hands. For him it was a "trifle" which had cost him altogether too much time. First of all, it must not affect German-Spanish relations. When Raschdau submitted to him on August 25 a draft of instructions to Solms, he noted in his own hand: "This is not a colonial question but a political one, belonging in the Spanish section; the Caroline Islands are a side issue and relations with Spain the main concern." The Chancellor would never have let the situation drift into a war. The *Hamburger Nachrichten* of February 3, 1892, asserted that a war with Spain was doubtful because commercial relations with Spain would have been interrupted and seriously damaged for many years as a result of Spanish sentiment against Germany's procedure. Nevertheless, Bismarck did not recognize a historical right on the part of Spain to possession of the Pelew and Caroline Islands: "If we did, we should make our procedure of this year an unlawful attack against a friendly power; if we admitted that Spain had been the former owner of the islands, our conduct in 1875 would

[60] Foster to Bayard, San Ildefonso, Aug. 20, 1885, Dept. State, *Despatches, Spain*, 114, no. 392.

[61] Bismarck's marginal note on telegram from German Legation, San Ildefonso, Aug. 23, 1885. A quite similar attitude is expressed in a telegram to Solms, Aug. 26, 1885.

[62] Not until Sept. 17 did Great Britain declare itself opposed to Spain's claims.

[63] Raschdau, *Meine ersten dienstlichen Beziehungen zu Fürst Bismarck*, 33f.

have to be adjudged admittedly ignorant, and our conduct in 1885 brutal."[64]
When instructions of August 17 from the Spanish Government to its Minister
in Berlin were communicated to him, the Chancellor changed his tactics. In a
marginal note he stated that the legality of the Spanish claims was not a
matter of feelings and moods but of facts of international law. "As far as
such facts exist and can be proved, we shall not maintain our claim. Adverse
public opinion has as much influence in Germany as in Spain, and the governments can do much toward influencing it by means of proper information."
On August 17 he sent word from Varzin to the Spanish Minister in Berlin
that Germany would naturally surrender her rights if Spain could prove hers
to be older. The hoisting of the flag was naturally done with reservation as to
earlier rights and not with the intention of violating the demonstrable rights
of others. However, to call the islands pearls of the Castilian crown was to
beg the question. The German Government had bound itself to a certain
extent through the protest of 1875 and would have to reach an agreement
with Great Britain. As a matter of fact, the régime in Spanish colonies made
trade impossible; for this reason, and because it seemed that Spain intended
to occupy the islands, the German Government had anticipated eventualities.
Herbert Bismarck remarked to the Kaiser that negotiations with France on the
same subject and the colonial controversies with Great Britain were of far
greater importance than the Caroline Islands, and yet Germany had reached a
most friendly understanding with Great Britain. Upon the Kaiser's reply that
the islands possibly were not worth all that ado, Bismarck wrote on the
margin of his son's memorandum: "Certainly; it was only Spain's insolence
that created it."[65]

The latter statement indicates the chief factor that retarded settlement of
the dispute. The Chancellor wished to await the subsiding of the noise and
excitement in Spain and their natural echo in Germany.[66] The attacks of the
Spanish press were extremely violent. Only the Spanish King kept his com-
posure. He clearly realized that Spain could not afford a war. "If you wish
to declare war without being forced to do so," he told his generals, "you can
wage it alone. I shall depart and retire to a foreign country because I prefer
to abdicate voluntarily four weeks earlier instead of being driven out of Spain
by force four weeks later, burdened with the crushing feeling of having
hurled my country into indescribable misfortune."[67]

On August 23 the German Government declared itself ready to enter into

[64] Marginal note on telegram from Madrid, Sept. 19, 1885.
[65] Memorandum of Herbert Bismarck, Aug. 28, 1885.
[66] Note of Rantzau for Foreign Office, Varzin, Sept. 2, 1885.
[67] Reports from Madrid on Aug. 22 and Sept. 11 and 16, 1885.

an examination of the Spanish claims to legal titles through friendly negotiations, and, if so agreed, to leave the decision to arbitration by a power
friendly to both parties. According to the Madrid correspondent of the
Kölnische Zeitung, September 18, the Spanish Minister of Education had
declared that his party (the Catholic Party) would only accept the mediation
of a successor of Alexander VI, the Pontifex Maximus. Bismarck surprised
the world by agreeing to that proposal.[68] By accepting arbitration he hoped to
make a good impression on the Catholics and at the same time, with reference
to the ecclesiastical controversy, intended to prejudice the Pope against the
influence of the Catholic Democrats headed by Windthorst.[69] It was an
objective of German policy to work for Spanish concessions with respect to
commerce. The commercial treaty of July 12, 1883, had caused considerable
difference of opinion with reference to the duty on rye; moreover, a more
favorable renewal of the treaty was hoped for. The decision of the Pope on
October 22 assigned the Caroline Islands to Spain but enjoined her to establish a stable administration there at once. Germany was granted special
commercial privileges with the right to maintain a port and coaling station
on the islands. A renewal of the German-Spanish commercial treaty was
promised. The German Government loyally supported the British negotiations
with Spain, which were expected to give the British equal economic advantages.[70] Spain, however, was not willing to concede a coaling station to Great
Britain also, on the ground that in such a case the United States might raise
the same demand (Solms to Bismarck, December 19).

The principles of American policy in the matter of the Caroline Islands
were expressed in the Presidential message of December 8, 1891, which stated
that the American Government did not intend to interfere, but insisted on
protecting the trade of peaceful American citizens.[71] In October the American
Government had made inquiries in Madrid as to how Spain, in the event of
American recognition of her claims, would treat the American Protestant
missions on the islands. The Spanish Government, thinking even the mere
inquiry implied recognition of its claims, solemnly promised protection of
the missions.[72] In general, however, American public opinion inclined toward
the Germans throughout the dispute. The press showed little sympathy for
Spain, excepting the *Courier des États-Unis,* which was under Spanish influ-

[68] Hagen, *Bismarcks Kolonialpolitik,* 563.
[69] Bismarck to Kaiser Wilhelm, Berlin, Sept. 21, 1885, telegram; cf. Poschinger,
Fürst Bismarck, neue Tischgespräche, I, 309f.
[70] Note of Rantzau to Foreign Office, Friedrichsruh, Oct. 31, 1885.
[71] Cf. Moore, *Digest,* V, 863.
[72] German Legation in Madrid to Chancellor, Oct. 19, 1885.

ence, and the *New York Herald,* which suspected Germany of aspirations with regard to Cuba.[73] Nor was the American Government unfriendly. The Secretary of State admired the way in which the Imperial Government had dealt with the situation. The sympathies of the United States, he told Count Leyden, the German chargé d'affaires, would be with that nation which was willing to perform the greatest service to the cause of civilization and humanity in those unexplored regions. "An additional interest of the United States in a stable government on the islands," the Secretary said, "results from the presence for many years of American missionaries who, by the way, carry on some trade, though on a modest scale, using a steamship of their own for communication between the various islands." Leyden inferred from the Secretary's friendly tone that personally he would have been glad to see Germany definitely occupy the Caroline Islands. In November the Secretary once more praised the policy of the German Government because of its conciliatory and generous spirit.[74]

The American public was interested in the future of the Caroline Islands inasmuch as the American missionaries had developed a brisk activity on some of the islands. But the hoisting of the German flag on the island of Yap by the gunboat *Iltis* was observed with a degree of anxiety. The question was raised as to whether a war between Spain and Germany would not necessarily lead to occupation of Cuba by the German Navy.[75] The *New York Herald* expressed that apprehension in strong terms on September 8. It published the correspondence of April 20 and May 11, 1868, between the commander of the *Königin Augusta,* Captain Kinderling, and the German consul in San José, Costa Rica, in which establishment of a German port in the West Indies was mentioned.[76] A commentary of the *New York Herald* ironically compared the official repudiation of the arbitrary procedure of the commander of the *Iltis* with earlier attempts of the German Government at denying intentions of getting a foothold in the West Indies. German acquisitions on the western coast of Africa, in the northern half of New Guinea, and in the Caroline

[73] Leyden to Bismarck, Washington, Aug. 31 and Sept. 10, 1885; Hohenlohe to Bismarck, Paris, Sept. 9, 1885.

[74] To Bismarck, Oct. 1 and Nov. 17, 1885, extract.

[75] For preparations of the German Navy, cf. Schulthess, *Europäischer Geschichts-kalender,* 1885, 127. Bismarck later alluded to those preparations in an interview with the representative of the *Petit Journal* on May 22, 1890; Poschinger, *Fürst Bismarck, neue Tischgespräche,* I, 309.

[76] Leyden, who transmitted the article of the *New York Herald* with his report of Sept. 9, expressed the opinion that the Department of State must have assisted the writer in his study of the archives, but as a matter of fact, the correspondence was known years before; cf. *ante,* p. 211.

Islands, seemed to point to a decided change in German policy, when compared to the assurances of Minister von Schlözer of eleven years ago regarding an assertion that Germany, under certain conditions, might aspire to the possession of Puerto Rico.[77] The writer of this article inquired whether Germany's respect for the Monroe Doctrine could be expected to be greater than her friendship for Spain. Was not Germany's alleged consideration for the United States of a similar nature to her consideration for Spain in occupying one of the Caroline Islands? The *Norddeutsche Allgemeine Zeitung* of September 22 attacked this article. In the event of war, Cuba would indeed be an important objective, "but the American statesmen are too well informed of the tendency of our colonial policy to think that the German Government could conceive the idea of taking possession of an island which, in German hands, would require far stronger garrisons than the Spanish Government is compelled to maintain there."[78]

At the same time the American Government was worrying about another incident. During the farewell call on August 20, 1885, of John W. Foster, the American Minister to Spain, a Spanish Cabinet member bitterly complained of Germany's procedure as being opposed to Spain's indisputable sovereignty. He had reason to believe, he said, that Germany had suddenly decided to assume the protectorate of the Caroline Islands principally because she had information of intentions on the part of the United States of placing the islands under its own protection.[79] The Department of State at once took the bait so cleverly set out. Instructions of September 7 to George H. Pendleton, the Minister in Berlin, called that assertion surprising. The American Government could not for a moment assume that it had been seriously believed by the German Government, which knew so well American policy as proclaimed and practised for more than a century, a policy averse to acquisition of remote colonies, and practically forbidding it. The Minister was instructed to inquire of the Foreign Office whether the assertion of the Spanish Minister had any foundation. The allegation was true only in that Bismarck, during the preliminary negotiations, had taken into consideration the potential claims of the United States to the Caroline Islands. The Chancellor had commissioned his son Herbert to make occasional inquiries regarding such American claims. Herbert Bismarck had carried out his orders on October 10, in the course of a conversation with Coleman, the American chargé d'affaires. Nothing further had been done. Herbert Bismarck therefore was able to assure Pendle-

---

[77] The German Minister had energetically refuted the rumor, which dated back to 1874, that Germany had aspirations concerning Puerto Rico.

[78] Schulthess, *Europäischer Geschichtskalender,* 1885, 130.

[79] Solms to Bismarck, Oct. 13, 1885.

ton on October 22 with a clear conscience that there was no information as to United States claims to the Caroline Islands and that the assertion in question had evidently been made for the purpose of creating dissent and estrangement between the two countries. The inquiry of October 10 had been made only as a matter of precaution and out of very friendly consideration for the United States. Germany fully understood the American policy. Pendleton was received by the Chancellor on the following day. The Chancellor declared that he had not heard of any American claims for possession or control of the Caroline Islands, but he had indeed found, on an old German map, the word "American" opposite or over two or three of those islands. His son had been commissioned to make inquiries in a friendly spirit as regards American claims of ownership and the interests of individual Americans on the islands. The previous day's conversation had answered the question to his complete satisfaction. Speaking at length about the dispute with Spain and about Germany's colonial plans in general, the Chancellor cleverly put the question whether the United States, in view of the material interests of its citizens on the islands, would not join in the treaty which Great Britain and Germany were about to conclude with Spain.[80] The Chancellor promised to exhaust every possibility in order to reach an acceptable understanding with Spain. The islands were not worth a war. They would never cover the cost of one week of war or even of one week of war preparations. Germany's colonial policy was absolutely peaceful and was based on the methods of commerce. Commerce protected its own interests. It maintained itself by means of exchange between the mother country and dependent colonies, not by military power. "The character and disposition of the German people are opposed to a policy that would necessitate establishment of garrisons in foreign or far distant countries." But Pendleton held out little hope for American participation in the treaty. He spoke of the traditional American policy which was averse to "entangling alliances." In general, the United States preferred "to rely on the law of nations and the appreciation of equity and comity among peoples," and to strive for reparation of wrong committed from time to time. The United States believed that this method had its advantages. Bismarck, evidently anxious to have the United States as a party to the treaty, once more enumerated the advantages of participation: free trade, religious liberty, and elimination of a colonial policy which everywhere, as in Cuba above all, destroyed all trade, "as that cover extinguished that candle." Pendleton, however, only promised that he would transmit the statement of the Chan-

[80] According to a private letter of Sept. 25 to Bismarck from Sir Edward Malet, the British Ambassador, the Ambassador was consulted concerning possible participation by the United States. The British Government agreed.

cellor to his Government. The conversation yielded no positive results. In instructions to the Legation in Washington (October 19) Bismarck again had the assertion of the Spanish Minister designated as "taken completely out of nothing, and lacking any sort of substance." The American Government was satisfied.[81]

II. THE GREAT POWERS AND SAMOA

The United States abandoned its policy of aloofness only in the case of one group of Pacific islands. Samoa figured in American policy at an early period because of its geographic location. Located on the steamship route between San Francisco and Auckland, between Panama and Sydney, and between Valparaiso and China and Japan, and lying outside the zone of storms, the islands were of particular value for the Pacific trade.[1] Savaii, Upolu, Tutuila, and Manua are the most important of those islands. Since the forties the Americans had kept a commercial agent in Samoa, but their trade was insignificant. The captain of a Pacific steamship line called attention to the importance of Samoa, but Commander Richard W. Meade, who touched at Samoa on a cruise in 1872, was first to appreciate the immense commercial and strategic importance of the harbor of Pagopago on the island of Tutuila. The harbor furnished an ideal coaling station for navigation in the south Pacific. Halfway between Honolulu and Auckland, it actually controlled the Polynesian trade routes. Meade immediately concluded an agreement with a few Samoan chieftains which gave the United States title to Pagopago. Meade's report for the first time aroused the officials of the American Government. They did not fail to realize that upon completion of an interoceanic canal that group of islands would gain tremendously in importance. From the beginning, American policy was influenced by the apprehension that Samoa, and in particular the harbor of Pagopago, might fall into the hands of a foreign power in the case of war. In American opinion this would have meant complete paralysis of Pacific trade. The American Government unofficially sent Colonel A. B. Steinberger to Samoa with instructions to make a thorough study of local conditions. Playing the part of a disinterested friend,

---

[81] Pendleton to Bayard, Berlin, Sept. 22 and 23, 1885, Dept. State, *Despatches, Germany,* 39, nos. 72 and 73; note of Herbert Bismarck, Sept. 22; Leyden to Bismarck, Nov. 13, 1885.

[1] Cf. Keim, *German-American Political Relations,* 135. For Samoa's importance to the United States, cf. Muzzey, *American Adventure,* II, 220.

Steinberger easily succeeded in gaining the confidence of a few chieftains. The Samoans asked for his advice in organizing a government. On his first trip Steinberger seems to have talked of an American protectorate; at any rate, the natives strongly counted upon it. On his return to Washington Steinberger's proposal to place the islands under American control was rejected, although obviously with some reluctance. The Department of State could not have obtained the consent of Congress to such a measure.[2] In more than one respect Steinberger's second sojourn in Samoa was an obscure affair. Assuming the office of Prime Minister of the Kingdom of Samoa, he worked for American annexation, evidently on his own responsibility. At the same time he maintained business relations with the German plantation company. All Samoan representatives of the great powers looked upon his activity with suspicion, and even the American consul complained of him. When Malietoa, the newly elected king, accused Steinberger of fraud, the latter was forced to submit to criminal proceedings on a British warship whose commander was his declared enemy. Malietoa was compelled to discharge Steinberger from his service. Since the affair was reported to Congress, the American Government had no choice but to sacrifice its confidential agent.[3] But Steinberger's second sojourn in Samoa sufficed to entangle the Samoan knot in a hopeless fashion. The Samoans belonged to the Polynesian race: lazy, unreliable, martial, but also good-natured, chivalrous, and extremely hospitable. Two great clans, the Taimuas and the Faipules, had been fighting for supremacy for a long time, but it had been impossible ever to secure general recognition of a king elected by either of the two families. The battles of the natives were comparatively harmless so long as the whites did not meddle. Not until white civilization entered with its firearms and alcohol did clashes that resembled German student duels assume more serious dimensions. The great powers, during their controversies, referred to "the will of the people" in the support of their own more or less dubious claims. That, of course, had nothing to do with the real situation, for the natives, like children, could be talked into anything.

In Samoa there were two big German copra plantations, founded in the fifties by Godeffroy & Co. of Valparaiso for its copra trade in the Pacific. American and British interests could scarcely be compared to the German interests. Later on even the central administration of the South Sea Company was located in Apia. From here German activities were directed in the region

---

[2] Fish to Steinberger, Dec. 11, 1874, Dept. State, *Special Missions,* 3: 265ff.; *House Executive Documents,* 44th Cong., 2d sess., no. 44, "Agency of A. B. Steinberger in the Samoan Islands."

[3] For the Steinberger mission, cf. Keim, *German-American Political Relations,* 116f.

bounded on the north by the Gilbert Islands and on the south by the Tonga Islands.[4] Great Britain for obvious reasons later denied the predominant position of German trade. The British calculated on the basis of landed property, when, as a matter of fact, production was the decisive factor. From this point of view there was no question that Germany occupied by far the first place through the eighties. Only the Germans possessed real plantations. "Considering the island region as a whole, German commerce is still leading there," the German consul in Apia wrote on September 2, 1884. "Nearly one half of total production flows through its channels. Of competing companies of other countries, only the Chinese house of Ong-Chong in Sydney is of any importance in the trade of the Gilbert Islands. The interests of the British firm Henderson & McFarlane are secondary to German interests everywhere except in the Tokelau Islands, where production is insignificant. The Englishman O'Keefe has interests only in Yap next to those of German companies. The American firm of Wightman Brothers in Apia is a new enterprise whose life is not assured as yet. In view of the present upward trend of German commercial enterprises in the island region, there is no doubt that they soon will secure a large share of the increasing production."[5] Nevertheless, German aspirations were extremely modest in the beginning. Instructions of the Chancellor to Weber, the German consul in Apia, of November 1, 1875, defined his mission as "exclusive cultivation of German trade and navigation, protection of nationals from infringements of their rights." In every permissible way he was to assert claims based upon definite legal principles, be they treaties, legal provisions, or general rules of law. "Although you must pursue this policy with great energy, you will always stay within those limits that cannot be transgressed without disturbing mutual relations or without hurting our own position." The German Government's attitude toward the Steinberger mission was one of watchful waiting. There had been plans for acquiring the harbor of Pagopago as a coaling station, "but that might cause ill feeling in Washington, and moreover encourage American plans, now held in abeyance, for acquisition of that harbor." The Admiralty was particularly instructed to maintain friendly relations with the United States and Great Britain. At the insistence of the navy, the German Government first thought of the harbor of Vauvau (Tonga Islands) for a coaling station, and later considered with increasing seriousness a harbor in Samoa.[6] But even such a

[4] Cf. *Staatsarchiv*, XLIV, 321.

[5] For German interests in the Pacific, cf. report of Travers, Dec. 8, 1886, *Samoa Weissbuch*, I, 1ff.

[6] Foreign Office to Consul Weber, Berlin, June 25, 1876, very confidential; Foreign Office to Admiralty, Berlin, July 2, 1876.

coaling station, destined for commercial purposes exclusively, seemed too great a venture to Bismarck. Commenting upon a memorandum of July 2, 1876, on the treaty of friendship with Tonga, he wrote: "What is understood by 'coaling station'? Buildings? Fortifications? Are we to claim exclusive use of the harbor? If not, why any stipulations? As to granting authority, I am not without apprehension that, owing to usual procedure of the navy, we might in the end drift into an enterprise equivalent to an Imperial German colony. Do we need a treaty to rent or erect buildings there, or to deposit coal for our disposal? More about that orally. Trade to be protected by frequent appearance and permanent stationing of ships."[7]

However, when in 1877 the Taimua party, under Steinberger's influence, quite frankly sought an American protectorate and sent a special envoy to Washington to negotiate, German business circles were justly alarmed. The German Government, therefore, made inquiries in Washington on January 24, 1878, as to the extent of the negotiations in progress. The Government of the United States was asked not to take advantage of the Taimua mission to conclude agreements that might create a situation similar to the one created for the German Government as a result of the American reciprocity treaty with Hawaii. Apprehension was expressed that in such a case Australian plans for annexation might be carried out. The American Government, although entirely inclined to encourage the far-reaching plans of the Taimua party, was compelled to deny officially any plans of annexation. The American Government, it said, only wished for a return of peace and for organization of a stable and independent native government. A protectorate could not be accepted under any condition. Griffin, the American consul in Apia, was instructed, if necessary, to lend his assistance to the German and British representatives for the protection of peace and order in Samoa.[8] Berlin did not look with favor upon the treaty of friendship and commerce of January 17, 1878, between the United States and Samoa. It was feared that the Americans would claim the privilege of direct intervention and thereby damage the commerce of the other powers.[9] The treaty granted to the United States exclusive disposal of the harbor of Pagopago. By article 5 the American Government offered its good offices in the event of a conflict between the Samoan Government and another government.[10] Thus the Americans had secured an

[7] Marginal note in memorandum regarding protection of German interests in the Pacific, July 2, 1876. Poschinger inaccurately quotes it in *Kölnische Zeitung*, Aug. 31, 1906.

[8] Schlözer to Bülow, Jan. 3, 1878; Foreign Office to German consul in Apia, July 30, 1878; cf. Keim, *German-American Political Relations*, 124f., footnotes 38 and 39.

[9] Keim, *German-American Political Relations*, 133.

[10] Malloy, *Treaties*, II, 1574ff.

important strategic point and a great commercial advantage. On his return home the Samoan envoy was escorted by a certain Mr. Goward who was to extend the greetings of the American Government to the people of Samoa. Goward's behavior was not very pleasing to the Germans. He allowed himself to be fêted by the Samoans and told the German consul that the German agreement with Samoa of 1877 was canceled; its article 4, granting preference to Germany, should be considered only as polite phraseology. Samoa was no longer in need of treaties with the other nations represented there. Finally Goward went so far as to offer his mediation for a German-Samoan treaty, an imposition which the German consul vigorously rejected.[11] Goward was supported by the American consul, who likewise wished to crowd out the other powers.

Not without difficulty did the German Government succeed in concluding a treaty with Samoa. The preliminary agreement of 1877 was not observed by the Samoans because of their American plans. Germany consequently seized the harbors of Saluafata and Falealili as security. Thereby, Germany wished to guarantee the independence of Samoa by treaty, as well as "strengthen the courage of our nationals for a continuation of their peaceful struggle with foreign competition."[12] Finally, on January 24, 1879, the German-Samoan treaty of friendship and commerce was concluded; it authorized German warships "to enter the harbor of Saluafata, to cast anchor there, remain, take in supplies, and to make repairs." The German Government, furthermore, was privileged to provide all such establishments and arrangements in that harbor as were required by the German warships and their men. Germany was allowed to establish a coaling station. All regulations affecting German nationals were to be discussed with an official of the Samoan Government by the German consul or other persons appointed by the German Government for that purpose. The Samoan Government promised not to grant to any other power in preference to the German Government any privileges with regard to the harbor of Apia and its shores.[13] The last stipulation was of especial importance to German trade. Germany rewarded the British for their support by loyally assisting them in their equally difficult negotiations for a treaty with Samoa. The British-Samoan commercial treaty, although not materially differing from the German treaty, did not grant the British a title to any special harbor. Simultaneously, a convention was concluded between Samoa and the consuls of the three treaty powers for the organization of a municipal

[11] Keim, *German-American Political Relations,* 133f.

[12] Foreign Office to the Chief of Admiralty, June 15, very confidential; to Bülow (in attendance on the Kaiser), June 22, 1876.

[13] Poschinger, *Die deutschen Handels- und Schiffahrtsverträge,* 348ff.

council in Apia. The harbor and city were neutralized. The council also was to take charge of the entire administration of the district of Apia. The Americans always denied that this implied a protectorate. This convention, never ratified by the United States, was destined to give rise to many disputes.

With the conclusion of these treaties ends the first phase of the Samoa question. Objective opinion must admit that the Americans advanced farthest during that period. Only the manœuvers of Steinberger injected an element into the Samoa affair that was to play so great a part in the future. The powers attempted to make the two big native parties serve their own interests by playing one against the other. Could Germany have forestalled later conflicts by quick action? That used to be said.[14] Possibly the British would not have offered serious resistance at that time, but the Americans, having realized the importance of the harbor of Pagopago ever since 1872, probably would have strenuously resisted Germany's effort to bring all of Samoa under its control.

The obvious menace to Germany's commercial interests in Samoa caused the German Government to realize that some radical action had to be taken. It submitted a Samoa bill to the Reichstag in the spring of 1880. The Godeffroy Company, which controlled the German trade in the Pacific, had become entangled in financial difficulties that ended in insolvency. In 1878 the company reorganized its jute business as a stock company, mortgaging a large part of its stock and of its land as well to non-German creditors. The Chancellor declared himself ready to assist when the Government was asked how the transfer of the mortgages into the possession of the mortgagor could be prevented. The German Maritime Commercial Company was organized and was to be subsidized by the Reich through the granting of an allowance to the stockholders of not to exceed 3 percent of the capital paid in or an annual amount of RM 300,000 during the first twenty years whenever the surplus did not permit a dividend of 4½ percent on the principal stock. According to the bill, the Chancellor was to approve the members of the board of directors and appoint a Reich commissioner who was to have broad powers regarding participation in discussions of the board of trustees and the general stockholders' meeting. In support of the bill it was stated that the commerce, navigation, and industry of the nation enjoyed greater and more permanent advantages in independent regions, that is, those lying outside the exclusive sphere of influence of other countries, than in regions where the free movement and the benefits from products of German labor were restricted by national and fiscal considerations and claims of other powers. The national importance of the case was given particular emphasis. The bill pointed out

[14] Hagen, *Bismarcks Kolonialpolitik,* 72; Reventlow, *Deutschlands auswärtige Politik,* 138ff.

the significance of developing trade in the southern Pacific and especially with Australia. Should the bill fail, the Government feared that German prestige with the natives would be undermined, Germany's commercial situation in the Pacific menaced, and her national honor among the powers diminished.[15]

The Reichstag did not discuss the facts objectively. The Center, embittered by the ecclesiastical conflict, joined the Progressives in opposing the bill. Bamberger accused the Godeffroy Company of improper business transactions and attempted to create the impression that the Government wished to participate in dishonorable speculations. On April 28, 1880, the bill was killed by a vote of 128 to 112. No doubt differences in domestic politics were responsible, for the opposition wanted the Chancellor to suffer a parliamentary defeat.[16] Bismarck thereupon declared that an active colonial policy was doomed, since the necessary support by public opinion was lacking. Even though there was an element of strategy in that statement, the Chancellor did act accordingly. In reply to a memorandum of Herr von Hansemann concerning German colonial plans in the Pacific, he had his office state on February 15, 1881, that in view of the failure of the Samoa bill it did not seem feasible to take vigorous initiative in the direction suggested. "An energetic support of German trade in those regions, such as Herr von Hansemann wishes, can be given by the Government only if there is adequate support by public opinion. The vote on the Samoa bill, however, indicates lack of interest on the part of a majority of the representatives of the nation. In view of the attitude of the Reichstag, the Government cannot carry on an active policy in the southern Pacific. Under the circumstances private enterprise must proceed alone. The Government will employ the navy and consular service to protect property acquired by private enterprise."[17]

The trend of affairs, however, soon put an end to that reservation. The rejection of the Samoa bill proved to be a strong factor in awakening national interest in colonial affairs. Within a few years the Chancellor gained the public support he had lacked in 1880. Above all, developments in the Pacific called for new decisions. The Australian colonies urged their mother country with increasing insistence to add unclaimed islands to the British possessions. Annexations were to include all islands between the 141st and 155th degrees, that is, New Britain, New Ireland, and the Solomon Islands.[18] These claims were advanced on the grounds that the British civilized and Christianized the natives. The natives would welcome annexation because of their sympathies

---

[15] Hagen, *Bismarcks Kolonialpolitik,* 72ff.

[16] *Ibid.,* 78ff. The Samoa bill was acted upon on Apr. 22 and 28.

[17] *Staatsarchiv,* 1884, XLIV, 161.

[18] *Ibid.,* XLIV, 170.

for Great Britain. Most of the islands were rich in tropical products, and sooner or later they would inevitably become an "Australian India." Because of their proximity to the Australian colonies they might be a source of danger in the hands of another great maritime power. Moreover, annexation by Great Britain would be the best way of regulating, if not stopping, the illegal traffic in labor in Polynesia, which in many respects was hardly less barbarous or inhuman than the African slave trade.[19]

The latter argument played an especially conspicuous part. Again and again the colonies raised the banner of humanity. The greatest vehemence was displayed in their campaign against the intended annexation of the New Hebrides by the French; as a Catholic power, France was strongly criticized because of her toleration of a system of compulsory colonial labor. Indeed, labor trade was an open sore in South Sea colonization. Since the Polynesians were unfit for plantation work, the required labor had to be imported from other islands, and the captains of labor ships were in the habit of exercising some coercion in hiring labor. The British, although no whit better than other nations, cleverly exploited that argument to discredit the colonial aspirations of other powers.[20] By such means they organized their resistance to Germany's colonial policy. The Germans, though not denying certain abuses, protested against exaggerations. A memorandum concerning the German Commercial and Plantation Company in the Pacific pointed out that in judging the labor trade it was a mistake to be too sensitive or to regard it as a covert form of slave trade. "The vast difference from the old slave trade is that the laborers, after expiration of their terms of service, are transported home free of charge, and that their service is controlled as well as possible during the life of contracts. Above all, it should be remembered that their living conditions do not become worse by their employment and that not only does the laborer absorb elements of civilization while staying abroad, but those elements are transmitted to his people after his return. . . . Treatment, care, and food of the plantation workers deserve credit. Their houses are airy and clean. Board mainly consists of vegetable food to which the men are accustomed, such as bananas, yams, taro, and breadfruit, some of which are raised on the plantations. . . ."[21]

[19] American consular report from Melbourne, May 21, 1884, cf. *Commercial Relations,* 1884, 174.

[20] Cf. *Staatsarchiv,* XLIV, 179f.

[21] Cf. *Deutsche Interessen in der Südsee,* I, no. 1, appendix 1. Even a none too sympathetic observer like Sewall, the American consul general in Samoa, on Aug. 15, 1888, admitted that Germany and Great Britain had done much toward mitigating the horrors of the labor trade. "As a rule, however, the labor trade is humanely conducted by the German labor vessels coming here." *Consular Reports,* 1888, XXVII, 410.

There was more cause for Australian apprehension about the convict colonies on the neighboring islands. They indeed constituted a serious menace to the safety of the British colonies. The Australians fought for their reputation, for only thirty years before the British had looked down upon them, as it was customary at that time to send criminal elements to Australia. But Germany had nothing to do with convict colonies. Australian criticism was really directed primarily against France, since New Caledonia was a convict colony pure and simple. The assertion that British commercial interests in general were greater in the Pacific than those of any other power was quite disputable during this period. The German consul general in Sydney thought that the colony of Victoria had connections only with Fiji. It neither imported nor exported anything to any of those South Sea islands that it desired to have protected from the covetousness of foreign nations. Commercial interests in southern Australia were limited to supplying flour to the French convict settlement in New Caledonia, while Western Australia and Tasmania had never endeavored to establish connections with the Pacific islands. As yet New Guinea was without any importance whatsoever for Australia's trade.[22]

German commercial organizations were justified in feeling disturbed. A particularly unpleasant impression was created by a resolution of the Intercolonial Conference in Sydney in 1883, by which no sales of land were to be recognized if effected actually or allegedly before establishment of British jurisdiction or sovereignty in New Guinea or on other islands of the Pacific not possessing a recognized government. Such a measure was certain greatly to diminish the trade value of the several thousands of acres of property of the German Plantation Company. Messrs. Hansemann and Bleichröder also complained that the plan of organizing the company for larger undertakings had to be deferred because Queensland attempted to take possession of New Guinea and the adjoining islands.[23] Bismarck thereupon decided to act. He proposed to the British Government an understanding regarding general principles to be followed as well as the demarcation of those regions which the two countries intended to place under their protection. The German Government was in favor of carrying on negotiations in the Pacific, but Great Britain preferred London. Space does not permit detailed description of the negotiations. They are intimately connected with the general colonial controversies between Great Britain and Germany that were then beginning. At times they

[22] German consulate general in Sydney to the Chancellor, Aug. 20, 1884, *Staatsarchiv*, XLIV, 201f.

[23] Administration of the German Commercial and Plantation Company in the Pacific to Bismarck, Hamburg, Jan. 30, 1884, and petition of Hansemann and Bleichröder, Berlin, June 27, 1884, *Staatsarchiv*, XLIV, 183ff.

were strongly affected by developments in general politics; the estrangement that led to a Franco-German rapprochement in 1885 naturally influenced negotiations regarding Pacific problems. Germany was represented by Krauel, Great Britain by Thurston. At the same time Meade, Under Secretary of State in the Colonial Office, communicated directly with Bismarck, and Herbert Bismarck was sent to London at critical moments.[24]

An agreement on principles involved did not offer serious difficulties. But the British colonies interfered again and again so that a definite settlement was delayed. New Guinea in particular was an obstacle. Since Great Britain had annexed the southern coast as early as October 1884, the Reich, on December 23, 1884, declared "a protectorate of His Majesty the Emperor for the northern coast of New Guinea lying east of the Netherland frontier, and for the islands in the New Britannic archipelago, with reservation as to legitimate rights." The British Colonial Office was taken by surprise. It was irritated to the point of inquiring of the Foreign Office whether in such circumstances agreements concluded with the German Government were still valid and whether the negotiations should be continued further.[25] In the Australian colonies excitement ran still higher. The government of Victoria protested in the name of the present and future of Australia. The British Government reproached Germany for violating her obligation for maintaining the *status quo* pending a definite settlement. The German Government denied that any such obligation existed since the measure had been decided upon in the summer of the preceding year. Urged by the Colonial Office, the British Government took possession of the remainder of New Guinea to which Germany in turn raised objections.[26]

From the very beginning, the Samoa and Tonga Islands had played a special rôle in the negotiations for the demarcation of spheres of interest in the Pacific. Like two fierce watchdogs, New Zealand and Fiji were lying in wait, barking whenever a foreign power dared even approach. Originally the British Government had declared itself only slightly interested in Samoa. As far as at all possible it cooperated with Germany. When Consul General Zembsch assumed office in the Pacific in 1879, the British Admiralty was

[24] For the development of Anglo-German relations, cf. *Die Grosse Politik*, IV, 3ff. For negotiations in the southern Pacific, cf. Hagen, *Bismarcks Kolonialpolitik*, 455ff.; Zimmermann, *Geschichte der deutschen Kolonialpolitik*, 93ff.

[25] British Colonial Office to Foreign Office, Dec. 31, 1884.

[26] Cf. Hagen, *Bismarcks Kolonialpolitik*, 435ff. and *Staatsarchiv*, XLIV, 160ff. For the following account, British records in the Public Record Office, as made accessible for the period through 1885, were studied, but superficially, however, because of lack of time. As far as could be ascertained, there was no conflict between the Colonial Office and the Foreign Office in the matter of Samoa.

instructed to support him in all matters pertaining to the maintenance of peace and promotion of trade (August 14). The British consul in Apia likewise was to interfere as little as possible with the internal affairs of Samoa. During the German-Samoan treaty negotiations the British loyally supported German interests.[27] But it is certain, none the less, that at an early period most of the British officially representing their country in the Pacific desired annexation by Great Britain. Gordon, high commissioner and consul general in the western Pacific was openly in favor of it; occasionally he even quoted Zembsch to the effect that incorporation of Samoa into the British possessions would be the most expedient solution (to the Secretary of State for the Colonies September 13, 1880). Chief Justice Gorrie, on June 23, 1879, wrote to the Colonial Secretary that Great Britain must not decline a voluntary offer on the part of the Samoans. In 1877 the British consul in Samoa advocated annexation in the interest of Fiji. Churchward, the British consul who came to Apia in the eighties, worked particularly hard for a British Samoa. His reports were so much along that line and he spoke so frequently of the sentiment of the Samoans as being in favor of British annexation that it may easily be imagined how he interpreted his mission.

New Zealand, however, was first to advocate annexation. It evidently hoped to be able to extend its commerce considerably in that portion of the Pacific. The New Zealanders thought that their country was suited for an intermediate trading station because of its geographic location. Some New Zealand products were especially adapted for consumption by the island people; other products were superior to goods shipped from San Francisco or Sydney. But commercial interests alone cannot explain the extraordinary interest of the whole New Zealand population in the future of Samoa. They were no doubt dominated by the fear that those islands, if in foreign hands, would some time endanger the security of the Australian colonies. The question of security formed the main topic of discussion in the intercolonial conferences of that period. With great seriousness it was stated that the colonies, in view of their great interests in the Pacific, could not allow foreign nations to possess islands nearby that might be a source of danger.[28] But New Zealand by no means contented itself with passing resolutions in that sense and with overwhelming the mother country with petitions and occasional threats. A former member of the New Zealand Parliament, John Lundon, went to Samoa in 1883 ostensibly on private business and spread propaganda for annexation

[27] Instructions to the British consul in Apia, Jan. 2, 1879.

[28] American consular reports from Melbourne and Auckland in 1883 and 1884 describe the excitement and the threats of the Australian colonies to secede from their mother country unless their wishes were fulfilled.

by New Zealand. The New Zealand press eagerly took up Lundon's highly colored reports. A petition by Malietoa for the annexation of Samoa (drafted in New Zealand) was assiduously exploited at British Government offices as "the will of the Samoan people."[29] While the British Government rejected the New Zealand plans for annexation, it let it be known confidentially that nothing would be done about the islands that would be disadvantageous to the interests of the Australian colonies.[30]

As in the days of Steinberger, the situation in Samoa had become obscure as a result of Lundon's machinations. The king and some of the chieftains showed so much animosity to the Germans that Stübel, the German consul, thought only a German-Samoan special agreement could protect German commercial interests.[31] This proposed agreement provided for a German-Samoan council of state which was to control and enforce punishment for offenses against German nationals and plantations. The agreement was in no sense designed to interfere with the existing administration in which the three powers in Apia cooperated jointly. Nevertheless, excitement in New Zealand ran so high that the Governor was actually forced by his Cabinet to cable the text of the German-Samoan agreement to London, despite the great expense of £400. Simultaneously, the New Zealand Cabinet asked permission to enter the harbor of Samoa with a ship of its own so as to ascertain the wishes of the natives. The Governor had his doubts as to the feasibility of that measure since a British man-of-war had already been ordered to Samoa. But he was outvoted since his ministers made it a point to have their opinion considered in London. As was to be expected, the British Government's reply was in the negative. The British Government, it was declared, was convinced that the New Zealand Government realized the importance for Australasia as well as for other parts of the Empire, of openly recognizing the justifiable claims of a great, friendly power, and of cooperating with Germany for the protection and development of European trade in the regions where one of the two countries had such strong interests that the other could not declare its own

[29] For a good review of the New Zealand intrigues, cf. *House Executive Documents,* 50th Cong., 1st sess., no. 238, "American Rights in Samoa," 158ff. Another detailed report came from the American consulate in Auckland, Oct. 2, 1883, Dept. State, *Despatches, Auckland,* 7, no. 168.

[30] British Foreign Office to the Colonial Office, Feb. 23, 1884.

[31] The American vice consul reported from Auckland, Jan. 24, 1885: "It is reported from Samoa that the knowledge of Mr. Lundon's scheme incited the German Consul to endeavor to secure the interest of his countrymen by a new convention—and that King Malietoa, who is not overstrong minded, was bothered on both sides, and so signed both documents as the readiest way out of the difficulty." Dept. State, *Despatches, Auckland,* 7, no. 226.

sovereignty within that territory.[32] As the Samoan leaders continued to be refractory, Stübel hoisted the German flag in Mulinu, where most of the German plantations were located. His Government disapproved his measure, declaring to London and Washington that Germany did not desire a change of the *status quo*.[33] That was absolutely sincere, although it did not prevent the Germans in Samoa in their turn from trying to arrange matters to meet their own purposes. But they were in a difficult situation. Lundon's machinations and the intrigues of the British and American consuls put the Germans on the defensive.

Bismarck, too, finally realized that conditions had become intolerable. On December 1, 1884, he had protests made in London against the New Zealand annexation plans.[34] Granville was willing to comply with the contractual obligation of not annexing Samoa, if Germany assumed the same obligation (Münster to Bismarck, London, December 5). Bismarck agreed, planning at the same time to negotiate with Great Britain for a German protectorate. He had inquiries made in Washington as to whether the United States would object. The reply as transmitted by Alvensleben was not encouraging. The American Government would see no cause for anxiety in a closer connection of those islands with the Australian system but would not accept with the same indifference any action for the annexation of Samoa (March 3). On the other hand, Krauel sent word from London that Great Britain, though on conditions not as yet formulated, was ready to let Germany have a free hand. "In my modest opinion this means that it would be advisable for us first to make sure of Samoa and to delay discussion of further plans of allotting the other independent island regions of the south Pacific." Krauel evidently thought Thurston's views were identical with those of the British Government. Thurston had from the beginning recognized Germany's predominant commercial position in Samoa. He even suggested that his Government officially acknowledge that predominance so as to facilitate a friendly and adequate settlement of the question.[35] Thurston and Krauel had agreed on a solution that would actually have transferred the administration of Samoa to

[32] Governor of New Zealand to Lord Derby, Jan. 17, confidential; Foreign Office to the Governor of New Zealand, Apr. 15, 1885.

[33] Kasson to Frelinghuysen, Berlin, Feb. 9, 1885, Dept. State, *Despatches, Germany,* 37, no. 165.

[34] A German note of Jan. 28 defended the special convention with Samoa, but promised not to ratify it if it should not agree with former declarations. The situation, it stated, had been aggravated by the fact that the Australian petitions had not been refuted.

[35] Thurston to Granville, Apr. 29, 1885, *British State Papers,* LXXIX, 970.

Germany, although it would not have been formally annexed out of consideration for Australian sensitiveness on the subject.[36]

But the opinions of the Foreign Office and Colonial Office were quite different. Lord Derby had cabled to Australia that neutralization of the islands as formerly intended would still best meet British interests.[37] But the British Government was not inclined to give due consideration to the German point of view, although the British among themselves admitted the far superior value of German trade.[38] They illogically evolved from that admission the proposal that the Samoan administration should be transferred to one power, namely, Great Britain. Samoa, it was said, could be administered most economically from Fiji. Needless to say the German Government did not appreciate that "disinterested" consideration for its treasury. It replied that Germany could organize the Samoan administration without increasing expenditures. The British Government thereupon responded that it was unable to agree and that consequently joint administration would have to be continued.[39] Krauel and Thurston had already prepared various proposals in that direction. One of them transferred the entire authority of government to one of the treaty powers; another left the present dynasty intact, giving it a council of state consisting of natives and representatives of the treaty powers. Germany wished to have two members on the proposed council, but Great Britain would not consent.[40]

At any rate, the British Government in 1885 does not seem to have been sure about the most advantageous policy regarding Samoa. On February 11, 1885, Lord Derby rejected annexation of Samoa by New Zealand, stating that Bismarck had declared in the Reichstag that the *status quo* in Samoa would have to be maintained. As late as November 11, 1885, the Colonial Office urgently submitted to the Foreign Office that it was impossible to change the British policy concerning Samoa.[41] But Hervey's memorandum for Pauncefote

[36] Bismarck to Münster, Dec. 11, 1884; to Alvensleben, Jan. 3; Krauel to Bismarck, Apr. 13, 1885.

[37] Cf. Hagen, *Bismarcks Kolonialpolitik,* 458.

[38] "The number of German subjects in the navigators and the bulk of German trade are reported to be largely in excess (nearly double) of the British population and trade"; Foreign Office to the Governor of New Zealand, Apr. 15, 1885.

[39] Foreign Office to Scott, Aug. 12, 1885, separate letter; note of reply from the German Government, Oct. 10, 1885.

[40] Krauel to Bismarck, London, Apr. 22, 1885.

[41] "We shall have a hot colonial attack if we now surrender the position built up by so many steps. The islands are practically of small commercial and political value and importance and there really should be no difficulty in keeping them independent . . ." Colonial Office to Foreign Office, Nov. 11, 1885, personal.

dated December 29, 1885, says: "Is it worth while resisting the German desire to take the Samoan administration into their own hands, if we could obtain complete freedom of commerce, most-favored-nation treatment for ourselves and for the colonies, and if the United States agree—a course which Thurston would think most expedient? The United States have shown anxiety lately to secure in the western Pacific freedom of commerce which they hold should be independent of any one power. We may conclude, I think, that they would be very willing to take common action with us to attain that object. But unless there is a fair prospect of gaining our end, *viz.*, the exclusion of Germany from the sole administration of Samoa, would it not be better to give way at once, and by so doing obtain all we and the colonies can reasonably desire? On the other hand it may be fairly contended that with United States aid we might succeed in making arrangements for securing Samoan independence. But I submit that it is no use continuing our efforts in that direction unless it is very certain that we shall persevere and not give way in the end." [42]

The allusion to the United States refers to a conversation in November between Sackville-West, the British Minister, and the Secretary of State. Bayard mentioned the commercial importance of the South Sea islands, owing to the construction of the big railroad lines. The Secretary thought it was natural for Germany, after achieving its unification, to extend its trade. But other states, including the United States in particular, participated in the trade with the islands; they could not allow any one power to have commercial preference. The United States would like to see independence assured for those islands that were suited for commercial enterprises because of their geographic location. [43] In other respects the United States and Great Britain did not agree sufficiently to permit their cooperation for any length of time. On the contrary, it was Schlözer's impression that the American Government was still very sensitive in its relations with Great Britain. On January 8, 1880, he wrote to the German Foreign Office: "Nearly every time when, in representing our special German interests in Nicaragua or Mexico or elsewhere, I submit a request to the American Government for diplomatic support, I meet with the greatest courtesy. As soon as Great Britain is involved, however, the old aversion of the Yankee to his British cousin appears, and the idea that the Star-Spangled Banner should join the Union Jack in any foreign action is distasteful to any American statesman." The extent to which British and American representatives were drawn together in the Pacific is a different

[42] Foreign Office memorandum, Dec. 29, 1885.
[43] Sackville-West to Salisbury, Nov. 6, 1885, confidential.

matter, however. It has already been mentioned that there the lines of demarcation had been largely obscured.

During that period the United States may be said to have remained in the background. An understanding with Great Britain regarding spheres of interest in the Pacific was the more important for German policy as this problem was only one part of general colonial and political discussions. When Hawaii began to interfere, the British Government indeed thought it noticed a growing interest in the United States in events in the western Pacific, and suggested that the American Government should be consulted in such problems of the Pacific Ocean as had not been settled.[44]

Germany had not altogether neglected the United States. As stated, she had given the United States a satisfactory explanation following the arbitrary procedure of the German consul, and the American Government seemed satisfied. Instructions of June 19, 1885, to the American consul in Apia are extremely cautious: A sound basis must be found for the neutrality of Samoa. America has a moral right to expect that no change of native government shall destroy the independence of the islands. A protectorate by one power is theoretically as contrary to American conceptions of justice as a protectorate of three, the usefulness of which the United States was asked to examine on former occasions. The United States was positively assured by the German Government that it would not interfere with the independence of the islands or disturb the relations of other powers hitherto maintained in conjunction with Germany. The British Government publicly declared itself opposed to any movement by the natives to incorporate Samoa in the Fiji system. It is hardly necessary for the American Government to make a similar official declaration. American policy in respect to transoceanic possessions has been known too long and too well to require a special declaration to the effect that it has no intentions concerning the acquisition of territory in Samoa. For this reason it is advisable that the American representative in Samoa should avoid any appearance of being opposed to Germany in the pending negotiations or of sharing the general impression that Germany actually desired to attain that power which was officially disclaimed by the German Government. "Your efforts should, however," the instructions concluded, "be directed to the maintenance of harmony and good will, when these may be threatened, and to their restoration, if by any untoward course of events they should be disturbed. To your discretion and tact (a fitting opportunity arising) may be due

[44] See *ante,* p. 216.

a satisfactory exit from the present embarrassing situation in Samoa, with credit and honor to all parties concerned."[45]

Since Malietoa continued to be antagonistic to German interests, the German consul removed him from his residence in Mulinu. Tamasese, the former viceroy, revolted and established, not without German aid, a counter-government. The Department of State at once protested formally, the policy of the United States being a "guarded reserve" (January 12, 1886). Again the German Government did not support its consul. The American Minister was told that Berlin was not informed of the incident and that any wrong committed would be repaired.[46] The exiled Malietoa appealed to the American consul for protection, referring to article 5 of the American-Samoan treaty of 1878 by which America had offered mediation in the event of a dispute between Samoa and another power. Greenebaum, the American consul, thereupon hoisted the American flag in Apia next to the Samoan flag. Possibly he considered the moment favorable for carrying out American annexation of Samoa by means of a *fait accompli.* There were some people in the United States who welcomed Greenebaum's action and did not understand their Government's disapproval. The Samoa *Times* of January 12, 1889, wrote: "A very favorable opportunity for America was missed when our Government refused to support Consul Greenebaum who proclaimed a temporary protectorate on the islands. That measure proved a grand success. It showed that the pistol of the highwayman was not loaded. When a German squadron of three warships was about to depose Malietoa, the aggressors were driven away by the sight of the American flag without a single ship in port for its protection, and the pirate fleet sailed away. Had not the Government so strictly adhered to the paralyzing tradition of nonintervention, taken over from fifty years of peaceful administration, the consul would have been supported, and Bismarck would have to look out for a different field for his colonial ambitions."[47] This statement is mentioned merely to show the extent to which the Samoa conflict was confused and exaggerated by local conditions and by more or less aggressive interference on the part of individual groups of interests.

The situation had indeed become more than ripe for a friendly discussion between the three powers. Washington took the initiative. The American

---

[45] *House Executive Documents,* 50th Cong., 1st sess., no. 238, "American Rights in Samoa," 9ff.

[46] *Ibid.,* 15f.; Pendleton to Bayard, Berlin, Jan. 16, 1886, Dept. State, *Despatches, Germany,* 40, no. 168.

[47] *Samoa-Weissbuch,* II, no. 45, appendix 1; *Sten. Berichte,* 1888-89, V, no. 138, 877.

plan was as follows: Election by the natives of a new head of the government, who then would be supported by the three powers; appointment of three new consuls for Samoa and regulation of all other questions in a conference of the German and British Ministers with the Secretary of State in Washington.[48] In April the British Government had suggested an investigation in Samoa by British warships. Bismarck, however, was in favor of a civilian inquiry.[49] The German Government accepted the American proposal on June 6, 1886, but requested sufficient time to get an accurate report on the state of affairs on the islands. Thereupon the three governments appointed special commissioners who were to ascertain the cause of the recent trouble and dissatisfaction among the natives. Bates, the American commissioner, had his course of procedure circumscribed. The Samoan Islands, the Secretary of State wrote him on July 22, 1886, were the only remaining neutral region in Oceania. Moreover, Samoa's neutrality was guaranteed. The American Government, although opposed to a protectorate of any one power, recognized the necessity of common action for maintenance of order and establishment of a stable government under the existing circumstances.[50] As was to be expected, the commissioners arrived at very different conclusions. Travers, the German representative, wished to have one of the treaty powers given charge of the Government with the consent of the other powers. In view of the predominance of German interests, he said, that one power should be Germany. The German Government should appoint an administrator and three principal officials, a chief justice, a director of finance, and a judge of first instance. The native king should be limited to functions of representation. The parliament should give advice concerning Samoan manners and customs; its resolutions should be considered only as far as expedient. The municipal council of Apia should be dissolved. The British commissioner, Thurston, recommended an experimental native government with the cooperation of representatives of the three powers; a board of administration, consisting of the king, viceroy, chieftains of various districts, and three officials appointed by Great Britain, Germany, and the United States; a municipal council in Apia composed of nine members, each of the three consuls appointing three of them. The American proposal resembled the British one; it transferred executive power to a council consisting of one representative of each of the

---

[48] Bayard to Pendleton, June 1, 1886, Dept. State, *Instructions, Germany,* 17: 658; *House Executive Documents,* 50th Cong., 1st sess., no. 238, "American Rights in Samoa," 19f.

[49] *British State Papers,* LXXIX, 975ff.

[50] *House Executive Documents,* 50th Cong., 1st sess., no. 238, "American Rights in Samoa," 29ff.

three powers. Bates personally was skeptical of his own proposition, which he had adapted to meet the instructions of his Government. He fully realized the dangers of an administration of three. Like his German colleague he considered administration by one power the best plan. That power, however, was to be the United States, not Germany or Great Britain. The American Government, having no intention of acquiring land, was in the best position to satisfy the wishes of the natives.[51]

In the meantime the London negotiations regarding the south Pacific proceeded. An improvement was noted in the atmosphere of coolness between Germany and Great Britain which had continued throughout 1885. Great Britain was so much in need of Germany's support in Egypt and Turkey and was so greatly concerned about the Franco-German rapprochement that it was ready to yield more concessions. Bismarck endeavored to solve the Samoan problem in close cooperation with Great Britain. His Foreign Office wanted British support for the following demands: Malietoa's removal from office as not being compatible with satisfactory development; preponderant German influence in the proposed commission of administration (chairmanship for at least three years), and special agreements with the Samoan Government for protection of German plantations. Bismarck did not agree to the second point of the instructions intended for London, October 14. The chairmanship, he held, was to be given powers which would make the whole arrangement dangerous for Germany. It would be acceptable only if the chairmanship also continued to be in German hands after the first three years. Such an arrangement would be unacceptable to the other powers, however, and the chairmanship should alternate and be merely a matter of form.

Then for the first time a plan was seriously considered for compensating Great Britain with Tonga if the former gave up its claims in Samoa. The Chancellor, to be sure, feared American protest against a German protectorate in Samoa. A year earlier, he said, those objections might possibly have been overcome. "But, after public opinion in the United States has been considerably wrought up by the Greenebaum incident with all its ramifications, we can hardly expect the American Government to acquiesce in an agreement dividing up Anglo-German interests in Samoa."[52] But, as Alvensleben also had recommended a bilateral understanding with Great Britain, attempts were made in that direction. It was planned to concede Great Britain the controlling influence in Tonga, if American approval of German administration in Samoa could be obtained in the Washington Conference. For the moment, however, it was not necessary to direct the heavy artillery of Tonga against London.

[51] For the commissioners' reports, cf. *ibid.*, 137ff.
[52] Rantzau to Foreign Office, Varzin, Oct. 21, 1886.

Hatzfeldt's impression from the very first discussion in London was that Great Britain would consent to German administration as a mandatory of the treaty powers. He therefore asked permission to keep all other proposals in reserve. Bismarck agreed, but expressly stated that Germany was interested in administration not ín domination.

At first the negotiations proceeded very slowly. They were conducted by Lord Iddesleigh and his representatives on behalf of the British Government. Iddesleigh wished to delay the decision until Thurston's report had arrived. The British advanced such vague phrases as: Greater accord between Germany and Great Britain in the commission could be counted upon; and the United States would accept any arrangement eliminating the danger of interference with American commercial interests. But British policy remained so obscure that Krauel, becoming impatient, was ready to depart. Salisbury acted at once. Hatzfeldt, in a personal letter to Herbert Bismarck on November 11, writes: "Salisbury, whom I saw today, was actually beside himself over the possibility of having the Samoa negotiations broken off and would not hear of Krauel's departing." He complained of the pedantry of his colleague and assured Hatzfeldt that he was willing to make concessions. As for Samoa, he wished only a guarantee of free trade for Great Britain and a form of agreement which, by veiling the preponderance conceded to Germany as much as possible, would protect him from attacks by the colonies. Salisbury not only agreed to the removal of Malietoa and the protection of the German plantations, as demanded, but he suggested of his own accord that administration should be transferred to one official who was to be chosen from the subjects of the power most interested there, instead of an international commission. The British Cabinet persisted only in one point—it wanted the head of administration appointed for a limited term. Great Britain wished to be able to say to its colonies: The power possessing preponderant interests at present is Germany. But it is not improbable that relations may change in the course of time, and that at the close of the German period of administration American or British interests will have gained predominance.

The British and German plans for administrative reorganization of Samoa differed considerably only in that the British plan provided for possible discharge of the adviser. Germany at once declared that to be out of the question. On March 16, the British Foreign Office withdrew that provision on the condition that complaints brought against the adviser by the other two treaty powers were to be examined carefully. The convention as finally formulated included all matters necessary for maintenance of safety and order in the islands. The harmless title of "adviser" was deliberately chosen for the executive; in reality this adviser was to be invested with full authority. He was to control all measures for public order, particularly for protection of the plantations, land, and other property of foreign subjects. Great Britain declared itself willing to work for the election of a new king, but was anxious to avoid the impression of having dropped Malietoa. A special clause was included which provided that the existing treaties with Samoa were to remain in force and that "the former declarations of Germany, Great Britain, and the United States concerning the independence of Samoa were confirmed in order to avoid the appearance of any intention to prepare for the annexation of Samoa by a foreign power in connection with the present interference with the administration of Samoa." After such concessions it was but natural for the British Government to present its bill. Salisbury and Pauncefote wanted German concessions in Tonga in order to defend themselves to the colonies. Germany, they pointed out, had no special interests in Tonga. Bismarck replied that there was no analogy between the Tonga Islands and Samoa, Great Britain not having so dominant a position in Tonga as Germany then had in Samoa. The Chancellor would not in principle decline an understanding with Great Britain about Tonga, however. "In consideration of the difficulties, fully appreciated by us, which the South Sea chauvinism of the Australian colonies creates for the British Government, I am quite ready for further negotiations, should British commerce at some future date succeed in acquiring the same predominant position as German commerce now possesses in Samoa. . . . We may possibly agree to British annexation of the Tonga Islands, provided that they concede to us freedom of action in Samoa" (to Hatzfeldt February 3, 1887, confidential). Before the Conference there was no occasion for further discussion of that question. Germany's policy was undoubtedly successful in that it influenced Great Britain at least to the extent of having it approve administration by one power and put the British Government under obligation to support this proposal in the Conference.[53] Administration by three powers was unacceptable to Germany. The Plantation Company, in a petition of May 13, 1887, called such a solution as sterile as the triumvirate of consuls. For this reason Alvensleben was instructed to suggest at the Conference the election of an official nominated by Germany, as well as dissolution of the municipal administration of Apia.[54] In this connection it was fortunate for the

[53] Besides the reports mentioned in the text, cf. Foreign Office to Krauel, Berlin, Oct. 26, 1886; Krauel to Bismarck, Nov. 3, 1886; Hatzfeldt and Krauel to Foreign Office, Nov. 15, 1886, telegram, very confidential; Herbert Bismarck to Hatzfeldt, Jan. 15, 1887; Hatzfeldt to Bismarck, Jan. 23, 1887; note from British Foreign Office, Mar. 16, 1887; Hatzfeldt to Bismarck, Apr. 13, 1887; cf. *Die Grosse Politik*, IV, 155, 172.

[54] Herbert Bismarck to Hatzfeldt, June 5; to Alvensleben, June 13, 1887.

German policy that Great Britain also considered that continuation of administration by three representatives of the powers would be disastrous.

During the months preceding the Conference in Washington, the Samoan situation had undergone a change inasmuch as Tamasese was gaining ground. German support of Tamasese as revealed by simultaneous letters of introduction to both Malietoa and Tamasese presenting the new German consul, Dr. Becker, evoked vigorous protests from the American Secretary of State. In its reply, the German Government pointed out the fact that Tamasese had four times as many followers as Malietoa.[55]

New and very serious interference came from different quarters. The Government of Hawaii, ambitious to imitate the example set by New Zealand in 1883, had been urging the American and British Governments since 1885 to guarantee the independence of the ownerless islands. The Hawaiian King was intensely interested in a few groups of islands more or less near his country, particularly the Marshall, Gilbert, and Caroline Islands. He inquired in Washington as to what attitude the Government would take toward independent governments on those islands, which then would have to be protected from annexation. Hawaii's interest was explained by a brisk movement of missionaries and laborers throughout the islands. On November 24, 1885, the Hawaiian Legation presented an official note on the subject in London. It demanded recognition of Hawaii as best suited to help, with the aid of the great powers, the populations of those islands in organizing such political communities and governments as were adapted to their requirements. The neutrality and governments of those commonwealths were to be duly recognized. London rejected that proposal. The British Government did not wish to interfere in the affairs of islands which, as a result of negotiations with the German Emperor, were situated within the German sphere of influence. But Hawaii would not be silenced. In September 1886 it appointed the former American consul to Samoa, Berthold Greenebaum, as vice consul in Apia with the intention of following American policy in Samoa. In this respect Hawaii was disappointed, since Greenebaum, in October 1885, had ceased to be American consul in Samoa. In February 1887, the Hawaiian representative in Washington presented one of many friendly letters from Malietoa asking for an Hawaiian Minister to Samoa. The Hawaiian Government asked permission of the American Government to establish diplomatic relations with Samoa, inquiring at the same time whether it approved of the Hawaiian policy in Polynesia. The Department of State was wise enough to give a positive warning: Owing to the distance between Samoa and Hawaii such relations would be difficult to maintain. Expenditures for a fleet would encumber Hawaiian finance. At the moment Samoan affairs were being examined by the Governments of the United States, Germany, and Great Britain. Interference on the part of the Hawaiian Government might disturb the efforts of the three powers to find a solution for domestic and foreign questions in Samoa.[56] Bismarck was greatly vexed over the Hawaiian intrigues in Samoa, the more so since they were by no means stopped by the American reprimand. At one time he bluntly expressed his anger: "We should not have to put up with the insolence of the Hawaiians any longer; if a German squadron were at anchor before Samoa, it could sail for Hawaii, and King Kalakaua could be told that, unless he desisted from his insolent intrigues in Samoa, we should shoot his legs in two, despite his American protection."[57]

The Conference, which opened in Washington in June 1887, was ill-starred from the very beginning. In October 1886, Bayard indeed promised the German chargé d'affaires an agreement. It was Zedtwitz's impression at that time "that the Secretary of State, with a sort of personal ambition, is working for the successful completion of the plan that originated from his initiative." But the nearer the Conference approached, the more did Bayard find himself restrained by consideration of the forthcoming elections. The British Minister actually thought that the Secretary of State regretted having suggested the plan for a Conference.[58] From the beginning the latter fought like a lion against the Anglo-German proposal for an adviser. In the second session on July 2, he argued about as follows: The United States refrained from any acquisitions in the south Pacific and vicinity. Its traditional policy was opposed to expansion. Its attitude toward those regions caused no disturbance to the commerce of other countries. On the other hand, the importance of the Samoan Islands, particularly in view of the future interoceanic canal, had increased considerably for all mercantile nations and for the United States especially, in view of its proximity as compared with the European powers. Moreover, the American Government had concluded the first treaty with those islands, and under such circumstances the United States, being the least interested power, expected its proposals for an organization of government in Samoa to be readily approved by the other two powers. This Ameri-

---

[56] Sackville-West to Salisbury, Washington, Nov. 6, 1885, confidential; Hawaiian Legation to Secretary of State, London, Nov. 24, 1885; Foreign Office to Hawaiian Legation, London, Dec. 11, 1885; Merrill to Bayard, Honolulu, Sept. 6, 1886; Bayard to Merrill, Oct. 25, 1886; Merrill to Bayard, Honolulu, Feb. 15, 1887; Bayard to Hawaiian Legation, Washington, Apr. 12, 1887; cf. *House Executive Documents,* 50th Cong., 1st sess., no. 238, "American Rights in Samoa," 37ff.; Ryden, *Foreign Policy of the United States in Relation to Samoa.*

[57] Rantzau to Foreign Office, Aug. 1, 1887.

[58] Alvensleben to Bismarck, Washington, June 2, 1887.

can point of view was unacceptable to Germany. The Samoan commission only perpetuated European rivalries. In accordance with his instructions Alvensleben spoke against Malietoa and on behalf of an adviser, which office should first be filled by a German. The other German demands were the recognition of absolute equality of commercial navigation, jurisdiction, and all other matters involving the safety of German nationals. The British representative seconded Alvensleben. Since Germany had the largest interests in Samoa, the office of adviser should be given to a German for the first five years. Bayard remained obdurate. He openly said that acceptance of such a plan would result in handing over possession of the islands to Germany.[59] The German Foreign Office therefore faced the question of whether it should await the moment when Bayard would consider the Conference a failure. Should not a *fait accompli* be created? That question was settled by Bismarck's statement that such violent actions were outside the sphere of colonial problems, unless there were a prior agreement with the other powers concerned.[60] American sentiment regarding Samoa between 1885 and 1888 was decidedly influenced by the attitude of President Grover Cleveland, a Democrat who opposed for idealistic reasons any sort of imperialistic policy.[61]

On July 26, the Conference adjourned until fall in order to give the several governments time to adjust their differences of opinion. In view of the discouraging result of the Conference Bismarck adopted a somewhat stronger tone. He sent word to Washington that the American Government could not take it amiss if Germany proceeded without American cooperation, taking its own interests in hand. Perpetuation of an inefficient government in Samoa could not be tolerated. The American proposals offered no remedy for the existing abuses. Germany was not seeking greater influence than Great Britain and the United States, except in so far as it would be readily conceded to her in the interest of all. It was impossible, however, to let the honor of the German Reich and the security of her nationals be forever disregarded as had been done by Malietoa. Even a hidden threat was added: "We do not intend to make trouble for the American interests in Hawaii, but we could not help doing so, if the United States created trouble in Samoa." Bismarck even went further by asking his Foreign Office for suggestions as to how the United States might be molested in the Sandwich Islands or elsewhere. When war was finally declared against Malietoa, who refused to make reparations for an incident on the birthday of the German Emperor, the Chief of Admiralty,

[59] Alvensleben to Bismarck, Washington, July 16; British Foreign Office to Sackville-West, Apr. 30; Hatzfeldt to German Foreign Office, Oct. 21, 1887, telegram.
[60] Foreign Office memorandum, July 23, with marginal note by Bismarck.
[61] McElroy, *Cleveland,* I, 240ff.

in a personal letter of August 10 to Herbert Bismarck, discussed the military possibilities of war with Hawaii. He considered as feasible the plan of a blockade of a few ports of the Sandwich Islands or occupation of Honolulu, unless Hawaii officially or unofficially received aid from the United States. But Berlin applied the brakes and assumed a merely defensive attitude toward Hawaii. Resistance against measures in Apia was to be broken; aggressive actions against the Sandwich Islands, however, were reserved for decision by the Imperial Government.[62] Definite action was undertaken against Malietoa, who was captured and taken away on a German warship. Tamasese, under protection of the German Navy, proclaimed himself King of Samoa. The American consul thereupon resigned under protest from the municipal council in Apia while the British consul, according to instructions, recognized Tamasese as the *de facto* ruler of Samoa. The German Government did not let the London thread break. Herbert Bismarck suggested to Salisbury that the Americans seemed to interpret the Monroe Doctrine in the sense that the Pacific Ocean was to be considered as an "American lake"; "not only did they want Hawaii (in which, as Salisbury said, Great Britain was not in any way interested) to be under its exclusive influence, but also Samoa and Tonga as stations between the future interoceanic canal and Australia. There were even some American visionaries dreaming of a forthcoming fraternization and consolidation of the various Australian colonies with the United States." Salisbury, deeply impressed, declared that the Americans would have to be watched closely at any rate. He recognized the German procedure as justified,[62a] and was on the verge of having British ships participate, but Bismarck decidedly did not want that.[63] Hatzfeldt requested the British Foreign Minister to prevent at all hazards any immediate and serious differences between the British and German representatives in Samoa. Salisbury promised to instruct his consul accordingly but refused to mediate in Washington, on the ground that British-American relations were not particularly good at that time.[64] Under pressure from the Hawaiian Legation, the American Government displayed much interest in the continued neutrality of the Samoan Islands. Alvensleben in fact gained the impression that an extension of that

[62] Rantzau to Foreign Office, Aug. 1; Caprivi to Herbert Bismarck, Aug. 10; Herbert Bismarck to Caprivi, Aug. 13, 1887, secret.

[62a] Memorandum of Herbert Bismarck, London, Aug. 24, 1887; cf. *Die Grosse Politik,* IV, 175ff.

[63] Hatzfeldt to Foreign Office, Aug. 13, 1887, telegram; Herbert Bismarck to Hatzfeldt, Aug. 14, telegram.

[64] Note of Herbert Bismarck, London, Aug. 24, 1887; Rantzau to Foreign Office, Friedrichsruh, Oct. 29; memorandum of Herbert Bismarck with marginal notes of the Chancellor of Oct. 29, 1887.

principle to all unoccupied islands of the Pacific was being contemplated. At least he had been informed by a responsible person that the United States in the near future would approach the powers in this sense concerning Hawaii. Bismarck endeavored to set the American Government at peace. The German procedure only meant settlement of personal accounts with Malietoa; no change was planned in regard to the neutral position of the Samoan Islands or to the contractual equality of the United States. The German squadron was strong enough to protect the Americans also and to prevent a civil war.[65] The commander-in-chief of the Pacific squadron received special instructions to avoid conflicts with the Americans. Berlin likewise objected to occupation of Apia by a German detachment. "Even if no collisions should occur with resident Englishmen and Americans," Zedtwitz was informed on November 8, "it will give the press in the Australian colonies and in the United States an opportunity to cast suspicion on our Samoan policy and to insinuate that we intend territorial expansion and violation of the treaty rights of other States interested in the southern Pacific."[66] Bayard feared that Samoa might come under the influence of the German Plantation Company. He would never agree to a partition that would terminate the autonomy of the islands. Nearly all other islands of the Pacific were in the possession or under the protection of European powers. In the event of a European war Samoa would be the only possible natural bulwark for protection of international trade in the Pacific. For this reason he was striving for neutralization of the islands. The policy of the United States in this direction was wholly unselfish; it might have annexed Samoa thirteen years earlier but had not seized that opportunity. He had been informed recently, not only from American but also from other sources, that the German Plantation Company aspired to domination of the islands. The history of the continents offered numerous examples of the ultimate results of such tendencies on the part of commercial companies in more or less civilized countries. If an American company ever displayed such intentions in Samoa, he as Secretary of State would take measures to suppress them. The German Minister again assured him that Germany did not intend to alter the neutrality of the Samoan Islands or the contractual parity of the United States with the other powers. Protection of its commercial interests was the sole objective of Germany's policy.[67] While the American press in general showed little concern, there were a few influential papers that severely attacked Bayard's policy, chiefly for reasons of domestic politics. Thus the *New York Tribune* on October 18 criticized the Secretary of State

[65] Alvensleben to Bismarck, Aug. 29; Bismarck to Alvensleben, Sept. 24, 1887.
[66] *Samoa-Weissbuch*, I, no. 13, *Sten. Berichte*, 1888-89, V, 569.
[67] Zedtwitz to Bismarck, Sept. 23 and Nov. 11, 1887.

for his masterly inactivity that had deprived the United States of the chance either to secure dominating influence in the islands or to keep open the question of whether American acquisition of the islands at a later date might not seem desirable. Likewise the *New York Herald* of November 10 described the advantages of an active American policy but foresaw an unfavorable reaction on the German-Americans. In the meantime the exchange of opinions was continued regarding the best possible administration of Samoa. In October, Coleman, the American chargé d'affaires in Berlin, proposed an early election of a king and viceroy. Herbert Bismarck, however, objected: A king had already been elected, Malietoa had violated German property, and the German Government was determined to wage war against him. But the Government wished to protect the rights and interests of foreign nationals, especially the Americans and British. He asked for some delay so as to learn how things were progressing. On November 4, Herbert Bismarck, on instructions from his father, informed the American chargé d'affaires that the Chancellor was astonished and grieved to see the United States and Germany quarrel over so unimportant and remote a place as Samoa, in view of the excellent and cordial relations of the two countries that were connected by so many different ties and whose citizens and officials otherwise maintained such pleasant relations. The Chancellor had instructed him to write to the German representative in Washington in that sense, and had expressed himself with deep emotion. Thereupon Count Bismarck repeated his request that Tamasese be granted a period of probation.[68]

Germany's principal grievances were directed against Consul General Sewall. Closely allied to commercial companies interested in Samoa, he followed an extreme policy on behalf of American interests. Controversies occurred in the municipal administration of Apia, and Sewall arbitrarily interfered with the jurisdiction of the foreign police and refused to participate in the election of a new chief of police. Bismarck, in a detailed instruction to Zedtwitz on November 18, 1887, complained of the behavior of the American consul general: "In view of the so friendly relations which have continued undisturbed for more than a century between Germany and the United States, it is remarkable that on that remote realm of islands, where neither America nor Germany has any political interests to defend, we are exposed to the continual ill-will of a series of American representatives." There were far more important differences with Great Britain and France. Great Britain had far more occasion to be jealous of the spread of German influence and moreover was compelled to consider claims and prejudices of her colonies which,

[68] Herbert Bismarck to Zedtwitz, Oct. 17, *Samoa-Weissbuch,* I, no. 9, *Sten. Berichte,* 1888-89, V, 567.

educated for the idea of British hegemony in overseas countries, were inclined to regard foreign neighbors as intruders in their spheres of interest or as a menace to their security. "I fail therefore to find *in the facts themselves* any reasons that could explain the continual ill-will shown towards us in Samoa by the American representatives of the past and of the present, and I should be thankful to Mr. Bayard if he would lend me his assistance in the investigation of this strange fact. Should my supposition be right that those difficulties have their origin in the personal disposition of the American representatives in Apia, and not in their instructions, I am convinced that the American Government will cause the necessary redress to take place." [69] The Department of State presented a defense on January 17, 1888. Germany's efforts toward creating order in Samoa did not always meet with the opposition of the American consuls. The chief cause of differences of opinion was the fact that Germany wished to establish a strong government, while the United States wished to defend the independence of the native government. The methods of the German representatives in Samoa were criticized on the basis of some of the incidents cited. [70]

Despite this frank discussion, the year 1888 did not bring a clarification of the situation. The Germans were of the opinion that there were no traces of political movements or discontent among the natives. [71] The Tamasese government, advised by Brandeis, a German, while admittedly accomplishing much good, could have maintained itself only in the case of complete unity among the treaty powers. [72] But that was out of the question. Sewall asserted that all measures of the Brandeis administration benefited only the interests of the German plantations. In an interview published in the San Francisco *Daily Examiner* on September 2, he discussed the great strategic importance of Samoa for the United States. America, he said, had no coaling station in the Pacific; after the prospective completion of the interoceanic canal, the value of Samoa, situated on the direct route to China and controlled by the United States, could hardly be overestimated. Germany respected only force. Had it

[69] *House Executive Documents*, 50th Cong., 1st sess., no. 238, "American Rights in Samoa," 96ff.

[70] *Ibid.*, 107ff.

[71] Report from Apia, Feb. 23, 1888, *Samoa-Weissbuch*, I, no. 18, *Sten. Berichte*, 1888-89, V, 573.

[72] Robert Louis Stevenson, not overly friendly to the Germans, remarks on the Brandeis régime: ". . . the more I learn of his brief term of rule, the more I learn to admire him and to wish we had his like. . . ." *Footnote to History*, 97. An American consular report from Sydney, Oct. 2, 1888, considers Germany's support of Tamasese as prudent, since he had many more adherents than Malietoa, Dept. State, *Despatches, Sydney*, 12, no. 266.

not been for an American warship, the German flag probably would have been floating over Samoa then. Bayard expressed this idea more guardedly: Samoa must be an oasis which in the event of war might offer a safe refuge to menaced merchantmen of the belligerent nations. Knappe, who had relieved Becker in the middle of November, inferred from a conversation with the American captain and the British consul that Tamasese was definitely to be overthrown. Thus there soon developed a party opposing Tamasese. Malietoa's son-in-law, Mataafa, secretly supported by the commander of the American warship, revolted. His party went so far as to attack German property.[73] Knappe, declaring a state of war, had a detachment of marines landed to protect the German plantations. He committed the grave mistake of not informing the other powers in advance of his intentions, thereby putting Germany in the position of the wrongdoer. The forces landed were quite inadequate, and a serious defeat near Fangalili cost the Germans not only fifty dead and wounded but their prestige with the natives. This incident was serious in a double sense. The American flag was burned in the course of a bombardment,[74] and the rebel forces fighting against the Germans were commanded by an American citizen, Klein. This time equally emphatic protests were lodged by both the American and the British consuls, while the German Government protested in Washington against Klein. Bismarck did not approve at all of Knappe's procedure. "Referring to your telegram of January 23 I remark that you are not authorized to deprive foreigners of the jurisdiction of their consuls," he wired on January 31. "The protest of your English colleagues against the measures taken is well founded. In the case of conflicts resulting from that occasion, you would be in the wrong. Your demand that Germany take charge of the administration lies outside your instructions and our intentions. Rescind it at once. Except for the surrender of criminal aggressors, no demand is to be made for which you have no authority."[75] The Chancellor insisted again and again that Germany was bound by treaties and was not entitled to proceed independently. When Knappe wired from Auckland on January 5, 1889, suggesting that Germany should obtain a mandate of annexation from the other powers, the Chancellor wrote on the margin: "Out of the question; this seems objectionable to me in the face of increasing American chauvinism and existing agreements. We pledged our word to Great Britain and the United States not to annex Samoa." On the following day Rottenburg informed the Foreign Office: "His Serene Highness wishes our representatives to respect international treaties more than the enclosed

[73] Knappe, Mar. 21, denied the report; cf. *Samoa-Weissbuch,* IV, no. 50.
[74] *Ibid.,* IV, no. 31.
[75] *Ibid.,* III, no. 48, *Sten. Berichte,* 1888-89, VI, 1235, footnote.

telegram would indicate. He is surprised that a Prussian official of training could expect him to violate the conventions with America and Great Britain. It is our right to protect property and to oppose force by force, but it lies outside political possibilities to break treaties." On February 21, Bismarck wrote to Knappe that it was his impression that the catastrophe might have been prevented, "if you had carried out your instructions, realizing the limitations of your competence without instructions and authorization from headquarters. If such had been the case, you would not have got into a situation of having to prove that you were absolutely mistaken, both as regards your own influence on the Samoan parties and the elements of resistance on the side of the opponents, and the country would not have had to pay for your error with a severe sacrifice of lives, whereby, in anticipation of the Imperial martial law, you forced us to make amends and jeopardized our peace with a friendly power." Knappe was dismissed and replaced by Stübel. Instructions to the latter, dated April 16, read: "The regrettable fact remains that Consul Knappe, without authorization from headquarters, without cogent reasons, and without a likelihood of success, undertook military measures on December 17 of last year, resulting in loss of lives on December 18, in an undesirable change of the situation of our planters in Samoa, and in endangering the peace with America. Had Consul Knappe not issued his requisition of the 17th, the former condition, not exactly satisfactory but at least tolerable, might still exist."[76] The Chancellor scathingly criticized the reports of Knappe, which did not arrive in Berlin until the end of February and the beginning of March. Knappe's report of January 31 was commented upon with numerous marginal notes of disapproval. Responding to the consul's proposal that Germany assume the administration of Samoa, Bismarck asked the questions repeatedly: "Without England?" "Why, then, a conference in Berlin?" "Knappe seems to think that depends on us exclusively. Does he not know the treaties?" The Chancellor questioned Knappe's assertion that all natives, including the rebels, would prefer annexation by Germany; that seemed to him a great illusion. Elsewhere he remarked about Knappe's idea of annexation: "This *idée fixe* is the *proton pseudos.*" The consul's sentiments suggested that he represented a policy different from the policy of the Reich. "I fail to understand," Bismarck wrote to Stübel on March 9, "why Mr. Knappe referred again to the idea of annexation, after his work in the Foreign Office, his instructions, and the latest correspondence should have told him that all plans of annexation concerning Samoa are directly contradictory to

<hr />

[76] *Ibid.*, III, no. 49, *Sten. Berichte*, 1888-89, VI, 1236.

the policy which I am pursuing according to Imperial intentions."[77] Bismarck's opinion of the situation from the standpoint of international law was about as follows: Germany is in a state of war in Samoa; but, in the sense of international law, it is not a war against Samoa or recognized rulers. Considering the difficulties of the problems of international law involved, strict adherence to the limitations of German rights is required. "The more firmly we are resolved to insist upon our rights within those limits, the more consistently must we avoid any transgressions."[78] Similarly, he commented upon a Foreign Office note of January 31, 1889, on subjecting the foreigners in Samoa to martial law as proclaimed there, with the statement that it was a *de facto* state of war. "We are not at war with Samoa; our friend Tamasese rules there (for us) ; our fight against rebels does not bring to bear upon the foreigners the legal effect of war in the sense of international law."

The American Minister in Berlin was told that Knappe had evidently lost his head and the American Government was assured that the fight forced upon Germany by Mataafa and his followers would be conducted with due consideration for American and British interests.[79] Any suspicion that Germany would not content herself with a neutral position in the Samoan Islands was unfounded. Germany desired only to "obtain a guarantee for ending bloodshed and executions."[80] The Department of State was by no means inclined to press matters too far. Bayard complained that the American press lacked a sense of responsibility. He welcomed Germany's suggestion for a new conference; this would afford an excellent occasion to allay excitement over the Samoan question. The Secretary of State thought that election of a new king by the natives was the best security and guarantee for peace. In view of the coming conference he advised instructing the three consuls in Samoa to postpone military action and to await the measures to be decided upon by the conference.[81] As for the public, the position of the Department of State was rather difficult. A majority of the American Senate wanted an aggressive policy. The commercial companies on the Pacific Coast which were particularly interested had strong support in the Senate. "Situation aggravated by the fact," the German Minister cabled on January 25, 1889, "that Bayard leaves

[77] Bismarck's marginal note on report from Apia, Jan. 4, 1889; Bismarck to Stübel, Berlin, Mar. 9, 1889, *Samoa-Weissbuch,* II, no. 47, *Sten. Berichte,* 1888-89, V, 890.

[78] Bismarck to Vice Admiral von der Goltz, Berlin, Feb. 5, 1889, *Samoa-Weissbuch,* I, no. 41, *Sten. Berichte,* 1888-89, V, 583f.

[79] Bismarck to Alvensleben, Berlin, Jan. 13, 1889; Bismarck, *Politische Briefe,* II, 351f.

[80] Arco to Bismarck, Washington, Jan. 21 and Feb. 1, 1889. *Samoa-Weissbuch,* V, no. 4, *Sten. Berichte,* 1890-91, appendix, I, no. 64, 553.

[81] Bayard to Arco, Feb. 5, 1889, *Foreign Relations,* 1889, 194f.

management of policy entirely to a Republican chauvinist Senate majority influenced by party interests. . . . Since the American press asserts that America can rely on British support, it seems desirable, for setting excited public opinion at ease, to disclose our convention with Great Britain regarding Samoa (yes) through London and Berlin, and possibly German consular reports incriminating Americans (no)." American papers harshly criticized the administration. In the *Washington Post* of January 21, Senator Morgan, Bayard's personal enemy, said that Germany had reached the climax of its policy. The Government had neglected to avail itself of the advantages of the American-Samoan treaty. This explained the present situation. The San Francisco Chamber of Commerce and the members of Congress dependent on it were particularly active.[82] It was only natural for the Pacific coast to take a keen interest in commercial relations with the islands of the Pacific. Although American business in Samoa was relatively insignificant, it was mainly San Francisco companies that participated. For this reason the Chamber of Commerce had passed resolutions in 1888 demanding an energetic policy in Samoa on the part of the American Government. Even during an earlier stage of the Samoa question it had demanded annexation. The German Minister reported on August 26, 1879, "about a coterie of speculators and adventurers who would not leave a stone unturned to force their Government into annexing the Samoan Islands." The press was at their service and, the Germans being considered the most dangerous rivals, they incited the public against the "German intruders."[83] The same people succeeded in having their confi-

[82] Arco, Dec. 29, 1888, and the German consulate in San Francisco, Jan. 3, 1889, report on the influence of the Chamber of Commerce on the Senate.

[83] The resolution of the Chamber of Commerce of Jan. 17, 1888, reads in part as follows: "That the so called equality of American interests at Samoa is a delusion evident to all merchants cognizant of the results of German armed occupation, and that this Chamber of Commerce earnestly protests against a repetition at the Hawaiian Islands of occurrences at Samoa, under any flag or any pretence whatever. . . ." In a petition to Congress on Dec. 20 of the same year, the Chamber of Commerce states: "Under these circumstances, The Chamber of Commerce of San Francisco as representative of the Commercial interests of the Pacific Coast, respectfully urges upon Congress such a decided policy in Samoa, that American interests may be considered, American citizenship respected and the agreement made by Germany with the Governments of Great Britain and the United States in regard to the independence of the Samoan Islands held inviolable. It is well understood that a policy of inaction by the United States Government, in Samoan affairs, will be followed by the same aggressive policy on the part of Germany in the Hawaiian Islands, and we respectfully represent that the time has arrived, when the United States must maintain its just rights, or sacrifice its selfrespect and its proper influence among the Islands of the Pacific." Dept. State, *Miscellaneous Letters,* Jan. and Dec. 1888, pt. II. It was the Chamber of Commerce in San Francisco that later was the strongest advocate of the annexation of Hawaii.

dential agent Sewall called before the Senate to report on the situation. Sewall's account, January 11 to 14, 1889, was of course biased. He asserted that the Germans intended to exploit the islands for an adventurer, Brandeis, and a German company. They were always antagonistic to the Americans and had made it a point from the beginning to attack Malietoa. The Samoans had restrained themselves until the German provocation occurred. Negro workers on the plantations were played against the natives. The Samoans desired an American protectorate.[84]

The affair came before the Senate on January 24. Senator John Sherman gave a full account of the origin of the trouble. He called attention to the importance of the harbor of Pagopago but concluded his address with a rather conciliatory statement: Whatever the newspapers may say, there is nothing in the situation that would justify either of the two nations breaking the peace until every possibility of peaceful settlement of the conflict was exhausted. It seemed to him the most insignificant dispute in which the United States was involved or ever had been involved. "It does not seem to me that Germany, whose people are like our own, and Great Britain, with their boundless empire, will ever allow the disgrace to be inflicted upon our civilization of having a single man of either of these nations killed in war or contest over this puerile controversy." A considerably stronger wind blew in the second debate of January 30. Senator Dolph, speaking on that date, also related the development of the conflict at length and read a letter from New York, written by a certain Mr. John C. Henderson, which put much stress on the strategic importance of Samoa. In the event of war, he said, Germany, possessing Samoa, might have a fortress there, thousands of miles nearer the Pacific Coast than the United States would like. "The Samoan Islands are strategically of vast importance to the United States in controlling an interoceanic canal. The United States can not afford to let European military powers own every strategic position commanding the interoceanic canal. . . . Even commercially the Samoan Islands must soon be of far more importance owing to their geographic position than they can be to Germany. It would be a great calamity to the United States to permit Germany to fortify a single position in those islands. It would be sowing the seeds of much trouble to the United States in years to come." So much for Henderson's letter. The fact that it was put on record shows how much importance the Senate attached to it. Mr. Dolph interpreted the Monroe Doctrine very liberally; he included in it all islands in the Western Hemisphere, naming the Sandwich Islands, Cuba, and Puerto Rico as examples. Conditions in Samoa, he said, were quite

[84] Statement of Harold M. Sewall, of Maine, consul general of the United States at Samoa, before the subcommittee of the Committee on Foreign Relations.

similar to those in the Sandwich Islands, being in like relation to southern California, the coast of Central America, and the interoceanic canal. The speaker demanded the *status quo* in Samoa and protection of American citizens. He did not want war with Germany, but to sacrifice the honor of a great nation was much worse than war. "The sacrifice of the rights of its citizens, the humiliation of its officers in the face of an arrogant power, is worse than war; and I would not submit to it." Congress let deeds follow words. The harbor of Pagopago hitherto had been rather neglected. Now $100,000 was appropriated for construction of a warship and a considerable sum for sending it there. In addition, two more war vessels were ordered to Samoa. Bismarck had refrained from increasing the German forces at Samoa "because we wish to steer clear of any responsibility for impairing the mutual confidence of both nations."[85] The crisis showed more plainly than ever to what extent the community of interests between the United States and the Australian colonies had developed. The Australian press vigorously seconded American agitation against Germany. Arco, on February 22, reported from Washington: "The American press pays much attention to all utterances from Australia which condemn our Samoan policy and suggest cooperation with the United States, and, after including the entire American continent in the sphere of influence of the United States, the recently developed megalomania of this young nation is flattered by the idea of coming sometime into closer relationship with the Australian colonies."

As a consequence the Samoan situation became serious. The three consuls openly fought among themselves, supported by the commanders of their war vessels. Bismarck coined the phrase *"furor consularis,"* which exactly fitted the period.[86] Seven warships lay at anchor in the small port of Apia. The men of the American and German warships regarded each other in the light of future enemies. There were rumors about shots having been fired from one of the ships. This newspaper fiction created so much excitement in San Francisco that the German consulate feared mob attacks if such reports should continue to be published (January 11, 1889). The possibility of war was in the atmosphere but not on Bismarck's desk. At a parliamentary dinner on February 22, 1889, he emphatically declared that he considered it out of the question for so small an affair to disturb in any way the friendly relations that for a hundred years had linked Germany with the kindred people of the United States. In self-defense he had the *Hamburger Nachrichten* declare later that he who waged war would have to be able to prove upon its conclusion that the

[85] *Congressional Record,* 1889, XX, pt. 2, 1283ff. and 1325ff.
[86] Sass, *Die deutschen Weissbücher,* 144.

war had furthered the interests of his country despite all the sacrifices it had made in the meantime.[87]

Carl Schurz, too, ever ready to mediate in times of trouble, had a long conversation with Arco on January 30, 1889. Arco called the dispute a war of newspapers and consuls and complained of the conduct of the American consuls. Schurz offered the opinion that public excitement would be appeased if Germany declared that the invitation for a conference would be based on parity of the three treaty powers and on the pledge that the autonomy of the Samoans would be preserved. Schurz believed that such a promise would make it absolutely impossible for future secretaries of state to support potential adventurous attempts looking toward an American protectorate of Samoa.[88] He reported the results of his interview to the Secretary of State on January 30 and offered his services.[89] It seemed quite feasible for Schurz to negotiate directly with the German Government as he had been Bismarck's guest on May 4, 1888,[90] and the Samoa problem had been discussed at that time. Schurz, very much concerned, warned Arco, in a letter of February 3, 1889, against taking a break between the two nations too lightly. "On the one side the best army in the world and an efficient, rapidly developing, navy; on the other side a nation of more than sixty millions, without a large standing army, it is true, and even without a considerable fleet of battleships, but with an abundance of money; with inexhaustible resources of all kinds; with an exceptionally inventive spirit of enterprise; with self-sacrificing patriotism and greatest perseverance once engaged; actually unassailable in its territorial possessions, and the only great power with its hands entirely free—these belligerent nations separated by the Atlantic Ocean. It would be no war of quick decisions. There would be no battles on land or naval battles either at first. But the United States would send a host of fast cruisers [we too!][90a] out into all seas to destroy German commerce. Germany would retaliate with similar measures, although under less favorable circumstances, since American overseas trade is relatively insignificant [America's merchant marine has 2.8 million tons, ours 1.3] and coastwise navigation, which is developing considerably, can more easily be guarded from loss. Thus the two nations would for a long time try to damage each other without a decision, and drive their maritime trade into the hands of England which certainly would attempt to

---

[87] Poschinger, *Fürst Bismarck und die Parlamentarier*, I, 227; Hofmann, *Fürst Bismarck*, II, 19.
[88] Schurz, *Speeches, Correspondence, and Political Papers*, V, 1ff.
[89] Arco to Herbert Bismarck, New York, Jan. 30, 1889 (copy).
[90] Poschinger, *Fürst Bismarck, neue Tischgespräche*, I, 151.
[90a] Bismarck's marginal notations appear in brackets.

preserve a neutrality so advantageous for her. Possibly the Germans would try to bombard American cities on the coast [certainly], being induced by the deficient fortifications of harbors; but American inventive genius [!] might yet offer all sorts of surprises in that respect. However, it would be doubtful if such attempts could be undertaken at all, for a French alliance will be forced upon the United States [?], and the German Navy would be engaged in European waters [and how about the British Navy?]." Thus such a war would be a long-drawn-out struggle of attrition between two powers, one of which was practically inexhaustible. Schurz, thereupon, spoke of restive elements, of speculators and, above all, of Southerners who thought that participation of former rebel States in a foreign war would improve the situation of their States, and of a few Northerners who believed that the Union would be more closely welded together, and finally of a national feeling, naturally both patriotic and honorable, but with many Americans too entirely sensitive and too inclined to meddle in world politics [Piratical brawling! Buccaneers]. The writer apologized for the length of his letter [God only knows!], but excused himself because of his warm interest in the cause of peace and friendship between Germany and America. He did not wish to impose himself as an adviser [But as an advocate for America]. Bismarck answered this letter, writing confidentially to Arco on February 24. Attacks, he said, had originated from already existing opponents. He did not think that events in Samoa had cost Germany many friends. "Chauvinist adventurers, unscrupulous speculators and fanatics, for whom Mr. Schurz claims a leading part in the event of war, are even now influencing public opinion in the United States to a degree not without danger." America's resources were not inexhaustible and a French alliance was problematical. The Chancellor refuted criticism of the Germans in Samoa. The Minister was instructed, however, to inform the American Government confidentially that Knappe had exceeded his authority. "But this is no justification for the murderous attack against our marines." In February or March 1889, Herbert Bismarck granted the representative of the *New York Herald* an interview for the express purpose of calming American public opinion. The Secretary of State pointed out the triviality of the affair, stating that there was a general desire to settle the question peaceably and rapidly.[91]

Nevertheless, unpleasant incidents might have happened in Samoa despite Germany's conciliatory policy, but they were prevented by a great catastrophe of nature. In the afternoon of March 15, 1889, the barometer dropped to 29.25 in., indicating the approach of a storm. In consideration of the danger-

---

[91] Schulthess, *Europäischer Geschichtskalender,* 1889, 38.

ous reefs in the harbor, the ships at anchor should have made for the open sea at once. The commander of the American squadron, however, made no move, and the Germans, to save their prestige, followed his example. Because of a misunderstanding, the British ship likewise remained at anchor. Thirteen smaller vessels were also in the harbor. The storm broke about midnight, and increased to a hurricane of unheard-of violence on the morning of the sixteenth. The smaller vessels were smashed on the reefs like matchboxes. But the large warships were also exposed to extreme danger. The German gunboat *Eber* sank first, with nearly her entire crew, only five men being saved. The *Adler* was saved from the same fate by her commander's desperate manœuver in seizing a favorable moment to run his ship on a reef. Even then twenty men lost their lives. Only the *Olga* suffered no loss of lives.[92] The American *Vandalia* and the British *Calliope* came near colliding. In the nick of time the *Calliope* succeeded in reaching the open sea. Thus not only this ship, but the *Vandalia* as well, which followed the British example, escaped certain destruction. Some of the men, after floating on wreckage through the terrible stormy night, were rescued with the aid of natives, who generously forgot all animosities. When the storm subsided, only Great Britain had a warship worthy of the name left in that part of the Pacific.[93]

But even so great a misfortune did not relieve the tension between Americans and Germans in Samoa; the men had to be given separate shelters on the island. The British and Americans, on the other hand, became friendly. In the note of thanks from the American Admiral Kane to the British commander of the *Calliope* for his bravery, there occurred the words that blood was thicker than water.[94] The catastrophe, at any rate, hastened preparations for the Berlin Conference; at last the powers were ready to come to an agreement about reduction of military forces in Samoa.[95] In the middle of April they agreed to station one ship each in Samoa. That Bismarck was very anxious to create a favorable atmosphere for the Conference was demonstrated by the early publication of the second part of the *Samoa-Weissbuch*, containing the instruction for Stübel of April 16 with its severe arraignment of

[92] Poschinger, *Bismarck-Portefeuille*, III, 122ff.

[93] For Knappe's report of Mar. 25 on the catastrophe, cf. *Samoa-Weissbuch*, IV, 51, *Sten. Berichte*, 1888-89, VI, 1360f. A fine description of the storm appears in Stevenson, *Footnote to History*, 244ff. Stevenson advances the theory that the modern navy was founded by that storm, inasmuch as the German and American vessels proved inadequate. For reports of eyewitnesses, cf. Obermüller, *Samoa*, 36ff. Ryden, *Foreign Policy of the United States in Relation to Samoa*, 443.

[94] Stevenson, *Footnote to History*, 266.

[95] Arco to Bismarck, Mar. 12, copy. Personal letter from Malet to Herbert Bismarck, very confidential; Arco to Bismarck, Apr. 11, 1889.

Knappe.[96] Contrary to all expectations, James G. Blaine, the successor of Secretary of State Bayard, did not prove at all irreconcilable. He said that everything should be avoided that might hurt German sensibilities. He shared the opinion that it would be wholly unreasonable to endanger the good relations between Germany and the United States because of Samoa. On March 18, he expressed himself even more explicitly. He wished the Samoa problem settled in such a way as not only to remove forever any danger of a conflict but also any kind of ill feeling between Germany and the United States. The instructions he was drafting for the American delegates to the forthcoming conference were worded in a most friendly tone, so as to bring about, insofar as Samoa was concerned, the same harmony that so gratifyingly existed between the two countries in all other respects.[97] Consul General Sewall was instructed not to return to Samoa. However, the Americans stubbornly stuck to the *status quo* of 1887. This was clearly stated in the instructions of April 11, 1889, to the three American delegates. The delegates were to insist chiefly on the *status quo,* but not in the form of an ultimatum. They were to oppose appointment of an adviser, since any violation of Samoan independence was contrary to American friendship for the natives. The principal basis for the attitude of the United States was, however, the port of Pagopago.[98] John Kasson, Walter Phelps, and George Bates were appointed as delegates.

Kasson, through a personal interview with Salisbury in London, sought to bring about an understanding on some principal points. The freedom of action of the British delegates, he hoped, would be somewhat greater than that of Lord Sackville at the Washington Conference. Salisbury laughingly remarked that Sackville certainly was not famous for talking. Kasson suggested to the British Minister that the English-speaking race was better fitted for promoting civilization and peace among the natives than the Germans "whose arguments had too visible a force with sword and helmet." He thought such cooperation in the Samoa affair was natural. But Salisbury answered evasively, saying that Great Britain had too little interest in Samoa

[96] Sass, *Die deutschen Weissbücher,* 145f.

[97] Arco to Bismarck, Mar. 4, 12, and 18, 1889 (extract).

[98] "We can not consent to the institution of any form of government in Samoa subject directly or indirectly to influences which in the contingencies of the future might check or control the use or the development of this American right. Nor can the Government of the United States forget, what we are satisfied the other treaty powers will cordially recognize, that our interest on the Pacific is steadily increasing; that our commerce with the East is developing largely and rapidly; and that the certainty of an early opening of an Isthmian transit from the Atlantic to the Pacific (under American protection) must create changes in which no power can be more directly interested than the United States." *Foreign Relations,* 1889, 201.

to participate actively. No doubt the Australians had some special interests there, and to a certain extent he would of course be glad to encourage their point of view, but German interests in the islands were greater than those of Great Britain. Both men joined in condemning the conduct of the consuls. Nevertheless, Salisbury was skeptical about a tripartite administration, although being willing because of American insistence to give up the mandate system. One reason for this concession probably was Salisbury's opinion that Bismarck was tired of the whole matter.[99] Generally speaking, however, Germany and Great Britain were in accord.

The Chancellor greeted the American delegates with great cordiality. Chatting genially with them, he related various reminiscences of his American student friends and of American diplomats he had known in the course of his career. As for Samoa, he said he thought it impracticable to organize a joint administration of foreign and native officials as had formerly been proposed by the American Government. In conclusion he wished the delegates a pleasant sojourn in Berlin; "if you want a good time here, turn to this gentleman, and if you want to work, turn to that gentleman," mentioning the names of two officials in the Foreign Office.[100] This pleasant atmosphere facilitated negotiations. Great Britain made a very wise proposal. Germany was to get Samoa; America, Hawaii; and Great Britain, Tonga. But the Americans were inflexible, asserting that such a solution would violate their obligations to Samoa.[101] Kimberley, the American Rear Admiral, succeeded in bringing about an armistice between the Samoan chieftains during the Conference. Germany insisted that Mataafa, being chiefly responsible for the conflicts, be permanently excluded from elections for king. The principal difficulty for the moment lay in veiling Germany's retreat in the question of the king, for abandoning Tamasese no doubt amounted to a retreat, since as late as October 1888 the German Government had been disinclined to do that.[102] Kasson, wishing to save Germany's face, proposed in a conversation with Herbert Bismarck that the German Government should take the initiative of its own accord.[103] After some hesitation this was done. In the very first session of the

[99] Kasson to Blaine, London, Apr. 24, 1889, Dept. State, *Samoan Conference at Berlin,* 1889, no. 2; cf. A. F. Tyler, *Blaine,* 233f.; for the preliminaries of the Samoa Conference, cf. *ibid.,* 218ff.

[100] Krauel, *Persönliche Erinnerungen an den Fürsten Bismarck,* 18f.

[101] Kasson to Blaine, Berlin, Apr. 27, 1889, Dept. State, *Samoan Conference at Berlin,* no. 3; Hatzfeldt to Bismarck, Jan. 16, 1889.

[102] Foreign Office memorandum on conversation with American chargé d'affaires, Oct. 30, 1888.

[103] Kasson to Blaine, Berlin, Apr. 28, 1889, confidential, Dept. State, *Samoan Conference at Berlin,* no. 4.

Conference on April 29, the German delegate declared that Germany did not object to Malietoa's return. But this did not mean complete surrender by the Germans. No attempt was made to have the mandatory system brought up for discussion. According to a story circulated later, a telegram from Blaine to his commissioners in Berlin, saying that the irritability of the Chancellor could not be a criterion for American rights, had decisively influenced the negotiations. But the telegram only concerned an exchange of opinions between the Department of State and the American delegation, certain members of which were ready to yield minor points so as not to risk the success of the entire Conference. The attitude of Bismarck was not at all affected.[104]

Negotiations proceeded rather smoothly, aside from some disagreement about the chief justice. Great Britain and Germany had agreed to select a British judge in the event of lack of unanimity among the powers, while the United States insisted on an appointment by a neutral power (the King of Sweden and Norway). By the protocol of June 14, 1889, Samoa was declared neutral territory, and the chief justice was to be appointed by the treaty powers in mutual agreement, but if they could not agree, he was to be appointed by the King of Sweden and Norway. Decisions of the chief justice, within the scope of his competence, were to be final, but the right was reserved to dismiss him by a majority of votes. Disputes during elections as well as conflicts between a treaty power and the Samoans were to be submitted to the chief justice. The treaty powers agreed to recognize his decision and abide by it. A municipal council of six members was provided, the chairman having only one vote; under certain circumstances he was to be appointed by a neutral power. He was to assist the Samoan king as an adviser. A large number of minor regulations, especially regarding allocation of land, need not be discussed in this connection. On December 10, Malietoa was again proclaimed king.[105]

The settlement was far from being satisfactory to Germany, nor did Bismarck consider it so. A handwritten, confidential letter to Arco from Varzin on July 12, 1889, shows his irritation at a remark of the American Minister, who had spoken of the victory of American diplomacy. He could not, he said, submit Arco's report to the Emperor. He did not attach such importance to the ratification of the resolutions of the conference by the United States Senate as the American Minister seemed to think. Should ratification be refused, the situation in Samoa would remain the same as before, and it would not be any more difficult for the Germans to endure than for the Americans. The German public considered the outcome as a defeat, while the Americans rejoiced at

[104] For details, cf. A. F. Tyler, *Blaine*, 247ff.
[105] Samoa Protocol, *Samoa-Weissbuch*, V, no. 8, *Sten. Berichte*, I, 1890-91, appendix, I, 560ff.

Bismarck's retreat.[106] All the American delegates, however, did not approve the outcome. Kasson, impressed with Bismarck's good will throughout the conference, was ready to yield on minor points. Phelps had nothing of importance to criticize. Bates, on the other hand, was of the opinion that the demands of his Government had not been met. He entertained grave apprehensions because of the possibility of dismissing the chief justice at the demand of the treaty powers. By such an arrangement, American influence would be inferior to European influence. Moreover, according to the text of the protocol, the liberation of Malietoa did not appear as an act of justice but as an act of grace. Such complaints may be due in part to a desire to present an independent opinion; nevertheless, Bates was not altogether wrong. So long as Germany and Great Britain were united, peace in Samoa was assured. The *status quo,* however, had not been completely restored. An important new factor had appeared whereby the three governments directly shared responsibility for the Samoan administration, and the inconveniences resulting from that provision no doubt were instrumental in convincing the powers that the situation was untenable. Moreover, general political considerations after 1890 affected the Samoan situation even more than did local affairs. In judging the settlement of 1889, it must be remembered that Bismarck's main objective was to prevent a united Anglo-American front. In that respect he succeeded. The situation was such as to prevent American acceptance of the German proposal for a mandate and to make effective British support doubtful. Possession of Samoa, however, did not seem important enough to Bismarck to provoke a conflict with the United States; indeed he probably would have preferred to drop the entire affair. At any rate, we may infer as much from a telegram to Arco, the contents of which Eckardstein reports in his memoirs. He was in favor, Bismarck said, of "withdrawing from Samoa entirely, if such were possible in an honorable way, for Samoa will never be of substantial value to us but will probably endanger our relations with America, and later perhaps those with Australia as well and consequently those with England." [107] Information from other sources point in the same direction. Thus Malet told Kasson he thought that Bismarck wished to discontinue entirely the active support of the Plantation Company, which had cost the Government such serious losses. Herbert Bismarck complained of increased expenditures for administration as required by the protocol, and suggested that possibly the German Government would recall

[106] Coolidge, *United States as a World Power,* 198.

[107] Eckardstein, *Lebenserinnerungen,* II, 34. This telegram was not found in the archives.

its vice consul.[108] Precisely as in the case of the Caroline Islands, Bismarck later declared that Samoa had not been worth a war.[109] The greatest objection to the protocol was the fact that official duties were not clearly defined nor local conditions sufficiently taken into account. Governmental authority in Samoa was conferred upon the chief justice, while the chairman of the municipal council was responsible for the administration of Apia. Because of the smallness of the country, the representatives of different authorities were apt to trespass on each other's competences. They would inevitably come into conflict whenever the interests of the Samoan Government were not directly identical with the interests of the administration of Apia. The chairman of the municipal council in turn frequently found himself in an embarrassing position with regard to foreign business men, for they considered the council an institution representing their interests. No sooner did the chairman of the council, in his capacity as a Samoan official, attempt to enforce a regulation in favor of the natives but unfavorable to the foreigners than a storm of indignation would break in the council where the merchants had their representatives. Thus it did not take long to return to the old state of affairs. The consuls, being the natural representatives of the whites, interfered with functions of the administration from which they were theoretically excluded. Moreover, their influence was stronger since they were supported by the several treaty powers, while the officials of the Samoan Government were constantly struggling with financial difficulties.

Nevertheless, it is surprising to see the United States plan to withdraw from Samoa shortly after the Conference; surprising, because such renunciation could hardly have been expected of Blaine, the imperialist.[110] The change was brought about chiefly by the fact that Blaine, because of his larger plans— Pan America and a Far Eastern policy—found Samoa an encumbrance likely to lead to unpleasant controversies with Great Britain and Germany. In addition the Americans had overestimated business opportunities; this may be inferred from a gradual change in public opinion.[111] On August 31, 1890, therefore, Blaine told the German Minister that he had been forced to take over the Samoan question from his predecessor Bayard, and the sooner the United States settled it, the better. Interference in Samoan affairs and the re-

[108] Kasson to President Harrison, Berlin, June 5, 1889, confidential, Dept. State, *Samoan Conference at Berlin,* 1889.

[109] Cf. Penzler, *Fürst Bismarck nach seiner Entlassung,* I, 367f.

[110] *Der Hamburgische Korrespondent* of May 17, 1889, thought that after the completion of the Panama Canal the importance of Samoa to the United States would decrease.

[111] For Blaine's policy in the Pacific, cf. *Foreign Relations,* 1881, 635ff., and Bemis, *Secretaries of State,* VIII, 119ff.

sulting disputes with Great Britain and Germany did not harmonize with the traditional foreign policy of the United States and was a source of continual conflicts. Samoa was not worth much to the United States, and if he, Blaine, were not hindered by consideration for public opinion, he would even then propose that the United States transfer its Samoan claims to Germany. Blaine hoped to accomplish such a transfer in the course of time and pledged the Minister to strict secrecy regarding his intentions, the realization of which would have to be carefully prepared (Mumm to Caprivi, Bar Harbor, August 31, 1890). A few months later the Secretary of State repeated that statement coupled with the reservation that the port of Pagopago would have to be guaranteed to the United States (Mumm, October 6). One year later, however, he was far more reserved, but he still complained that cooperation of three great powers within so small a territory had come to be a continuous source of friction and differences (Arco, December 12, 1891). Meanwhile public opinion was changing noticeably. Senator Morgan, the chairman of the Senate Committee on Foreign Relations, declared himself opposed to the condominium. It was impossible, he said, to keep three women locked up in one room and avoid jealousy and quarrels. Secretary of State Walter Q. Gresham went so far as to say that the Samoan Islands were lying quite outside the United States sphere of interests, requiring many sacrifices without the least advantages (Samoa, April 1, 1894). The Presidential message of December 3, 1894, frankly admitted the failure of the existing arrangement. American participation in the Samoan administration was contrary to the teachings and warnings of wise and patriotic men who had created free laws. The President requested Congress to examine the measures initiated by the Government in order to reach an agreement freeing the United States from its obligations to the other powers but without surrendering existing rights. A survey of the Secretary of State concluded on May 9, 1894, found that an autonomous government existed in name only.

In the face of such facts it was only natural for Germany to hope for the ultimate success of her policy. First the Washington hint was followed up, but when the promises of the Americans did not materialize, on pretense of British resistance, the British Government was approached. The German Foreign Office thought it possessed wonderful articles for exchange—Hawaii for the United States and Tonga for Great Britain. But Hawaii was already in American hands, its incorporation into the United States showing ever more clearly on the political horizon. Germany's consent was not needed. An attempt to induce London to undertake joint action in Washington concerning Hawaii failed utterly. London pretended not to be interested and failed to show any inclination toward getting into difficulties with the United States. The Tonga bait was not alluring. Louder and louder complaints were being heard from Australian colonies which would never give their consent to the surrender of Samoa. As a matter of fact New Zealand again had new schemes, going so far as to dream of establishing a "Lesser Britain," which was to include New Zealand, the Fiji Islands, Tonga, and Samoa. Hence German progress was slow. In a conversation between Hatzfeldt and Lord Rosebery on May 10, 1894, the latter advised the former not to be so insistent about Samoa. Because of the colonies, British difficulties were as great as those of Germany. There was only one solution, and that was to let matters alone.[112] As a matter of fact the situation had changed radically since 1887. Great Britain was no longer inclined to have the Samoan administration transferred to Germany alone. Hatzfeldt, in a report of June 1, 1894, expressed his doubts as to whether Rosebery would be at all willing to concede Germany any colonial advantages.[113] The Samoa problem consequently was merged with the general discussion of Anglo-German relations. It was finally settled in an atmosphere of tension between Great Britain and Germany, and of evident irritation between Germany and the United States because of the Manila incident. Not only with respect to Samoa but also in the political treatment of colonial questions in general, there developed more and more that common front between Great Britain and the United States that made it so difficult for Germany's policy to have its just demands fulfilled.

Time and again there had been fights among the natives, but a crisis was finally reached in the autumn of 1898. Malietoa died on August 22 and succession to the throne was disputed at once. The Germans proposed that Mataafa be recalled from exile, while numbers of natives objected. At the end of December 1898, a majority of chieftains agreed on the election of Mataafa. Chief Justice Chambers, an American, however, at the beginning of January 1899, ruled that election to be in violation of the Berlin treaty and appointed Tanu, Malietoa's son, as king. Clashes were renewed immediately, Mataafa's followers being victorious. The consuls thereupon established a provisional government with Mataafa at its head. Since the chief justice refused to recognize that arrangement, the president of the municipal council, as the head of the provisional government, closed the supreme court. The British consul protested, declaring the closing of the supreme court to be contrary to treaty and reopened it by force, in agreement with the American consul. In vain did the German Government endeavor to bring about an understanding in Washington. The United States ordered a squadron of warships to Samoa, and

[112] *Die Grosse Politik,* VIII, 426.
[113] *Ibid.,* VIII, 435ff.

its commander on March 11 proclaimed the provisional government, Mataafa deposed, and the supreme court in operation. British and American ships bombarded Apia and damaged the German consulate. Tanu was crowned king on March 23.

Matters could not possibly continue in such a fashion. A joint commission was sent to Samoa, and all parties then agreed that the existing form of administration had not stood the test in any respect. Even the American commissioner, Bartlett Tripp, said that each of the great powers could easily rule the islands in the form planned, but hardly all of them together; he therefore considered it necessary to dissolve the partnership of nations.[114] The tension between the United States and Germany because of the Manila incident, and the great irritation of the Germans toward the British were reflected in the fact that the United States and Great Britain cooperated more closely than ever. The American Admiral in Samoa was thus commissioned to enforce majority decisions, that is, those agreed upon by the American and British consuls. Germany, regarding Great Britain as the chief culprit and the United States as its agent, handled the situation badly. Threats of breaking off diplomatic relations with Great Britain because of Samoa were certain to have an undesirable effect and were as un-Bismarckian as possible. Germany then proposed a plan of partition by which the United States was to receive the island of Tutuila with Pagopago, Germany Upolu with Saluafata and Savaii, and Great Britain the Tonga Islands (August 29). But Great Britain at first would not accept that solution. Britain wanted above all to keep the island of Upolu and offered Savaii and partition of the Tonga and Savage Islands as an alternative. After considerable bargaining, Germany finally agreed in return for a number of other concessions. At the last moment Great Britain again hesitated and dropped its claims to Samoa. An Anglo-German convention was concluded and signed on November 14, 1899. It gave Germany Upolu and Savaii as well as Jendi in the neutral zone. Great Britain received the Tonga Islands including Vauvau, the German neutral zone excluding Jendi, and the German Solomon Islands, excluding Bougainville. Commercial agreements in regard to Togoland, the Gold Coast, and Zanzibar were inserted in the convention. On December 2, 1899, the United States, Germany, and Great Britain concluded a treaty whereby the latter two powers renounced all rights to the island of Tutuila and all other islands in the Samoa group east of the 171st degree and in return the United States recognized the Anglo-German convention. All three powers guaranteed to one another most-favored-nation privileges for trade and navigation in the Samoan Islands. A protocol to the agreement on November 7, 1900, provided that arbitration by the King of

[114] Keim, *German-American Political Relations,* 209.

Sweden and Norway was to fix indemnities for losses of white residents in Samoa incurred during the fights.

The Germans rejoiced at the acquisition of Samoa. But it is questionable whether that success was as great as it appeared on the surface. Great Britain had received a big prize indeed, and for the United States also the solution was most favorable. Strategically as well as commercially Tutuila was of equal importance to Pagopago. Such was the opinion held in particular by John Hay, American Secretary of State.[115]

[115] Thayer, *Hay*, II, 282ff.

OUTLOOK

T HE final settlement of the Samoa conflict reflected many changes on the
horizon of world politics. The tension between Germany and the United
States, perceptible at that time, cannot be fully appreciated without simultaneous consideration of events during the Spanish-American War. In Manila,
it will be remembered, a very serious incident occurred between the American
and German admirals. It is not without a touch of piquancy to observe that
the year 1898, so extremely important for American policy and marking a
new phase in American-German relations, is also the year of Bismarck's death.
Not until that year does the era of Bismarck really end. His very existence
had until then exercised a powerful, if indirect, influence.

Bismarck did not live to see the end of the Spanish-American War. We
are not informed of his true opinion about it, but if a report of the *Leipziger
Neueste Nachrichten* may be trusted, Bismarck's sympathies were not very
strong on either side.[1] Realizing that his every word still reverberated throughout the world, he used considerable discretion in speaking to representatives
of the foreign press. The news of the death of the first German Chancellor
was received with surprisingly great attention in the United States, particularly
in view of the fact that the war with Spain was still in progress. His dismissal
itself had not made much impression in America. In March 1890, Freiherr
von Eckardstein, attaché at the German Legation in Washington, had a conference with Carl Schurz and when conversation turned to Bismarck's resigna-
tion, Schurz remarked that the American people, after that fateful event,
had quickly passed on to other matters. The Americans simply thought: "The
Emperor and Bismarck are both hardheaded chaps, they could not work to-

[1] Poschinger, *Also sprach Bismarck,* III, 359.

gether, one of them had to go and as the Emperor could not go, Bismarck had to go." Others would even say: "The Emperor is a fine plucky young fellow, he kicked out Bismarck, as soon as it suited him, and he will kick out many of the chancellors to follow." [2] The American Ambassador in Berlin, Andrew D. White, also regarded the dismissal of Bismarck as a proof of the Emperor's strength of character and independence. As in Great Britain, only a few people realized the full significance of the event. "The Prince was an Atlas," the correspondent of the *New York Herald* wrote from Berlin on April 20, 1890, "who for forty years has carried a world upon his shoulders." Nevertheless, the death of the great Chancellor was the occasion for long articles and biographical sketches in American newspapers. Between July 31 and August 3, 1898, the event even seemed to attract more attention than the war. So far as articles written on that occasion are concerned, the war clearly had widened the general understanding of political realities. A country about to embark upon a new imperialism had no cause for indignation at the man of "blood and iron," a headline that actually appeared over many articles. While there were comparisons between Gladstone, the "man of the people," and Bismarck, "the man of power," the prevailing tendency was one of admiration for the achievements of the founder of the Reich. "One must go back to Charlemagne to find his equal," declared the New York *Herald* on July 31, 1889. "The Reich founded by Charlemagne disintegrated while the Reich of Bismarck is built on a rock." The *New York Tribune* of the same date called Gambetta the greatest of modern tribunes, Gladstone the most capable and conscientious citizen of the world, "but as regards historical importance Bismarck is the greatest man in political history since the death of Napoleon."

It might be an interesting task to trace parallels in those obituaries with the decisive transformations in the world's political situation and public opinion. The Americans keenly sensed at that moment that a whole era had come to an end. At the bier of the great Chancellor they bade farewell not to the friend of the United States but to the symbol of a powerful European state, the strongest exponent of European politics in the second half of the nineteenth century.

What were the general outlines of American-German relations from 1890 to the World War? On the whole, all of the questions concerning both countries and influencing mutual relations, positively or negatively, remained the same as the questions discussed in this book. Nothing absolutely new was added. The element of German emigration remained of importance as before, although emigration in the twentieth century did not by any means reach the

---

[2] Eckardstein, *Lebenserinnerungen,* I, 111f.

extent that it did during the last few decades of the nineteenth century. Economic rivalry also continued, asserting itself in reciprocal measures of protection or in direct competition in Central and South America, and in the Far East. Likewise there continued the menace of conflicts in the Pacific Ocean. Yet there also remained the possibility of occasional cooperation in the Far East, as in Bancroft's time. Even a minor problem like Venezuela came up again.

.   .   .   .

After 1890, it may be repeated, there were no new problems to disturb American-German relations. The tensions of 1898 and 1902, serious though they appeared at the moment, differed only in degree and not in principle from the controversies that had occurred as early as the eighties of the last century. They resulted from the same cause: German and American policies of expansion directly confronted each other in the Pacific area or on the American continent. The good intention of cultivating friendly relations likewise continued as of old, particularly from the German side. Not until the twentieth century were systematic attempts made to deepen the existing friendship. In this connection there might be mentioned Germany's efforts to use the German-Americans as a connecting link, the mission of Prince Henry in 1902, the exchange of professors, and innumerable speeches on American-German friendship.

Conditions materially changed in only two respects. One was the elimination of the great German statesman. How decisively that one personality influenced even such matters as seemingly lay outside the course of general relations could easily be demonstrated. The consistency of Bismarck's policy shows most clearly in those cases when subjects apparently wholly irrelevant were subordinated to his general system. But after his retirement the coherent totality of his creation was dissolved into separate parts, the building so ingeniously constructed tottered, and this fact no doubt affected American-German relations.

The other point was a complete change in the atmosphere between the two countries. Some people may ascribe that change chiefly to ideological causes. Democratic and peace-loving America, they may say, differed too much from the autocratic government of militarist Germany. The basic principles of policy contrasted too widely, with Germany on the one hand basing her policy on power and the United States on the other hand being contented with influencing other countries by peaceful means. Ideology, or rather belief in such ideas, should not indeed be underestimated. The present book has repeatedly called attention to differences in the respective states of mind attributable to diverse conditions, both geographic and ethnographic. But after all this ideology was only of secondary importance. The decisive factor was that two ambitious young powers that had entered the arena of world politics in 1896 and 1898 respectively, realized more and more that they disturbed each other and might possibly be mutual menaces. This sentiment cannot be clearly analyzed but was a very real fact.

Andrew Dickson White, when in 1897 he again took charge of the American Embassy in Berlin, was surprised to find a sentiment of vexation toward the United States, and ascribed it to the growth of economic rivalry. But it was more than that. The rivalry included all matters, and in that atmosphere even the German element in the United States lost its power of conciliation, becoming itself a part of the latent American-German tension.

This, however, would never have sufficed to replace traditional friendship with temporary enmity. For the ultimate cause of Germany and the United States drifting so widely apart in their relations, we must consider the connection of shifting world constellations and the transformation in Anglo-German and Anglo-American relations since the nineties. The final word on American-German relations after 1890 has not as yet been spoken. But all investigations dealing with that subject and particularly the most recent one, a very careful study by Ilse Kunz-Lack, *Die deutsch-amerikanischen Beziehungen von 1890 bis 1914*, unmistakably indicate that events can be understood only by considering Great Britain.

Beginning with the Danish crisis of 1864, Anglo-German relations were never free from tensions. Bismarck had made it one of the fundamental principles of his policy to prevent Anglo-German antagonism, and either to promote friendly relations or indirectly to keep Great Britain from making the forces of her Empire available to Germany's continental opponents. Even his diplomatic skill, however, was unable to minimize the fact that the German nation everywhere found its colonial aspirations frustrated by Great Britain while the latter in its turn was disquieted by Germany's predominant position on the Continent. Nevertheless, because of Bismarck's genius, British policy until 1890 had never been sufficiently unrestrained to make the future development of Anglo-German relations dependent on it alone—and this involved the real danger. It was disastrous for Germany that Great Britain regained her freedom of action after 1890, just when world politics forced the British Empire to make fundamental decisions.

These were required by the changed conditions in the Far East. As early as the seventeenth century the occidental powers had begun the political penetration of China. Divergent interests of the rival states developed in an ever-increasing degree. The Sino-Japanese war of 1894 marked the beginning of the eastern Asiatic question. Great Britain, possessing the most vital interests, succeeded in having other European powers concerned with eastern Asiatic affairs participate in joint action in Tokio, and a peace was concluded that largely satisfied British interests. At the same time Russia's advance in Manchuria came to be an ever greater menace to Great Britain, while differences with France became increasingly critical and drifted toward an open break in 1898. Great Britain faced the imminent danger of a universal alliance of the powers interested in the Far East, in addition to the overwhelming pressure upon its commerce by its rivals with Germany in the vanguard. It was but natural, therefore, for Great Britain to seek support; Germany and the United States were first considered, since both of these nations, as compared with France and Russia, were newcomers in eastern Asia. Understanding with the United States could be achieved the more easily, as in the Pacific area, as pointed out before, a spontaneous Anglo-Saxon community of interests had developed that diplomacy needed only to resume and encourage.

In view of the complexity of commercial relations at the time, it would have been too difficult, if not altogether impossible, for the United States to turn against Great Britain. An agreement, on the other hand, promised a guarantee for more effective competition against other rivals, principally Germany and secondly Japan. One need not go so far as to speak of a gentlemen's agreement; moreover there is no conclusive evidence of it. Probably the understanding was achieved by a less formal method. Years before the Spanish-American War, during which time British policy so conspicuously differed from that of the continental powers, leading American and British periodicals discussed the question of an entente of the Anglo-Saxon powers. Great Britain, by recognizing the Monroe Doctrine in the spring of 1896, took the last decisive step.

Germany on the other hand ran no small risk in that Great Britain challenged at a moment when the former's relations to the world powers were in a state of obscurity or even hostility. France, through the Fashoda affair and the subsequent settlement with Great Britain, had given evidence of the fact that cultivation of the spirit of revenge against Germany was considered more important than world-wide differences with Great Britain regarding political interests, and therefore had to be regarded as an irreconcilable enemy. As a result of its tactless conduct in Tokio in 1895, Germany, more than the other powers, had incurred the ill-favor of Japan. Russia was not ready to draw the logical consequences from the good services that the Reich had rendered in the matter of eastern Asiatic interests. Relations with the United States, finally, were necessarily influenced by the development of Anglo-German relations. It is of little importance to know whether or not Great Britain, in challenging Germany, intended to include the United States and Japan in an alliance. As soon as Great Britain, as an eastern Asiatic power, approached Germany, any decision of the latter would inevitably determine the grouping of all powers interested in eastern Asia. German diplomacy at that time believed it had a free choice. As a matter of fact it was faced with a dilemma that should at least have induced the German Government to make certain concessions even if convinced that the British overtures were not sincere.

The period from 1898 to 1902, then, was of the greatest importance in the development of American-German relations. Neither the Manila incident nor the Venezuela conflict of 1902 was a decisive factor. There followed times when the two countries were outwardly on the best of terms. The important point rather was that, once the British overtures had failed, the tension between Germany and Great Britain was increased to the degree of world-wide political enmity. Germany, most actively engaged in eastern Asiatic affairs since the acquisition of Kiaochow, automatically met a solid Anglo-Saxon front. From that time on the British conception of German policy perceptibly gained more and more ground in the United States. Not until then did the common language attain its full significance. Numerous channels enabled the British press and literature to influence American public opinion against Germany. It is a characteristic fact that one of the principal concerns of the British Government, anxiety over Germany's naval armament, to some extent spread to the United States. Ilse Kunz-Lack points out that in congressional debates on the development of the American Navy reference was no longer made to Great Britain but to the growth of Germany's naval force. The distrust prevailing between Germany and the United States could have been removed only through a decided improvement in Anglo-German relations.

It is not for us to analyze the causes that led to the entrance of the United States into the World War. No doubt there were special reasons not at present known to us. But Germany's failure to see that its relations with the United States were closely connected with the development of Anglo-German and Anglo-American relations was one of the grave errors of Germany's pre-war policy.

APPENDIX

I. THE REVOLUTION OF 1848

J. C. Calhoun to Baron von Gerolt.[1]

Washington, 28th May, 1848.

My dear Sir:

I have examined with as much attention and care, as my engagements would permit, the fundamental law of the German Empire, proposed to the Diet by the Committee of seventeen; and agreeably to your request, I herewith communicate the suggestions, which occurred to me in reference to it. I call them suggestions, because I have not that full, accurate knowledge of the existing institutions of Germany, nor of the character, feelings and opinions of the German people, or of the different interests of the communities of which they are composed, that is indispensable to form a Constitution, which would suit them, or to pronounce with any certainty, whether the proposed plan, or any other, would. Every constitution to succeed, must be adapted to the community for which it is made, in all respects; and hence no one, in forming a constitution for itself, can derive much aid from that of others.

With, then, the imperfect knowledge, which I have, and which all must have, who have not long resided in the country, it seems to me, that the project errs in proposing to base the Constitution on *national unity* and to vest the Union, or Empire, as it is called, with so vast an extent of power, as it does. It strikes me, that it would be impossible to induce the several communities, of which Germany is composed, to adopt it. To pass over all other difficulties, would the two great Monarchies of Prussia and Austria agree to it? Would

[1] See also letter from Calhoun to Gerolt, May 28, 1848, as printed in *American Historical Review*, XL, no. 3 (Apr. 1935), 477f.

the Sovereign of either of them agree to be elected Emperor, if his elevation to that high office would necessarily involve the relinquishment of his present crown? Or, if it would not, would either agree, that the other should add the imperial to his present crown? Or would either agree, that an inferior potentate, or any individual, however distinguished, should be elevated to a power and dignity vastly greater than his own? It seems to me not; and that if there was no other difficulty [*sic*] in reconciling either of these powers to the project, this of itself would defeat it.

But, if it could be adopted, it strikes me, that it would not be advisable. A Constitution based on national unity, and with such extensive powers, would, it seems to me, form too intimate and close a union, for a people divided into communities, with political institutions so very different and interests so very conflicting. The union would be much closer than that between the states of our union, and the powers possessed by the Empire would be much greater than those possessed by our federal Goverment [*sic*], although our State Governments are far more homogenous than the several German communities and the diversity of interest much less. And yet, experience has shown, that the tendency to concentrate all powers in the federal Government is far stronger than that towards dissolution, contrary to the anticipation of many of the most experienced and wise of our statesmen, when the Government went into operation. Judged, then, by our experience, the constitution proposed for Germany, would end either in absorbing all the powers belonging to the Governments of the several communities and concentrate the whole in the Empire; or what is more probable, a conflict would follow between it and them, resulting from the Union being closer, than what interest and the sympathy of the parts would permit, which would end in the dissolution of the former.

With these impressions, I am inclined to think, that the existing confederation should be preserved, but improved and strengthened. What improvement should be made in the formation of the Diet, I am not prepared to say, but am of the opinion, that the powers in article 2 marked f. g. h. i. k. so far as it relates to currency, weight and measures, might safely be vested in the confederation. I am of the opinion, that it would be advisable to vest it with powers, connected with the foreign relations of Germany and its defence against aggressions from abroad and with the interior relations of its several communities and the preservation of peace and harmony between them, but with no more, than may be indispensable for either purpose. I am also of the opinion, that no further change should be made in the formation of the Diet, than may be necessary to make it the safe depository of these and such other powers, as may be conferred in it. It would be safer, at first, to give too little rather than too much power. It would be easier to add, whatever power experience might show to be necessary, than to divest the Diet of such as may be found to be mischievous.

I look to Germany with deep interest. If France has taken the lead in pulling down the old Government, it is reserved for Germany, if I do not mistake, to take the lead in the more glorious task of constructing the new on true principles. The character of the people is well suited to establish and maintain constitutional Governments, and she has ample and excellent materials wherewith to construct them,—far better than France or any other country on the continent of Europe. On her success will depend, not only the successful consummation of what the recent revolutions aimed at in Germany, but in the rest of Europe. If she fails all others probably will.

II. THE REVOLUTION OF 1848

A. J. Donelson to James Buchanan, September 14, 1848
(No. 4)

> Frankfort, September 14th, 1848.
> [Received October 10, 1848]

Sir:

I was admitted to an audience yesterday at 12 oclock [sic] with the Vicaire of the German Empire for the purpose of presenting my letter of credence. My observations and the reply made to me on that occasion you will find in the annexed papers.

In the conversation which ensued afterwards I ventured to ask his Highness whether he thought the recent changes in his Cabinet and those which had been made at Berlin and Vienne [sic] seriously threatened the success of the Central Power. His answer, very prompt, was that such difficulties were not unexpected—that they were the naturel [sic] product of the fomentation caused by the effort to reform the institutions of Germany, and that they only pointed out more clearly the nature and the extent of the compromises to which I had adverted as characterising those that formed the basis of the American Constitution. He said very emphatically that both the people and Princes of Germany must yield much to this spirit of compromise but that come what might he would adhere faithfully to the principle on which he had accepted office. The crisis in his judgement [sic] had not reached, and he did not believe it would, a point to authorize despair of the success of the Central Power: and that such must not be the inference if he went to the Right, Centre, or Left for the members of his Cabinet.

In this conversation also with the view of ascertaining the extent of the powers His Highness might regard as appropriate to the sphere of a Federal Government I enumerated such as we had found indispensable in our experience, and particularly that in reference to the regulation of duties on Foreign imports. On these subjects he seemed to have formed matured opinions, and I am gratified to say to you that they are such as might be concurred in by our own statesmen. In other respects the audience was most gratifying, as I am sure his official speech will be to the President.

You will remark the compliment paid to our institutions when they are characterised as worthy of the imitation of Germany not only as a system but for the welfare they secure to the people. If I mistake not this is the first instance in which the Chief of a Government, of which the majority of the Crowned Princes of Europe forms a part, has recognised the principle which places soverignty [sic] in the hands of the people, and holds it up to the nations of the Earth, not as an experiment, but as a safe example.

Such language could not but excite in my bosom a thrill of satisfaction, which, if flattering to my pride as an American citizen, must in an equal degree impress me with the responsibility of my official duties. Sincere as has always been my gratitude to the great men who formed our constitution I never realized before, so clearly, how important is the trust it confides to us, as an example to other nations, who without its influence would abandon the hope of liberty. But for this example I do not beleive [sic] that the constituent assemblies which are now organised throughout Germany would have been formed. Instead of making an effort to establish this Federal Government the probability is that public opinion would have tended again towards the system of absolutism, and not to that of written constitutions limiting the powers of the Government.

Mr. Beckerath has been called to Berlin by the King to form a new ministry. He is distinguished for talents, but cannot be expected to settle the issue which has been raised at Berlin on the Army question. The point in this question is that the Assembly claims the right of determining the obligations of the officer, and that his oath hereafter shall bind him not merely to the King but to the constitution, or rather to the legality of the existing Government. The question will enter into the agitations of the future, which we are not yet certain will subside without civil war.

The final vote is not yet taken on the Armistice: and this Cabinet cannot be formed until it is.

IIA. THE BANCROFT - BISMARCK INTERVIEW

Wednesday August 28, 1867.

A little before 2 o'clock Count Bismarck called for me in his carriage. I met him as he came up stairs and joined him. I thanked him for his goodness in giving up so much of his time to me, he said it was very agreeable to him, he wd. a great deal rather be so employed than be shut up in his workingroom. We drove out of the Brandenburg gate and as we passed the garden to his house wh. runs down to the old boundary of the city, he pointed it out to me. Discourse naturally fell on the rapid increase of the city of Berlin. He said it was increasing in every direction; that he was accustomed to ride in summer to the other side of the city in order to get a bath in the morning in the Spree where its waters were pure, that he had to ride very far the city having increased as much in that direction quite as much as in the other.

The reform bill in England was spoken of as having the support of the conservative party in Parliament; that catholic emancipation and the repeal of the corn law were carried under cons. adminis; those of the Duke of Well. and Sir Robt. Peel. He himself said that the great change effected in the last few years in England, have been effected only under the lead of a conserv. ministry,—under the lead of any other they wd. have excited too much apprehension and must have failed.

Thursday September 26, 1867.

Went to dine with Count Bismarck,—invited at five. The company which consisted of about sixteen persons arrived punctually and the dinner was served without any delay. The count led me into dinner and placed me at his right hand, The dinner was excellent and of many courses. The wine was excellent and liberally served. In about an hour and a quarter the company rose. Coffee and liquors were then served and cigars in the large receiving room and by seven o'clock every one of the company had taken leave. Such I understand is the custom at Bismarck's entertainments. His time is too precious to spend much of it at the table and this is well understood by his guests. During dinner he was exceedingly courteous, directing a word to one and another but talking with me more than the rest. I reminded him of the strong points of resemblance between our constitution, and the constitution of the North German Union, and asked him if it was the result of imitation or that the same necessity led to the same results. He said, "a little of each." The Bundesrath he regarded as in fact a Chamber. It had the power of proposing laws, amending them and negating them. The members of it were indeed subject to recall, but then though they appeared as the representatives of various sovereigns those sovereigns were restrained by their respective constitutions representative assemblies and responsible ministries so that there was none of them likely to send a delegate who should not substantially represent the opinion of the state to which he belonged.

As to his late circular, it was but a repetition of what he had all along said and its object was to give assurance to the South German states, so that they might feel that nothing had been changed in their position by the interview of the Emperors at Salzburg.

I alluded to the superiority which Prussia possessed over England and Italy by its large class who were proprietors of land. He said that England was a landless people, the people of Prussia a landed people. He said that though he might not have been forward to urge the measure he was satisfied that it was a wise one. "And if I do not express myself with enthusiasm on the subject" said he, "it is because I am one of those who suffered by it in my estate."

On my saying that my journey through Spain had assisted to convince me that the ecclesiastical system of catholic Rome was inconsistent with the good administration of a country. He agreed that there were principles in the catholic religion which made it unfavorable to political freedom. But he observed that in all catholic countries the government was politically corrupt. In Italy the navy had such preparations as should have made it far superior to the Austrian; but there had been dishonesty in selling stores which should have been used in fitting out the fleet and consequently the Italian fleet was defeated where it ought to have been successful and it was defeated in consequence of administrative corruption. That on the contrary was not the case in protestant countries, not in Holland, nor in Denmark nor in Sweden nor in Prussia and in England no public measure and no judicial decision can be carried by a bribe.

Something having been said of Roumania he spoke of Prince Charles of Hohenzollern. "The Prince" said he "came to me to know if he should go to Bucharest, I said to him 'How do you feel, have you courage to take its risks?'. He hesitated and spoke about speaking to the king. If you speak to the king I said the king will arrest you." He still hesitated. Bismarck told him "you run no risk, the day is gone by where the throats of princes were cut or they suffered from any personal cruelties." At last the prince got up courage to go, he passed thro' Austria with a passport calling himself Lehavan and so he got through. But Bismarck says he is too much under the influence of his mother who is a catholic. I said he must be a catholic. He answered "Yes after a fashion" but he said he was one like that man who on being questioned on to whether he was a catholic said "yes I'm a cath. but I don't make much use of that." But he said again he was too much under the influence of his mother who was a more devoted catholic.

Count Bismarck spoke favorably of the purchase of the North West America from Russia. Russia could not turn it to any account. The enterprising men of the United States would do so. He had lately heard that the region was well wooded, if so it would be valuable for its forests and then for its furs. On my speaking of the United States as a wine growing country he compared California to Hungary in that both produce gold and wine. Happening to say that I had been the night before to hear the Afrikanerin and that the opera did not seem to me one of the best and contained things evidently repeated from the Huguenots he said yes, and that in naming the Huguenots I had named the best of Meyerbeers operas and added that he had made very free use of the old church melodies. On my saying that was new to me he at once instanced the music of "Eine feste Burg ist unser Gott," and immediately hummed the air, as one which Meyerbeer had appropriated in the Huguenots.

Thursday November 7, 1867.

This was the day when the electors met to choose representatives to the Prussian Landtag. The election was held in the large saloon of one of the principal Hotels in Unter den Linden. Going to the Hotel in the midst of the election I found it crowded with men interested in the election. Politicians chatting and smoking or taking refreshments filled all the passages and rooms on the way to the great hall. That was crowded by men who were evidently much interested in the progress of the elections. Bismarck had been one of the electors and had given his vote, in every instance, for the conservative candidate. Two representatives have already been chosen and the party of the progress an ultra liberal party had triumphed by so vast a majority that there could be no doubt of their ultimate success on the vote that was then taking for a third representative. Bismarck had voted throughout the conservative ticket but it was said that he was ready to cast his vote for the National Liberal, Twesten, should the conservative candidate evidently fail. The Prussians are careful to protect the vote for the Imperial Diet by the use of ballot, but here where the electors voted for their constituents they did so by word of mouth, passing before the president as they pronounced their choice. After walking some time among the crowd of the lookers on and observing the progress of the voting I went into the room where count Bismarck was sitting on a sofa waiting to learn the result of the vote. I found him engaged in reading a

little book. He said that it was difficult for him to give the day to his duties
as elector but having been chosen [sic] he had done so. That he had taken
with him papers, gone through them all and was then whiling away the hour
that remained before the election should be completed with reading a novel
at the same time he held the book towards me and showed me that it was
"Drei Novellen" by Storm, printed in 1862, I said the author was unknown
to me. He spoke of him as rather sentimental and a writer pleasing to the
ladies. I said I had read Auerbach. He said Auerbach excelled in descriptions
of peasant life but seemed to think his novel "Auf die Höhe" extravagant.
He then explained to me the nature of the illness under which he had been
suffering. St. Petersburg, said he, has neither physicians nor apothecaries and
woe to the man who gets unwell there. He said he was suffering there from
rheumatism; that a man came to him and put on a plaster under the knee;
that he fell asleep and awaking he found that in four hours the plaster had
eaten not only through the skin but into the flesh; in pulling it off not the skin
only but bits of flesh came with it, laying open the veins and that in consequence one of the veins on the left side of the left leg was destroyed. As a
consequence the blood had to find for itself other channels and these new
channels were some times insufficient. This would cause an effusion of blood
of an erysipelas character. When this happened he was debarred from his
usual exercise, could not ride on horseback and so his sleep at night was
disturbed. He spoke of the matter as nothing serious but it seemed to me that
he regarded it as more serious than he was willing to confess.

Turning the conversation on the state of affairs in Italy he answered me
with the frankness which he has always used when I have heard him speak
of public affairs. He said that an emissary of Garibaldi had come to him last
summer to ask for assistance especially money. He named the name of the
emissary but I have forgotten it. The emissary had a paper from Garibaldi,
signed by Garibaldi, but it might have been a forgery and who could know
certainly that he was not a secret agent of Louis Napoleon or of Austria.
"However" he said "the emissary was what he pretended to be. I told him
to apply to his own government and to do nothing but in connection with
that government and intimated that I should communicate his application to
that government this he desired should not be done although he pretended
to act on an understanding with the Italian government and also professed
to be indirectly assured that the Emperor Napoleon would make no objections
to their proceedings." Bismarck observed that Napoleon must have acted with
duplicity; that if he had spoken as plainly to the Italian government in the
beginning as he did in the last Garibaldi's enterprise would have been
prevented.

1868

On Saturday the fifth of December Count Bismarck called upon me at 11½ and stayed with me an hour. His health seemed restored. On his way to me he had made the circuit of the Thiergarten on foot for exercise. He described to me his estate of Pomerania. A forest containing exceedingly old trees of great beauty. He described himself as very unfit to manage such an estate for he couldn't bear to have a fine tree cut down. Of game there was a plenty of wild boar. But the deer had been killed off to a great degree and in order to replenish the forest he and his neighbors had agreed to kill none for three years and to kill no female for seven. Of birds they had cranes also black cocks the large game known in Scotland. The character of the country was not mountainous but undulating. He gained health by riding and walking. He explained very fully his relations with Russia, Roumania and Hungary. He told me that he had written a letter to Prince Charles of Roumania telling him to take for his model King Leopold of Belgium; that he must administer his government with strict respect for treaties existing with European nations, he must give up every idea of an extension of his territory or a change of his relations to other powers and should content himself with a wise regulation of his own dominions. That if he could not succeed with such a policy he had nothing to do but retire and go home to his father. As to the relation of friendship between Russia and Hungary it was a very natural one and grew necessarily out of the existing state of things; the alliance between Prussia and Russia was an alliance for the establishment and security of peace. It had no relation to Russia as a party undertaking a war. With regard to the future admission of the Southern powers of Germany into the Confederation he had taken care to leave it to the option of the Southern powers themselves and it would not be long before they would come knocking at the doors for admission. Meantime they would aim at uniformity in legislation, and by means of the Zollparliament they would all be drawn nearer to each other.

He should take as much care of his health as was possible but he could not dispose of his work to keep himself free in the evening. His work was so great he was obliged to engage in labor both morning and evening; neither was he disposed to make over his work to others; took too much interest in the business he undertook to leave it to others.

March 4, 1869

Count Bismarck and others, all Germans but my stepson, dined with me to day. B. was entirely at his ease: talking, chatting, joking, telling anecdotes of himself at Göttingen: e.g. that in his last year at the University, he did not dine in the Krone; he had reduced the state of his finances too low for that.—

Among other things he assured to me his passion for country life; I never heard any one speak of country life with more rapture.

After dinner he spoke a while with me apart. I told him of the remarks of Andrassy, that at Nikolsburg, he Bismarck had been before all others distinguished for his moderation. He said there was truth in the remark: that the king wanted a cession of the north part of Bavaria, of a part of Bohemia, of Austrian Silesia in whole or in part, and of all Saxony, that he had renited: Had spoken of the good qualities of the old king of Saxony, and had advised against driving him from his throne; had spoken to the king (William of Prussia) against demanding cessions from Bavaria and against demanding them from Austria; that the king of Prussia received then moderating counsels with aversion, threw himself on the sofa, wept bitterly for half an hour, complained of desertion; would not be comforted, and with the utmost difficulty was made to yield. He went on and said that Afterward in meeting the Landtag of Prussia he (Bismarck) proposed to the king to ask for his ministers a bill of indemnity for their infraction of the laws: the king renited: would not hear of it willingly: that he was obliged to reason with him long, in order to persuade him to yield; that it was for his good to remain in a state of antagonism with the parliament and with liberal principles and parliamentary government. The king gave way but most reluctantly.

Of the Queen Bismarck complained: she was such a "coward," that was the word.

(Min. Moltke had told me of the difficulty of getting the king in 1866 to consent to the movements that led to war. He was renitent and held back but was carried along.)

III. THE NATIONAL PROBLEM

George Bancroft to William H. Seward, December 24, 1868.
No. 87.

> American Legation,
> Berlin December 24, 1868.
> [Received January 12, 1869]

Sir:

On the fifth of December, soon after his return from the country, Count Bismarck paid me a visit of an hour's length or more. He explained to me the policy which governed all the relations of North Germany to the states which now are usually spoken of as South Germany. On the one hand he holds inflexibly to the purpose of doing nothing, directly or indirectly, to control the deliberations of South Germany with regard to the greater nearness of relations which they may choose to hold to North Germany. Any closer approximation than now exists by treaties, if it should take place at all, must be the result of the free unbiased wishes and request of the Southern governments and branches of the German nation. On the other hand he maintains that it is the undoubted right of the Southern branches of the German nation to connect themselves more closely with the North if it should be the desire and judgment of both parties. The right of the German governments and people to improve their government he holds to be a subject for their own decision free from foreign intervention or influence.

With regard to the Austro-Hungarian Monarchy he considers the connection of Austria and Hungary to be definitively settled, so that no question of nearer relations can arise with regard to the Germans of Austria.

With regard to the East the policy of this government is most friendly towards Austria and Hungary. Every just cause of offence is most carefully avoided and every opportunity of manifesting good will is improved. The alliance between Russia and Prussia is an alliance of peace, not of aggression. The advice of this government to the ruling prince of Moldavia and Wallachia is to avoid all schemes of ambition and to apply himself diligently and exclusively to the establishment of the free institutions and the development of the great resources of his provinces taking as his model the late King Leopold of Belgium.

Since this interview I have read a speech of Baron von Varnbühler delivered in the Württemberg House of Deputies in which that minister declares in the clearest language that no attempt whatever has been made by North Germany to sway the deliberations of the government of Württemberg. All this was already known to you from my previous reports and otherwise; but I thought it would be interesting to you to receive direct and authentic information of the spirit of moderation which rules in the Foreign Department of North Germany.

IV. PRUSSIA'S POLICY IN THE WAR OF SECESSION

George Bancroft to William H. Seward, February 26, 1869.

> American Legation,
> Berlin February 26, 1869.
> [Received March 15, 1869]

Sir:

The conduct of the Prussian government towards us in the time of our civil disturbances has seemed to me an object worthy of the most exact and thorough inquiry. The political papers of those days are for the most part already removed from the Foreign Office to the Archives; and, as the policy of this government since Count Bismarck has been the first minister has been frank and open beyond that of any government in Europe, I am able to make to you a report, which is the fruit of a thorough search of the documents and of other inquiries made with the best opportunities of obtaining trustworthy information.

As there were two ministers of Foreign Affairs, viz.; Count von Schleinitz and Count von Bernstorff after the inauguration of Mr. Lincoln and before Count von Bismarck-Schönhausen in October 1862 took the seals of the Foreign Office and the presidency of the Ministry the opinions of the King are of the most importance as showing the policy that was scrupulously observed during the whole period of our long struggle. The king from the first took the ground, that the question involved in our war was a question of right and wrong, that there is but one right and but one wrong; that the right was with the established government of the United States which represented their union and that the wrong was with the seceding states which placed themselves in rebellion against their just government. The ministry did indeed lay down the principle of non-interference and neutrality; but on the part of Prussia there was no concession of belligerent rights to the South either on the Ocean or elsewhere. This government pays the closest attention to military movements everywhere, and it had observers in various parts of the United States to take notice of the wonderful improvement in the science of war which grew out of the application of American enterprise to that subject. But every request of officers for a leave of absence in order to serve in the Southern army was sternly refused. As the war was protracted, there grew up in the aristocratic squiralty a sympathy for the South; and those who piqued themselves on their religious orthodoxy and piety forgot the wrongs of slavery and sympathized with the South which they described as the land of gentlemen. Against this opinion the King steadfastly declared that it was not a question between landowners or so-called gentlemen and the industrial classes under the appellation of mechanics and shopkeepers; that the question was simply a question of right and wrong and that without a doubt the right was entirely on the side of the North. When some of this fraction of the Prussian landed aristocracy gave a dinner to two officers of the Southern Confederacy who happened to be in Berlin, the King expressed his extreme displeasure at the act. Baron Gerolt the Prussian Minister at Washington always in his despatches supported the right of our government and steadfastly held the belief that it would succeed in putting down the Rebellion. For this conduct the King honored him with his special approbation and, as a distinguished mark of it gave him at the end of our war an order of the kind which is most in request among the Prussian statesmen and generals. I may cite as one of my authorities in this matter the king himself who at my audience of reception said to me that Prussia from the first existence of our government had never failed on its part to cultivate the most friendly relations with the United States of America.

All the papers that issued from the Foreign Department from the inauguration of Lincoln to his death are marked by this spirit. It regulated the conduct of Counts von Schleinitz and von Bernstorff, who were both remarkably reserved and silent men; it came out more clearly during the ministry of Count Bismarck who maintained unreservedly the view that the North was right. If the sympathy of the squiralty of the kingdom manifested itself socially, or, as it once did, through the press, it served only to make the fixed and immovable attitude of the Minister more conspicuous. Especially when on one occasion one or perhaps two remarkable articles appeared in a very able Prussian newspaper strongly favoring the cause of the South, Count Bismarck regarded it as a symptom of incipient opposition to the government of which he was the head; and the knowledge of his displeasure and the earnestness of his remonstrances checked the further publication of such articles.

No formal overture was made by any European power to this government to recognise the independence of the Southern Confederacy. To hints, insinuations and rumors to do so this government gave no encouragement; but remained true to the simple principle that the government of the union had the right on its side; that the Southern Confederacy was in the wrong, and that therefore the government of the North was entitled to the best wishes of all powers, friendly to order and justice.

V. THE HOHENZOLLERN CANDIDACY

D. E. Sickles to Hamilton Fish, Madrid, July 11, 1870.
No. 127

> Legation of the United States,
> Madrid, July 11, 1870
> [Received July 26, 1870]

Sir:

The situation is warlike. It is said that France has sent her ultimatum to Prussia, and if the answer is not immediate and satisfactory, war will follow. This action indicates a determination not to wait for the action of the Córtes, already convened for the 20th instant. My impression is that with less impatience on the part of France, the candidature of Prince Leopold, left to its fate in the Córtes, would fail. But it seems that France chooses to make a direct issue with Prussia,—and perhaps the question of the Spanish succession is more the occasion than the cause of her belligerent attitude.

It will be difficult for Spain to keep aloof from the struggle. In the event of her becoming a party to it, the fate of Cuba and Porto Rico will present one of the most important questions involved in the contest, regarded from an American point of view. Spain cannot hope to hold her Colonies against the powerful navy of France. It may be assumed that the insurgents in Cuba will seize the opportunity to form an alliance with France in order to gain their independence. I have not yet ventured to make any suggestion to this Government on the subject, and although General Prim in a recent conversation, spoke of the gravity of the complication, he said nothing to me of its possible bearing on Cuba. I shall endeavor to find an opportunity to ascertain his views on this aspect of the question, and may have occasion to communicate them to you by Cable.

Meanwhile I look anxiously for your instructions, as I presume you are already informed of all that has transpired.

VI. THE HOHENZOLLERN CANDIDACY

D. E. Sickles to Hamilton Fish, Madrid, July 13, 1870
No. 131

> Legation of the United States,
> Madrid, July 13, 1870.
> [Received July 28, 1870]

Sir,

The intimations of the President of the Council and of the Minister of State, in my interviews with them, coincide with the impressions of the diplomatic corps, and of the press in regarding hostilities between France and Prussia as imminent. Yesterday a communication was received by this Cabinet from the French Government, in reply to the note of the Minister of State announcing the candidature of Prince Leopold, which is represented to be more conciliatory towards Spain than was anticipated. It seems that while France is disposed to treat the election of the German Prince to the Spanish throne as an affront, it will not be resented against Spain as an injury. And judging from the air of relief visible today in all quarters, Spain is quite content to disengage herself from the complication, if she can have her way and let Prussia fight her battles. It may be said that this is not the Spain of Charles the Fifth whose crown is offered to a Hohenzollern, but it is an illustration of the restraints imposed on Cabinets by public opinion. A very large part of the population of this country do not want a King at all;—and it may be confidently affirmed that a great majority are unwilling to accept Prince Leopold at the cost of an European war in which Spain may be forced to take sides,—to be followed in all probability by internal conflicts not less destructive to her prosperity and the beneficial results anticipated from the Revolution of 1868.

France appears to be unwilling to wait for the action of the Spanish Córtes in determining her attitude towards Prussia. This circumstance, in view of what I have just related of the more pacific tone at Madrid, tends to confirm the opinion I have already intimated that the Spanish succession is more the ostensible than the real motive for the recent demonstrations of France. It may be that finding herself better prepared for immediate operations than Prussia, France hopes to seize the left bank of the Rhine, the boundary so long coveted, before Prussia can take the field in sufficient force to resist a sudden and formidable movement against her frontier. And this conquest, if held by France, would be claimed as a just compensation in the subsequent adjustment of that ever vacillating situation called the European equilibrium.

Prussia has so far maintained a haughty reserve, and with great tact suffers the provocations offered by France to betray her ill-concealed jealousy of the great German Power.

I inclose a copy of Mr. Sagasta's note to the representatives of Spain abroad, dated the 7th inst, in relation to the candidature of Prince Leopold, which you will no doubt receive through Mr. Roberts; and also a copy of a paper on the same subject signed by Mr. Salazar, the envoy employed by General Prim in his negotiation with the Prince, sent to me from the Ministry of State.

VII. THE FRANCO-GERMAN WAR, 1870–71

John Jay to Hamilton Fish, July 16, 1870.
No. 136

> United States Legation,
> Vienna, July 16, 1870.
> [Received August 3, 1870]

Sir,

I have had today conversations in reference to the War, with Lord Bloomfield; Baron Schweinitz; the Marquis de Cazean, the Chargé d'Affaires of France; Mr. von Hoffmann of the foreign office, the Count Andrassy, Minister of Foreign Affairs in Hungary, and the Count Potocki, the Chief of the Austrian Ministry.

They all agree in regarding War between France and Prussia as certain, although no formal declaration has been yet made on either side. My first visit was to Lord Bloomfield who received me with his usual cordiality and talked with me for an hour. He had just seen the Count de Beust who he said had behaved as well as possible in the whole matter. He believed that the Chancellor had been as much surprised as any one at the decided tone of the Duke de Gramont in reference to the candidateship of the Prince Leopold of Hohenzollern for the Spanish throne, that he had done all he could to effect a pacific arrangement between France and Prussia; and that he was now resolved to maintain Austria in a position of absolute neutrality.

Lord Bloomfield spoke of the wisdom of this course in view of the difficulties still existing in the Empire, and expressed himself in terms of more distinct approval than I have heard him use before in regard to the policy of Count de Beust. He said that during the last four years Austria had made immense progress in civilization and good government; and that if no third power intervened in the war she would be safe. He added even if Russia should intervene, why need Austria go in at all.—He asked me how the United States would like a blockade of Bremen and Hamburg. I said it would be extremely inconvenient and injurious as our commerce with that port was large and important. He replied that the trade of England with the Prussian ports was still more direct immediate and constant; and that a blockade would be a very serious matter—and then he added "they must arrange it so as not to interfere with our Commerce". I said what sort of a blockade would that be? He said well—well, it is a mere matter of force, and they must manage it so as not to interfere with us.

My next visit was to U. S. Prussian Minister who lives next door to the British Embassy. Baron Schweinitz begged me to excuse him as he had that moment received a despatch from Berlin—and then as I was going, he insisted on my sitting down for a few minutes. He said the war was inevitable, and that Austria would be neutral unless Russia interfered. I asked Will Russia intervene? He said *"No! not so long as she can aid us by keeping quiet."* He added that the South German States would go as a unit against France—that one spirit of Nationality pervaded them all, and that he had received visits from Germans of all parts and classes, giving him this assurance.

I remarked that I had seen by the *"Correspondance Autrichienne"* of the Evening before that he had paid an official visit to the Chancellor, to thank him in the name of his Government at Berlin for his friendly efforts for mediation and his policy of neutrality. The Baron said yes and that Count de Beust had received him very cordially. He added that two young Austrian Officers had with the approval of their Government applied for leave which had been granted—or would be—to accompany the Prussian Army. The Baron hardly disguised his anxiety about the permanent neutrality of Austria. If she kept out of the war, it would be a contest simply between France and Germany, and would not extend to the rest of Europe. It all he said depended upon Austria.

At the Foreign Office Count de Beust being away I had a few words with Mr. von Hofmann. His language confirmed what Lord Bloomfield had told me as said by the Chancellor, that there was no hope left of mediation, the haughty spirit and angry feeling both at Berlin and Paris rendering useless all the endeavours of England and other powers to settle the quarrel. He said "Austria will rest neutral". Count de Beust has been accused by his enemies of intermeddling in affairs that did not concern him. Now Europe will see on his part the most perfect inactivity. No movements, of troops—no army, but absolute neutrality. I said "Does France understand and approve of this?" He said *"Yes! It is the best service we could render to France, for if we intervene Russia will intervene. It is better as it is."* I remarked should Russia intervene she may arouse your Slavic populations on the Danube. He said yes, and the highest motives of the preservation of the state require us to be neutral.

The Marquis de Cazean at the French Embassy to my question if there was still room for mediation replied no, that an offer had been made by Lord (A.) Loftus, the English Ambassador at Berlin, which Prussia might have been perhaps inclined to accept because she wanted time. Prussia he said will have her army ready in ten days. France is ready now.

I said I suppose it is too early to ask whether there will be any blockade of Hamburg and Bremen, which would be inconvenient to American Commerce. He replied "I dont know the plan of the Campaign, except that it is to be localized as much as possible. It is to be a duel between the two nations—Austria will not intervene unless Russia intervenes. It is better so. It will disturb Europe less."

As I was leaving he said perhaps you would like to see the instructions which I have just received from Paris, and he shewed me some paragraphs explaining the just claims of France upon the neutrality of the South German States especially of Bavaria and Würtemberg—that this was not a case within the meaning of the Military Treaties, and instructing the Chargé that they expected the Austrian Government to enlighten the ministers of those states upon the subjects. He said as I concluded the reading—"I have communicated this desire of my government to the Chancellor." And he added that the Chancellor had responded that altho' the people of those states might be misled by the cry of nationality, the Governments perfectly understood the position.

The Marquis referred to the demand of the Duke de Gramont that the King of Prussia as the head of the Hohenzollern family should distinctly refuse his consent to the Prince Leopold accepting the throne of Spain, and said— England made a similar demand of Louis Philippe when the Duke de Nemour was proposed for the Belgian throne, and the Duc de Gramont used the identical words used towards England when Prince Alfred was named for the throne of Greece, but no offence was then taken by the English Cabinet for the reason that there was no angry feeling on either side.

My conversations with the Count Andrassy who has arrived here from Perth and with the Count de Potocki developed nothing of importance unless it were the perfect harmony of their views in regard to the policy and necessity of Austrian neutrality, and the emphatic assent of Count Andrassy to my suggestion that I supposed that if Russia should intervene in the war, Hungary would be ready to fight with a will.

In reference to the South German States Ct. Andrassy observed that while there might be a good deal of talking among their people on both sides he doubted if they would take much part in it one way or the other.

I should perhaps add that when I called at the English-German and French embassies I said frankly "I am about writing to my government and I come to ask what I may say of your views touching the war."

From these conversations of which I have given but a brief outline, I think it may be assumed 1st that France and Prussia are at present desirous that the war should be simply a duel between them without interference on the part of other nations. 2. That Russia and Austria both acquiese for the present in this view. 3d. That there is reason to suppose that Russia may be drawn into the quarrel, notwithstanding her supposed desire not to be withdrawn at present by an European war, from the prosecution of her Eastern projects and the completion of her Railway System towards the South. 4. That such a step on the part of Russia would probably lead to a reconsideration of the present decision of neutrality on the part of the Austro-Hungarian Empire.

The appearance of Russia in the field would tend to arouse all the war-like ardour of the Hungarians, who cherish the most bitter enmity to the Court of St. Petersburg for having lent its assistance to Austria in subduing them in 1849. That Russian intervention so important at the moment to the Habsburgs was repaid by what the Russians denounced as the "splendid ingratitude" of Austria, during the Crimean war of 1854. 5. So that should Russia intervene in the present war on the side of Prussia, and Austria follow on the side of France, there is reason to anticipate a conflict of the most embittered character, one which may involve in its calamities nearly the whole of Europe, and possibly in its opening of the Eastern question a part also of Asia and Africa.

In view of so grave a contingency, it occurs to me that the Government of the United States may with great propriety, and without departing at all from its settled policy of avoiding entangling alliances, or mixing in European disputes, bring to bear as the common friend of all parties its great moral influence—an influence which is being felt more and more by the Cabinets and the people of Europe, to prevent the war now commencing between France and Prussia from assuming continental proportions.

*   *   *   *   *   *   *

VIII. THE BURNSIDE MISSION

E. B. Washburne to Hamilton Fish, October 9, 1870.
Confidential.
No. 303

> Legation of the United States,
> Paris, October 9, 1870.
> [Received November 9, 1870.]

Sir:

I came to the Legation last night to write you a despatch to send out by the Minister of the United States of Columbia, who was to have left this morning. On my arrival I was both surprised and gratified to learn that General Burnside and Mr. Forbes had returned to the city. They very soon afterwards reported themselves and explained the reason of their visit. In several interviews with Count Bismarck he expressed the idea that it would be well to have certain suggestions conveyed to Mr. Jules Favre in relation to an armistice, for the purpose of enabling the French people to elect a constituent assembly. You will recollect that was a matter which was talked of in the interview between Favre and Bismarck, and that the former rejected it, because it was insisted that as a condition to such an armistice, the Prussian army should have possession of some of the forts about Paris. It is evident that both powers desire a convention of the people of France; Prussia, because she wants a more substantial power to treat with than the present provision government; France, because the Government of the National Defence do not want to take the responsibility of making a treaty, but desire that any treaty to be made should be made by a power emenating directly from the whole people acting through a constituent assembly. Count Bismarck authorized

General Burnside to suggest to Mr. Jules Favre that he would yield the question of the forts and would grant an absolute armistice of forty-eight hours for holding an election, and give every facility for a fair election; for the distribution of tickets and circulars; for a committee to go out of Paris, as well as for the departure of the members elected from the city of Paris, to render themselves wherever the convention should be held, &c. &c. In addition it was suggested that a sort of *semi-armistice* might be agreed upon to extend over a sufficient time to permit the convention to be held—that is to say, there should be no firing, but that the Prussians should be permitted to bring up their guns and provisions and that every thing in Paris should remain *in statu quo.*

I accompanied the two gentlemen this morning to see Mr. Jules Favre and we had an interview of an hour. The whole subject was gone over and Mr. Favre stated the objections to Count Bismarck's suggestions. He is, however, to see his colleagues on the subject to-night, and we are to have another interview with him to-morrow morning in season, I hope, to give you an account of it before Genl. Burnside shall leave to-morrow noon. I trust some *starting point* may be found so that negotiations, with a view to peace, may be entered upon. In accordance with your instructions, if *both* parties shall signify a desire for the good offices of our Government, disconnected with the European powers, I shall feel authorized to extend them in a proper manner.

Monday noon,
Oct. 10, 1870.

I have this moment returned from a long interview between Genl. Burnside and Mr. Forbes, Mr. Jules Favre and Genl. Trochu. As the flag of truce is waiting to take our countrymen into the Prussian lines, I have time to say but one word, and that is, that the parties are a long way apart and that there is hardly a probability that anything will be accomplished. The door, however, is left open, and it is barely possible that something may be accomplished in the future.

IX. THE MONROE DOCTRINE

Bismarck to Schlözer
Copy II, 35061.

Berlin, den 18. Dezember 1871.

Ew. pp. werden aus meinem an Ihren Herrn Amtsvorgänger gerichteten Erlasse vom 13. Mai d. J. entnommen haben, wie sehr die in Venezuela wohnhaften Deutschen und die mit ihnen in Geschäftsverbindung stehenden Handlungshäuser in Deutschland unter den Parteikämpfen zu leiden haben, welche die Republik zerrütten. Darin ist keine Besserung eingetreten; die von der Regierung vertretenen Reklamationen sind nicht liquidiert, die schwebenden sind nicht erledigt, die Unzulänglichkeit der Rechtspflege, die Unsicherheit von Eigentum und Leben der Fremden sind durch den zwischen den Gelben und Blauen ausgebrochenen Bürgerkrieg grösser als je geworden. Nachdem die Regierung in Washington unsere vertrauliche Anregung gemeinschaftlicher Schritte zum Schutze der Fremden abgelehnt hatte, wurde Sr. M. in den westindischen Gewässern stationierte Corvette »Gazelle« angewiesen, sich an der Küste von Venezuela zu zeigen, um die dortige Regierung daran zu erinnern, dass unsere Reichsangehörigen nicht schutzlos seien. Die »Gazelle«, von deren Sendung Mr. Bancroft vertraulich benachrichtigt worden war, ist Anfangs v. M. in Guaira eingetroffen; ihr Erscheinen hat aber auf die Disposition der Regierung keine ersichtliche Wirkung gehabt.

Inzwischen sind zu unserem Bedauern auch mit anderen südamerikanischen Staaten Unannehmlichkeiten entstanden. Die peruanische Regierung zögert noch immer, den Entschädigungsansprüchen der Deutschen ebenso gerecht zu werden wie den gleichartigen Ansprüchen von Bürgern anderer Staaten und hat ihrer ultramontanen Neigung zu Gefallen, einen angeblichen päpstlichen Delegaten eine weder in Verträgen, noch in der Praxis begründete Stellung zu dem diplomatischen Corps angewiesen. Unser Vertreter in Peru war angewiesen, sein Verhalten nach dem des amerikanischen Gesandten einzurichten. Der Letztere hat aber, bis er seinen Posten in Urlaub verliess, keine Stellung zur Sache genommen.

In Rio de Janeiro sind Mannschaften eines deutschen Kriegsschiffes von der Polizei in einer Weise behandelt worden, welche falls durch weitere noch nicht abgeschlossene Ermittlungen die ersten Anzeigen bestätigt würden, den Charakter rechtswidrigen und gewalttätigen Amtsmissbrauchs trug[en].

Wir sind es den persönlichen Interessen unserer Nationalen und unserer staatlichen Würde schuldig, auf gerechte und gesetzmässige Behandlung derselben zu halten, und glauben um diesen Zweck zu erreichen, die Regierungen und Bevölkerungen daselbst an die ihnen bisher fremde Vorstellung gewöhnen zu sollen, dass die deutsche Flagge eine Marine repräsentiert, welche entschlossen ist, das Völkerrecht ihrerseits sorgfältig zu achten, aber auch durch den geringen Umfang ihrer Streitkräfte sich nicht abhalten lässt, für die Achtung desselben Rechtes den Deutschen gegenüber nötigenfalls einzutreten.

Ew. pp. ersuche ich ergebenst, dem Herrn Staatssekretär von dem Vorstehenden vertraulich Mitteilung zu machen. Die bekannten Anschauungen des Kabinetts von Washington, die vielleicht noch nicht erloschene Erinnerung an falsche Gerüchte von deutschen Absichten auf Erwerbung irgend eines

Hafenplatzes in Südamerika machen es nötig, an diese Mitteilung noch folgende Erläuterungen zu knüpfen. Es liegt uns ganz fern, irgendwo in Amerika Fuss fassen zu wollen und wir erkennen in Betreff des ganzen Kontinents den vorwiegenden Einfluss der Vereinigten Staaten als in der Natur der Dinge begründet und unseren Interessen am meisten zusagend unumwunden an. Wir haben dort keine politischen, nur kommerzielle Interessen und also keinen anderen Wunsch als geordnete Verhältnisse, Schutz für Person und Eigentum der Fremden hergestellt zu sehen. Ich habe deswegen den deutschen Geschäftsträger in Lima abberufen, sobald mir schien, dass er seine Aufgabe nicht in der ausschliesslichen Pflege der Handelsinteressen, sondern in Erstrebung politischen Einflusses suche, und der Präsident Grant ist auf unser Ersuchen, die einstweilige Vertretung der Deutschen durch den amerikanischen Gesandten zu genehmigen, in dankenswerter Weise eingegangen. Für die Bereitwilligkeit dazu wollen Ew. pp. bei dieser Gelegenheit meinen verbindlichsten Dank ausdrücken und die Erklärung wiederholen, dass wir uns freuen würden, in Fragen, in denen wir dasselbe Interesse haben, wie in Betreff der Reklamationen in Venezuela und der Etiquettenfrage in Peru, unser Verhalten nach dem der Vereinigten Staaten einrichten zu können. Aus dem Berichte des Legations-Sekretärs von Alvensleben vom 18. Juli d. J. wollen Ew. pp. ersehen, dass Herr Fish der italienischen Regierung zu erkennen gegeben hat, die Vereinigten Staaten könnten eine Kollektivexpedition europäischer Mächte gegen Venezuela nicht mit Gleichgültigkeit ansehen, und dies ist uns neuerdings aus Florenz bestätigt worden. Auf der anderen Seite ist Herrn von Gülich die ganz vertrauliche Andeutung gemacht worden, dass unsere Anregung vom 13. Mai in Washington einen besseren Erfolg gehabt haben würde, wenn sie in anderer Weise geschehen wäre. Wenn der Freiherr von Gerolt, wie aus seinem Berichte geschlossen werden könnte, bei jener Gelegenheit von der »Monroedoktrin« gesprochen haben sollte, so wäre sein Misserfolg erklärlich. Wir haben keinen Beruf, von einer bei einem Teile der amerikanischen Staatsmänner herrschenden Doktrin in unserem Verkehr mit der amerikanischen Regierung Notiz zu nehmen, wenn wir sie auch bei unseren Erwägungen zu berücksichtigen haben. Eine Erwähnung derohalben würde um so mehr zu bedauern sein, als auch in der Sache selbst keine Veranlassung dazu vorlag. Die Stelle in der Botschaft des Präsidenten Monroe vom Jahre 1823, aus der sich die Doktrin entwickelt hat, ist veranlasst durch die damals obwaltende Besorgnis, dass europäische Mächte Spanien in seinem Kampfe gegen die empörten Kolonien unterstützen könnten. Monroe erklärt es für unmöglich, dass die alliierten Mächte (die heilige Allianz) ihr politisches System auf irgendeinen Teil des amerikanischen Kontinents ausdehnen könnten, ohne das Glück und den Frieden der Vereinigten Staaten in Gefahr zu bringen, und will den amerikanischen Kontinent nicht als Gegenstand künftiger Kolonisation durch europäische Mächte betrachtet wissen.

Weder das eine noch das andere lag in unserer Anregung; und wenn man in Washington bei irgendeiner anderen der beteiligten Mächte dergleichen Hintergedanken voraussetzte, so gab es kein besseres Mittel, ihre Realisierung zu verhüten, als die von uns gewünschte gemeinsame Haltung Deutschlands und der Vereinigten Staaten. Nach der Aufnahme, welche Ew. pp. Mitteilung und die daran zu knüpfende Erläuterung bei Herrn Fish finden, wollen Sie beurteilen und mir gefälligst berichten, ob Sie einen Versuch, den abgerissenen Faden wieder aufzunehmen, für angezeigt halten. Zu Ihrer Orientierung füge ich hinzu dass der amerikanische Gesandte in Caracas Herrn von Gülich gesagt hat, wenn er auch seinen eigenen Weg gehe und sich an der von den Vertretern Deutschlands, Englands, Spaniens, Italiens, Dänemarks unter dem 11. v. M. an die Regierung gerichteten Kollektivnote nicht beteiligen wolle, so verfolge er doch ganz dasselbe Ziel, die Lage aller ausländer in Venezuela sicherzustellen.

X. CONVERSATION WITH BISMARCK.
PRUSSIAN UPPER CHAMBER

George Bancroft to Hamilton Fish, January 25, 1873.
No. 453.
Secret and Confidential.

> American Legation,
> Berlin, January 25, 1873.
> [Received February 15, 1873.]

Sir:

I was last evening with the Prince of Bismarck. He complained of being ill and having but one sound leg, the left one giving him much trouble and pain. His physicians, he said, had advised for him a sea-voyage, which led me to say that he would find a warm welcome in the United States, from the Atlantic Coast to San Francisco. "Next to San Francisco," rejoined he, "are the Sandwich Islands which I should be heartily glad to see in your pos-session." I dwelt upon the remark in order that I might be certain of under-standing him rightly, and he repeated his words saying, he should be glad to see the Sandwich Islands a part of the United States.

Nothing could exceed the clearness and emphasis with which he spoke and the remark proves his unfailing desire to cultivate friendly relations with the United States.

The illness from which the Prince suffers is Ischias, or Sciatica, which for at least fifteen years has most grievously disturbed his nervous system. In 1859, on his way to Russia, he was at Berlin a great sufferer from this cause. At St. Petersburg, as he himself once told me, a physician applied to the left leg, below the knee, a plaster composed of such ingredients that in two hours it ate deeply into the flesh, and when excessive pain compelled him to tear it off, several of the veins, nearest the surface, were destroyed, so that the blood had to seek new channels. Since that time, he has been liable to intense suffering and disturbance of the nervous system, whenever he has been forced to excessive labor or been exposed to troublesome resistance and contradiction.

The late changes in the Prussian Cabinet have as yet led to no very decisive or very important results. The constitution of Prussia was granted by the late King, Frederick William the Fourth, elder brother of the present King. He was a man not so much reactionary, as whimsical and fanciful. He was fond of English precedents, and in Church matters showed a leaning to the British Episcopal system.

In constructing his House of Lords, there was in Prussia no aristocracy analogous to that of Great Britain, and the piebald chamber which he constituted, represented rather the peculiarities of his own mind, than the wants or capacities of the Kingdom. His House of Lords was composed partly of hereditary members after the English model and partly of the representative holders of a Knight's estate; but members of this class could vote for its representatives and if elected could take their seats only in case their families had been in uninterrupted possession of the estate for one hundred years. Some of the Universities, some of the Cities elect members and a large power was reserved to the King of naming members for life. The House so reconstructed was not likely to perform its functions to the satisfaction of the country and was constantly in conflict with the Lower House; but when the Kingdom of Hanover, when Hesse Cassel, when Nassau were added to Prussia the organization of the House of Lords was manifestly more than ever at variance with the wishes and wants of the country. According to the best opinion which I am able to form the Prince of Bismarck has long since perceived the inadequacy of the present House of Lords. Its rejection of the moderate, and I might almost say, conservative bill granting something more of self-government to the Circles of the Kingdom, offered an opportunity for proposing such a reform, and the power of the King to name members for life was thought to be sufficient to secure in the House of Lords itself, a bill putting an end to its own existence, and in its stead calling into being a true Senate. To accomplish this result, a reconstruction of the Prussian Ministry was necessary, but this reconstruction, the Emperor who hates to part from tried friends refused to concede. A creation of Peers was made only sufficient to carry the bill which the Upper House had rejected.

The Prince of Bismarck, as it would seem, did not consider the new law as important enough to call for a creation of Peers. He would have no new creation, or, one large enough to change the character of the Upper House. Failing to be permitted to reconstruct the Ministry and to reform the House of Lords, Achilles who was President of the Prussian Ministry retired to his tent. Now there was no one who dared supplant the Prince of Bismarck, and no one who wished his place; but as the Prince retaining his position as Chancellor of the Empire, and as Minister of Foreign Affairs for Prussia, insisted on retiring from the post of President of the Ministry, and as the King would not make the concessions which were necessary to bend his will, the office of President of the Prussian Ministry was conferred on the Count von Roon. Now the Count von Roon stood at the head of the War Department, with the applause of the army and of all the Kingdom. He was satisfied with his honors and his post, and hated the very thought or appearance of superseding the Prince; and it was only through his obedience to the King that he consented as senior Minister to take the chair of President of the Council.

Meantime it is announced to the world that as to the measures that are to be pursued, the Prussian Ministry is entirely united; but the recent constitution of the Ministry is not generally regarded as likely to continue for any great length of time.

The nation generally shares his desire for a thorough reform of the House of Lords, but if the House of Lords conducts itself now with discretion the reform will be indefinitely postponed.

XI. CONVERSATION WITH BISMARCK

George Bancroft to Hamilton Fish, May 25, 1874.
No. 593.
Private.

> American Legation,
> Berlin, 25 May, 1874.
> [Received June 11, 1874.]

Sir:

On Wednesday evening I spent an hour with the Prince of Bismarck. He greeted me with the kindest words, which were all the more welcome to me as they were mixed with the strongest expressions of a desire that the most friendly relations between my country and the new German empire may be maintained.

As to his health he described it as much improved "but," said he, "what I need for recovery is solitude." So he would go as soon as he could to Varzin for a few days, then pass through Berlin to the baths of Kissengen according to the directions of his physicians. His sleep, he said, was good but he did not fall asleep before four o'clock in the morning. He digested very slowly and therefore could not eat but once a day, nor sleep until the process of digestion was over. The left side was that where the weakness formerly lay and still lies; but this winter neuralgic pains had attacked him in the right side more than in that in which he had formerly suffered. As to gout he made no mention of it.

Of the present strife with the usurping disposition of the Vatican priesthood he said he had long ago represented it as the same in substance as the strife between Calchus and Agamemnon, the priest of that day, pretending to powers superior to the state, would be contented with no less sacrifice from the King of men than that of his daughter. He had once, he related, been discussing questions of this sort with Bishop Ketteller [sic] and the bishop had turned upon him with the question, "so then you think that no Catholic can be saved?" and he answered with a laugh, "As to the Catholic people they certainly may be saved; but as to the priesthood certainly not." From his conversation I could perceive that he aimed at a reform in the Catholic church, which should after ancient precedents and in conformity to a practice introduced in some parts of Switzerland secure to the congregation (Gemeinde) some share in the choice of the ecclesiastics that were to be connected with it. As to France he seemed to have no political purpose but to cultivate friendly relations with any government that the French might establish for themselves, and no wish but that they might attain to a government which would assure to them quiet and prosperity.

With regard to the Orient he spoke somewhat at large, and I believe I represent to you his policy with regard to it correctly, when I describe it as one of passive observation.

On the whole I can say that the policy of the prince is a policy of peace, that his connections with other powers have always in view its preservation, and that there is no power on the globe whose friendship he is more disposed to cultivate than that of the United States.

XII. CONVERSATION WITH BISMARCK

J. C. Bancroft Davis to William M. Evarts, September 24, 1877.
Confidential
No. 759 via Hamburg.

Legation of the United States,
Berlin, 24 September, 1877.
[Received October 11, 1877.]

Sir:

Prince Bismarck returned to town from Gastein day before yesterday. Yesterday morning I received a note from Mr. von Bülow saying that the Prince would be glad to see me in the evening. I answered the invitation at the appointed hour. After a few minutes delay the Prince came into the ante-room, and led me to his working room, and placed me at his table. He said that learning that I was about leaving, he wished to see me and say good bye. He spoke of the pleasant relations which had always existed between Germany and the United States, and he was pleased to say that he thought they had not sufferred under my administration of this Legation. I replied that I had found the relations excellent and had endeavored to keep them so; and that it afforded me the greatest pleasure to be able to assure him, from the general tenor of your instructions, that the new administration was no less anxious than its predecessor to preserve and increase good relations between the two countries. He expressed great pleasure at hearing this and said that he was pleased to know that an effort was about to be made to bind the two countries still closer by new treaty arrangements. He spoke warmly of Mr. Bancroft, and said that the naturalization treaties which he had been instrumental in concluding had proved a great benefit to both countries. I said that I was of the same opinion and added that it was well known that I thought it would be well if we could unify them. He thought so too, but said that it would require the assent of the Bundesrath, which I regarded as an intimation that possibly there would be difficulties in the way on this side, which, however, might not be insuperable.

He spoke of his admiration of the political wisdom which the Americans had shown in the settlement of the disputed Presidential election. He said that the questions adjusted there would have been difficult to manage in Germany.

He spoke of the increase of Roman Catholics in America, and of the efforts of the Jesuits to convert the Southern Negroes, and said that he had been told that the Jesuits expected to make America their stronghold, and perhaps eventually to remove the Papacy there, and govern Europe from America.

The conversation turned upon the War, and he expressed his surprise at the successes of the Turks. He said he had not supposed that the Russians would get to Constantinople without difficulty: but that he supposed the difficulties would come from climate and topography, not from defeats in battle.

We talked about sundry other matters, personal to himself and to me. The interview lasted about three quarters of an hour. So far as I know it is the only interview which a representative of my grade has had with Prince Bismarck since I came to Berlin, with the single exception of an interview of the Belgian Minister, held in compliance with special instructions from his government. I look upon it as a new indication of the great desire of the Prince to maintain the most friendly relations with the United States.

XIII. BISMARCK'S POLICY, AN AMERICAN OPINION

John A. Kasson to T. F. Bayard, Secretary of State,
Washington, D. C., April 30, 1885.
No. 255.

> Legation of the United States,
> Berlin, April 30, 1885.
> [Received June 8, 1885.]

Sir:

In the closing days of my official term at the German capital I can perhaps render the Department no better service than to transmit some observations upon the spirit and tendencies of the present German Government, of its influence upon other nations, and of its bearing upon important American interests.

In speaking of the present German Government, Prince Bismarck must be understood as the equivalent title. He is not only its most eminent figure, but the absolute author and exponent of its policy. I do not say this in depreciation of the individuality or of the dignity of the Emperor, whose personal worth and high character are esteemed by all men. But while His Majesty has reserved to himself all military questions, including questions of war and of peace, yet in the conduct of interior and external nonmilitary affairs the Prince Chancellor is essentially omnipotent. His great national services in the past, his singular foresight and wisdom proved by a series of extraordinary successes in diplomacy and statesmanship during a period of twenty years, have won for him the profound confidence of his Imperial and Royal Master, as well as popular faith in his ability to manage the state. No civil Minister in any department would venture to enter upon any independent course of action, or to disregard the advice of the Chancellor. His counsel is the directing law in every division of the Government except the military branch. He is thoroughly German and deeply patriotic. His comprehensive common sense, his great intellectual ability, his keen perception of the moral as well as physical forces of his adversary, give him a steady power which is never relaxed by any indulgence of the imagination, or of other softening qualities usually found mixed in the human character. No creature endowed with the hunting instinct ever kept more closely the line of scent which leads to the object of pursuit than this great diplomatist keeps to the sure road which conducts him to his objective. No sentiment of pity, no regret for severity, detracts from his joy over the victories which he has won for Germany. When Thiers (as it is said) wept over the wounds inflicted upon the pride of France, and begged consideration for the sentiment of French patriotism and for the tax burdened people of France, he touched no responsive nerve of this Minister, and obtained no reduction of the milliards imposed on the French people. Fair phrases about traditional friendships, the progress of liberty and civilization, the brotherhood of nations, and the like, have no more practical significance for him than the blank margin of a state paper. "What will you give to me for what you want from me?"—is in effect his answer to all approaches for more favourable international arrangements. This must be remembered, Mr. Secretary, in any effort the President may be disposed to make for further treaty regulations on the two principal points of dissension now existing between our Government and Germany: and we must be prepared for an answer to that question. It is he who has introduced into modern diplomacy the condensed expression of that idea by his Latin phrase *do ut des*. But the dead language employed does not conceal the vivid life found in his application of the maxim. If we answer "I want it because it is just," he would only demand again "how much is it worth to you? If Germany has something to convey which you want, you must buy it with a price!"

This materialistic policy, this law of selfinterest pure and simple, is applied by him not alone in his own proper negotiations with other Governments. If his intervention is required by way of mediation and influence in behalf of another Government, from him comes still the demand, what will you give? or else, what can I take? To quote another of his phrases dedicated to such a relation of mediator, he is "an honest broker," and as such entitled to a commission on the transaction. It is possible that he learned this vantage from Lord Beaconsfield, who played in presence of Prince Bismarck this intervening role between Turkey and Russia, and for his brokerage took the Island of Cyprus. But he is capable of extending the rule far beyond the ideas of his

305

instructor. He will help a neighbour to take such a brokerage, when he has himself an object in view to which that may be auxiliary.

It is the Prince Chancellor who has given a new encouragement to violent national seizures by his liberal application of an other Latin phrase—*beati possidentes*. If it be a *fait accompli*, 'let it stand and seek compensations elsewhere.' If what he holds to be his just claims are refused, disregarded, or too long neglected, he wastes no threats; but at an unexpected moment, as in his quarrel with England, develops a complication which had not been dreamed of by his adversary. Wishing to distract the attention of France from her lost provinces of Alsace-Lorraine, he steadily encouraged her foreign adventures which seek the conquest and occupation of territories manyfold larger than that which was lost. This policy had the further advantage of scattering her military forces, and giving them an ever open field for costly employment. With wonderful skill and vigour, after aiding Russia to a position where she could safely move toward Afghanistan, after taking the side of France in her transmediterranean quarrel with England, with all continental Europe in close friendly relations with Germany, he brings England to terms upon his colonial policy, and obtains his long neglected demands. His prestige in both Europe and Asia at this moment is without precedent in European history.

His first reliance was upon the Prussian army, which, with the aid of Italy, who was paid at Austria's expense, won the North German Confederation from Austria; and next upon the German army, which enabled him to execute his plan for a German Empire, further aggrandized by the captured French provinces. It was next necessary to fortify his enormous acquisitions, beginning with Schleswig-Holstein and ending with Alsace-Lorraine. With the same unerring judgment, as his Northern flank was guarded by the Northern seas, he proceeded to guard the Southern flank of Germany. He inaugurated there a close alliance with Austria, for which after the Russian war he paid her a price at the expense of Turkey, by giving to her the North-Western Turkish provinces, with further expectations to the South and East. He thus paid his two successive allies without cost to Germany. There still remained a point of danger in the rear,—the Paris Government being always in the front of his vigilant observation. France was always easily excited by the idea of a Franco-Russian alliance in aid of the recovery of her lost departments, and her hopes were sustained by this possibility. Having belted Europe from North to South, including Italy, against French aggression, he turned to Russia, whose Czar was finally brought into the Austro-German understanding, with an undoubted future advantage to herself. The price of this accession remains to be developed. Probably it was to be paid in Asia, and not alone at the cost of the Central tribes. It is probable that unhappy Turkey will yet pay the chief figure of this compensation.

Thus Prince Bismarck has obtained security on both flanks and in the rear, and can henceforth look squarely and only in front. Why not diminish, if he cannot abolish this last danger? The first conspicuous movement to this end was a surprising confidential interview with the French Ambassador here, and the subsequent introduction of France as the European leader in the adjustment of various African questions, the backing of France against England in Egyptian questions, the ready agreement to push Paris to the front in negotiations in which Europe was interested, and the general moral support of French claims abroad, to which he brings not only German imperial, but triimperial support, utilizing the solidarity of the views of the three Empires. This *Drei-Kaiser-Bund* is an amazing power, in presence of which French anti-German feeling has become silent, and the voice of *Revanche* is rarely more heard. Even Italy, which has shown a kindly feeling toward England in the recent difficulties of the latter country, has felt obliged to avow that this kindness was limited by her attachment to the alliance of the Central Powers.

The resulting influence of such colossal successes in diplomacy, supported by a military strength in the back ground which none can question, is evident in the moral position acquired by Prince Bismarck as an international counsellor, even as an admitted arbitrator, perhaps I should say Dictator, in all international complications. Germany, almost unknown in Asia twenty years ago, is now a great moral power there, of which the oldest Asiatic nations stand in awe. At that period equally unknown in Africa, she is now an African colonial power, and one of the dictators in Egyptian affairs. At that date unknown in the Pacific ocean, she is now the proprietor of islands and harbours there for the founding of colonies, and for the extension of her commerce. Then known to the United States only as a sympathetic national and commercial friend, and without a navy, she is now known to us by her calculated hostility to our agricultural and commercial development, by her aggressions in the Samoan Islands, and by one of the ships of her navy which in a distant sea illegally violated one of our unarmed commercial vessels, in the absence of any American navy to resent it.

It is to be remembered that the first point of Prince Bismarck's policy is the rounding out of the Empire, and the securing of its safety against continental hostilities, especially against France. Next, providing for the external development of German industry, and for the emigration of her surplus population at the same time by the establishment of colonies on other continents and islands, where Germans shall retain their allegiance and lend strength to the mother country, instead of leaving her weaker by their withdrawal to an alien land. In the execution of this second point he was already in accord with France; and by quarreling with England he has now also obtained the consent of the latter. The new German subsidized steamship lines to distant seas are now inviting the colonial extension of Germany in imperial rivalry with England.

This review, Mr. Secretary, is not written for publication. It is not intended to be a Platonic essay, nor a mere contribution to general literature. It is offered in the hope—not so strong as I could wish it to be—that it may tend to persuade my Government of the *necessity* of foresight, and of energetic action at an early day, in two directions:—First, to obtain a navy strong enough, in presence of new elements of international complication, to secure respect for our flag, and to maintain our asserted rights. Secondly, to anticipate and provide against the coming hostile European action which will be directed to the overthrow of our much vaunted, and newly imperilled "Monroe Declaration."

If it may possibly induce more confidence in my views of European tendencies at this time, I venture to refer to my later Despatches as Minister in Vienna, in which I urged the then Administration to prepare for a coming European reaction against our agricultural interests,—a war of tariffs or prohibitions against our great line of exports. That forecast proved correct, our Government took no decisive measures, and we remain today the victims of that policy, without prospect of relief.

Based upon the like careful observations, I now venture to submit the following forecast; and it is always to be borne in mind as a quality of Prince Bismarck that events do not develop his policy. His policy develops events. He is not a mere manipulator; he is a creator. With the world's globe before him he indicates the national lines and colours which *ought* to be there. He then seeks the hands which are to put them there, whether his own, or another's.

Remembering this, I invite your attention to the fact that there remains at the moral disposition of Prince Bismarck, for the final quieting of France, a precious compensation, which shall at once soothe her for the loss of the Suez Canal and console her for the loss of Alsace. The compensation will this time be forced from neither Austria, nor Denmark, nor Turkey, nor France, nor China, nor Tunis, nor Afghanistan, nor England, all of whom have in turn been obliged to contribute either to the territories of Germany, or to those of the allies whom Germany from time to time has been pleased to favour in support of her own aims. The control by France of the Central American Isthmus, and its interoceanic canal, commanding the commerce between the Atlantic and Pacific oceans, and one of the only two direct routes to Australia and Eastern Asia, would be a domination of which any nation might be proud, and would carry with it to France a prestige, and a possible naval and commercial advantage, far greater than the restoration of her two lost departments. For its possession she would voluntarily lay at the feet of the donor her doubtful hopes to regain the keys of the captured fortresses. When the ripe moment shall have come, I do not entertain the least doubt that Prince Bismarck will say to the French Government,—"why should there not be a permanent adjustment and peace between us? You know how far my friendship has already helped you to recover your prestige in Europe, and enlarge your territories in Asia and Africa. What can you do in Europe against the three Emperors? Germany has now possessions and colonies in the Pacific ocean. French capital has bought the railroad and has built the Panama canal, and both demand your protection against the local revolutionary elements there. Give me equal rights for German commerce and navy in that canal, and I will support you in obtaining and maintaining possession of that Isthmus. You will control that route as England does that of Suez. Your real competitor and rival is England. With this route in your hands you equalize positions with her." When this suggestion shall be made,—there are signs that it may have already been made,—France, with the European Dictator at her back, will undertake it far more readily than she moved into Mexico, and with far greater assurance of success. The French spirit of aggression is eternal.

When this first step shall have been taken, *if the United States maintain their present attitude,* I further anticipate another aggressive movement from England or France under the iron plea of national necessity, upon the other transisthmian route. For it is not to be forgotten that Europe has justice on her side when she claims that this interoceanic route *must* be utilized for the commerce of the world; and that the United States cannot be permitted to obstruct every great nation willing to open it, while refusing themselves to turn a spadeful of soil. In President Monroe's time single passengers required many weeks for transit between the two continents. In President Cleveland's time whole regiments of troops will be able to make the same transit in as many days. Interests were then widely separated. They are now in close contiguity. Occasions for alien intervention by local provocations are as easily found now as trees in a Central American forest. Our naked American "Declaration", unsupported by possession or long-range guns, is mere vapour in presence of European self-interest, backed by Krupp cannon and a purely materialistic diplomacy. I have more reasons to give in support of my views, but not in this already too long Despatch.

I regret to make of my last political communication to my Chief a note of warning. But I strongly distrust the future of European relations to America. I wish to impart this distrust to my Government. For there is yet time, and there are still means, for thwarting unexecuted purposes, and for fortifying the future of our vital interests.

XIV. THE CAROLINE ISLANDS DISPUTE

George H. Pendleton to T. F. Bayard, Secretary of State, Washington, D. C., September 22, 1885.

No. 72.

Legation of the United States,
Berlin, September 22, 1885.
[Received October 12, 1885.]

Sir:

In pursuance of your Instruction No. 44, in which you quote the statement made by the Spanish Minister of State in an interview on the subject of the sovereignty of the Caroline Islands with Mr. Foster, as reported by him, to the effect that one of the reasons "alleged by Germany for sending the recent expedition of occupation was the fear that possession of the islands would be taken by the United States. This reason he said had been given no later than yesterday to the Spanish Minister in Berlin", I sought an interview with Count von Bismarck today at the Foreign Office.

The conversation reported in my Despatch No. 61 led me to believe that he would deny there had ever been, on the part of Germany, the statement quoted in Mr. Foster's Despatch. As I could see no good to result in any direction, from a controversy on this point, but rather, perhaps, an unpleasant personal embroilment, I thought it best not to state the channel through which the information came to the Department, but only to ask the question, and, according to the answer, to make the explanation propounded by you.

I said to him that a report had reached my Government that Germany had alleged as one of the reasons for the recent expedition for the occupation of Caroline Islands, a fear that they would be taken in possession by the United States, and I was instructed to ask whether the facts were so, and if so, on what such an apprehension was based. He at first did not quite catch the purpose of the question and said, that is not true, but it seems to me your question is rather academical [sic] than practical.

I replied, that perhaps would depend somewhat on the statement which I should make after an answer to the enquiry.

He then said, the statement is utterly without foundation. No such intimation could have been made, as no such thought ever existed. It had never been suggested to the Imperial Government that the United States made any claim to the possession of those Islands, and it was only from excess of caution, and from a most friendly and loyal regard for the United States, that the Chancellor had directed him to makes the enquiries in his conversation with me of the 10th instant. He then asked for the authority of such statement, but I avoided the question and it was not pressed. Continuing he repeated that the statement was absolutely without foundation, and said it was evidently intended to create distrust and alienation where there was now, and always ought to be a frank and friendly confidence: that it was inconsistent with the tone and spirit of his conversation with me; and he seemed to feel that there was an implication of want of candor on his part, which he was desirous to remove.

I did not interrupt him to make the obvious remark that if there were any such implication, it was in the statement itself and not in your communication to me, as at the date of your instruction, my report of the conversation with him had not reached you. This occurred to him later however, and he mentioned it with evident satisfaction.

I then expressed to him the satisfaction which I knew my Government would feel to hear that the statement was without truth. I said my Government had felt the statement to be so directly in the face of the assertions, and acts of the United States against territorial aggrandizements of this nature, of its traditions and history, of its policy declared and pursued for more than a century discountenancing distant colonial acquisitions even to the extent of refusing to avail itself of voluntary offers made by other powers to place territories under its sovereignty or protection, which must certainly be well known to the enlightened sovereign and statesmen of Germany, that it had instructed me to make the enquiry whether the statement had any foundation in fact, and if so, or if there were any misapprehension on the part of Germany as to the real motives and designs of the United States, to give to the German Government a most emphatic and earnest denial.

I was careful to confine myself very closely to the letter of your Instruction, avoiding all that related to the authority for the statement, and whatever might seem harsh to a susceptibility which was evidently aroused, believing that, in this way I might best carry into effect its spirit.

Count von Bismarck expressed himself greatly gratified by this expression of the policy and attitude of my Government, saying that Germany was fully aware of its general policy, and had believed its attitude to be, in this particular case, as now authoritatively represented.

I then read to him your Instruction No. 43 in relation to the work of the

Board of Foreign Missions in the Islands, and left with him a copy. He seemed to recognize the extent of that work, and to appreciate the justness of its appeal for the beneficent protection of whatever enlightened Government may govern the Islands. Of course this conversation serves as a reply to the questions contained in my Despatch of September 10th.

I neglected to say in the beginning of this Despatch that as I entered his room, and before I had mentioned the object of my visit Count von Bismarck expressed his satisfaction at seeing me, as he was in the act of writing me a note inviting me on behalf of the Prince Chancellor to an interview tomorrow afternoon, the special purpose of which was not stated.

XV. THE CAROLINE ISLANDS DISPUTE

George H. Pendleton to T. F. Bayard, September 23, 1885
No. 73.

> Legation of the United States,
> Berlin, September 23, 1885.
> [Received October 12, 1885.]

Sir:

This afternoon I had an interview with Prince Bismarck according to his own appointment. It was the first time I had ever seen him. He seemed strong and vigorous, and to have entirely recovered from the illness, which public rumor attributed to him in the early summer.

After pleasant remarks about the Americans whom he had known intimately and esteemed during his university life, and many enquiries about Ohio and Cincinnati, and the many Germans who have settled there and become citizens of the United States, the Chancellor approached the subject of the interview to which he had invited me, and of which I had been till then ignorant.

He spoke of the existing differences with Spain in regard to the Caroline Islands. He said that his son (Count von Bismarck) had reported to him the conversation, which he had with me yesterday, (given in my Despatch No. 72). That it maintained the traditional policy and attitude of the United States, and, while only what he expected, none the less, gave him pleasure. He then explained the action of the German officers which gave rise to the present condition of affairs, asserted that Germany had no desire or design to take possession of any of the islands already in the possession of any other nation, that its officers had instructions to interfere with no flag, but to confine themselves to territory which was without an owner. (Herrenlos) :

One Holcombe an American, who had married a native wife, and been guilty of cruel and barbarous practices had stimulated the Spanish officers and government to assert ownership of the islands and to take possession, in the hope that his activity in behalf of a new regime would cover up a past which he certainly had every reason to regret, and for which he would naturally desire protection.

His desire now is to find proper terms of accomodation with Spain, and he would exhaust every effort to that end. Germany could not be inconsistent with the action which itself had heretofore in 1875 taken, in conjunction with England and recognize in Spain the past ownership and possession of the Islands, but would do every thing that is compatible with its own dignity and interests, to arrange for the future; he had proposed arbitration, and had hoped that it might be accepted by Spain in any sense most agreeable to herself, but in vain; finally he had proposed to submit all questions to the arbitration of the Pope, who, he supposed, would not be unacceptable to Catholic Spain, and would be willing to undertake the office in the interests of peace among men—to this suggestion he had as yet received no response.

He spoke of the colonial policy of Germany, that it was peaceful and friendly, following the lines of commerce, and taking care of its interests, maintaining itself by the interchange of benefits between the mother country and the dependent colonies, not by military occupation and the force of arms; neither the genius nor tastes of the German people favored a policy which would require the establishment of garrisons in foreign or far-off lands.

He spoke of the stress and distress of war, its costliness of blood and treasure, its heavy burthen of taxation and bitter, long enduring estrangement of peoples whose interest and real advancement require them to be friendly.

And finally, he said there would be no war with Spain about these Islands; they were not worth it; they would never repay one week of war, or even one week of preparation for war, that if there could be no arbitration, there should be a treaty which would close the differences between the two countries.

I was struck by the apparent freedom and frankness with which all this was stated at great length. I have not attempted to give his statements in detail, or in the exact order and language used, or my part, which was brief, in the conversation, yet I believe the above is a faithful resumé of the thought, and, as far as I can remember, of the general expression of the Chancellor.

After a pause he continued; that he had never heard of any assertion by the United States of ownership or sovereignty over these Islands, although on an old German map he had found the word American opposite to, or over two or three of them, and had known that the American missionaries had done much and good work among the savage inhabitants of one or more of them. That he had therefore, in a spirit of perfect friendliness and loyality requested his son to make the enquiries as to the attitude of our Government in regard to the claim of its own ownership of the Islands, and the individual interests existing in our people, and that the conversation with his son yesterday had answered fully both enquiries in the sense which he had expected and fully appreciated.

We will make a treaty with Spain, said he, taking up a large sheet of paper on which were several sub-headings, we will recognize the present ownership of Spain on these terms:

That she shall keep the peace and preserve order, giving us the right to interfere only in case she shall fail to do so.

That the jurisdiction over our own people shall remain with us until Spanish Courts shall be fully established and settled in the administration of justice.

That free trade shall be allowed us with the Islands.

That liberty of conscience and freedom of religious worship shall be maintained.

This is my general idea of the treaty we shall offer to Spain. England will join with Germany in this treaty. England and Germany will act together, and no treaty will be made by us not acceptable to England.

I do not know that Spain will accept it. The question which I wish to submit to you, is whether the United States, in view of the material interests of her citizens, would desire to become a party to this treaty which we will make, England and Germany on the one side and Spain on the other.

I said that the policy of the United States had been uniformly not only against distant colonial possessions, but also against "entangling alliances" of any kind, that they had generally preferred to rely on the law of nations, and the appreciation of equity and comity among peoples, and special application for redress of wrongs when committed, and were not without reason to believe that this course had some advantages.

But, said the Chancellor, interrupting, this will secure to your people free trade, religious liberty, and relief from a colonial policy, which everywhere, as in Cuba, has crushed out all commerce, as that cover extinguished that candle.

I repeated in a different form the statement I had just made, adding, that this policy had caused the United States, to refrain from becoming party to treaties, whose general object and purpose they highly approved, and which might at times, and in some aspects be very advantageous to the material

314

interests and the moral and beneficent work of their citizens. I said that I would report the conversation to my Government, and would in due time advise him of any instructions I might receive.

The manner of the Chancellor was agreeable, his frequent allusions to our country were of a pleasant character, and his method very direct. Of course I took no memorandum as the conversation progressed; but I have written this out within a few hours, and feel confident that it contains the substance of his part in it.

XVI. BISMARCK'S DISCHARGE

William Walter Phelps to James G. Blaine, April 2, 1890.
No. 93.
Confidential.   Legation of the United States,
                                           Berlin, April 2, 1890.
Sir: [Received April 21, 1890.]

* * * * * * *

The immediate causes of the rupture were,—so far as one who reads only from the outside can tell;—The actions of the Emperor in the cases of personalities, which were unpleasant to the Chancellor, or which became so when done without consultation with him; such, for example, as bringing von Berlepsch, the young Saxon, into the Ministry of Trade and Commerce, and the conspicuous decoration of von Bötticher, the next in civil rank to Prince Bismarck, with the Black Eagle;—The Emperor's determination to receive the reports of his Ministers directly, and not through his Chancellor, as the Chancellor claimed was the constitutional practice and the obligation of the law of /52:—The Emperor's recent relations to Socialism and Labor, where the preliminary Proclamations were without the witness of Chancellor and Minister, and where the Chancellor wished for longer consideration and discussion before such a departure from the old traditions of Hohenzollern policy was inaugurated.

Before briefly stating what may be considered the natural consequence of this great political change, I would like to state for the information of the Department what I believe to be the facts as to the manner in which Emperor and Chancellor and Secretary of State parted.

The Emperor made no effort to induce the Chancellor to stay, which went far enough to indicate that, to obtain this result, he would in any way modify his political purposes so as to make them endurable to Prince Bismarck.

The Emperor wished Count Herbert Bismarck to stay, and made as many and as earnest efforts in that direction as became a sovereign. These went so far that nothing but the condition of the Secretary of State's health, which notoriously needs amelioration, would, in courtly convention, excuse Count Bismarck's persistent refusal to yield an assent.

I think we may expect, as the results of the young Emperor's freedom from all control, a series of surprises. Young, ambitious, restless, having obtained for himself the position of actual as well as nominal Ruler, so that he is sure to gain all the credit of all his acts, it is believed that he cannot resist a desire to rapidly inaugurate changes which he believes to be for the good of Germany and of mankind. He is earnest, courageous and animated by lofty aspirations to associate his name with great reforms, moral, social, industrial and political, and he is likely to waste little time in using the great resources which Prince Bismarck has gathered for him, in the effort to obtain a speedy gratification of his ambitions.

BIBLIOGRAPHY[1]

Abbott, John Stevens Cabot. Prussia and the Franco-Prussian War . . . Including Biographical Sketches of King William and Count von Bismarck. Boston, Philadelphia, 1871.

Adams, Charles Francis. Studies Military and Diplomatic, 1775-1865. New York, 1911.

——, Trans-Atlantic Historical Solidarity; Lectures Delivered before the University of Oxford in Easter and Trinity Terms, 1913. Oxford, 1913.

Adams, Ephraim Douglass. Great Britain and the American Civil War. 2 vols. London, New York, 1925.

Adams, Henry. The Education of Henry Adams; an Autobiography. Boston, 1918.

——, History of the United States of America, 1801-1817. 9 vols. New York, 1921.

——, Letters of Henry Adams (1858-1891), edited by Worthington Chauncey Ford. Boston, New York, 1930.

Adams, James Truslow. The Epic of America. Boston, 1931.

Adams, John. The Works of John Adams, with a Life, Notes and Illustrations by His Grandson, Charles Francis Adams. 10 vols. Boston, 1850-56.

Adams, John Quincy. Briefe über Schlesien. Aus dem Englischen übertragen von F. G. Friese. Breslau, 1805.

——, The Diary of John Quincy Adams, 1794-1845. American Political, Social and Intellectual Life from Washington to Polk. Ed. by Allan Nevins. New York, London, Toronto, 1928.

——, Letters from Silesia, Written during a Tour through that Country in the Years 1800, 1801. London, 1804.

——, Memoirs of John Quincy Adams, Comprising Portions of His Diary from 1795 to 1848. Ed. by Charles Francis Adams. 12 vols. Philadelphia, 1874-77.

——, The Writings of John Quincy Adams. Ed. by Worthington Chauncey Ford. 7 vols. 5 yet to appear. New York, 1913-17.

Adams, Randolph Greenfield. A History of the Foreign Policy of the United States. New York, 1924.

[1] Alphabetical order. For magazine articles, see authors' names. For U. S. official documents, see "United States".

Alcott, Louisa May. Louisa May Alcott, Her Life, Letters, and Journal. Ed. by Ednah B. Cheney. Boston, 1900.

America and Europe; a Study of International Relations. I. The United States and Great Britain, by David A. Wells. II. The Monroe Doctrine, by Edward J. Phelps. III. Arbitration in International Disputes, by Carl Schurz. New York, 1896.

Ames, John G. Comprehensive Index to the Publications of the United States Government, 1881-1893. 2 vols. Washington, 1905.

Anonymous. "German Socialism in North America", in North American Review, vol. 128, no. 269, pp. 372-387.

Anton, Peter. Masters in History. Gibbon, Grote, Macaulay, Motley. Edinburgh, 1880.

Aron, Joseph. Alsace-Lorraine. Monument to Grant. New York, Paris, 1885.

"Ausfuhr von amerikanischem Fleisch nach Europa" in Ausland. 1866. No. 47.

Baasch, Ernst. Beiträge zur Geschichte der Handelsbeziehungen zwischen Hamburg und Amerika. Hamburg, 1892.

——, Geschichte Hamburgs 1814-1918. Gotha, Stuttgart, 1924-25.

Bacourt, Adolphe F. de. Souvenirs d'un diplomate. Lettres intimes sur l'Amérique. Paris, 1882.

Badeau, Adam. Grant in Peace. From Appomattox to Mount McGregor. A Personal Memoir. Hartford, 1887.

——, Military History of Ulysses S. Grant, from April, 1861, to April, 1865. 3 vols. New York, 1868-81.

Baker, Thomas Stockam. Lenau and Young Germany in America. Philadelphia, 1897.

Baldwin, James M. Lecture III. "The Effects of the War upon American Opinion", in American Neutrality; Its Cause and Cure. New York, London, 1916.

Bancroft, George. The American Revolution . . . 4 vols. Boston, 1860-75.

——, Denkschrift über den Kanal von Haro, als Grenzlinie der Vereinigten Staaten, Wilhelm I., Dt. Kaiser, als Schiedsrichter übergeben von dem am. Bevollmächtigten G. Bancroft, 4 Okt. 1866.

——, History of the Colonization of the United States. 3 vols. Boston, 1838-57.

——, History of the Formation of the Constitution of the United States. 2 vols. New York, 1882.

——, History of the United States of America, from the Discovery of the Continent. 6 vols. New York, 1888.

——, The Life of William H. Seward. 2 vols. New York, London, 1900.

——, Literary and Historical Miscellanies. New York, 1855.

——, Memorial Address on the Life and Character of Abraham Lincoln, Delivered . . . in the House of Representatives at Washington Feb. 12, 1866. Washington, 1866.

Bartholdt, Richard. From Steerage to Congress, Reminiscences and Reflections. Philadelphia, n.d.

Bassett, John Spencer. The Middle Group of American Historians. New York, 1916.

Baylies, Nicholas. Political Controversies between the United States and Great Britain. Des Moines, 1885.

Beard, Charles Austin and Mary R. The Rise of American Civilization. 2 vols. New York, 1927.

Becker, Carl Lotus. The Eve of the Revolution; a Chronicle of the Breach with England. New Haven, 1921.

Belmont, Perry. Survival of the Democratic Principle, Including the Tariff Issue. New York, London, 1926.

Bemis, Samuel Flagg, ed. The American Secretaries of State and Their Diplomacy. 10 vols. New York, 1927-29.

Bernhardi, Theodor von. Aus dem Leben Theodor von Bernhardis. 6 parts. Leipzig, 1893-97.

Bible, George W. Great European Conflict. Franco-Prussian War . . . New York, 1870.

Bigelow, John. France and the Confederate Navy, 1862-1868; an International Episode. New York, 1888.

——, France and Hereditary Monarchy. London, New York, 1871.

——, Retrospections of an Active Life. 5 vols. New York, 1909-13.

——, American Policy; the Western Hemisphere in Its Relation to the Eastern. New York, 1914.

Bigelow, Poultney. History of the German Struggle for Liberty. 4 vols. New York, 1896-1905.

——, Prussian Memories, 1864-1914. New York, London, 1915.

Bismarck, Otto Fürst. Anhang zu Gedanken und Erinnerungen II. Hrsg. von Horst Kohl. Stuttgart, Berlin, 1901.

——, Die Gesammelte Werke. Friedrichsruher Ausgabe. 14 vols. Berlin, 1924-33.

——, Politische Briefe aus den Jahren 1849-1889. 2 vols. Berlin, 1889, 1890.

Bismarck-Jahrbuch hrsg. von Horst Kohl. 6 vols. Berlin, 1894-99.

Bittinger, Lucy Forney. The Germans in Colonial Times. Philadelphia, London, 1901.

Bogart, Ernest Ludlow. An Economic History of the United States. New York, London, 1912; new ed. New York, 1922.

Bolles, Albert Sidney. The Financial History of the United States, from 1861 to 1885. New York, 1886.

Boutroux, E. Les États-Unis et la France. Paris, 1914.

Boynton, Charles B. English and French Neutrality and the Anglo-French Alliance, in Their Relations to the United States & Russia . . . Cincinnati, Chicago, 1864.

Bradford, Gamaliel. American Portraits 1875-1900. Boston, New York, 1922.

Bradley, Arthur Granville. The Fight with France for North America. New York, 1900.

Brandenburg, Erich. Von Bismarck zum Weltkriege . . . Berlin, 1925.

Bratter, Carl Adolf. Amerika, von Washington bis Wilson. Berlin, 1916.

Brauns, Ernst Ludwig. Ideen über die Auswanderung nach Amerika . . . Göttingen, 1827.

Breffken, Constantin. Amerika in der deutschen Literatur. Cologne, 1917.

Brinkmann, Carl. Geschichte der Vereinigten Staaten von Amerika. Leipzig, Berlin, 1924.

——, Wirtschafts- und Sozialgeschichte. Munich, 1927.

Brockett, Linus Pierpont. The Great War of 1870 between France and Germany. Comprising a History of its Origin and Causes . . . New York, 1871.

Brodnitz, Georg. Bismarcks nationalökonomische Anschauungen. Jena, 1902.

Burgess, John William. Germany and the United States; an Address Delivered before the Germanistic Society of America, January 24, 1908. New York, 1913.

Busch, Moritz. Tagebuchblätter. 3 vols. Leipzig, 1899.

Busching, Paul. Die Entwicklung der handelspolitischen Beziehungen zwischen England und seinen Kolonien bis zum Jahre 1860 . . . Stuttgart, Berlin, 1902.

Cadogan, Edward Cecil George. Makers of Modern History; Three Types, Louis Napoleon, Cavour, Bismarck. London, 1905.

Calhoun, John C. Correspondence of John C. Calhoun, ed. by J. Franklin Jameson, in Annual Report of the American Historical Association, 1899, vol. II.

Callahan, James Morton. American Relations in the Pacific and the Far East, 1784-1900. Johns Hopkins University Studies in History and Political Science, Series 19. Baltimore, 1901.

Calwer, Richard. Die Meistbegünstigung der Vereinigten Staaten von Nordamerika. Berlin, 1902.

Cambon, Jules Martin. France and the United States; Essays and Addresses. New York, 1903.

The Cambridge History of American Literature. 4 vols. New York, Cambridge, 1917-.

The Cambridge History of the British Empire. Cambridge, 1929-.

The Cambridge History of British Foreign Policy, 1783-1919. Ed. by A. W. Ward and G. P. Gooch. 3 vols. London, New York, 1922-23.

The Cambridge Modern History. Vol. VII. The United States. Cambridge, 1903.

Carnegie, Andrew . . . Deutschland und Amerika in ihren wirtschaftlichen Beziehungen zueinander unter besonderer Berücksichtigung Englands. Deutsch von J. M. Grabisch. Berlin, 1907.

Carnegie Endowment for International Peace. Division of International Law . . . Opinions of Attorneys General, Decisions of Federal Courts, and Diplomatic Correspondence Respecting the Treaties of 1785, 1799 and 1828 between the United States and Prussia. Washington, 1917.

Chadwick, French Ensor. The Relations of the United States and Spain, Diplomacy. New York, 1909.

Channing, Edward. A History of the United States. 6 vols. New York, 1905-25.

Channing, Edward, and Albert Bushnell Hart. Guide to the Study of American History. Boston, 1896.

Charles, Heinrich. The Commercial Relations between Germany and the United States. New York, 1907.

Chevalier, Louis E. La marine française et la marine allemande pendant la guerre de 1870-1871 . . . Paris, 1873.

Churchward, William Brown. My Consulate in Samoa; a Record of Four Years' Sojourn in the Navigators Islands . . . London, 1887.

Circourt, Adolphe, Comte de. France and the United States. Historical Europe. Boston, 1877.

Cleveland, Grover. Presidential Problems. Rev. ed. London, 1904.

——, Writings and Speeches of Grover Cleveland. Selected and ed. by George F. Parker. New York, 1892.

Cobbett, William. The Parliamentary History of England from the Norman Conquest 1066 to the year 1803. 36 vols. London, 1806-20.

Condorcet, Jean A. Marquis de. "De l'influence de la revolution de l'Amérique sur l'Europe", in vol. II, Oeuvres de Condorcet publiées par A. Condorcet O'Connor et M. F. Arago. 12 vols. Paris, 1847-49.

Coolidge, Archibald Cary. The United States as a World Power. New York, 1908.

——, Die Vereinigten Staaten als Weltmacht. Eine Betrachtung über internationale Politik. Berlin, 1908.

Corti, Egon Caesar. Maximilian und Charlotte von Mexiko . . . 2 vols. Zürich, Leipzig, Vienna, 1924.

Corwin, Edward Samuel. French Policy and the American Alliance of 1778. Princeton, 1916.

Culbertson, William Smith. International and Economic Policies, a Survey of the Economics of Diplomacy. New York, London, 1925.

Curti, Merle Eugene. Austria and the United States 1848-1852. A Study in Diplomatic Relations. Smith College Studies in History, vol. XI, no. 3, April 1926.

——, "Young America", in American Historical Review, vol. XXXII, no. 1 (Oct. 1926), pp. 34-55.

Curtis, Eugene Newton. "American Opinion of French Nineteenth Century Revolutions", in American Historical Review, vol. XXIX, no. 2 (Jan. 1924), pp. 249-270.

——, The French Assembly of 1848 and American Constitutional Doctrines. New York, 1917.

Curtis, George Ticknor. Life of James Buchanan, Fifteenth President of the United States. 2 vols. New York, 1883.

Curtis, William Eleroy. The United States and Foreign Powers. New York, 1899.

Curtius, Frederick. "Germany's Right to Alsace", in North American Review, vol. 146, May 1888.

Daenell, E., and A. Hasenclever. Geschichte der Vereinigten Staaten von Amerika. (Natur und Geistesw.) Leipzig, Berlin, 1923.

Dannehl, Otto von. Carl Schurz: ein deutscher Kämpfer. Berlin, Leipzig, 1928.

Darmstädter, Paul. Die Vereinigten Staaten von Amerika, ihre politische, wirtschaftliche und soziale Entwicklung. Leipzig, 1909.

Davis, Jefferson. The Rise and Fall of the Confederate Government. 2 vols. New York, 1881.

Davis, John Chandler. Mr. Fish and the Alabama Claims; a Chapter in Diplomatic History. Boston, New York, 1893.

——, Treaties and Conventions Concluded between the United States of America and Other Powers Since July 4, 1776. Washington, 1889.

Day, Clive. History of Commerce of the United States. New York, 1925.

Dehn, Paul. England und die Vereinigten Staaten. Hamburg, 1915.

De la Gorce, R. Histoire du second Empire. 7 vols. Paris, 1894-1905.

Delbrück, Rudolph von. Lebenserinnerungen. 2 vols. Leipzig, 1905.

Dennett, Tyler. Americans in Eastern Asia: A Critical Study of the Policy of the United States with Reference to China, Japan and Korea in the 19th Century. New York, 1922.

De Ricci, James Herman. The Fisheries Dispute, and Annexation of Canada. London, 1888.

Deutsche Auswanderung und Kolonisation. Erster Rechenschaftsbericht des Berliner Vereins zur Zentralisation deutscher Auswanderung und Kolonisation. i. A. des Verwaltungsrats D. von Gaebler. Berlin, 1850.

Deutsche Interessen in der Südsee, vol. I, no. 1, appendix 1.

Der deutsche Pionier. Erinnerungen aus dem pionierleben der Deutschen in Amerika.

Die Deutschen in Amerika und die deutschamerikanischen Friedensfeste im Jahr 1871. . . . New York, 1871.

Deutsches Handelsarchiv hrsg. vom Reichsamt des Inneren. Berlin, 1886.

Die deutschen Handels-, Freundschafts-, Schiffahrts-, Consular- und literarischen Verträge. Zusammengestellt und herausgegeben vom Generalsekretär des Centralverbandes deutscher Industrieller, Regierungsrat a. D. Beutner. Berlin, 1883.

Die Deutschen Kolonien der Provinz Rio Grande do Sul (Südbrasilien). . . . Hrsg. vom Zentralverein für Handelsgeographie . . . Berlin, 1881.

Dewey, Davis Rich. . . . Financial History of the United States. New York, 1915.

Dewey, John. China, Japan and the U. S.; Present Day Conditions in the Far East and Their Bearing on the Washington Conference. (New Republic Pamphlet No. 1.) New York, 1921.

Dietz, Alexander. Frankfurter Handelsgeschichte. 4 vols. Frankfurt, 1910-25.

Dix, John A. Memoirs of John Adams Dix. Compiled by his Son, Morgan Dix. 2 vols. New York, 1883.

Dodd, William Edward. The Cotton Kingdom. A Chronicle of the Old South. (Vol. 27—Chronicles of America Series, 1919.)

——, Expansion and Conflict. Boston, New York, 1915.

——, . . . Jefferson Davis. Philadelphia, 1907.

——, Lincoln or Lee; Comparison and Contrast of the Two Greatest Leaders of the War between the States . . . New York, London, 1928.

——, Robert J. Walker, Imperialist. Chicago, 1914.

Douglass, Frederick. "Haiti and the United States", in North American Review, vol. CLIII (Sept. 1891), pp. 337-345.

Dudley, Thomas Haines. ". . . Three Critical Periods in Our Diplomatic Relations with England During the Late War", in The Pennsylvania Magazine of History and Biography, vol. XVII (1893), pp. 34-54.

Duniway, Clyde Augustus. "Reasons for the Withdrawal of the French from Mexico", in the Annual Report of the American Historical Association, 1902, vol. I, pp. 313-328.

Dunning, William Archibald. The British Empire and the United States; a Review of Their Relations During the Century of Peace Following the Treaty of Ghent. New York, 1914.

Dwight, Henry Edwin. Travels in the North of Germany in the Years 1825 and 1826. New York, 1829.

Eckardstein, Hermann Freiherr von. Lebenserinnerungen und politische Denkwürdigkeiten. 3 vols. Leipzig, 1919-21.

Edmundson, George. Anglo-Dutch Rivalry During the First Half of the Seventeenth Century. Oxford, 1911.

Emerson, Ralph Waldo. Correspondence between Ralph Waldo Emerson and Hermann Grimm. Ed. by Frederick William Holls. Boston, New York, 1903.

——, Emerson's Complete Works. Riverside ed. 12 vols. Boston, 1883-93.

——, Journals of Ralph W. Emerson with annotations ed. by Edward W. Emerson and Waldo E. Forbes. 10 vols. Boston, New York, 1909-14.

Encyclopedia Americana. 30 vols. New York, Chicago, 1931-32.

Everett, Edward. Academical Education. An Address Delivered at St. Louis 22 April, 1857 at the Inauguration of Washington University of the State of Missouri. Boston, 1857.

——, Importance of Practical Education and Useful Knowledge . . . Boston, 1840.

——, Selections from the Works of Edward Everett, with a Sketch of His Life. Boston, 1839.

Eye, A. von. Der Auswanderer. Winke und Weisungen für Ansiedler in den deutschen Kolonien Südbrasiliens nach eignen Erfahrungen zusammengestellt . . . Berlin, 1885.

Fabri, C. Europäische Einwanderung in Brasilien, kolonialpolitische Betrachtungen zur augenblicklichen Lage Brasiliens. Hamburg, 1894.

Falconer, Sir Robert. The United States as a Neighbour, from a Canadian Point of View. Cambridge, 1925.

Faulkner, Harold Underwood. American Economic History. New York, London, 1928.

——, Amerikanische Wirtschaftsgeschichte. 2 vols. Dresden, 1929.

Faust, Albert Bernhardt. Das Deutschtum in den Vereinigten Staaten . . . 2 vols. Leipzig, 1912.

——, The German Element in the United States, with Special Reference to Its Political, Moral, Social and Educational Influence. 2 vols. 2d ed. New York, 1927.

——, "Vergangenheit und Zukunft der deutschen Sprache in Amerika", in Monatshefte für deutsche Sprache und Pädagogik. 17. Jhrg. Milwaukee, 1916.

Favre, Jules. Gouvernement de la défense nationale. 3 vols. Paris, 1871-75.

Fay, Theodore Sedgwick. Die Sklavenmacht. Blicke in die Geschichte der Vereinigten Staaten . . . Berlin, 1865.

Festreden bei der Erinnerungsfeier an Edward Everett, George Bancroft, H. W. Longfellow und John L. Motley. Gehalten in der Aula der Georgia Augusta. Göttingen, July 4, 1890.

Fish, Carl R. American Diplomacy. New York, 1915.

Fisk, George Mygatt. Die handelspolitischen und sonstigen völkerrechtlichen Beziehungen zwischen Deutschland und den Vereinigten Staaten von Amerika. Stuttgart, 1897.

——, "Most-Favored-Nation Relations, German-American", in the Journal of Political Economy, vol. 11, no. 2 (Mar. 1903), pp. 220-236.

Fiske, John. "Athenian and American Life", in Collected Works, vol. 18, pp. 395-441. Ed. by the Riverside Press. Boston, 1902.

Fitzmaurice, Lord Edmund. Life of Granville, George Leveson Grower, Second Earl Granville 1815-1891. 2 vols. London, 1906.

Foreign Policy Association. The Seizure of Haiti by the United States. New York, 1922.

Foster, John Watson. Diplomatic Memoirs. 2 vols. Boston, New York, 1909.

France, Ministère des affaires étrangères. Les origines diplomatiques de la guerre de 1870-71, recueil de documents publié. Paris, 1910-.

France–États-Unis; revue mensuelle du Comité France-Amérique. 6 vols. Paris, 1919-24.

Franke, Otto. Die Grossmächte in Ostasien von 1894-1914 . . . Brunswick, Hamburg, 1923.

Frankfurt-Amerika. Hrsg. vom Wirtschaftsamt der Stadt Frankfurt a. M., Abt. für Werbe- und Ausstellungswesen, anlässlich der Ausstellung Frankfurt-Amerika. Frankfort on the Main, 1926.

Frankfurter Zeitung. Geschichte der Frankfurter Zeitung. Volksausgabe. Frankfort on the Main, 1906.

Franklin, Benjamin. The Autobiography of Benjamin Franklin and Selections from His Other Writings; ed. and with an introduction by Nathan G. Goodman. New York, 1932.

——, Benjamin Franklin and the University of Pennsylvania. Ed. by Francis Newton Thorpe. Bureau of Education Circular of Information No. 2, 1892. Washington, 1893.

——, The Works of Benjamin Franklin . . . with Notes and a Life of the Author, by Jared Sparks. 10 vols. Chicago, 1882.

Frankreich und der deutsch-französische Krieg in den Jahren 1870-71 . . . New York, 1871.

Franz, Günther. Bismarcks Nationalgefühl. Leipzig, 1926.

Friedjung, Heinrich. Das Zeitalter des Imperialismus 1884-1914. 3 vols. Berlin, 1919-22.

Friedrich III. Das Kriegstagebuch 1870-1871. Hrsg. von Otto Heinrich Meisner. Berlin, Leipzig, 1926.

Frisch, Hans. Monroe-Doktrin und Weltpolitik der Vereinigten Staaten von Nordamerika. Vienna, Leipzig, 1917.

Fröbel, Julius. Amerika, Europa und die politischen Gesichtspunkte der Gegenwart. Berlin, 1859.

Fueredi, Arnold. Deutschland und Amerika Hand in Hand . . . Berlin, 1914.

Fuess, Claude Moore. Carl Schurz Reformer (1829-1906). New York, 1932.

Funke, Alfred. Aus Deutsch-Brasilien. Bilder aus dem Leben der Deutschen im Staate Rio Grande do Sul. Leipzig, 1902.

Garlepp, Bruno. Bismarck Memorial . . . Akron, Chicago, 1898.

Gazley, John Gerow. American Opinion of German Unification, 1848-1871. New York, 1926.

Geisberg, Wulf Dietrich. Bismarck und das Kriegsvölkerrecht. Ein Beitrag zur Geschichte Bismarcks und des Völkerrechts. Leipzig, 1913.

Generalakte der Samoa-Konferenz. Berlin, 1899.

Geschichte der Handelskammer zu Frankfurt a. M. 1707-1908. Beiträge zur Frankfurter Handelsgeschichte, hrsg. von der Handelskammer zu Fr. a. M. Frankfort on the Main, 1908.

Gladstone, William Ewart. The Speeches and Public Addresses of the Right Hon. W. E. Gladstone. 10 vols. London, 1894.

Goebel, Julius. Der Kampf um die deutsche Kultur in Amerika. Aufsätze und Vorträge über die deutschamerikanische Bewegung. Leipzig, 1914.

——, "Carl Schurz als Deutschamerikaner", in Deutschamerikanische Geschichtsblätter. Jahrbuch der deutschamerikanischen Gesellschaft von Illinois. Hrsg. von Julius Goebel. (Vol. XXIX) Chicago, 1929.

Golder, Frank A. "The Russian Fleet and the Civil War", in American Historical Review, vol. XX, 801-812.

Görlach, Wilhelm. The Life of Prince Bismarck. New York, 1882.

Graham, F. D. "International Trade under Depreciated Paper. The United States, 1862-79", in Quarterly Journal of Economics, vol. XXXVI (Feb. 1922), 220-273.

Grant, Ulysses. Personal Memoirs of U. S. Grant. 2 vols. New York, 1885. New ed. rev. 1895.

Great Britain, Foreign Office. British and Foreign State Papers, 1841-. London, 1841-.

——, Cattle Disease (United States of America). Further Correspondence and Reports Relating to Disease of Animals in the United States of America. Presented to both Houses of Parliament by command of Her Majesty. London, 1882.

Greeley, Horace. Glances at Europe . . . New York, 1852. 3d ed.

Green, Samuel Swett. George Bancroft. Worcester, 1891.

Greene, Evarts Boutell. Lieber and Schurz, Two Loyal Americans of German Birth. Washington, 1918.

Greene, George Washington. The German Element in the War of American Independence. New York, 1876.

Die Grenzboten. Zeitschrift für Politik, Literatur und Kunst. Leipzig, Berlin, 1845-.

Die Grosse Politik der europäischen Kabinette 1871-1914; . . . Hrsg. im Auftrage des Auswärtigen Amtes. Berlin, 1922-.

Grothe, Hugo. Die Deutschen in Übersee. Berlin, 1932.

Grund, James Pemberton. "Bismarck and Motley—With Correspondence Till Now Unpublished", three parts, in North American Review, vol. 167, part I (Sept. 1898), 360-376; part II (Oct. 1898), 481-496; part III (Nov. 1898), 569-572.

Hagen, Maximilian von. Bismarcks Kolonialpolitik. Stuttgart, 1923.

Halle, Ernst von. Amerika, seine Bedeutung für die Weltwirtschaft und seine wirtschaftlichen Beziehungen zu Deutschland, insbesondere zu Hamburg. In Einzeldarstellungen herausgegeben. Hamburg, 1905.

——, Die Blockade der nordamerikanischen Südstaaten. Die Baumwollenhungersnoth in Lancashire. Berlin, 1900. (Jahrbuch für Deutschlands Seeinteressen II. Jahrgang v. Nauticus.)

——, "Deutschland und die öffentliche Meinung in den Vereinigten Staaten", in Preussische Jahrbücher, 1902.

Hamburger Handelsarchiv. Sammlung der auf Handel und Schiffahrt bezgl. Hamburgischen Verträge, Verordnungen und Bekanntmachungen. Hamburg, 1864.

Handels- und Schiffahrtsverträge einzelner deutscher Staaten mit Dänemark, Schweden, Norwegen und den Vereinigten Staaten. Zusammengestellt vom Reichsamt des Inneren. Berlin, 1897.

Die Handelspolitik Nordamerikas . . . sowie die Deutsche Handelsstatistik von 1880 bis 1890. Berichte und Gutachten veröffentlicht vom Verein für Sozialpolitik. Leipzig, 1892.

Hanfstaengl, Ernst F. S. Amerika und Europa von Marlborough bis Mirabeau . . . Munich, 1930.

Hansen-Taylor, Marie. See Taylor.

Harper's Weekly; a journal of civilization. New York, 1857-1916.

Harring, Harro Paul. Russland und die Vereinigten Staaten Nordamerikas. New York, 1854.

Hart, Albert Bushnell. The American Nation, editor. New York, London, 1904-18.

——, Extracts from Official Declarations of the United States Embodying the Monroe Doctrine 1789-1891. New York, 1892.

——, The Foundation of American Foreign Policy. New York, 1901.

Hartmann. Die Bancroft-Verträge. Pr. Verwaltungsblatt 35. Jahrg. 1913-14. 36. Jahrg. 1914-15.

Hashagen, Justus. Ostasienpolitik der Vereinigten Staaten von Amerika. Bonn, 1917.

Hasse, Adelaide Rosalie. Index to United States Documents Relating to Foreign Affairs, 1828-1861 . . . Washington, 1914-21.

Haswell, John H., compiler. Treaties and Conventions Concluded between the United States of America and Other Powers since July 4, 1776 . . . Washington, 1889.

Hatfield, J. Taft, and Elfrieda Hochbaum. "The Influence of the American Revolution upon German Literature", in Americana-Germanica, vol. III, no. 1 (1899), 338-385 (New York, Berlin, London).

Hatschek, Julius, and Karl Strupp. Wörterbuch des Völkerrechts und der Diplomatie. 3 vols. Berlin, Leipzig, 1924-29.

Hawgood, John A. Political and Economic Relations between the United States of America and the German Provisional Central Government at Frankfurt am Main in 1848-1849. Forest Gate, 1928.

Haworth, Paul Leland. "Frederick the Great and the American Revolution", in American Historical Review, vol. IX, no. 1 (Apr. 1904), 460-478.

Hay, John. Letters of John Hay and Extracts from His Diary. 3 vols. Washington, 1908.

Hazen, Charles Downer. Contemporary American Opinion of the French Revolution. Baltimore, 1897.

Hehl, R. A. "Die Entwicklung der Einwanderungsgesetzgebung in Brasilien" in Schriften des Vereins für Sozialpolitik, LXXII. Leipzig, 1896.

Heinz, Georg G. Die Beziehungen zwischen Russland, England und Nordamerika im Jahre 1823. Beiträge zur Genesis der Monroedoktrin. Berlin, 1911.

Hemans, H. W. "Prussia and Germany", in North American Review, vol. 112 (Jan. 1871), 113-159.

Henderson, John Brooks. American Diplomatic Questions. New York, 1901.

Hendrick, Burton Jesse. The Training of an American; the Earlier Life and Letters of Walter H. Page, 1885-1913. Boston, New York, 1928.

Hepner, Adolf, tr. America's Aid to Germany in 1870-1871. An abstract from the official correspondence of E. B. Washburne, U. S. Ambassador to Paris. St. Louis, 1905.

Herrick, Hugh M. William Walter Phelps, His Life and Public Services. New York, 1904.

Heusinger, Otto. Amerikanische Kriegsbilder. Aufzeichnungen aus den Jahren 1861-1865. Leipzig, 1869.

Hiestand, Henry. Travels in Germany, Prussia and Switzerland . . . New York, 1837.

Hildt, John C. Early Diplomatic Negotiations of the United States with Russia. Baltimore, 1906.

Hill, Charles Edward. Leading American Treaties. New York, 1922.

Hirst, Francis W. Life and Letters of Thomas Jefferson. New York, 1926.

History Circle. British-American Discords and Concords; a Record of Three Centuries. New York, London, 1918.

Hoche, Jules. The Real Bismarck. New York, 1898.

Hofmann, Hermann. Fürst Bismarck 1890-1898 . . . 3 vols. in 2. Stuttgart, Berlin, 1922.

Hohlfeld, Alexander R. Der Einfluss deutscher Universitätsideale auf Amerika . . . Philadelphia, 1904.

Holmes, Oliver Wendell. Ralph Waldo Emerson, John Lothrop Motley; Two Memoirs. Boston, New York, 1906.

Holst, Hermann. Verfassung und Demokratie der Vereinigten Staaten von Amerika. 3 vols. T. I. Düsseldorf, 1873-81.

——, Die Verfassungsgeschichte der Vereinigten Staaten von Amerika seit der Administration Jacksons. 4 vols. Berlin, 1878-91.

Howe, Mark Antony De Wolfe. The Life and Letters of George Bancroft. 2 vols. New York, 1908.

Hübener, Erhard. Die deutsche Wirtschaftskrisis von 1873. Berlin, 1905.

Hundert Jahre amerikanisches Generalkonsulat in Frankfurt am Main 1829-1929. Frankfort on the Main, 1929.

Hundert Jahre Deutschtum in Rio Grande do Sul. 1824-1924. Hrsg. vom Verband deutscher Vereine. Porto Alegre, 1924.

Hyde, James Hazen. Les États-Unis et la France; les relations historiques franco-américaines (1776-1912). Paris, 1913.

Hyde de Neuville, Guillaume baron de. Mémoires et souvenirs. 3 vols. Paris, 1888-92.

Ide, Henry C. "The Imbroglio in Samoa", in North American Review, vol. 168 (June 1899), 679-693.

Isham, Charles. The Fishery Question; Its Origin, History and Present Situation. New York, London, 1887.

James, Henry, Jr. Transatlantic Sketches. Boston, New York, 1903.

James, William. The Letters of William James, ed. by his son, Henry James. 2 vols. Boston, 1920.

Jay, John. Correspondence and Public Papers of John Jay, ed. by Henry P. Johnston. 4 vols. New York, 1890-93.

Jefferson, Thomas. The Writings of Thomas Jefferson, collected and edited by Paul L. Ford. 10 vols. New York, 1892-99.

Jennings, Walter Wilson. A History of Economic Progress in the United States. New York, 1926.

——, Introduction to American Economic History. New York, 1928.

Johann, König von Sachsen. Briefwechsel König Johanns von Sachsen mit George Ticknor, hrsg. von Johann Georg Herzog zu Sachsen im Verein mit E. Daenell. Leipzig, Berlin, 1920.

Johnson, Emory Richard, and others. History of Domestic and Foreign Commerce of the United States. 2 vols. Washington, 1915.

Johnson, Willis Fletcher. America's Foreign Relations. 2 vols. New York, 1916.

Johnston, Alexander. American Political History 1763-1876. 2 vols. New York, London, 1905.

Johnston, Mary. Pioneers of the Old South; a Chronicle of English Colonial Beginnings. New Haven, 1921.

Jones, Howard Mumford. American and French Culture, 1750-1848. Chapel Hill, London, 1927.

Jordan, Donaldson, and Edwin J. Pratt. Europe and the American Civil War. Boston, New York, 1931.

Joseephy, Fritz. Die deutsche überseeische Auswanderung seit 1871 . . . Berlin, 1912.

Kapp, Friedrich. Aus und über Amerika. Tatsachen und Erlebnisse. 2 vols. Berlin, 1876.

——, "Der deutsch-amerikanische Vertrag vom 22. Februar 1868", in Preussiche Jahrbücher, vol. XXXVI, 1875.

——, Die Deutschen im Staate New York während des achtzehnten Jahrhunderts. New York, 1884.

——, European Emigration to the United States. A Paper Read Before the American Social Science Association at New York, October 27, 1869. New York, 1869.

——, Friedrich der Grosse und die Vereinigten Staaten von Amerika, mit einem Anhang: die Vereinigten Staaten und das Seekriegsrecht. Leipzig, 1871.

——, Leben des amerikanischen Generals Friedrich Wilhelm von Steuben. Berlin, 1858.

——, Life of John Kalb, Major-General in the Revolutionary Army. New York, 1884.

——, Life of Frederick William von Steuben, Major General in the Revolutionary Army. New York, 1859.

——, Der Soldatenhandel deutscher Fürsten nach Amerika. Ein Beitrag zur Kulturgeschichte des achtzehnten Jahrhunderts. 2. verm. und umgearb. Berlin, 1874.

Kasson, John A. "The Hohenzollern Kaiser", in North American Review, vol. 146 (Apr. 1888), 361-378.

——, "Otto von Bismarck", in North American Review, vol. 143 (Aug. 1886), 105-118.

Kaufmann, Wilhelm. Die Deutschen im amerikanischen Bürgerkriege. Sezessionskrieg 1861-1865. Munich, Berlin, 1911.

Keim, Jeanette. Forty Years of German-American Political Relations. Philadelphia, 1919.

Keith, Arthur Berriedale. Selected Speeches and Documents on British Colonial Policy 1763-1917. 2 vols. Oxford, 1918.

Keudell, Robert von. Fürst und Fürstin Bismarck. Erinnerungen aus den Jahren 1846-1872. Berlin, Stuttgart, 1901.

Keyserling, Graf Alexander. Ein Lebensbild aus seinen Briefen und Tagebüchern. Zusammengestellt von seiner Tochter, Freifrau Helene von Taube von der Issen. 2 vols. Berlin, 1902.

Kingsford, William. The History of Canada 1608-1841. 10 vols. London, 1887-98.

Koerner, Gustav Philipp. Das deutsche Element in den Vereinigten Staaten von Nordamerika, 1818-1848. Cincinnati, 1880.

——, Memoirs of Gutave Koerner, 1809-1896, Life-sketches Written at the Suggestion of His Children; ed. by Thomas J. McCormack. 2 vols. Cedar Rapids, 1909.

Kohler, Max James. An Important European Mission to Investigate American Immigration Conditions and John Quincy Adams' Relation Thereto (1817-1818). Chicago, 1919.

Krauel, Richard. Deutsche Interessen in Brasilien. Hamburg, 1900.

——, "Prince Henry of Prussia and the Regency of the United States, 1786", in American Historical Review, vol. XVII, no. 1 (Oct. 1911), 44-51.

Kraus, Herbert. Die Monroedoktrin in ihren Beziehungen zur amerikanischen Diplomatie und zum Völkerrecht. Berlin, 1913.

Krause, William E. The German-French War of 1870 and Its Consequences upon Future Civilization. San Francisco, 1872.

Kunz-Lack, Ilse. Die deutsch-amerikanischen Beziehungen von 1890 bis 1914. Stuttgart, 1935.

Lammers, A. "Reform des Seekriegsrechts", in Preussische Jahrbücher, vol. 26. Berlin, 1870.

Langenbeck, Wilhelm. Geschichte des deutschen Handels seit dem Ausgang des Mittelalters. Aus Natur und Geisteswelt 237. Leipzig, 1909.

Larned, Josephus Nelson. The Literature of American History. A Bibliographical Guide . . . Edited for the American Library Association. Boston, 1902.

Latané, John Holladay. America as a World Power, 1897-1907. New York, 1907.

——, The Diplomatic Relations of the United States and Spanish-America. Baltimore, 1900.

——, A History of American Foreign Policy. New York, 1927.

——, The United States and Latin America. Garden City, 1920.

Learned, Marion Dexter. Guide to the Manuscript Materials Relating to American History in the German State Archives. Washington, 1912.

Leusser, Hermann. Ein Jahrzehnt deutsch-amerikanischer Politik (1897-1906). Beiheft 13 der Historischen Zeitschrift. Munich, Berlin, 1928.

Lieber, Francis. Letters to a Gentleman in Germany, Written after a Trip from Philadelphia to Niagara. Ed. by Francis Lieber. Philadelphia, 1834.

——, The Life and Letters of Francis Lieber. Ed. by Thomas Sergeant Perry, Boston, 1882.

——, The Stranger in America . . . Sketches of Manners, Society and National Peculiarities of the United States. London, 1835.

Lingley, Charles Ramsdell. Since the Civil War. 2d ed. New York, 1926.

Litchfield, Henry Percy. The Franco-German War of 1870. Gracehill, 1872.

Lodge, Henry Cabot. One Hundred Years of Peace. New York, 1913.

Lodge, Sir Richard. Great Britain and Prussia in the Eighteenth Century. Oxford, 1923.

Loë, Freiherr von. Erinnerungen aus meinem Berufsleben 1849 bis 1867. Stuttgart, Leipzig, 1906.

Loftus, Lord Augustus William. The Diplomatic Reminiscences of Lord Augustus Loftus 1862-1879. 2d series, 2 vols. London, 1894.

The London Index. 1861-65.

Longfellow, Henry Wadsworth. Life of Henry Wadsworth Longfellow, ed. by Samuel Longfellow. 3 vols. London, 1886-87.

Lord, John. Two German Giants: Frederick the Great and Bismarck. The Founder and the Builder of the German Empire. To Which are Added a Character Sketch of Bismarck by Bayard Taylor and Bismarck's Great Speech on the Enlargement of the German Army in 1888. New York, 1894.

Lord, Robert Howard. The Origins of the War of 1870, New Documents from the German Archives. Harvard Historical Studies 28. Cambridge, 1924.

Loring, Nathaniel Hall. Prussia; Its Position and Destiny, Due to Frederic II, the Great . . . New York, 1887.

Lowe, Charles. Prince Bismarck; an Historical Biography. 2 vols. New York, 1886.

Lowell, Edward Jackson. Die Hessen und die anderen deutschen Hilfstruppen im Kriege Grossbritanniens gegen Amerika 1776-1783. Dtsch. hrsg. von Prof. O. C. Verschuer. Brunswick, Leipzig, 1901.

——, The Hessians and the Other German Auxiliaries of Great Britain in the Revolutionary War. New York, 1884.

Lowell, James Russell. Letters of James Russell Lowell, ed. by Charles Eliot Norton. 2 vols. London, 1894.

Loyson, Charles J. M. France and Germany: a Discourse Pronounced at London, Decem. 20, 1870, for the French Relief Fund; by the Reverend Father Hyacinthe. Baltimore, 1871.

Luckwaldt, Friedrich. Der Aufstieg der Vereinigten Staaten zur Weltmacht. Eine Geschichte ihrer Aussenpolitik. Berlin, 1935.

——, Geschichte der Vereinigten Staaten von Amerika. 2 vols. Berlin, Leipzig, 1920.

Lutz, Ralph Haswell. Die Beziehungen zwischen Deutschland und den Vereinigten Staaten während des Sezessionskrieges. Heidelberg, 1911.

——, "Rudolph Schleiden and the Visit to Richmond, April 25, 1861", in the Annual Report of the American Historical Association, 1915, pp. 207-216. Washington, 1917.

Malloy, William, compiler. Treaties, Conventions, International Acts, Protocols, and Agreements between the United States of America and Other Powers. 3 vols. Washington, 1910-23.

Marckes, Theo. von. The Franco-German War . . . Philadelphia, 1870-71.

Marcks, Erich. Bismarck. Eine Biographie. 1 vol. 6th ed. Stuttgart, Berlin, 1909.

——, Erinnerungen an Bismarck. Aufzeichnungen von Freunden und Mitarbeitern des

Fürsten mit einem Anhang von Dokumenten und Briefen in Verbindung mit A. Brauer gesammelt von Erich Marcks und Karl Alexander von Müller. Stuttgart, Berlin, 1915.

Maxwell, Sir Herbert Eustace. The Life and Letters of George William Frederick, Fourth Earl of Clarendon. 2 vols. London, 1913.

May, Arthur James. Contemporary American Opinion of the Mid-century Revolutions in Central Europe. Philadelphia, 1927.

Mayo-Smith, Richmond. Die Einwanderung in die Vereinigten Staaten von Amerika. Schriften des Vereins für Sozialpolitik LXXII. Leipzig, 1896.

McCabe, James Dabney. History of the War between Germany and France . . . Philadelphia, 1871.

McCrane, R. C. "American Position in the German Revolution of 1848", in The Historical Outlook, vol. XI, no. 9 (Dec. 1920).

McElroy, Robert McNutt. Grover Cleveland, the Man and the Statesman, an Authorized Biography. 2 vols. New York, 1923.

McMaster, John Bach. History of the People of the U. S. from the Revolution to the Civil War. 8 vols. New York, 1883-1913.

Meyer, Hildegard. Nordamerika im Urteil des deutschen Schrifttums bis zur Mitte des 19. Jahrhunderts eine Untersuchung über Kürnbergers "Amerika-müden", mit einer Bibliographie. (Übersee-Geschichte III.) Hamburg, 1929.

Meyer, Richard. Die Ursachen der amerikanischen Konkurrenz. Ergebnisse einer österreichisch-ungarischen Studienreise. Berlin, 1883.

Miller, Hunter. Treaties and Other International Acts of the United States of America. Vols. 1-4. Washington, 1931–34.

Mills, Joseph Travis. Great Britain and the United States; a Critical Review of Their Historical Relations. London, New York, 1920.

Mitchel, John. Ireland, France, and Prussia, a Selection from the Speeches of John Mitchel. London, 1918.

Moore, John Bassett. American Diplomacy, Its Spirit and Achievements. New York, London, 1905.

——, A Digest of International Law. 8 vols. Washington, 1906.

Morley, John M. The Life of William Ewart Gladstone. 3 vols. New York, London, 1913.

Morris, Gouverneur R. The Diary and Letters of Gouverneur Morris . . . Ed. by Anne Cary Morris. 2 vols. New York, 1888.

Mosher, Robert Brent, compiler. Executive Register of the United States, 1789-1902 . . . Baltimore, 1903.

Motley, John Lothrop. Der Abfall der Niederlande und die Entstehung als holländischer Freistaat. Aus dem Engl. 3 vols. Dresden, 1858.

——, Briefwechsel von John Lothrop Motley. Aus dem Engl. übersetzt von A. Eltze. 2 vols. Berlin, 1890.

——, The Causes of the American Civil War. A Letter to London Times. New York, 1861.

——, The Correspondence of John Lothrop Motley, ed. by George William Curtis. 2 vols. New York, 1889.

——, Historic Progress and American Democracy: An Address Delivered Before the New York Historical Society. . . . December 16, 1868. New York, 1869.

——, History of the United Netherlands: From the Death of William the Silent to the Twelve Years' Truce—1609. 4 vols. New York, 1861-68.

——, John Lothrop Motley and His Family; Further Letters and Records, ed. by His Daughter and Herbert St. John Mildmay. London, New York, 1910.

——, Peter the Great. New York, 1877.

——, The Rise of the Dutch Republic. A History. 3 vols. New York, 1856.

——, The Writings of John Lothrop Motley. Netherlands ed., 17 vols. New York, London, 1900.

Mowat, Robert Balmain. The Diplomatic Relations of Great Britain and the United States. New York, London, 1925.

Munde, Charles. The Bancroft Naturalization Treaties with the German States, Being a Collection of Documents and Opinions Relating to the Subject. An Appeal to the German-American Citizens. Würzburg, 1868.

Muzzey, David Saville. The American Adventure. 2 vols. New York, London, 1927.

Nearing, Scott, and Joseph Freeman. Dollar Diplomacy; a Study in American Imperialism. New York, 1925.

——, Dollar-Diplomatie. Eine Studie über amerikanischen Imperialismus. Übers. von Paul Fohr, Geleitwort von Karl Haushofer. Berlin-Grunewald, 1927.

Neuhaus, Georg. Deutsche Weltwirtschaftsgeschichte im neunzehnten Jahrhundert. Munich, 1907.

Nevins, Allan. Henry White, Thirty Years of American Diplomacy. New York, London, 1930.

Newton, Thomas Wodehouse Legh. Lord Lyons; a Record of British Diplomacy. 2 vols. London, 1913.

Nimmo, Joseph. The Production of Swine in the United States . . . Quarterly Report of the Bureau of Statistics on the Foreign Commerce . . . 1883 Suppl. Washington, 1884.

North, William. Memoir of the Baron von Steuben. Deutschamerikanische Geschichtsblätter. Jahrbuch der deutschamerikanischen historischen Gesellschaft in Illinois. Hrsg. von Julius Goebel. 1929 (vol. XXIX). Chicago, 1929.

Nouette-Delorme, Émile. Les États-Unis et l'Europe; rupture de l'union, reconnaissance du Sud, abolition de l'esclavage. Paris, 1863.

Oberholtzer, Ellis Paxson. Jay Cooke, Financier of the Civil War. 2 vols. Philadelphia, 1907.

Obermüller, Julius. Samoa. Zur Geschichte der deutschen Kolonien in der Südsee mit besonderer Rücksicht auf die Kämpfe um dieselben und die Ereignisse von 1888-1889, nach Quellen. Leipzig, 1889.

Ollivier, Émile. L'empire libéral; études, récits, souvenirs. 18 vols. Paris, 1895-1918.

——, The Franco-Prussian War and Its Hidden Causes. Trans. from the French, with an Introduction and Notes by George Burnham Ives. Boston, 1912.

Oncken, Hermann. Amerika und die grossen Mächte. Eine Studie über die Epoche des amerikanischen Imperialismus. Studien und Versuche in neuerer Geschichte. Max Lenz gewidmet. Berlin, 1910.

——, Die deutsche Auswanderung nach Amerika und das Deutschamerikanertum vom 17. Jahrhundert bis zur Gegenwart (1911). Historisch-politische Aufsätze und Reden I. Munich, Berlin, 1914.

——, "Der Kampf um die Einheit in Deutschland und in den Vereinigten Staaten von Amerika", in Die Glocke (Chicago), vol. I, 1906.

——, Die Rheinpolitik Kaiser Napoleons III. von 1863-1870 und der Ursprung des Krieges von 1870-71; nach den Staatsakten von Österreich, Preussen und den Süddeutschen Mittelstaaten. 3 vols. Stuttgart, 1926.

Owsley, Frank Lawrence. King Cotton Diplomacy. Foreign Relations of the Confederate States of America. Chicago, 1931.

Paasche, H. Über die wachsende Konkurrenz Nordamerikas für die Produkte der mitteleuropäischen Landwirtschaft. Jahrb. für Nationalökonomie und Statistik. Vol. 33. Hrsg. von Johannes Conrad. Jena, 1879.

Parsons, Frank. The Story of New Zealand; a History of New Zealand from the Earliest Times to the Present. Ed. by C. F. Taylor. Philadelphia, 1904.

Paullin, Charles Oscar. Diplomatic Negotiations of American Naval Officers 1778-1883. The Albert Shaw Lectures on Diplomatic History. 1911. Baltimore, 1912.

Peez, Alexander von. Die amerikanische Konkurrenz. Vienna, 1881.

Penzler, Johannes. Bismarck und die Hamburger Nachrichten I. Geschichte des Fürsten Bismarck in Einzeldarstellungen. Vol. XIII. Berlin, 1907.

——, Fürst Bismarck nach seiner Entlassung. Leben und Politik des Fürsten seit seinem Scheiden aus dem Amte auf Grund aller authentischen Kundgebungen. 7 vols. Leipzig, 1897-98.

Perkins, Dexter. The Monroe Doctrine, 1823-1826. Harvard Historical Studies 29. Cambridge, 1927.

——, The Monroe Doctrine, 1826-1867. Baltimore, 1933.

Persigny, Jean de. Mémoires du duc de Persigny. Publiés avec des documents inédits, un avant-propos et un épilogue par M. H. de Laire, comte D'Espagny, anc. secrétaire intime du duc, orné d'un portrait de l'auteur. Paris, 1896.

Pfeffer, Karl H. England im Urteil der amerikanischen Literatur vor dem Bürgerkrieg. Leipzig, 1931.

Philippovich von Philippsberg, Eugen v. Auswanderung und Auswanderungspolitik in Deutschland . . . Schriften des Vereins für Sozialpolitik LXXII. Leipzig, 1896.

Pierce, Edward Lillie. Memoirs and Letters of Charles Sumner. 4 vols. Boston, 1877-93.

Pohle, Ludwig. Die Entwicklung des deutschen Wirtschaftslebens im 19. Jahrhundert. Leipzig, 1908.

Pollard, Edward Albert. Life of Jefferson Davis with a Secret History of the Southern Confederacy . . . Philadelphia, 1869.

Poole, William Frederick. An Index to Periodical Literature. 3d ed. with assistance of William I. Fletcher. Boston, 1882. 5 Supp. 1888-1908.

Poore, Benjamin Perley. A Descriptive Catalogue of the Government Publications of the United States, September 5, 1774-March 4, 1881, Compiled by Order of Congress. Washington, 1885.

——, The Life and Public Services of Ambrose E. Burnside, Soldier,—Citizen,—Statesman. Providence, 1882.

Poschinger, Heinrich v. Aktenstücke zur Wirtschaftspolitik des Fürsten Bismarck. Berlin, 1890.

——, Bismarck-Portefeuille. Stuttgart, Leipzig, 1898, 1900.

——, Fürst Bismarck als Volkswirt. Dokumente zur Geschichte der Wirtschaftspolitik in Preussen und im Deutschen Reich. 3 vols. Berlin, 1889-91.

——, Fürst Bismarck und der Bundesrat. 5 vols. Stuttgart, Leipzig, 1897-1901.

——, Fürst Bismarck und die Diplomaten 1852-1890. Hamburg, 1900.

——, Fürst Bismarck und die Parlamentarier. 3 vols. Breslau, 1894-95.

——, Fürst Bismarck, neue Tischgespräche und Interviews. Stuttgart, Leipzig, 1895-98.

——, Neues Bismarck-Jahrbuch, vol. I. Vienna, 1911.

——, Die wirtschaftlichen Verträge Deutschlands. 2 vols. Die deutschen Handels- und Schiffahrtsverträge. Berlin, 1892.

Powers, Harry Huntington. America and Britain; the History of the Relations between Two Peoples. New York, 1918.

Prager, Ludwig. Die Handelsbeziehungen des Deutschen Reiches mit den V. St. v. A. bis zum Ausbruch des Weltkrieges im Jahre 1914. Dazu einen Nachtrag über d. Entwicklung der Verhältnisse in der Nachkriegszeit bis 1924. Eine kritisch-historische Wirtschaftsstudie. Weimar, 1926.

Prenzler, ——. Jugendgeschichte des Fürsten Bismarck.

Quellen zur Geschichte von Hamburgs Handel und Schiffahrt im 17., 18. und 19. Jahrhundert. Hrsg. von E. Baasch. Hamburg, 1910.

Randon, Jacques. Mémoires du Maréchal Randon. 2 vols. Paris, 1875-77.

Raschdau, L. Meine ersten dienstlichen Beziehungen zu Fürst Bismarck.

Rathgen, Karl. Englische Auswanderung und Auswanderungspolitik im neunzehnten Jahrhundert. Schriften des Vereins für Sozialpolitik LXXII. Leipzig, 1896.

Ratschläge für Auswanderer nach Süd-Brasilien . . . herausgegeben von Dr. Robert Jannasch, unter Mitwirkung von Karl Koseritz, 4, umgearb. und vermehrte Aufl. Berlin, 1898.

Rattermann, Heinrich Armin. Gustav Körner, deutschamerikanischer Jurist, Staatsmann, Diplomat und Geschichtsschrieber . . . Separatdruck aus dem 11. Vol. der gesammelten Werke. Cincinnati, 1902.

Rauers, Friedrich. Bremer Handelsgeschichte im 19. Jahrhundert. Bremer Handelsstatistik vor dem Beginn der öffentlichen administrativen Statistik in der 1. Hälfte des 19. Jahrhunderts. Hrsg. vom Bremer Statist. Amt. Bremen, 1913.

Ravold, Jean Baptiste. Français et Allemands aux États-Unis d'Amérique pendant l'année terrible (1870). Conférence fait à Gerbévillier le 14 Juillet 1883. Nancy, 1884.

Raymond, Mrs. Dora Neill. British Policy and Opinion During the Franco-Prussian War. New York, 1921.

Readers' Guide to Periodical Literature 1901 to date.

Reddaway, William Fiddian. Frederick the Great and the Rise of Prussia. New York, London, 1904.

——, The Monroe Doctrine. Cambridge, England, 1898.

Reimann, Eduard. Neuere Geschichte des preussischen Staates. 2 vols. Gotha, 1888.

Rein, Adolf. Der Kampf Westeuropas um Nordamerika im 15. und 16. Jahrhundert. Stuttgart, Gotha, 1925.

Remont, B. S. L'Union Américaine et l'Europe. Paris, 1861.

Reuter, Bertha Ann. Anglo-American Relations During the Spanish-American War. New York, 1924.

Reventlow, Graf Ernst zu. Deutschlands auswärtige Politik 1888-1914. 4th ed. Berlin, 1916.

Rheindorf, Kurt. England und der Deutsch-Französische Krieg 1870-71 . . . Bonn, Leipzig, 1923.

——, Die Schwarze-Meer- (Pontus-) Frage vom Pariser Frieden von 1856 bis zum Abschluss der Londoner Konferenz von 1871 . . . Berlin, 1925.

Rhodes, James Ford. History of the Civil War, 1861-1865. New York, 1917.

——, History of the United States from the Compromise of 1850. 4 vols. New York, 1895-99.

Rice, Allen Thorndike, ed. Essays from North American Review. New York, 1879.

Richardson, James Daniel. A Compilation of the Messages and Papers of the Confederacy Including the Diplomatic Correspondence, 1861-1865. 2 vols. Nashville, 1905.

——, A Compilation of the Messages and Papers of the Presidency, 1789-1897. Published by authority of Congress. 10 vols. Washington, 1866-99.

Rippy, James Fred. The United States and Mexico. New York, 1926.

Ritter, Gerhard. Bismarcks Verhältnis zu England und die Politik des "neuen Kurses." Berlin, 1924.

Rittner-Lübeck. Die Landwirtschaft in den Vereinigten Staaten von Amerika. Das Ausland 1889, nos. 34 and 35.

Robertson, Sir Charles Grant. Bismarck. New York, 1919.

Romero, Matias. "The Fall of the Second Empire as related to the French Intervention in Mexico", in the Century Magazine, vol. 54, no. 1 (May 1897), 138-139.

Roosevelt, Nicholas. The Restless Pacific. New York, London, 1928.

Roosevelt, Theodore. Theodore Roosevelt: an Autobiography. New York, 1919.

Roscher, Wilhelm, and Robert Jannasch. Kolonien, Kolonialpolitik und Auswanderung. Leipzig, 1885.

Rosengarten, Joseph George. Frederick the Great and the United States. A Paper Read before the Pennsylvania German Society at the Annual Meeting . . . 1904. Lancaster, 1906.

——, The German Soldier in the Wars of the United States. Philadelphia, 1886. 2d ed. rev. and enl., 1890.

——, Sources of History, a Paper Read before the German-American Historical Society of New York and the Pionierverein of Philadelphia. Philadelphia, 1892.

Rothan, G. Les origines de la guerre de 1870. Paris, 1879.

Rothfels, Hans. Bismarcks englische Bündnispolitik. Stuttgart, Berlin, Leipzig, 1924.

Rowe, Newton Allan. Samoa under the Sailing Gods. London, New York, 1930.

Russell, Lord John. The Later Correspondence of Lord John Russell, 1840-1878; ed. by G. P. Gooch. 2 vols. London, New York, 1925.

——, Recollections and Suggestions, 1813-73. London, Boston, 1875.

Ruville, Albert von. William Pitt Graf von Chatham. 3 vols. Stuttgart, Berlin, 1905.

Ryden, George Herbert. Foreign Policy of the United States in Relation to Samoa. New Haven, 1933.

Salomon, Felix. Britischer Imperialismus von 1871 bis zur Gegenwart. Leipzig, 1917.

——, Englische Geschichte von den Anfängen bis zur Gegenwart. Leipzig, 1923.

Samoa unter deutscher Herrschaft. Globus vol. 80, 1901, no. 4. Brunswick, 1901.

Sartorius von Waltershausen, August Freiherr. Das deutsche Einfuhrverbot amerikanischen Schweinefleisches. Jena, 1884.

——, Deutsche Wirtschaftsgeschichte, 1815-1914. 2. ergänzte Aufl. Jena, 1923.

——, Deutschland und die Handelspolitik der Vereinigten Staaten von Amerika. Schriften der Zentralstelle für Vorbereitung von Handelsverträgen. Berlin, 1898.

Sass, Johann. Die deutschen Weissbücher zur auswärtigen Politik, 1870-1914 . . . Berlin, Leipzig, 1928.

Savidge, Eugene Coleman. The American in Paris; a Biographical Novel of the Franco-Prussian War; the Siege and Commune of Paris, from an American Standpoint. Philadelphia, 1896.

Spiegel, Käthe. Kulturgeschichtliche Grundlagen der amerikanischen Revolution. Beiheft 21 der Historischen Zeitschrift. Munich, Berlin, 1931.

Staatsarchiv, Das. Sammlung der offiziellen Aktenstücke zur Geschichte der Gegenwart. 86 vols. Hamburg sp. Leipzig, 1861-1919.

Stanton, Theodore. General Grant and the French. Extracted from "The Cornell Magazine", October 1889. Paris (?), 1891.

Staudinger, Julius von. Sammlung von Staatsverträgen des Deutschen Reiches über Gegenstände der Rechtspflege . . . vol. 1. Munich, 1895.

Stearns, Frank Preston. The Life of Prince Otto von Bismarck. Philadelphia, 1899.

Stevenson, Robert Louis. A Footnote to History. Eight Years of Trouble in Samoa. New York, 1897.

Stillman, William James. The Autobiography of a Journalist. 2 vols. Boston, New York, 1901.

Stöcklin, Jules. Les colonies et l'émigration allemande . . . avec préface par R. Postel. Paris, 1888.

Stolberg-Wernigerode, Otto Graf zu. "Bismarck and His American Friends", in Virginia Quarterly Review, July 1929.

——, "Die Deutschen und die Amerikanischen Einigungskämpfe und die Presse", in Festschrift of the Zeitungsverlag, 1931.

——, "Unbekannte Gespräche mit Bismarck", in Süddeutsche Monatshefte, Feb. 1930.

Stone, William Leete, trans. Letters of Brunswick and Hessian Officers during the American Revolution. Albany, 1891.

Straus, Oscar Solomon. The United States and Russia: Their Historical Relations. New York (?), 1905.

Stuhlmacher, Walter. Bismarcks Kolonialpolitik nach den Aktenveröffentlichungen des Auswärtigen Amtes. Halle (Saale), 1927.

Sturz, Johann Jakob. Suggestions for the Encouragement of Emigration by Theoretical, Financial and Practical Means. Washington, 1866.

Sumner, Charles. The Duel between France and Germany, with Its Lesson to Civilization. Lecture by Hon. Charles Sumner. Boston, 1870.

——, Our Foreign Relations: Showing Present Perils from England and France . . . Speech of Hon. Charles Sumner, before the Citizens of New York, at the Cooper Institute, Sept. 10, 1863. New York, 1863.

——, The Works of Charles Sumner. 15 vols. Boston, 1870-83.

Tansill, Charles Cellan. The Purchase of the Danish West Indies. Baltimore, London, 1932.

Tardieu, André Pierre. France and America; Some Experiences in Cooperation. Boston, New York, 1927.

Taylor, Bayard. Life and Letters of Bayard Taylor. Ed. by Marie Hansen Taylor and Horace E. Scudder. 2 vols. Boston, 1884.

——, "Weimar in June", in Atlantic Monthly, vol. 39, no. 231 (Jan. 1877), 61-69.

Taylor, Marie Hansen. Aus zwei Weltteilen; Erinnerungen von Marie Hansen-Taylor . . . mit bildnissen von Bayard Taylor und Marie Hansen-Taylor. Stuttgart, Leipzig, 1905.

Thayer, William Roscoe. The Life and Letters of John Hay. 2 vols. Boston, New York, 1915.

Théry, Edmond. . . . 1890-1900. Histoire économique de l'Angleterre, de l'Allemagne, des États-Unis et de la France. Paris, 1902.

Thornton, Percy Melville. Foreign Secretaries of the XIX. Century to 1834. 2d ed. 3 vols. London, 1881-83.

Thouvenel, Louis. Pages de l'histoire du second empire d'après les papiers de M. Thouvenel, ancien ministre des affaires étrangères (1854-1866). Paris, 1903.

Thwing, Charles Franklin. The American and the German University. One Hundred Years of History. New York, 1928.

——, A History of Education in the United States since the Civil War. Boston, New York, Chicago, 1910.

Ticknor, George. Life, Letters and Journals of George Ticknor. 2 vols. New York, 1909.

Tonnelat, Ernest. L'expansion allemande hors d'Europe. États-Unis—Brésil—Chantoung—Afrique du Sud. Paris, 1908.

Townsend, Mary Evelyn. Origins of Modern German Colonialism, 1871-1885. Columbia University Studies in History, Economics, and Public Law. Vol. 98, no. 1; whole no. 223. New York, 1921.

——, The Rise and Fall of Germany's Colonial Empire, 1884-1918. New York, 1930.

Tuttle, Herbert. "The German Empire", in Harpers' New Monthly Magazine, vol. 63.

Tyler, Alice Felt. The Foreign Policy of James G. Blaine. Minneapolis, 1927.

Tyler, Lyon G. England in America, 1580-1652. New York, London, 1904.

United States. Congress. American State Papers, Class I: Foreign Relations 1789-1828. 6 vols.

——, ——, Congressional Documents Published by the United States Congress. Washington, 1870-1910.

——, ——, The Congressional Globe . . . 23d Cong. to the 42d Cong. Dec. 2, 1833, to Mar. 3, 1873. 46 vols. Washington, 1834-73.

——, ——, Congressional Record 1873 to date.

——, ——, Joint Committee on Printing. Biographical Directory of the American Congress 1774-1927. Washington, 1928.

——, Department of Agriculture. Bureau of Animal Industry. D. E. Salmon, Chief. Bulletin No. 30. Trichinosis in Germany. Washington, 1901.

——, Department of Commerce. Bureau of Foreign Commerce. Commercial Relations of the United States with Foreign Countries. Washington, 1855-1908.

——, ——, Consular Reports from the Consuls of the United States on the Commerce, Manufactures, etc., of Their Consular Districts. Washington, 1880-1903.

——, Department of State. Correspondence Concerning the Claims Against Great Britain . . . 7 vols. Washington, 1869-71.

——, ——, Diplomatic Correspondence, 1783-1789. 7 vols.

——, ——, Diplomatic Correspondence, 1861-1868 (no volume for 1869).

——, ——, Papers Relating to the Foreign Relations of the United States, 1870-1921. Washington, 1870-1937.

——, ——, Report of the Secretary of State, with Accompanying Correspondence in Relation to the Proposed Interoceanic Canal between the Atlantic and Pacific Oceans. Transmitted to the Senate in Obedience to a Resolution. Sen. Ex. Doc. 112, 46th Cong., 2d sess. Washington, 1880.

——, ——, Bureau of Rolls and Library. Documentary History of the Constitution of the United States of America, 1787-1870. Washington, 1894-1905.

——, House of Representatives. American Rights in Samoa. Message of the President of the United States with Enclosures in Response to the Resolution of the House of

Representatives in Relation to the Affairs in Samoa. House Ex. Doc. 238, 50th Cong., 1st sess., 1888.

——, Library of Congress. Legislative Reference Service. Documents Illustrative of the Formation of the Union of the American States. House Doc. 398, 69th Cong., 1st sess. Washington, 1927.

——, Navy Department. Official Records of the Union and Confederate Navies in the War of the Rebellion. Series II, vol. 3. Washington.

——, Senate. Documents Relating to the Interoceanic Canal. Sen. Doc. 357, 57th Cong., 1st sess. Serial 4245. Washington, 1902.

——, ——, Immigration Commission, 1907-1910. Statistical Review of Immigration, 1820-1910. Distribution of Immigrants, 1850-1900. Sen. Doc. 756, 61st Cong., 3d sess. Washington, 1911.

——, ——, Swine Products of the United States. Sen. Report 345, 48th Cong., 2d sess., March 19, 1885.

——, ——, Committee on Foreign Relations. Compilation of Reports of Committee on Foreign Relations, United States Senate, 1789-1901. 8 vols. Washington. Government Printing Office, 1901.

——, ——, Select Committee to Inquire into the Sale of Arms. Report and Testimony. Washington, 1872.

——, Superintendent of Documents. Checklist of United States Public Documents 1789-1909 . . . Washington, 1911.

——, ——, Document Catalogue 1893 to date.

——, Treasury Department, Bureau of Statistics. Statistical Abstract of the United States, 1889. Washington, 1890.

Vagts, Alfred. Mexiko, Europa und Amerika unter bes. Berücksichtigung der Petroleumpolitik. Eine Wirtschaftl. diplomatische Untersuchung. Berlin-Grunewald, 1928.

Van Tyne, Claude Halstead. The Causes of the War of Independence, Being the First Volume of a History of the Founding of the American Republic. Boston, New York, 1922.

Victoria, Queen of Great Britain. The Letters of Queen Victoria, a Selection from Her Majesty's Correspondence between the Years 1837 and 1861. Ed. by Arthur Christopher Benson, M. A., and Viscount Esher. 3 vols. New York, 1907.

——, The Letters of Queen Victoria. Second Series. A Selection from Her Majesty's Correspondence and Journal between the Years 1862 and 1878, ed. by George Earl Buckle. 3 vols. London, 1926-28.

Victory, Beatrice Marguerite. Benjamin Franklin and Germany. Ph.D. Thesis. Americana-Germanica No. 21. University of Pennsylvania, 1915.

Villard, Henry. Lebenserinnerungen. Berlin, 1906.

——, "Political Career of Karl Otto von Bismarck-Schönhausen", in North American Review, vol. 108 (1869), 165-221.

Villate, Achille. Economic Imperialism and International Relations During the Last Fifty Years. New York, 1923.

Vocke, William. The Relations of the People of the United States to the English and the Germans. Chicago (189-?).

Wagner, N. Die Vorgänge auf den Samoa-Inseln. Dargestellt mit besonderer Berücksichtigung der veröffentlichten deutschen amtlichen Aktenstücke. Hrsg. von d. Abt. Graudenz der deutschen Kolonialgesellschaft. Graudenz, 1889.

Walker, Robert James. American Slavery and Finances. (3d ed., with appendix.) 9 vols. London, 1864.

——, An Appeal for the Union. Letter from the Hon. Robert J. Walker, New York, Tuesday, Sept. 30, 1856, to Hon. Charles Shaler and others, Democratic Committee, Pittsburgh, Pennsylvania. New York, 1856.

——, Letter of Hon. R. J. Walker, in Favor of the Reelection of Abraham Lincoln. London, Sept. 30, 1864. New York, 1864.

——, Our National Finances. Letter of Hon. Robt. J. Walker, Ex-Secretary of the Treasury. Washington, 1867.

Walter, Rudolf. Deutschland und die Vereinigten Staaten in ihrem gegenseitigen Warenverkehr seit der Wende dieses Jahrhunderts. Greifswald, 1921.

Wappäus, Johann Eduard. Deutsche Auswanderung und Kolonisation. Leipzig 1846.

Washburne, Elihu Benjamin. Franco-Prussian War and the Insurrection of the Commune. Washington, 1878.

——, Recollections of a Minister to France, 1869-1877. 2 vols. New York, 1887.

Washington, George. The Writings of George Washington, Being His Correspondence, Addresses, Messages, and Other Papers, Official and Private, Selected and Published from the Original Manuscripts, with a Life of the Author, Notes, and Illustrations, by Jared Sparks. 12 vols. Boston, 1838-39.

Wätjen, Hermann. Aus der Frühzeit des Nordatlantikverkehrs. Studien zur Geschichte der deutschen Schiffahrt und deutschen Auswanderung nach den Vereinigten Staaten bis zum Ende des amerikanischen Bürgerkriegs. Leipzig, 1932.

Weber, Paul Carl. America in the Imaginative German Literature in the First Half of the Nineteenth Century. New York, 1926.

Webster, Charles Kingsley. The Foreign Policy of Castlereagh, 1815-1822, Britain and the European Alliance. London, 1925.

Webster, Daniel. The Letters of Daniel Webster . . . ed. by C. H. Van Tyne. New York, 1902.

——, The Writings and Speeches of Daniel Webster. 18 vols. National edition. Boston, 1903.

Wendte, Charles William. America and Germany, Their Mutual Relations. Boston, 1910.

Werner, B. von. "Die erste Kreuzung deutscher und amerikanischer Interessen auf Samoa" in Unsere Zeit, 1889, vol. I, part 2.

West, Warren Reed. Contemporary French Opinion on the American Civil War. Baltimore, 1924.

Westphal, Ernst. Bismarck als Gutsherr. Leipzig, 1922.

Wharton, Francis. The Revolutionary Diplomatic Correspondence of the United States. Edited under direction of Congress . . . 6 vols. Washington, 1889.

White, Andrew Dickson. Address at the Funeral of Edward Lasker. Ithaca, 1884.

——, Aus meinem Diplomatenleben. Übers. von H. Mordannt. Leipzig, 1906.

——, Autobiography of Andrew Dickson White. 2 vols. New York, 1905.

——, A Fourth Series of Lectures on Modern History. The Greater States of Continental Europe. Ithaca, 1874.

——, The New Germany. Bulletin of the American Geographical Society, No. 4. New York, 1882.

——, The President of the United States. Address. Leipzig, 1898.

——, Seven Great Statesmen, in the Warfare of Humanity with Unreason. New York, 1910.

White, Elizabeth Brett. American Opinion of France from Lafayette to Poincaré. New York, 1927.

Whiteman, Sidney. Personal Reminiscences of Prince Bismarck. New York, 1903.

——, Teutonic Studies. London, 1895.

Wilkens, Frederick H. "Early Influence of German Literature in America", in Americana Germanica, vol. III, no. 2, 103-205.

William, James. Gesandter d. Vereinigten Staaten bei der Pforte: Die Rechtfertigung der Südstaaten Nordamerikas. Deutsche Ausgabe mit einem Vorwort von E. M. Hudson. Berlin, 1863.

Williams, Benjamin Harrison. Economic Foreign Policy of the United States. New York, 1929.

Willson, Beckles. America's Ambassadors to France (1777-1927). A Narrative of Franco-American Diplomatic Relations. New York, 1928.

Wilson, Woodrow. Division and Reunion. New York, 1921.

Wirth, Max. Die Krisis in der Landwirtschaft und Mittel zur Abhilfe. Berlin, 1881.

Witte, Emil. Aus einer deutschen Botschaft. Zehn Jahre deutsch-amerikanischer Diplomatie. Leipzig, 1907.

Wülffing. Der Erwerb von Ackerbau- und Handelskolonien durch das Deutsche Reich. Cologne, 1881.

Young, John Russell. Around the World with General Grant . . . 2 vols. New York, 1879.

Zeitlin, Leon. Fürst Bismarcks sozial-, wirtschafts- und steuerpolitische Anschauungen. Leipzig, 1902.

Der Zerfall der Vereinigten Staaten von Nordamerika. Münster, 1864.

Zimmermann, Alfred. Die europäischen Kolonien. Schilderung ihrer Entstehung, Entwicklung, Erfolge und Aussichten. 6 vols. Berlin, 1896-1914.

——, Geschichte der deutschen Kolonialpolitik. Berlin, 1914.

——, Kolonialpolitik. Hand- und Lehrbuch der Staatswissenschaften . . . Abt. I, vol. 18. Leipzig, 1905.

Zorn, Ph. "Zur Frage des besten Staatsform", in Deutsche Revue (Apr.-June 1878), 219-228.

INDEX

Date Due

6499	Apr 16		
6499	May 5		
6842	Mar 31		
7423	Apr 26		
8971	Nov 2		
OCT 3 0 '50			
NOV 1 5 '50			
MAY 2 '57			
MAY 2 '58			
OCT 2 4 '58			
MAR 6 '64			